FIRE IN THE SKY

FIRE IN THE SKY

The Walton Experience

Travis Walton

MARLOWE & COMPANY
NEW YORK

Published by Marlowe & Company
632 Broadway, Seventh Floor
New York, New York 10012

ISBN 1-56924-710-2

Library of Congress Card Catalog Number: 96-075582

Printed in the United States of America

Contents

FIRE IN THE SKY

Foreword

by Tracy Torme, Screenwriter/Producer, *Fire in the Sky*

It was November 5, 1985, and the significance of the date hadn't escaped me. As the jetliner descended toward the Valley of the Sun, my mind reeled back, ten years to the day.

I'd been sitting in the library at Beverly Hills High (in the days before its zip code became a household word), listening to the radio on headphones, pretending to study. A five-minute newsbreak interrupted the rock and roll, and the last item caught my distracted attention. . . .

An Arizona man named Travis Walton was missing—and his coworkers came up with the craziest excuse for his disappearance: He had been blasted by a ray of light and taken away by a flying saucer, they said. It was clear from the tone of the report that no one believed them. Murder was already being mentioned. The local newsmen threw in the standard line about "little green men" . . . then the Stones returned with a song about tumbling dice. But I wasn't listening. I was thinking about Travis Walton.

Now, ten years later, I was touching down in Phoenix, on my way to Snowflake, Arizona, and a face-to-face meeting with Travis. As I hurried to catch a commuter flight, I ran into the pilot, who informed me that his plane was grounded. There was a storm over the White Mountains, and I was out of luck. I offered to double the money. No go.

Storm? What storm? I looked up at the cool blue sky in frustration. My time was limited; I had to be back in L.A. in three days, and I was determined to reach Snowflake.

So I rented a car—a very *special* car according to Hertz—a brand-new four-wheel-drive Peugeot—and I was off to Snowflake. For two hours I headed east across the desert, enjoying the sunshine and scenery in a way only a city boy can.

And then it started to snow—in a big way.

As ice, sleet, and snow pelted my little French car I made an interesting discovery: The windshield wipers didn't work. I drove on in exasperation, sticking my head out the window and trying my best to follow the highway, then glancing back through the mist for the racing flatbed that was sure to run me down at any moment.

Near the old mining town of Superior, I pulled off the road and waited for the storm to abate. I thought of Travis and the first time we'd spoken, a few days earlier. I'd gotten his number from Snowflake Information; I later discovered it had been unlisted for ten years—he'd just put it back in the phone book a day or two before I called. I took that as a good omen. The call had been spurred by a discussion I'd had with producer Robert Strauss a week previous. The Walton case was so interesting, so spectacular, why hadn't anyone made a movie about it? In my preliminary talks with Travis, the answer became clear.

The Travis Walton I knew only by voice seemed extremely suspicious of anyone from Hollywood. In fact, he seemed suspicious of anyone, period. So I was journeying to Snowflake for two major reasons: to convince him that I was sincere in my pledge to make a film that told his story truthfully, and to see for myself if the case was a hoax. In my mind, the latter wasn't a deal breaker. If the Walton incident was an elaborate ruse, I still felt that made for a great story that could be translated to the screen.

The storm never ended; I arrived in Snowflake three hours later, half amazed still to be in one piece. Over the course of the next few days and several more trips to the area, I interviewed Travis and Dana Walton, Mike Rogers, Kenny Paterson, John Goulette, Allen Dalis, Glen Flake, Marlin Gillespie, etc. I spoke with believers and disbelievers, well-wishers and scornmongers. In the end there was only one conclusion I could possibly reach.

The woodsmen had been telling the truth.

Something built by nonhuman hands really did appear on the mountain that night. A piece of unreality had become all too real and had changed seven young men's lives forever. I was amazed by the skeptics' lack of a reasonable alternative, and I was impressed by the amount of *suffering* the incident had caused the woodsmen.

Six and a half long years later, *Fire in the Sky* went into production. Why did it take so long? In the film business, things that should take a week take a month. And every time we said, "Could we please have twenty million dollars to make this movie?" . . . someone with twenty million dollars said no.

It was my sad duty to report to Travis all the roadblocks and false alarms we experienced during those years. I encouraged him to maintain the hope and expectation that our film would eventually be made. Travis hung in there with us until we finally hit pay dirt. As the film was produced, shot, and edited, I could sense his growing excitement, as well as the satisfaction he felt at finally having the opportunity to have a large, nationwide audience vicariously relive his experience. I know this book will enlighten and amaze the reader, just as the story of the Walton Seven first captivated me, half my lifetime ago.

Travis Walton has changed since the time I first met him. His qualities of quiet truthfulness and deep introspective thinking are still the same, but the chip on his shoulder has evaporated. He holds his head high now, confronts his critics directly and readily accepts the fact that there are some who will always disbelieve. He is a family man of quality, at peace with himself and his experience. I'm proud to call him my friend.

Preface: Context

To perceive is to suffer.

—Aristotle

It was many years ago that I got out of a crew truck in the national forest and ran toward a large glowing object hovering in the darkening Arizona sky. But when I made that fateful choice to leave the truck, I was leaving behind more than just my six fellow workmen. I was leaving behind forever all semblance of a normal life, running headlong toward an experience so overwhelmingly mind-rending in its effects, so devastating in its aftermath, that my life would never—could never—be the same again.

Nothing in this naive country boy's life up to that moment could have prepared me for what followed. But what I didn't know then, I think I know now. It's been a real education! And with this new book I try to share those insights. When I first wrote *The Walton Experience* (Berkley Books, 1978), the book which Paramount Pictures' movie, *Fire in the Sky*, is based on, I stated my desire that the book put the reader where we were when it happened. My hope was that if people could vicariously *live* it—somehow actually experience it as if they were there in my stead—perhaps they could take a more open-minded and objective approach to their evaluation of it all.

However, nothing approaches the goal of allowing people to live someone else's experience nearly so well as a movie. I think most people knew better than to expect a documentary, and although some dramatic license was exercised, I believe that the movie succeeded in conveying the emotional essence of what we went through. Public response to the film fulfilled all reasonable expectations of its makers. And it satisfied my goal of imparting my experience on the gut level, so I feel free now in this updating to emphasize other areas. I provide an accurate, undramatized chronicle of events, and I account for the main departures that the film took from what actually happened. I try to satisfy the interest which so many people have expressed concerning why, after all this time, I finally consented to a movie being made, and what the process of its creation was like.

One of the most neglected areas in the earlier book was the controversy surrounding the whole episode, the attacks by people who for various reasons felt compelled to try to deny that it had ever really happened. Many of those attacks were so ridiculously baseless that I naively believed a cursory rebuttal would be sufficient. I thought those inclined to doubt could easily be pointed in a direction that would lead them to discover there was no truth in the alleged scenarios which had me or my coworkers hallucinating on drugs, creating a hoax, suddenly becoming psychotic, etc. I wrote as if all these claims could be as easily refuted as the charge that the report was a cover story for a gory chainsaw murder.

I could not have been more mistaken. The onslaught not only did not go away, it grew. Refuted claims were continuously resurrected and, like a child's game of gossip, became more embellished with each telling.

Therefore I devote my greatest efforts here to critical analysis of the myriad attempts to explain away what was otherwise recognized as the most spectacular, best-documented UFO incident ever.

Another emphasis in this book is the context in which this incredible event occurred. People need to know more about the prior lives of the people involved and the community in which it happened in order to understand its impact and aftermath. And the years of the aftermath are a story unto themselves, a story so excruciating that my memories of what I have lived through because of some people's reaction to what happened are a hell which nearly overshadows the experience itself.

Take a sleepy little Western town steeped in conservative, traditional values. Drop into its midst an event so shocking, so anomalous, that by its very nature it challenged conventional beliefs and attitudes, at the same time being impossible to dismiss, demanding to be confronted. That, pardner, was the makings of some serious turmoil.

The UFO incident caused me to come in contact, directly or indirectly, with many people from all over the world whom I otherwise would never have known anything about. It so happened that most of them came from the larger cities. In many of those people I detected the attitude that it was good that this event occurred in such a place. If anything could make a bunch of hicks wake up and smell the coffee, make them realize "there are more things in heaven and earth" than allowed for in their pantheon of dear illusions, it was this sort of event; it was just what these close-minded rubes needed to shake up their smug orthodoxy, to pull their blinders off so they might also begin to see a little more of the modern world outside their little corn-row rut.

Perhaps. But I believe their attitude is metrocentric, their own dear illusion that small towns are backward and cities are populated solely with hip, sophisticated, open-minded people with a much more accurate picture of "the real world."

I have news for them. I've seen both sides and I can tell you that rural communities have no corner on tunnel vision. Admittedly, these mountain communities are somewhat more homogeneous in their views, but there is far more diversity here than metrophiles assume. They seem to forget we're plugged into the same national media they are, not sitting here watching reruns of local news from the 1950s. Granted, people here can be very certain of their truths, but no more so than elsewhere. Living among people with a greater variety of viewpoints doesn't necessarily impart an openness to *consider* those viewpoints. Tolerance doesn't translate into open-mindedness. A diversity of self-certitudes is still self-certitude.

The more I discover of the world, the more I see how fundamentally alike people everywhere actually are. In a broad sense we all share the same basic strengths and failings, although to varying degrees. And it is this array of traits which some realists regard as being the cause of what is referred to as "the human condition."

I've come to realize that the biggest problem anywhere in the world is that people's perceptions of reality are compulsively filtered through the screening mesh of *what they want, and do not want, to be true.* People see what they expect to see. Preconceptions seem to predetermine judgment of everything. It's not solely because this human failing played such a big part in the experiences I recount here that I consider it so important in the overall scheme of things. If you look, you'll find this human proclivity at the root of every single personal problem or social ill humanity has ever endured. These mountain communities are more a microcosm of the world than some would expect.

Snowflake, Arizona. To some people from out of state, these two words sound like an oxymoron, a contradiction in terms. Many times I've had to persuade those on the other end of long-distance phone lines that I was not joking. They just "know" that it never snows here in the Desert State, and besides, who would really name a town Snowflake? Well, it does snow, quite enough, thanks. Not as much as some places in Arizona, but then, that isn't where the name comes from anyway. When I tell them the town was named for two of the founding families—the Snows and the Flakes—and that the

Snows have all drifted away but there are still plenty of Flakes here, they become certain I'm kidding.

But Snowflake, ever since its founding in 1878, has been a town that people have been forced to take seriously. Rugged Mormon pioneers came into this area when it was virtually wilderness and founded a number of towns here on the mountain. They hunted game, fought off wolves, bears, and lions, dammed streams, cut timber, quarried rock, and built homes for their families. They farmed the land and herded sheep, cattle, and horses over large tracts of the surrounding area. They tamed their piece of the American West at a cost of great hardship and loss of life.

My wife Dana's great-grandparents, Smith D. Rogers and Eliza Snow Smith, were among the earliest settlers. Her grandfather Wilford was born in a log cabin here in 1888. Snow blew through cracks in the cabin onto the bed where he came into this world, as the seventh of fifteen children, four of whom died before reaching adulthood. He led a robust life full of hard work in the outdoors, but made time for music and theater. He survived being buffeted by the elements, sickened by diptheria, rolled over by a horse, and run over by a bus. The grand old man passed away a while back at the age of ninety-eight, able to outwork most younger men nearly until the end of his life. Only the strongest survived.

Snowflake has always held a disproportionate influence over larger towns in the region. A high percentage of Snowflake residents are descended from the original settlers. There have been times when Flakes and other Snowflake founding-family names have filled nearly every position of power and status in the county. There was once talk of moving the county seat to Snowflake.

For a very long time Snowflake Union High School was the only one, attended from nearly a dozen of the surrounding towns, some more than thirty miles away. One by one the other towns are building their own high schools, but the SHS Lobos continue to win a larger portion of sports competitions, including the wolf's share of state championships. SHS has also had great success in orchestra, choir, marching-band competitions, spelling bees, and debate competitions. The school places in the top three every time the academic decathlon team competes.

When the UFO incident happened in 1975, the town's population was around 2,500, less than half its present size. Main Street is still basically about twelve blocks long; one whole block for the LDS (Mormon) church, one bank, a post office, a few small businesses. Most of the buildings are single-story; a few lots on Main Street still haven't been built on. All but one of the four service stations have been supplanted by quick-stop mini-marts. Snowflake has yet to get its first stoplight.

The years have seen a slow waning of the old lines of power. Outside influences continue to come in and take hold, some for the better, others not. The percentage of non-Mormon residents has continued to grow. Many of the traditional ways remain, however. When I first moved here, two lawmen—a resident county deputy and one town marshal—were all the law enforcement the whole area had. Now there's a police force of ten and a number of resident county sheriff's officers. Even in a town where the smallest incidents are reported (unlike cities where people are so jaded they often don't even bother to report being the victims of major crimes), Snowflake still has an astonishingly low crime rate. A rash of broken windows can make the local newspaper. Although drug abuse used to be virtually nonexistent here, we still have the lowest incidence in the state. Some of the kids may complain that "nothing ever happens here," but their parents say, "Thank heavens for that."

The train is gone now. The Santa Fe Railroad pulled up the tracks through town a while ago. Ranching isn't nearly what it once was. Now the total output raising pigs is more than double that of cattle; the nation's largest pig farm is located here. But forest product–related jobs have dominated the area's economy for a long time. This way of life may be in for an abrupt change here, along what's been called "America's last frontier," because of timber cutbacks due to environmental concerns.

The old joke about rolling up and putting away the sidewalks at nine o'-clock still applies, except on Saturday dance nights. Journalists and movie people often call this a *"Last Picture Show"* kind of town. Western-style dress, though still popular and in current revival, no longer completely dominates the fashion scene. But the annual Sweet Corn Festival, Pioneer Days Celebration, and the Fourth of July Rodeo are still the biggest events of the year. The Homecoming Game Parade gets almost as big a turnout, since high-school football is taken very seriously here. The year of the UFO incident, Snowflake defeated nearby Round Valley during future gridiron star Mark Gastineau's last year of high-school play there. A number of athletes have left here for the pros.

I think it was Robert Service who said that big spaces seem to produce big men. Arizona has always been a place of big spaces and probably always will be, since only a tiny percentage of the state is privately owned. The rest is Indian reservations, state and federal land, and national forest.

Arizona has been called a land of contrasts, and many of the borders of those contrasts seem to fall in the area around Snowflake. The region, called the White Mountain/Mogollon (*moe* gee on) Rim area, extends from the center of Arizona where the Rim begins and runs eastward into the White Mountains near the New Mexico border. It ranges south from the high desert near the lower boundaries of the Petrified Forest, the Painted Desert, and the Navajo and Hopi Indian Reservations, continuing south to the still higher elevations of the wetter, alpine-forested Sunrise Ski Area up near the timberline on the Apache Indian Reservation.

Snowflake lies midway, in the scrub cedar and rolling prairie at the northern edge of the largest ponderosa pine forest in the world. In ages past, Snowflake's valley was a vast lake, drained by a huge crack that opened up from Snowflake to the Little Colorado River back about the time a space visitor of another sort impacted, sixty-some miles to the northwest, forming the world-famous Meteor Crater. (Some speculate that the crack, as well as the big sinkholes just northwest of town, happened *because* of the meteor.)

There aren't many such places, where you can snow-ski in the morning and water-ski in the heat of a desert lake the afternoon of the same day. Turkey Springs, where the incredible series of events begins, is so high up on the Mogollon Rim that it's often inaccessible to workers or film crews for three or four months of the year. The 7,500-foot-high ridge of the forested Mogollon Rim, twenty miles southwest of Snowflake, forms a long natural barrier to the prevailing winds. This shields the town and the surrounding area from the brunt of storms, which makes for the milder, if dryer, high desert climate.

These open vistas and windswept sagebrush grasslands have been called lonely. Remote, yes. But loneliness is a subjective experience. A man working by himself in the forest, miles from anything human, can feel more at one with the world and far less lonely than another man sitting in his house in the middle of a community from which he feels set apart. What is to one man a rich, expansive refuge of peaceful, reflective solitude, is to another man a bleak empty prison of drab isolated boredom. Some men live in both. Pity the man of either perspective who is blind to the other.

It's inevitable that we find ourselves on one side of the lock or the other. Whether you think of yourself, or those on the other side, as locked in or locked out, may be only a matter of perspective, with the one who seems to control the key being a minor irrelevance. The satisfied see themselves as either sheltered or liberated. The dissatisfied see themselves as either inmates or exiles. To each his own.

Fall, 1975. Nixon was out, Ford was in, and Watergate wouldn't go away. The historic Apollo/Soyuz joint mission of '74 was still being toasted. Sakharov had just won the Nobel Peace Prize. But the towering threat of instant nuclear annihilation by a monolithic Soviet Union was still a perpetual shadow over the world. More than one million died in the Khmer Rouge takeover of Cambodia. Scientists at the University of California at Irvine had recently announced their findings that chlorofluorocarbons are rapidly depleting the earth's protective ozone shield against ultraviolet radiation from space. Squeaky Fromme, Patty Hearst, and the Symbionese

Liberation Army were in the news. Congress passed the Freedom of Information Act. The movie *Jaws* broke all box-office records, and Jack Nicholson came into his own with an Academy Award for *One Flew Over the Cuckoo's Nest,* which also took Best Picture. Pete Rose helped the Cincinnati Reds win the World Series, and the Pittsburgh Steelers won the Super Bowl. My best friend, Mike Rogers, and I were very "into" martial arts and still pondering the mysteries of the recent death of Bruce Lee and the seeming invincibility of Muhammad Ali. Olivia Newton-John's "Have You Never Been Mellow" and John Denver's "Thank God I'm a Country Boy" were at the top of the pop charts. They were okay, but we preferred what might seem an unlikely mix of music which included the easy country of Don Williams, some classical, early Cat Stevens, and especially the Moody Blues.

In Snowflake, social trends have a way of lagging behind the rest of the nation. Even here, however, by late 1975 the fashion of longer hair on men had lost much of its sixties countercultural statement, having become so mainstream that many country-western music stars were letting their hair grow. As a result, many of the men on our woods crew, even Mike and me, had longer locks than some of the more traditional town fathers considered respectable for red-blooded American males, although it barely overhung our collars. Only one of our crew, Ken Peterson, maintained the neatly cropped conventional haircut. We *were* red-blooded American males, but after the UFO incident, all it took were little signs such as these to confirm the notion for many locals that we were some living example of why the golden ways of the past seemed to them to be eroding.

It may seem quaint to speak of how hard labor builds character, but I've seen the process in action too much not to believe in it. It's more than the balancing effect on brain chemistry of vigorous exercise. Occasionally men new to such work came to us from the city or from less-demanding jobs. Then the outcome of the struggle between the demands of the job and the character with which they arrived would play itself out before us. Living on the "mean streets" seems to harden only the *exterior,* the part that relates to other people, the cultivated look of "badness."

For a man out there on the mountain, his battle, in a way, really isn't with the baking sun, chilling winds, steep terrain, thorn bushes, or dangerous equipment. His battle isn't with the rough roads, mud holes, biting insects, or gnarly thickets. The real struggle is with his inner self. Call it fiber, backbone, or grit: true toughness is internal.

The ability to keep going when he's hot, thirsty, out of breath, when his hands hurt and his muscles ache, while bark, bugs, pine needles, and sawdust are falling down his shirt to stick in his sweat. The ability to say yes to more of this and no to the beckoning shade tree, because he knows he ought to and because that's what he said he'd do. This can help give a man the power to say yes or no—in the right instances—to just about anything and to act consistently with what he says. And, to confront daily the inflexible realities of a "real world" that has teeth and bites back with immediate logical consequences, regardless of sophistical argument or politically correct rationalization, can teach something else now in short supply—common sense.

In my case, hair past my collar wasn't the only excuse for the local establishment to look a bit askance at me. I'm going to tell you some things about myself I'm not particularly proud of, but I'll mention them only because they shed light on why I reacted to the UFO the way I did, and because they help explain to a degree the community's reaction to what happened.

I was a little wild in my younger days. I pulled some risky stunts on my motorcycle that I cringe to look back on. I drove a number of very fast and unique cars in those days: a 1960 Pontiac Ventura that had a 389 engine with a *factory* three 2-barrel carburetor setup; a 1957 Chevy Nomad station wagon in nearly perfect original condition; a 1969 Mustang Mach I with a 428 Cobra Jet engine; and, briefly, a 1968 Corvette Stingray with the rare (500-plus horsepower) L-88 427 engine. These were cars I could have kept whose current worth would make collectors drool. I was no stranger to the quarter-mile strips earlier generations had marked off on the straight stretches of highway outside of town.

When my older brother was headed off to Oklahoma to attend world rodeo champ Jim Shoulders' bull-riding school, I, having never ridden a bull in my life, jumped in the pickup with him and off we went. I had no dreams of being a rodeo star myself, but took a bovine beating every day for a week, just for the experience.

When Barroom Brawlers promoters came to the mountain to stage their version of an amateur boxing, "tough man" contest, Mike and I went in and signed up. We did pretty well, so I also went and competed the next two years.

Karate schools came and went in the White Mountain area, and Mike and I signed up every chance we got, getting exposure to a variety of instructors, different martial-arts styles, and different classmates to spar with.

I'd take off to Mexico or thumb my way to Florida without much forethought.

I hiked, fished, and hunted some pretty remote Arizona back country and I scaled some pretty dangerous rock walls in the canyons in the area. One night when our group challenged us, a friend and I went over the fence and climbed the Tower, all the way to the top of a microwave antenna so high you can see it from thirty miles away. (Please, don't anyone else *ever* try this stupid stunt.)

I did some partying and acting out in ways I lived to regret. Yeah, there were fights. Did I always win? Is anyone a winner in these kinds of things?

A good while before the UFO incident, on another contract, Mike and I and another crew were on our way home from work one day. Suddenly a black bear ran across the road in front of the crew truck. Mike had to slam on the brakes to avoid hitting it. The bear stopped on the other side and looked back. I took advantage of the truck stopping to jump out and run straight toward the critter, roaring like I was an enraged grizzly. The bear fled as if its tail were on fire. I got back in the truck, as if nothing had happened, ignoring the looks on the guys' faces. I said in a low-key deadpan: "Huh. That one must've heard of me."

It might have seemed impressive at the moment, but it wasn't really anything. The bear was already intimidated by its near miss with the truck, and by the way it only half turned around, I could tell it was already all set to hightail it. Just in case it didn't, I was carefully gauging the relative distances between the bear, me, and the safety of my empty seat in the truck. Usually, if a predator isn't cornered, its reflex is to flee when chased, just as it will respond by giving chase if you run away from it.

Most of the foregoing was *years* before the UFO incident. I survived, surprisingly enough, without a single broken bone. I had a few isolated brushes with the law, mostly traffic offenses, but nothing that left me with any record. It was a small part of my life, a brief phase I went through, but I paid the prices and really learned my lesson, and had not received so much as a traffic ticket for a number of years before the UFO incident. In fact, it's been like that for all of the many years since my wayward phase.

I really don't like having to go into events of my wilder days. But I came to realize that, without the perspective provided by knowing these things about me, people will never understand the answer to what was for so many one of the more mystifying questions raised by my story: *Why?* The other men were either frozen in terror or frantically trying to find a way to crawl under the seats. *Why was I the only one brazenly to get out of the crew truck and approach such a fearsome unknown?* I kept getting this question, over and over again, for years. Perhaps now it's a bit clearer what kind of man it took to react in that way.

However, youthful bravado is only half the explanation for that apparent mystery. The acute embarrassment I feel in reviewing that time period will also be better understood from knowing something else about me. Another side to my personality ran deeper, more true to my real nature. I was possessed by a seemingly unquenchable thirst for knowledge, especially of a type others considered off limits—not bad things, just things hidden, regarded as best left for a few, or truths that many deny solely from bias or fear. My all-consuming curiosity was more powerful than my own fear, and at its zenith in my life the evening of November 5, 1975.

Many of those who disapproved of my ways were probably in the throes of backlash to the changes time had brought to their world, and needed a culprit, as if I were an agent of those changes. How little they really knew about me.

Small towns are always described as places where everyone knows everyone else. Actually, a small town is a place where people only think they know everyone. They know everyone's name—but not always *who* they really are. I've heard many rumors make the rounds about folks here that proved to be ridiculously false when I finally got verifiable word. The more hush-hush the "scoop," the further it's likely to be from the truth. I've learned to hold off on drawing any conclusions about late-breaking local news. Getting the facts straight right off is so rare that it amazes me how many people are willing to jump prematurely to conclusions that so often prove false.

However, it's human nature for most people to view their own pasts through a rosy haze, while their memories of the wrongs of others are indelible. I teach my kids about the fragility of one's reputation. Very old people might forget everything else about the early years, but few have any trouble recalling which girls were known as "easy" and the name and deeds of the school bully. When I was in high school I took part in a protest of the high-school dress code. Now that I have a son there with some of the same teachers, it's kind of funny to note the misgivings I felt when the school board recently voted to concede and relax standards on some of those same old issues.

There was a greatly underestimated intellectual side to me. I think I caused a little dismay in some of those who rarely would see me take a textbook home, would see me cut class, then on Friday rumble up to the high school on my motorcycle, walk in, and ace the test. It seemed a refutation of their ethic, especially for certain teachers who I'm sure felt they were seeing a living non sequitur—"People like that can't get high grades."

Still, there were a few times I just let things slide. I actually dropped out of high school with only a year to go; but I came back, buckled down, graduated, and obtained grants to attend all three of the universities to which I applied. I chose to attend NAU, Northern Arizona University (the Lumberjacks, of course!). I kept changing majors—electronic engineering, law, psychology, medicine, liberal studies—not because I lacked sufficient interest, but because I was so interested in *everything*.

I really had no reason to expect to be seen as I truly was. I made sure no one knew what I had been like before my family moved to Snowflake in

1968 from Payson, Arizona, where I'd been known as a goody-goody, sensitive, an egghead nerd! I was called "Einstein," "mad scientist," and nicknamed "the Professor." So I came here determined to leave that pigeonhole behind. But I only succeeded in getting myself into another, equally ill-fitting pigeonhole as a rebel. Nevertheless I privately continued my intellectual inquiries into a wide variety of subjects such as philosophy, religion, art, languages, music, science, and literature (including the works of Ayn Rand, beginning with *Atlas Shrugged,* but especially her nonfiction).

I recall that for my twelfth Christmas I received a copy of Isaac Asimov's *Intelligent Man's Guide to Science,* the first brand-new book I'd ever owned; it's still in my personal library, now grown to well over a thousand volumes. Though much of that edition is still relevant, it's interesting to read how dated some of science has become, what hadn't yet been discovered, and amusing to read how humanity was "aiming firmly for the moon." I've never read any of Asimov's fiction, but I've accumulated quite a few of his hundreds of other works.

It would be hard to characterize the particular subjects that intrigued me, because I don't subscribe to the usual limits. There is *nothing* that shouldn't be examined. Many people avoid reading the works of those with whom they disagree, but I find these to be some of the most stimulating.

I have some Cherokee in my immediate ancestry on my mother's side, so I delved into the language and history of the Cherokee nation. The Cherokee's status as one of the so-called "Five Civilized Tribes" didn't prevent President Andrew Jackson from ordering in the 1830s the forced foot march of the tribe from their homelands on the East Coast to reservations half a continent away in Oklahoma. There was tremendous suffering and death among those herded along by soldiers, on what became known as the Trail of Tears. My great-grandfather was a chief who escaped the procession and settled in Tennessee before later rejoining his people in Oklahoma.

I became a state-certified EMT (Emergency Medical Technician). I worked at the nearby Show Low airport to pay for my private-pilot ground school and flying lessons. I worked on a number of inventions I came up with for automotive applications. When midwives I knew told me they had been taking the college licensing preparation course and studying for the state midwife licensing examination, I borrowed their textbooks a few days before the test and read them. Since the statute permitted persons who had not taken the college classes to take the test, I took the exam with dozens of midwives from around Arizona, some of whom were registered nurses who had already been practicing midwifery for years under physicians' supervision. I received the second-highest score out of the entire group, just behind a lady who had actually taken the college course.

I was a person who seemed to be from two worlds. People from both worlds didn't know quite how to take me, each probably believing I was of the other. Adding to some of the friction between me and one or two guys on the crew was my attitude toward smoking and drinking. They seemed to miss the distinction between refusing to drink with them and simply refusing to drink.

Snowflake residents, I think, viewed me as an outsider. My moving to town from elsewhere and my church inactivity contributed greatly to that impression. I never told anyone, but my Mormon roots were as deep as anyone's. They didn't know it but, going way back, I'm actually related to some of them. My great-great-grandfather, Joseph Walton, was among the pioneer families to settle the Utah Valley with Brigham Young. Joseph Walton helped build, and lived in, Wordsworth Fort in Alpine, Utah. He served under Captain Carlisle and Sergeant John Langston as a soldier in the Fifth Tenn, a Mormon militia company, and later as a police officer. He saw a lot of trouble with Indian raids, including the Walker War and the Black Hawk War, and endured the same hardships as the other pioneers in taming the Utah Valley. His son, my great-grandfather, John James Walton, worked in Brigham Young's household to pay his way in becoming one of a small number in the very first graduating class of the Brigham Young Academy, later known as Brigham Young University.

I've gone through major changes. Now that I bring these things out, some of which I'd like to deny, I'm put in the position of counseling my kids to do as I do, not as I did. The UFO incident was a sharp turning point for me. There were other reasons, too, though . . . an accumulation of smaller lessons, general maturity, and the realization that such a background, smokescreen or not, can be the kind of thing that can put the lady of your dreams beyond reach.

I admit it wasn't easy for people to understand the complexities and apparent contradictions of my personality. How could the shy person they met one time be the same grandstanding guy they would see at another time? Now that I no longer have a reckless side, it's a little easier for people to understand me, or to think they do.

I still love and enjoy the outdoors, although I haven't been hunting in ages. I used to kill rattlesnakes whenever I came across them, just like everyone else. Now I just let them go their way and I go mine. I still try to stay fit and live healthy. I'm not so quick to anger or to try and resort to physical solutions to confrontations. First I'll exhaust every possible rational, logical solution, because the truth is, I've found that there usually *is* one. The thing to remember is that if you're living as right as you know how, if someone has a problem with you, chances are, the problem is their own, which should obviate emotional reactions born of defensiveness. In other words, you don't have to take it personally.

Don't get the idea I've lost any spark, however. I've just redirected those energies into more productive outlets. I'd prefer to be a thinker and a lover than a fighter—if others will let me.

I wouldn't want this personal reordering to give the impression that I buy into the anti-ego disease that is spreading through society. Vanity is a character flaw (actually a cloak for low self-esteem), but ego is the wellspring of the psyche. It's an inescapable fact of life. The person who criticizes you for taking pride in excelling is really implying this illogical nonsense: "You are saying you are good relative to someone else [probably me], and that is *bad*. I, however, am *not* taking pride in my good qualities; but that is *good*. Therefore, because I'm egoless *and* I have shown you the error of your ways, I am good relative to someone else [namely, you]."

Loggers are a competitive lot, and our crew was no exception, especially Mike and me. We were always really competitive on the job—and about the job itself, too. Who could cut the most trees, who could go the longest without dulling his chain on a rock, etc. The contract specifications based tree sizes on DBH—diameter at breast height—because diameters near the ground don't correlate well to actual size. We'd have moneyless wagers to see who could most closely guess what diameter the scale would read without touching the tree, and at various distances from the tree.

We were very competitive concerning ideas, too. We would debate all kinds of things, not just philosophy. Current events, things going on in our lives and in the lives of those around us—even job-related subjects. Logically proving our own position was the game, and the struggle brought us naturally to the rules of that game. The drives to and from work were always long, but we would fill the time with talk of many fascinating things.

The guys on the crew who didn't have a taste for all that found some of the talk a little bewildering. "Would you guys quit *arguing*, for hell's sake?" they'd say; and, "Who in hell gives a *damn* about why humans enjoy hearing music? Embryological neuro-artifacts of mathematical harmonics bullshit! Ain't it enough to know what sounds good to you? Why do you guys have to pry into everything? What's it ever going to get you? All you guys ever do is argue." But there were some who, although surprised, took a liking to it and jumped right in and held their own.

We would have challenges to see who could predict where a tree would fall without a nudge. Games of reaction time, little unspoken duels, such as seeing who could keep from being the first to say, "Let's break," or "Let's call it a day." Seeing who'd be first to get his saw started or race back to the truck. Who could most closely estimate the distance between two trees, or how many man-hours it would take to complete a given acreage.

As a ponderosa pine grows, its lower limbs die off and new ones are added to the top. Normally they get drier and drier until wind or snow breaks them off. As karate practice, we'd have matches to see who could snap-kick off the highest limb above our heads without falling on his can. Being taller, I always won this one. We would take one of the round files we sharpened our chains with and see who could throw it and stick it closest to the center of the end of a log. Mike usually won this one. We would compete to see who'd be fastest to get his saw through a log. Mike usually won this one, too.

I guess Mike has more sawdust in his veins. Mike's father, Lyle, became a logger in 1947, at first using the manual crosscut saws they called "Swedish violins," since engine-driven chainsaws hadn't yet come into use. When Mike was growing up, he helped his dad in the woods. Lyle has done tree thinning intermittently for the U.S. Forest Service since leaving the railroad, and is still doing it at the age of seventy-plus. Mike's grandpa, George Howard, planted trees in the forest in Nebraska before becoming a forest ranger in Colorado. After Grandpa George left the Forest Service, he was in timber-related work the rest of his life. And Mike's mother, Joyce, was born two months premature when her parents were snowed in at a ranger station near Yampa, Colorado, during the worst storm of the year. She spent her girlhood living in various lumber camps. Aside from being a born woodsman, all that competitiveness on the job probably helped Mike when he entered the big lumberjack contests, where he did well.

Mike had been bidding U.S. Forest Service thinning contracts since he was only nineteen years old. In the fall of 1975, I'd just helped him finish out his Candy Mountain contract up near the Blue Wilderness Area. Now *that* was some job. We were above 10,000 feet. There were times there when we found ourselves looking *down* at the clouds! It's beautiful green country, thick with wild berries and abundant with wildlife—but, brother! can that altitude make you breathe hard when you work. Heck, just carrying your saw back up the hill to the crew truck can make you gasp. No wonder. That's the altitude above which it is recommended for pilots to have pressurized cabins or to use supplemental oxygen.

Most of the Candy Mountain crew had left for one reason or another, and so for Turkey Springs Mike had been adding some men. Including Mike, there was a total of seven of us working on that contract at the time of the incident.

I first became friends with Mike while attending high school with Mike's younger brother, whom I had joined working for Mike during our summer recesses.

Ken Peterson I'd known for years. Mike had known him all his life, having grown up together. Everyone always thought of Ken as a really decent guy. A former high-school athlete, he was a quiet, introspective sort, always polite, a real straight arrow. Very conventional in his dress, manner, and behavior, but also a deep thinker, and religiously a bit restless, a searcher. He lived by his beliefs, but he wasn't pushy about it. He'd speak up about men smoking or swearing on the job, but it was more in defense of his right to his personal environment than about converting or imposing his beliefs on others. He was a steady worker and got along well with everyone, though he tended to talk more with Mike and me than the others.

Except for me, Allen Dalis had been there longest, outlasting a number of other men who came and went over the summer. He was more experienced, too, because he'd worked for Mike before. There had been a few rough moments between Allen and others on the crew, including a fistfight with Mike a month or so earlier. He'd led a troubled life growing up in Phoenix, but he could also be a real charmer when he chose to. My own troubles with him were forgotten as far as I was concerned. His dark side notwithstanding, he was downright likable much of the time. Besides, he was a heck of a good sawyer.

John Goulette was the closest thing to a sidekick for Allen in the crew. John had worked for Mike before on a couple of occasions when Allen had also. John and Allen had completed service in the navy, and they were friends, but John really wasn't a lot like Allen. Although he knew how to have a good time, he was quite a bit more easygoing. He got along well with the rest of the crew, but tended to pair off with Allen.

John Goulette had been living in Phoenix and he'd been back there the previous weekend. He brought back with him a gangly, six-foot-seven guy named Dwayne Smith, who was looking for a job. He was new to this sort of work and he'd only been there three days, so I didn't know much about him. Being new, he wasn't very outgoing, and tended to keep with Allen and John. There was a little heckling going on between him and "the kid," Steve Pierce, who returned fire by calling Dwayne "Herman Munster" because of his height. Steve's family weren't area natives, but his family owned land east of Snowflake. Steve had been with us for a few weeks. He was the youngest on the crew, but he was strong and big for his age. It looked as if he was going to work out okay.

So there we were. A mixed group of personalities, with various friendships and antagonisms, all headed off toward work in the mountains of northern Arizona, and the experience of a lifetime.

PART 1

The Incident

CHAPTER 1

First, an Open Mind

By reason only can we attain to a correct knowledge of
the world and a solution of its great problems.

—Ernst Heinrich Haeckel

Before giving the eye-witness account of the sighting and subsequent events, I want to appeal to reason and briefly explain why I go into the matter once more, after so much time.

For a while it seemed that everyone wanted to know more about the UFO incident. They wanted to know if anything so incredibly bizarre could actually happen. . . .

Could it? Well, it did, but unfortunately, often it was the tendency of a great many people to consider only those facts which supported their preconceived beliefs—not only the lay public, but also scientists, lawmen, and newsmen. Both the skeptics and even those who accepted the truth of our experience were often guilty of making up their minds on the basis of only part of the evidence. Scientific testing took time, and many people did not want to wait until *all* the facts were in before reaching a conclusion.

There was "something for everyone" in the early news reports of the incident. A controversy raged that offered evidence to confirm any particular bias a person might choose, and offering food for thought for the unprejudiced and more logical individuals.

Every time I read a newspaper or magazine article about my experience, it was with outraged exasperation. Not one of the written accounts of my experience was entirely correct. I'm not referring only to reports which took the disbelieving viewpoint. We're all entitled to our opinions in matters of opinion. However, in matters of fact we are not. I'm referring to those reports which garbled basic facts of an indisputable nature—names, ages, places, even the *sequence* of events; reports in which quotations from nearly everyone involved were pure invention. Reports that repeated the vaguest rumors and even things which a simple check could have disproved before they were put before millions of people.

A number of so-called experts appeared very foolish by coming out in the media and speaking too soon. They made public statements as if from established fact, which were proven totally false when the real evidence was publicized. Seeing these things, I would tell the next interviewer how no one ever seemed to get it right. He would sympathize, assuring me that *he* would straighten things out. Sure enough, when his article came out, words I hardly recognized would be enclosed by quotes and labeled "Walton said." I started really overemphasizing the problem, even asking interviewers to repeat the basic facts back to me. But the errors continued.

The difficulty was not lessened by the silence I maintained, at first, to the media. They printed what they could get, which was not much. So the problem was not entirely their fault, as the profession of journalism has its own built-in complications. An hour-long interview is condensed into a half page of shorthand notes. When those are expanded and organized into a full-length article, how can it possibly be accurate? The contrast is like that between reconstituted orange juice and the freshly squeezed stuff. The general flavor is there, but something is missing.

The difficulties the interviewers had became even more understandable to me after I began this book. I had my own share of troubles in trying to achieve absolute accuracy—and I'm the one it happened to. In researching the facts, I found that people's memories posed a problem. If it was only that their recall had *faded*, it would not be so bad. But people tend to remember things a little differently as time goes by. Even if they remember something exactly as they experienced it, they might not have perceived it correctly. A dozen people can witness the same automobile accident and all have a different recall of the event. I dealt with this problem by eliminating versions that did not agree with the majority, and by checking with written records.

I racked my brain for even the most insignificant detail about the sometimes enigmatic thing that had happened to me. The description of the incident and events immediately following it is as nearly accurate as I was able to make it, and it is repeated from an account that I wrote while the facts were fresh.

There were reasons for my writing this book other than the need to set the record straight. For one thing, my reserved nature made me want to avoid being eternally interviewed. But at the same time, I had experienced something that I felt should be shared and recorded. In this book I satisfy both those goals. When some people expressed so much intense curiosity, and others, out of fear, tried to explain away what had happened, I kept thinking, If only they could have been there! Therefore, I have tried to relate these experiences in a way that will allow you, the reader, to relive them and feel what we felt at the time it was all happening. Even in parts where I was not on hand, I have attempted, from careful interviews with those who were there, to reconstruct the scenes just as they occurred, to impart a sense of presence for the reader.

My coworkers were faced with similar problems, continually asked what they'd seen, or when they were told that they did not even *know* what they'd seen. To help explain it to others, and to demonstrate that they had no doubts about what they had witnessed, Michael Rogers brought the group's collective descriptions to life in the painting entitled *The Walton Experience.*

Mike Rogers was mysteriously inspired to paint better than he ever had before. This, after not having painted in over ten years! Mike had at first intended only to portray the original incident, but when I saw the precision of detail he expressed, I asked him to help me re-create my experience in art form. His most recent additions show how much his ability has grown. Mike knows me and he knows what I mean when I describe something. Still, in the drawings of the beings I encountered, Mike drew over twenty representations, all of which fit the verbal description, before I picked out the one closest to what they had actually looked like.

If only they could have been there! I thought. I hope that I have been successful in creating something that puts you where we were that November night.

My six coworkers and I did not set out to "prove" the truth of our experience. Circumstances at the time of the incident made it necessary to report it to law enforcement officials. The media picked it up and after that, it became simply a matter of defending ourselves against a wild variety of accusations. This is not to say that all the reports in the media were negative. Most of the news reports were positive, or at least gave unbiased coverage of the overall account. But for the record, all the misinformation and mistaken conclusions need to be set straight.

It is easy to sympathize with those who find it all difficult to accept. If they think they feel incredulous about it, then they should be able to appreciate how difficult it was for seven tree-cutters to adjust to. We were the ones it happened to. Yet we had our own share of difficulty accepting what our own senses adamantly told us we had experienced.

There were inevitably demands for proof. With little or no remaining physical evidence, absolute proof was impossible to produce. However, as we shall see, the additional testimony by law enforcement officials and scientific researchers offered overwhelming evidence that it did indeed happen just as we reported it.

Imagine our dilemma. If we could have produced hard physical proof such as bringing in a crashed saucer on the back of a truck, or dragging in an alien being in chains, we might possibly have found ourselves in a more believable position. Even if I could have brought back some piece of physical "proof," there were some hard-core disbelievers who still would not accept it. For example, there were many people who insisted that man would never make it to the moon. They swore that God would never allow it. Perhaps modern technology is frightening to them. If man were meant to go to the moon, he would have been put there, they said. When man did set foot on the moon in 1969, most of them conveniently forgot their previous predictions. But a few hard-core disbelievers insisted that man never did go to the moon and that it was all a television hoax on the part of the government!

Religious convictions are a considerable source of bias in the matter of extraterrestrial visitors. It is not necessarily a religious matter—no more than the question of simple life on Mars is a religious matter. Unless your particular religion denies that there are such things, it is an academic matter rather than a religious one. Nevertheless, people made unnecessary religious interpretations, pro *and* con, concerning the concept of visitation of earth by life from other worlds.

The average individual is going to believe what he wants to believe, regardless of evidence or facts. Those who believe we had a UFO experience are going to believe exactly that and those who scoff will continue to scoff. However, there is hope. There are alive today totally unbiased, rational individuals (you?) who make judgments solely on the basis of *logic*. People who are actually capable of withholding judgment *indefinitely* if there is insufficient evidence for them to base a conclusion on.

My six coworkers and I know that the incident did, in all reality, happen. We have our memories to help us accept the truth of our incredible experience. You are not so fortunate (or unfortunate, depending on where you're sitting). You have only your powers of reason. Here's the straight of it. The conclusion is yours.

"Condemnation without investigation is the height of ignorance."
—Emerson

CHAPTER 2

An Ordinary Day

One impulse from a vernal wood
May teach you more of man,
Of moral evil and of good,
Than all the sages can.

—Wordsworth

It was the morning of Wednesday, November 5, 1975. To us, the seven men working in Apache-Sitgreaves National Forest, it was an ordinary workday. There was nothing in that sunny fall morning to foreshadow the tremendous fear, shock, and confusion we would be feeling as darkness fell.

It often amazes people from out of state to discover these forests in Arizona—the "arid zone." Arizona conjures up to them a hostile image of bare rock, cactus, and sandy deserts. Yet we also have hundreds of square miles of green forests. A mixture of oak, fir, and pine covers over a quarter of the state. Arizona Rocky Mountain High! Television westerns probably make for some pretty wild ideas about the southwestern U.S. I once heard of a lady tourist inquiring as to whether we had much trouble with Indian attacks! Our many picturesque blue mountain lakes, forest meadows, and the stark white and emerald-green quaking aspen trees are just not in keeping with the parched mirage projected by the movies.

We were working on the Turkey Springs tree-thinning contract. Basically, thinning involves spacing and improving the thick stands of smaller trees to allow for their faster growth. Even a virgin forest has dense thickets of small trees that require many years for natural dominance to select which of the trees will survive. Thinning speeds up the natural selection by cutting the imperfect, diseased, and damaged trees, thereby spacing the remaining ones—all according to a set of well-researched specifications set down in the Forest Service guidelines.

The sign at the entrance to Apache-Sitgreaves National Forest bears the words "Land of Many Uses." Thinning assists nearly every one of the Forest Service programs for multiuse of all the forest resources. The decreased tree density allows for increased grazing. Watershed is increased by millions of gallons without increased erosion. Hunting, fishing, and even recreation are land-uses that benefit from thinning.

That day, November 5, we were cutting a fuel-reduction strip up the crest of a ridge running south through the contract. Fuel reduction is the process of cutting the thinning slash into lengths and piling it up to be burned in the wet season. The loggers who had cut the area before us had used their bulldozers to push their logging slash into huge piles on the same strip. The Forest Service burns all the piles, carefully keeping them under control, at a time when fire danger is lowest in terms of moisture and wind. This eliminates almost all of the flammable fuel in 150-yard-wide strips that section off nearly the entire forest. If a fire starts, it will not burn far before running into one of these fuel breaks and, hopefully, it will not be able to burn any farther.

When we are piling, some of the men run saws while the others pile. I was running a saw, as were Allen Dalis and John Goulette. Dwayne Smith, Kenneth Peterson, and Steve Pierce were piling behind the cutters as we worked our way up the strip.

Second break came (none too soon) after about three hours of work since first break. Mike shouted loudly over the noise and gave the signal, thumbs up, then pointed to his watch. We shut off our saws and the forest stillness returned. For half an hour, quiet would reign again. I stopped and wiped the sweat off my forehead before carefully setting my hot saw on a nearby stump. We charged down the hill to the truck parked in the road below and grabbed our lunches. Some of the men sat in the truck and others sat outside on the carpet of pine needles. Everyone started eating. I was starved—but that was nothing unusual. Hard work in high, thin air can really burn up the calories. I was the object of a lot of ribbing from the crew about my appetite on account of my oversized "lunchbox." I began carrying my lunch in a small suitcase after finding that even two ordinary lunchboxes could not handle the amount of food I required to be able to cut trees all day.

Those guys didn't have much room to talk. They ate a considerable amount themselves; most of them carried their own lunches in large, brown paper grocery bags. Besides, I only weighed 165 pounds, which was light for my height and frame. We all found it necessary to take two lunch breaks during the day. It was just too much to go for two four-hour stretches without eating. I never noticed any of *them* dragging their heels when break time finally arrived.

I sat and ate in the dusty old work-truck. It was a 1965 International double-cab, painted a dirty brown with a mud-stained white roof and hood, with some rough wooden sideboards on the back. This dented-up rattletrap was all that stood between us and a long walk back to civilization.

After the roads out there at Turkey Springs had finally finished off the '72 Chevrolet van we used to ride to work, we started using the International. Its first days had established a poor precedent by which to judge its future performance. We had trouble with it every day for two weeks, including flat tires, fuel-line problems, leaking radiator hoses, thrown fan belts, getting stuck, and running out of gas. Some of these problems resulted in getting home quite late, but worse yet were the long walks it forced us to make. More than once we began the trek up and down the hills back to Heber. Each time we were lucky enough to be picked up, tired and footsore, by a passing vacationer or one of the local ranchers. After those first incommodious weeks, we had no more malfunctions. Strangely, the truck settled down to function smoothly, mile after rugged mile. I began to place a tentative trust in the well-seasoned machine.

The pickup was parked on what might very loosely be called a primitive road. This dirt track was in terrible shape, as the battered gas tank on the underside of the truck could attest. The underchassis would scrape over water-bars in the road, which are called "thank-you-ma'ams" for some forgotten reason. (Maybe it's because of the *wham, bam* you get from crossing them too fast. Gratitude was the least of our feelings for them.) These humps of dirt prevented the road from washing out in the rainy seasons. But they also prevented practical travel of the road in anything less tenacious than a Sherman tank.

That "road" might have been more accurately termed "obstacle course." In addition to the water-bars, there were fallen logs and large, round boulders in the path—so many, it was more sensible to weave the truck around them than to clear the way. All this zigzagging made the half mile from the Rim Road to the work site half again as long. Maneuvering that long double-cab pickup over that tortuous trail was slow progress.

The short piece out to the Rim Road was the worst of the trip. From there it was a somewhat better dirt road winding the thousand feet back down to Heber, Arizona, fifteen miles to the north, and from there on, it was another thirty-three paved miles east to Snowflake.

The contract was bordered on the south by the Rim Road, which clings to the top edge of the 7,500-foot-high Mogollon Rim, a ridge extending nearly three hundred miles east-west through northern Arizona. The Mogollon Rim actually forms a high cliff in many places, and, in the area south of Turkey Springs, drops steeply into the Apache Indian Reservation. Land north of the Rim very gradually descends into a rolling plain known as the Mogollon Plateau.

These cool autumn days are some of the best of the year for working. The lack of heat and wind allows us to maintain a reasonably comfortable working temperature. Although it can get bitterly cold at night, it usually gets up to a pleasant forty or fifty degrees in the middle of the day—still cool enough to be bracing. During the summer rainy season, we have to worry about getting stuck and digging the pickup out of mudholes. Those unpredictable downpours will sometimes completely interrupt our workday, wasting our forty-eight-mile drive.

Allen Dalis and John Goulette were leaning against an old gray log in the sun, eating their sandwiches. Both were twenty-one, had recently served out their obligations in the navy. They tended to keep to themselves and did not join in talk much of the time. They preferred to swap stories about the partying they had done and the women they had met in various ports overseas.

Ken Peterson was a blond, blue-eyed six-footer—a typical clean-cut, all-American boy. He had been good in sports in high school. At twenty-six he still looked like an overgrown kid. Ken had gotten more serious about life lately. He had a new son by the pretty little señorita he had married from south of the border. I was engrossed in my apple and did not join in the religious discussion Mike and Ken had struck up.

We talked about everything under the sun during our breaks and on the long drive home. We had conversations about religion, politics, and, of course, women. We talked about karate a lot. We touched on just about every subject of interest to us. Lusty outdoor activity really brings the mind alive and stimulates interest in life.

Dwayne Smith was a quiet sort; I did not know too much about him. He looked to be about twenty-one. John had brought him up from Phoenix only two days before. He sat on a stump nearby and ate without talking much. He was more than six feet seven inches tall and his height did not lend easily to the repeated bending over involved in piling. But, for a green man, he was doing surprisingly well. He had been piling behind me and was good at keeping up, so far. I was going to wait to see how Dwayne panned out. A lot of new men jump out there and make like a ball of fire to impress the boss and the rest of the crew with what hard workers they are. Then they quit in a few days when the accumulating fatigue wears them down. Or some hit it hard, but cannot get themselves to work every day. They make some excuse to take off during the week to recuperate. I figure it's best to hit a pace that is fast but still easy enough to keep up day after day.

Steve Pierce was laughing at something John had said to Allen. Steve was a big, husky, dark-haired kid who looked older than he was. Mike did not know it, but Steve was only seventeen. Steve came from a family with a strong work ethic, so when he quit school he had to find a job.

The autumn sun slanting weakly through the tall stands of pine was failing to take the fall chill from the air. A large crow swooped close for a curious look at us, the sunlight flashing on its shiny black feathers. Its hoarse cawing announced our resting presence to the whole forest (as if our saws had not already done so) and it flapped higher on the crisp air. Not a solitary cloud cluttered the azure hemisphere arching overhead. For as far as I could see, there was nothing but clear blue sky. Sky that borders infinite space—as we so easily forget by day.

The conversation usually begins to pick up after we've eaten. During the first part of our lunch breaks, we concentrate on knocking the sharp edge off our appetite. The birds slowly regain their confidence and begin chirping and flitting through the trees. Only after things really quiet down do we become conscious of the ever-present whispering of the wind through the treetops. Just about the time the woods return to normal, when we get cooled down, start relaxing, and talk gets interesting, our break ends.

Abruptly the crew boss, Mike Rogers, let go an intermittent blast on the horn of the International. Our half-hour break was over: time to put our coats on and our noses back to the grindstone. We topped off our gas tanks and cranked up. This one-pint fueling would run the machine for almost an hour, cutting down hundreds of trees on less than twenty cents' worth of fuel. With all due respect for our sturdy lumberjack predecessors, this is not bad efficiency—when you consider trying to use an axe to do the same thing.

The chains on our saws are always filed razor-sharp for maximum cutting speed. With five horsepower behind them, those chains can rip a six-inch-diameter tree off its stump in less than one second. Building so much power into such a light tool makes it easy for the chain to grab the wood and kick back at the operator. It seems that everyone who works very long with a chainsaw gets cut—and a saw blade cuts flesh like a hot knife through butter.

A newly hired man usually cuts himself within the first few days. The ease with which those whirling, knifelike teeth can mangle flesh is always a stunning revelation to the uninitiated. Some of the most horrible wounds you can imagine have resulted from chainsaw cuts. The chain can shred the muscles in a man's leg into hundreds of bloody strips in a split second. It is a surgeon's nightmare to try to stitch these wounds back together, and they are slow in healing. New recruits are required to wear a tough guard on their left leg for the first few days on the job. The deep slashes that accumulate in the guard often fail to instill caution in the wearer. When the guard is removed, the man promptly cuts himself. Then . . . he learns. Often the man never cuts himself again after that first lesson. Some men get away with only minor nicks, but *all* the saw operators have scars—gruesome diplomas of lessons in practical experience.

The boss, Mike Rogers, was twenty-eight, the oldest of the seven men. He had been bidding these thinning contracts from the Forest Service for nine years. That had been long enough to learn (the hard way) all the tricky pitfalls of the business. He was getting to where he could fairly consistently gauge the price per acre that would underbid the other contractors and still allow a profit margin. Turkey Springs was the best contract, profitwise, Mike had ever been awarded. In fact, it paid the highest acre-price he had ever received.

It is production in terms of acres that determines how much profit you can make in thinning. Two factors affect this: the tree density relative to price-per-acre, and the amount of ground the crew can cover in a given span of time. Mike hired the fastest cutters he could get and paid the sawyers an hourly amount based on their cutting efficiency and speed.

I had worked with Mike off and on during the seven years I had known him. Mike never tried to dominate his men, unlike some of the other men I had worked for. Rather than ordering his men around, Mike gets cooperation by simply telling them what needs to be done. A man only gets paid if he does his job, so lording it over employees is an unnecessary ego trip for a practical man like Mike. The job was just the thing for my independent nature.

I had lived the first half of my life in the desert city of Phoenix, before moving with my family into the forested mountain area of the state. Before I got into thinning, I cut and loaded pulpwood logs for a year or two. However, pulpwood, thinning, and the other jobs I had held, had been only part-time work after school and for summer vacations. Up until I left school I held a wide variety of jobs, never getting in a rut. The changes of pace were good, but thinning was always the most likable work. It was then paying better than it ever had, so there I was at twenty-two, thinning trees for a living.

I enjoy seeing the deer and other animals in the woods, but I would see no deer that day, nor any other animal with any sense. It was deer-hunting season and the fools from the city would shoot at anything that moved. I had been hearing the crack of high-powered rifles from all directions that morning. The sound of our saws carries great distances, but the noise doesn't seem to bother the hunters. At such times one might wonder about the safety of being in the woods.

Actually, it's not that bad. Hunting accidents are rare in Arizona. There are three times as many accidents between vehicles and elk along the Rim as there are firearm-related hunting accidents in the entire state. These are mostly self-inflicted, by shotgunners after game birds, and all but one in the last five years was nonfatal. In the entire U.S. there are almost no recorded accidental shootings of people not accompanying the hunter. And in Arizona there has never been a nonhunter even *injured* by firearms in the wild.

I'm sure that responsible woodsmen exist . . . somewhere. Stories about hunters who kill livestock and mistake other hunters for game are for the most part just that, stories. But every season brings back those lunatics who shoot holes in signs and leave piles of broken glass bottles from their target-practice sessions. Every year there are those who leave their trash behind, even some who drive home blissfully unconcerned about the campfires left blazing away back in the woods.

Anyone who thinks I am overstating the natural beauty of the forest obviously has not been there. Even flowery words cannot re-create the clean, robust feeling a man can experience when he is surrounded by nature. You do not have to be a dainty, daisy-sniffing poet to appreciate the green planet God gave us. As with any manual labor, at times, thinning can be a dreary, ass-busting, backbreaking, bone-weary *grind*. But my deep love for the fresh wildness of the forest is why I chose to work there.

One minor hazard we had to put up with is those damned buckthorn bushes, or buckbrush. The tough, flexible stalks will not cut when a chainsaw hits them. Instead, they get caught on the chain and flip back at the worker with enough force to drive their long thorns through a heavy glove all the way to the bone. The scratches and punctures we received from those poisonous spines nearly always ached and drew blood, even when quite minor. Whenever we had to cut trees in a patch of that cursed brush, our legs and arms would start to feel like pincushions.

Dwayne Smith wasn't aware of it, but I had to be constantly careful to fell my trees so as to miss him. His inexperience, or maybe overeagerness, was causing him to work too close to me, instead of allowing a little accumulation of slash to put some distance between us. A couple of falling saplings bouncing off his skull would knock a little vigilance into him if he wasn't careful. But at least he was trying.

I could not say the same for Steve. I could see Mike far back down the strip, restacking some sloppy piles to bring them up to specification. Steve took advantage of the boss's absence to rest his can momentarily on a handy log. He was ordinarily a good worker, but was a little disgruntled today because Mike had blamed him for some bad piles Dwayne had made.

I was trying to keep my distance from the other men, but we were coming together on a thick place to one side of the piling strip. The noise of my own saw is loud enough, even with earplugs, without revving all three of them in one spot. Just then I saw a shadow and jumped barely in time to escape a falling tree. Damn! I looked to see who had cut it. Allen. His mocking grin let me know it was no accident. I didn't let on that he had needled me. I moved farther up the strip to work. Even when accidental, falling trees were another good reason not to work too close to another man.

Once, while thinning in a high wind, I heard a loud crack and looked up in time to see a giant dead tree blotting out the sun as it fell toward me. Dead trees, or "snags," as woodsmen call them, do not have a parachute of green limbs to slow their fall. The ancient bug-ridden tower fell so quickly I didn't have time to move. The brittle old tree landed in the midst of the crew with a crackling roar, shattering into dozens of jagged sections. The thunderous force with which it snapped off the smaller trees it fell on was enough to make a man need to change his pants. After the dust cleared and we recovered from the shock, we made a head count. We found everybody standing and in one piece.

Allen always cut like a crazy man. He would put his head down and slash everything in his path, not looking where the trees fell. He was a faster sawyer than anyone out there, even me. His speed helped acre-production, but it kept him from being up to working every day. His uncontrollable temper was probably what made him saw like that, taking his anger out on the trees. Allen had nearly come to blows with almost everyone on the crew, including me. He had a way of picking fights he never finished. Although our differences were forgotten as far as I was concerned, and we were friendly on the job, I suspected that Allen might have one or two lingering bad feelings toward me.

The afternoon sun was starting to cool as it began angling steeper down in the west. In the mountains, sundown comes early. It gets dark very quickly when old Sol slips behind the trees and out of sight behind the high ridges. That last part of the day always seems to crawl by. The gathering chill was beginning to numb my nose. We moved quickly in the late-afternoon nippiness. With summer ending, it was starting to get down to five or ten degrees at night. Activity helped me build up body heat inside my lightweight, blue denim jacket. I worked a little faster to ward off the chill, eagerly anticipating the reprieve of the day's conclusion. Not long to go before we could head for home and a nice hot shower.

Sunset had been fifteen minutes earlier, but we kept cutting in the waning light. I checked my watch again. It was six o'clock at last! Mike was still down the hill a little way, picking up and repiling. I yelled and took the liberty of giving the stop-work signal. The sound of the saws died; the final echoes absorbed into the deepening dusk.

"Time to go!" I announced loudly. The tired men were revitalized by the prospect of quitting for the day, and by their feelings of accomplishment. We had moved a pretty good distance up the strip in those eight hours of labor.

"Let's go home!" John said enthusiastically.

Allen grumbled, "It's 'bout time."

"We really hurt 'em today, boys," Ken exclaimed, rubbing his palms together with the characteristic ambitious mannerism he used when he talked about work.

"Hurt *me*, you mean!" Dwayne said, rubbing his lower back.

"One of you guys wanna help me carry this stuff?" Steve asked, gathering up the nearly empty gas and oil cans. John grabbed the water jug and an oil can. I carried the orange five-gallon plastic gas can in one hand and my saw in the other as we descended the hill.

We loaded the chainsaws and gas and oil cans into the back of the truck. After arranging the gas cans so they would not tip over and leak on the bumps, Mike slammed the tailgate tightly.

"You guys have got to start doing a better job on those piles," Mike said. "That mess I fixed up back there never would have passed inspection. I know who's making those mistakes by their position on the strip. So, not mentioning any names, let's tighten up on the specifications—all right?"

Nobody said anything. He was right. If our cutting failed to pass inspection, it would delay our payday until it did pass. It was in our interest to get it right the first time.

"Listen to that," Steve said. We could still hear the faint sound of shooting reverberating down the gullies somewhere in the distance. It is illegal to hunt after sundown, but there just aren't enough game wardens to go around. Maybe someone was doing a little target practice.

"Let's load up, men," Mike said.

The decrepit pickup groaned on its tired old suspension as everyone piled in. There was Dwayne by the left rear door, John and Steve in the middle, and Allen by the right rear door. In the front, I sat by the door, riding shotgun. Ken sat in the middle, and of course Mike was driving. The seven of us usually sat in the same place every day. Nonsmokers in front, smokers in back.

"Home, James," someone said, with mock elegance.

Mike started the old pickup and we climbed north up the ridge toward the Rim Road. It was 6:10. Barring any breakdowns, we should be home before 7:30. We left the windows down so we could cool off some. We were still warm from laboring, in spite of the evening air. Mike, Ken, and I do not smoke and we prefer to inhale genuine, unadulterated air. The four in the backseat lit up as soon as we were in the truck, eager after hours without a cigarette. The fresh air coming in my window was bracing. We usually nap on the way to work every morning, but none of us ever feels drowsy on the way back to town. The rousing activity on the job hones a keenness that stays with us all the way home.

"Why don't we all go swimming after dinner tonight?" I suggested.

Dwayne, new to Snowflake, looked doubtful. "You guys are crazy, it's too damn cold for that."

"There's a heated pool in town," I told him. Snowflake was a small town of only 2,500 then, but it actually had an indoor swimming pool.

"That would be a good way to soak out some of the crud and tiredness I'm feeling," Mike agreed.

"I'll bring a basketball," Ken volunteered.

Bouncing over the thank-you-ma'ams, the truck kept bottoming out on its springs with a dull clunking sound. The fellows started cracking jokes about the pickup.

"Peddle harder, everyone, we'll make it up this hill yet," Ken quipped.

"Hey Mike, do you like this thing better than a pickup truck?" one of the men called from the backseat.

The continual jouncing and bobbing of the vehicle, unencumbered with shock absorbers, caused me to add: "What he's got here is a rare specimen of Australian pogo truck!"

Everybody laughed.

Just then my eye was caught by a light coming through the trees on the right, a hundred yards ahead. I idly assumed that the glow was the sun going down in the west. Then it occurred to me that the sun had set half an hour ago. Curious, I thought it might be the light of some hunters camped there—headlights or maybe a fire. Some of the guys must have caught sight of it too, because the men on the right side of the truck had fallen silent.

As we continued driving up the road toward the brightness, we passed in sight of it for an instant. We barely got a glimpse through gnarled branches before we rolled past the opening in the trees.

"Son of a . . ." Allen started.

"What the hell was that?" I asked.

My eyes strained to make sense of the glimmering through the dense stand of trees blocking our vision. From my open window, I could see the yellowish brilliance washing across our path onto the road another forty yards ahead. Intrigued, I was impatient to get past the intervening pines.

"Hurry up! Drive on up there where we can see!" somebody urged.

From the driver's seat, Mike could not look up with the proper angle without leaning way over. "What do you guys see?" he demanded curiously.

Dwayne answered, "I don't know—but it looked like a crashed plane hanging in a tree!"

Finally, our growing excitement spurred Mike into wringing out what little speed the pickup could still achieve on the incline. We rolled past the intervening evergreen thicket to where we could have an unobstructed view of the source of the strange radiance. Suddenly we were electrified by the most awesome, incredible sight we had seen in our entire lives.

"Stop!" John cried out. "Stop the truck!"

As the truck skidded to a dusty halt in the rocky road, I threw open the door for a clearer view of the dazzling sight.

"My God!" Allen yelled. *"It's a flying saucer!"*

CHAPTER 3

Abduction!

*Just as yellow gold is tested by the fire, so is friendship
to be tested by adversity.*

—Ovid

Mike shut off the engine. We watched, spellbound. The men on the left side of the truck leaned over so that they could see. There, a mere ninety feet above the ground, a strange, golden disc hovered silently. Our attention was riveted on that object poised in the air. Impaled by the sight, we were held transfixed for one long, silent moment that felt like an eternity.

The cold, jarring reality of what we were witnessing struck fear and awe to the core of every one of us. Suddenly beholding its vivid, magnificent structure summoned all emotions at once. You could almost hear our hearts pounding above that suspended instant of silence. Less than thirty yards away, the metallic craft hung motionless, fifteen feet above a tangled pile of logging slash.

The craft was stationary, hovering well below the treetops near the crest of the ridge. The hard, mechanical precision of the luminous vehicle was in sharp contrast to the primitive ruggedness of the dark surroundings. Its edges were clearly defined. The golden machine was starkly outlined against the deepening blue of the clear evening sky.

The soft yellow haze from the craft dimly illuminated the immediate area with an eerie glow. Under the weird light, the encircling forest took on bizarre hues that were very different from its natural colors. The trees, the brush, and the grass all reflected subtle, peculiar new shades.

I estimated the object to have an overall diameter of fifteen or twenty feet; it was eight or ten feet thick. The flattened disc had a shape like that of two gigantic pie-pans placed lip to lip, with a small round bowl turned upside down on top. Barely visible at our angle of sight, the white dome peaked over the upper outline of the ship. We could see darker stripes of a dull silver sheen that divided the glowing areas into panel-like sections. The dim yellowish light given off by the surface had the luster of hot metal, fresh from a blast furnace.

There were no visible antennae or protrusions of any kind. Nothing that resembled a hatch, ports, or windowlike structures could be seen. There was no motion and no sound from the craft. It almost appeared to be dead in the air. There was no life visible anywhere. Nothing stirred. It seemed that even the wind held its breath. The entire scene—we the work crew, the pickup, and the spectacular intruder—seemed frozen for a single instant.

Ken shattered the silence. "Damnation! This is . . . really . . . happening!" he breathed hoarsely, in a voice fraught with awestruck fear.

Those words abruptly shook us from our reverie. No more than a second had passed since I had thrown open the door as the truck stopped. I glanced from one to another stricken face. Allen was hiding down low behind the doorsill. As Dwayne later expressed it: "He kissed his knees." Turning back to that impelling spectacle in the air, I was suddenly seized with the urgency to see the craft at close range. I was afraid it would fly away and I would miss the chance of a lifetime to satisfy my curiosity about it. I hurriedly got out of the truck and started toward the hovering ship.

The men were alarmed by my sudden action.

"Travis!" Allen called, low.

"What do you think you're doing?" Mike demanded in a loud, harsh whisper.

Placing my feet quietly, I quickly stalked closer to the mysterious vehicle. Stepping over a low-leaning fir sapling, I carefully picked my way through the opening in the trees. I put my hands in my pockets in response to the cooler twilight air outside the truck.

After I had traversed about fifteen or twenty yards, the men began urgently calling to me, in strained, hushed shouts, to return to the truck.

"Travis!"

"Hey, Travis!" the men warned insistently.

"Get back here, man!" one of the men called in a louder voice.

I stopped walking for a long, hesitant moment. I paused and turned to look back at the six men staring questioningly at me from the truck. The sober realization of what I was doing abruptly heightened the doubt I was already wrestling with. What should I do? I asked myself. Maybe I'm being foolhardy, I told myself. I won't get too close . . . but what if there's somebody inside that thing? I faltered. Finally I reassured myself with: I can always run away.

I was committed. Without replying to the guys, I resolutely turned and continued my brazen approach.

"That crazy son of a bitch!" I heard someone swear.

I moved more slowly, cautiously covering the remaining distance in a half-crouch. I straightened up as I entered the dim circular halo of light softly reflecting onto the ground under the craft. I was about six feet from being directly beneath the machine. Bathed in the yellow aura, I stared up at the unbelievably smooth, unblemished surface of the curving hull. I was filled with a tremendous sense of awe and curiosity as I pondered the incomprehensible mysteries possible within it.

I had become aware of a barely audible sound coming from the ship. I could detect a strange blend of low- and high-pitched mechanical sounds. There were intermittent high, piercing, beeping points overlaid on the distant, low rumbling sound of heavy machinery. The strange tones were so mixed that it was impossible to compare them to any sound I could remember ever hearing.

"Travis! Get away from there!" Mike yelled to me.

I shot a fleeting look at the pickup parked in the road, then turned my attention back to studying the incredible ship.

Suddenly I was startled by a powerful, thunderous swell in the volume of the vibrations from the craft. I jumped at the sound, like that of a multitude of turbine generators starting up. I saw the saucer start wobbling on its axis with a quickening motion, in a pattern like the erratic spin of an unstabilized top. The same side continued to face me as the craft remained hovering at approximately the same height while it wobbled.

I ducked into a crouch, down behind the safety of a nearby log. I expected the saucer to streak away. It didn't. Cringing there, I did some fast reassessments of my situation. I resolved to waste no time in getting the hell out of there!

I rose to go and was half out of my crouch when a tremendously bright, blue-green ray shot from the bottom of the craft. *I* saw and heard nothing. All I felt was the numbing force of a blow that felt like a high-voltage electrocution. The intense bolt made a sharp cracking, or popping, sound. The stunning concussion of the foot-wide beam struck me full in the head and chest. My mind sank quickly into unfeeling blackness. I didn't even see what hit me; but from the instant I felt that paralyzing blow, I did not see, hear, or feel anything more.

The men in the truck saw my body arch backward, arms and legs out-stretched, as the force of the blow lifted me off the ground. I was hurled backward through the air ten feet. They saw my right shoulder hit the hard rocky earth of the ridgetop. My body landed limply and lay motionless, spread out on the ground.

"It got him!" Steve yelled.

Dwayne screamed: "Let's get out of here!"

"Get this son of a bitch moving!" Allen shrieked hysterically.

Mike did not need to be asked. He was already desperately groping, fum-bling around for the ignition switch. His shaking fingers finally seized the key. The engine roared to life. He popped out the clutch and the truck lunged forward. The knobby mud-and-snow tires flung rocks and clouds of dirt backward as the International spun out of the clearing. Mike gunned the truck up the boulder-strewn track. He frantically spun the steering wheel one way, then the other, navigating the tortuous road.

"Is it following us?" he yelled over his shoulder. Nobody answered.

"Is it after us?" he shouted again.

When again no reply came, he turned to see the looks of stupefied shock on the faces of his crew. Their pale faces stared straight ahead, blankly. He knew then that it was entirely up to him to get them all to safety.

In reaction to the unbelievable horror of what they had witnessed, six hardened woodsmen were reduced to mindless terror. The truck bounced wildly in their panicked flight. It scraped loudly over the rocky water-bars. Mike sent the pickup careening off the road, crashing over bushes and small trees. He turned around to find the truck heading toward the thick trunk of a big pine tree. He jerked the machine back onto the track in a spray of dirt and gravel.

Mike was fearful that the saucer was pursuing them. He put his head out the open window to try to see behind and was stung in the face by the sharp pine needles of a passing limb. He kept hitting boulders and other obsta-cles in his attempts to look behind. The erratically vibrating rearview mir-rors only produced a blurred, flickering image, a faint yellow glow in the blackness. Goaded by a surge of terror, he stomped on the gas pedal.

The rattling truck shot forward at thirty-five miles an hour—far too fast for the condition of that road. A passing limb slammed into the right rearview mirror, bending it uselessly to the side of the truck. The old In-ternational went flying through the air over the dirt ramp of a high water-bar. As it landed, the pickup smashed down destructively on its weakened springs with a terrible crash.

The powerful jolt of metal on metal brought Mike to his senses. He was gripped by a sudden icy realization. If the truck broke down, they would be stranded and at the mercy of the unknown threat they were fleeing. He slowed the truck down to ten miles an hour. He was grateful to find the truck still working, capable of carrying them away.

The road turned east in a tight curve to the left. The men remained petrified in stunned silence. Mike was still badly frightened, and apprehensive of being pursued. He looked north, back across the curve of the road, and saw the startling glow of the saucer in the gathering darkness. It was still barely visible in the same clearing, two hundred yards back. He was very much relieved to find that their mad dash had put some distance between them and it.

The truck passed behind dense thickets of pine saplings, and the ship was once more lost from sight. In diverting his attention from his driving, Mike made the wrong approach to a water-bar in the road. It was the largest of the thank-you-ma'ams and the last one before the Rim Road, a hundred feet farther on. Unless that water-bar was crossed at the correct angle, the pickup would high-center and get stuck straddling the hump. Mike stopped the truck to back up and make another run at it.

"It doesn't look like it's after us," Mike shuddered as he shoved the gearshift into reverse.

The pause broke the men out of their shocked silence. They began to jabber hysterically. Instead of continuing on over the obstacle, they sat there with the engine running. They struggled to collect themselves and decide what to do. Everyone was yelling at once, in a confusion of high-pitched shouting. Allen uttered a loud string of profanity. They were all either crying, praying, or swearing. Some did all three. Steve was sobbing out a prayer, his young face streaming with tears.

Ken stammered, "I c-can't believe wh-what I just saw!"

Dwayne said in a wondering voice: "I've never seen a UFO before!"

"It l-looked like it k-k-killed him!" Allen stuttered.

Ken shook his head. "That poor guy!"

Mike anxiously asked: "I saw him falling back, but what happened to him?"

"Man, a blue ray just shot out of the bottom of that thing and hit him all over! It just seemed to engulf him." Ken's voice was solemn with awe.

"Good hell! It looked like he *disintegrated*!" Dwayne exclaimed.

"No, he was in one piece," Steve contradicted. "I saw him hit the ground."

"I do know one thing. It sure looked like he got hit by lightning or something!" Dwayne returned. "I heard a zap—like as if he touched a live wire!"

"Damn!" John swore. "It sure knocked the hell out of him!"

"It looked almost like a grenade exploded in front of him and just blew him back!" Ken cried.

"Hey, men, we better go back!" someone said.

Ken agreed. "Yeah, he could be hurt real bad!"

"No way, man. I ain't going back there!" Steve said.

Dwayne said, "No, we better go back. He could really need help!" He looked at Steve. "You don't want to stay here by yourself while we go, do you?"

Steve gave him a blank stare.

"I don't know if I want to go back, either!" John admitted.

"It's startin' to get dark, maybe we better go get some help," Allen faltered.

"All right," Mike interjected. "Let's build a fire so the guys who don't want to go can stay here in the clearing while the rest of us go back there."

Primitive instinct made the false security of a fire seem somehow comforting. Mike shut off the engine and they all got out into the deepening dusk.

Their hoarse yelling grew louder and more hysterical when they got out. They kept looking around nervously, up into the darkening sky. Mike went to the back of the truck to get gas to splash on some wood for a quick fire. The men followed. They aimed most of their ideas and questions about what they should do at him. Even though Mike did not insist on being bossy at work, they automatically turned to him to tell them what to do. Their diminished self-possession caused them to depend on Mike for answers he did not have.

Just as Mike was about to get the gas out of the back, they were startled by the sudden approach of headlights coming west on the Rim Road. The dim outline of a camper-pickup could be seen passing in the dark.

"Let's go catch that pickup and get help!" John yelped excitedly.

"We can't catch that guy," Mike said, dispirited. "He's long gone by now—but maybe he'll stop up the road somewhere," he added, brightening a little. "If we can't catch him, maybe we can find some other hunters or somebody."

"Yeah, let's go!" Dwayne agreed.

Everybody piled in the right side of the truck, Dwayne this time taking the recently vacated front seat, by the door. As Mike went around the driver's side of the truck, he exclaimed: "Look! Did you see that?"

The men scrambled to look. One of the men ran to the front of the pickup. "What was it?" he asked.

Mike told them he thought he had briefly seen the outline of the golden disc through the trees to the south. It had raised itself vertically to treetop level and streaked away toward the northeast at incredible speed.

They got in the truck, Mike pondering the unbelievable acceleration of that streak he had glimpsed. He angled the forgiving old pickup over the high water-bar and pulled out onto the Rim Road, heading west. He drove rapidly, half hoping to catch up with the camper that had passed.

"What do you guys think we should do?" Mike asked.

"I think we ought to go back!" Ken said vehemently.

Allen disagreed. "We oughta get some help—get some guns from some hunters or somebody—before we try that."

"I'll go if we can stay in the truck," Steve whined. "I don't want to get out."

"I guess we better go back," John said solemnly. He hadn't said much at all until now. He appeared still to be in a mild state of shock.

They argued on, rehashing what had happened. They did not find any hunters, or anyone else. They were still arguing a mile down the road, where they reached the turnoff that went north to Heber from the Rim Road. There, they finally worked their way around to the inevitable conclusion.

"Ken, do you think it's safe to go back and see about Travis?" Mike asked.

"That's what I've been saying we should do all along! He could be bleeding to death! Maybe he was only knocked down by that thing. We don't know. We ought to at least go back and check!"

Mike turned the truck around at the turnoff. He said firmly: "This truck is going back. Anybody who doesn't want to come can get out right here and now, and wait! We've been acting like a bunch of cowards. We're all scared, there's no denying that, but we've got to do what we should've done in the first place!"

The embarrassed men no longer protested returning to the site. Even if any were still reluctant, they were ashamed to say so. Also, the prospect of waiting alone at the turnoff in the dark was much worse then going back together.

Their courage had been reinforced by the time and distance away from the site. However, as they turned left, off the Rim Road toward the original scene, their apprehension began steadily to rebuild. They could not stop going over and over what they had seen. They began speculating on the dreadful possibilities of what they might find when they returned. The nearer they got, the more anxious they became.

"What if that thing is still there?" Dwayne questioned fearfully.

"We'll be able to see it before we get there," Mike said uncertainly. "If it *is* still there, we'll turn around and get the hell out of there."

"What if we find Travis's dead body lying out there?" was Allen's grisly question.

Nobody replied—nobody wanted to think about the answer to that.

They rounded the curve where Mike had last been able to see the saucer. They saw nothing. The pickup rolled hesitantly onward. Skittishly the men looked all about them. They quieted their motions inside the truck. Their subdued comments came less frequently.

"Get the flashlight out of the glove box, there," Mike directed. Dwayne handed it to him.

"I think it was right along here somewhere, you guys, so keep your eyes peeled." Mike drove on slowly, scanning the roadside.

"Hold it! It was right back there!" Ken exclaimed.

"Yeah! I think it was right about here!" Dwayne agreed. "I recognize that pile of slash over there!"

Mike sent the flashlight beam stabbing out into the darkness. He called loudly, "TRAVIS . . . !" Everybody listened intently. No answer.

Somebody suggested pulling the truck around and pointing the headlights toward the log pile above which they had seen the hovering ship. They backed up and pulled in, driving over the fir sapling leaning in the way. Their eyes searched the area illuminated by the headlights.

They found nothing. No dead body in the clearing.

"Maybe this ain't it," Ken suggested. "All these piles look alike."

"I thought it was farther down that way," Allen said, pointing north down the ridge.

"Naw, if anything, it was farther back up that way," Ken countered.

"No, I remember this spot," Dwayne insisted. "See that tree leanin' down over there?"

"We're just going to have to get out and look around," Mike cut in. "Before we do anything—who all's coming and who all is staying?"

Nobody wanted to remain behind alone. The woods were very dark.

"Leave it running," Steve suggested, as they got out of the truck. They left the doors open, too—everyone saw the sense of a quick getaway. Just in case.

They searched first in the security of the headlights. Everybody stayed together, huddling close behind Mike, who carried the only flashlight.

The tightly-knit group searched the immediate area thoroughly, foot by foot. The flashlight beam probed into the night, examining every dark shape. They searched behind every log, bush, and stump. They called repeatedly: "Travis! . . . TRAVIS!!" Except for their calls, the woods were deathly quiet.

Their eyes strained into the dark of the surrounding trees. They cast occasional apprehensive glances skyward. There was nothing but empty, star-dusted sky. Their frayed nerves were strained to the snapping point.

"Look out!" Dwayne cried, jumping.

Everyone jerked their heads this way and that, looking around them. "What's the matter?" the others asked urgently.

"Ohhh!" Dwayne heaved a relieved sigh. "That moon up there scared the hell out of me!" There had been a new moon the previous Monday, which had grown tonight to a thin, golden sliver only a little lighter in color than the flying saucer. "I caught it out of the corner of my eye and I thought it was that flying saucer coming back!" The adrenaline that had surged into everyone's bloodstream left them shaking uncontrollably.

Occasionally catching unexpected glimpses of the moon, and anticipating at any moment the discovery of a charred corpse increased every man's gut fear. They became more and more nervous as they searched.

"TRAVIS!" they called at intervals.

They looked farther north, as Allen had suggested, but there were no more slash-piles there. Also, the ground was steeper than they remembered the site being. They searched beyond the crest of the ridge and farther south, where there were more piles. None of the piles looked as much like what they remembered as the first one they had investigated.

"Maybe he ran after us when we took off!" Ken suggested. They searched for tracks in the soft, powdery dust of the road. There were no tracks but those of the truck. Looking in the trees on the steeply sloping ground east of the road, the men again found nothing.

They found no sign anywhere—no foreign objects or unusual markings. No burns, pad impressions, or disturbed ground. Not a trace of tracks and no evidence of a struggle.

"TRAVIS!"

The longer they continued, the more worried Mike became, more overcome with emotion. He stumbled, then stood, looking down, struggling to control his feelings. The loss of his friend, his guilt at driving away, and the pressure of the leadership being demanded of him all became too much to bear for a moment. He silently handed the flashlight to Ken.

"You all right, Mike?" Ken took him by the shoulder. "Take it easy, man. Come on, it's going to be okay."

After a few moments, Mike managed to regain his composure. Finally he could speak: "Okay, you guys, we're not doing any good here. Let's go!"

They got in the truck and began the long drive back to Heber. The farther they got from the spot, the more relieved they grew. Speeding slightly, they drove as fast as road conditions would permit. The memory of what they had so recently witnessed left them with a spectrum of strong emotional reactions.

"That ray was the brightest thing I've ever seen in my whole life!" declared Steve. "It almost blinded me for a second."

"You're never gonna catch me out here in these woods again!" vowed Dwayne.

Ken kept shaking his head. "Incredible, absolutely incredible," he pondered aloud.

Behind their excited talking, the men were nagged by the problem they knew they would have to face.

"What are we going to do now?" somebody finally asked.

"Let's get a buncha people together to go out there and help us look," Dwayne suggested.

Then Ken voiced the one thought they had all avoided so far. "We're gonna have to tell the authorities about this."

"The cops?" Allen exclaimed. "No way! They'll think we're nuts!"

"If we don't tell them, and if Travis can't be found, they might suspect *us*," Mike pointed out.

"If we tell anybody at all, they're gonna think we're crazy!" Steve said.

"I know!" John said, brightening. "We'll just say that Travis is lost, and not say anything about the UFO."

"He might well only be dazed and wandering around out there . . . but what if he's not?" Mike questioned ominously. The possibility of what else incredible might have happened that this question opened up, was one thing they did not want to think about.

"We'd better tell them everything and just pray that they believe us!" said Ken. "We've got to stay honest all the way through this. It's the only way we're going to be believed."

Just then the pickup rounded the bend. The comforting lights of Heber came into view. The oasis of civilization was the very symbol of salvation to them at that moment. They drove down the dark, quiet street of the sleeping town to the nearest telephone. The pale blue fluorescent light of that phone booth was a welcome sight.

They parked the truck and got out. Ken picked up the cold black receiver and dialed *O*. It was he who first broke the incredible news to the police.

CHAPTER 4

Night Search

Even the bravest are frightened by sudden terrors.

—Tacitus, 87 A.D.

Ken Peterson waited nervously for an operator to answer. He glanced at his watch. It was 7:35 P.M. He looked out the window, his breath fogging the cold glass. Just outside the booth, Mike and Allen were pacing up and down, occasionally casting anxious glances at him. They stamped their feet to ward off the creeping numbness of the cold November night. The others sat in the warm truck. All five men waited tensely while Ken talked.

"Well?" Allen said, as Ken stepped out of the telephone booth.

"He's coming," Ken announced.

"Who's coming?" Mike asked. "The sheriff?"

"No—Deputy Ellison," Ken replied. "He wants us to meet him up there." He pointed toward a parking lot a block up the street by the highway.

"What did you tell him?" Mike asked impatiently.

"Nothing," Ken answered. "I mean, at the last minute I got to thinking. If I was to tell him about the UFO on the phone, he might've thought it was a crazy joke or something and hung up on me." They started toward the pickup. "I just told him one of our crew got lost," he finished lamely.

The heater's noisy fan was blowing lukewarm air into the truck. Theirs was the only vehicle in the freshly paved parking lot. They did not talk much. The excitement had diminished into the numb silence of shock.

While they waited for Deputy Ellison, they struggled to think of a way to present their incredible report.

"You know," Dwayne said discouragingly, "it's gonna be awful hard for him to accept. We're gonna hafta expect that."

"Hell no, he ain't gonna believe us," Allen grumbled. "The pigs never believe anything."

This derogatory term for the authorities bothered the other men.

"Here we are, asking them for help," Ken reproached him, "and you sit here talking about them like that."

Allen ignored their disapproval.

"They've *gotta* know we're telling the truth," John insisted. "I sure don't know what the hell we're gonna do if they don't."

"Well, we're about to find out," Mike said grimly. "Here he is."

The shiny brown county car was pulling into the parking lot. It rolled up to the driver's side of the truck and stopped. The big deputy stepped out and sauntered around the car. Passing in front of the headlights, he sent long, shifting shadows out across the deserted highway.

Mike rolled down his window as the officer stepped up. He stood about five-ten, a strong two hundred pounds. He wore the brown, western-style uniform of the Navajo County Sheriff's Department. On the lapel of his heavy coat glinted the golden star of his badge.

"Okay, what's the problem here?" he demanded. There was a tone in his voice that made them certain he would not believe a single word of what they were about to say.

"Well," Mike began. "A friend of ours is probably lost. At least he might be lost, anyway. I mean, he may be dead!"

Ellison's interest sharpened. His eyes darted from one face to the other. Steve's reddened eyes and tear-streaked face, the various pale, taut expressions of the others, made him certain of at least one thing. Something very serious had happened.

"What do you mean, 'He might be dead'? You'll have to be a little more specific than that," the deputy said with stern authority. "What makes you think he might be dead?"

"Well, sir . . ." Mike groped for words. "It's kinda hard to explain. You may think we're . . . I mean . . . I don't really know where to start!"

"How about starting at the beginning?" Ellison ordered impatiently.

Ken came to Mike's rescue. He began relating what had happened. Ken's words were like a leak springing in a dam. The others joined in, adding more information and agreeing with Ken's descriptions. The impact of their recent experience was fresh in everyone's speech. Their voices broke at the recall of their nightmarish ordeal. Emotions overflowed at the first opportunity to tell someone who had not seen what they had seen. The dam obliterated, their words washed over Ellison like a flood tide.

The deputy exhibited exceptional cool and reserve. He did not interrupt the men the first time through the account. While they talked, Ellison studied each face with narrowed eyes. The longer the men talked, the more his attitude seemed to change. What it was changing to, the men couldn't be certain.

Finally, when they finished, Ken confronted the officer with what everyone considered obvious. "You don't believe us, do you?" he asked fatalistically. He looked Ellison squarely in the eye.

Surprised, Ellison replied: "No, I wouldn't say I don't believe you, though you've got to admit it sounds pretty wild."

The men were relieved that the deputy was taking them seriously. But that had only been a secondary source of their apprehension. The fate of their coworker was their prime concern.

The deputy continued. "No, I believe you enough to where I'm going to call in and get some deputies out here to look for this man. I want some of you to come up on the hill with me. I've got to radio in to the central office in Holbrook. Yes, you three," he said, nodding at Mike, Ken, and Allen— the more vocal half of the group. The other three men were still claimed by stunned silence for the most part. "The rest of you wait here," he ordered.

The three got in the police car with Ellison and rode the winding mile west on Highway 277 to the top of the hill. The radio did not have the power to transmit out of the canyon cradling Heber. Up on the hill, the deputy had a clearer shot at Holbrook, the county seat. Ellison radioed the dispatcher. He was informed that the sheriff was not in the office but would radio back.

While Ellison waited for his superior to return his radio call, he had the dispatcher connect him with County Deputy Glen Flake. He asked Deputy Flake to check at my home to see if I was there. He thought it was possible that I had somehow caught a ride into town after the others had left me behind. Ellison did not explain the request. But Deputy Flake reported back in a few minutes that there were no lights on, the house was locked up; no one was home.

Finally Sheriff Marlin Gillespie came on the radio. Ellison told him that he had a missing-person's report involving a UFO. He briefly related what he'd been told. Gillespie said he would come out immediately. Ellison explained there would be bad road conditions. Sheriff Gillespie responded that he and Undersheriff Ken Coplan would bring the Sheriff's Department's four-wheel-drive pickup.

After Sheriff Gillespie signed off, Deputy Glen Flake came back on the radio to ask: "What was that I heard about Travis Walton and a UFO?" He inquired whether any more men were needed. Ellison told him that it was best not to talk about the matter over the air until they had checked into it further. They did not want to start a panic with any wild rumor. Deputy Flake agreed, but said he would stand by.

Deputy Ellison drove the three men back to the parking lot where the other three men had remained. They all waited for Sheriff Gillespie to travel the forty-five miles from Holbrook.

An hour later, Sheriff Gillespie and his second-in-command, Under-sheriff Coplan, arrived in the county's four-wheel-drive pickup. The camper-truck was a big machine with at least a foot and a half of ground clearance. Ken Coplan got out and strolled over to where Ellison was questioning Ken Peterson, off to one side. Coplan was a big grizzly, even compared to the sizable Ellison. However, the truly commanding figure was Sheriff Gillespie. His character more than compensated for his smaller frame. He approached Mike's window. The well-seasoned sheriff's eighteen years in law enforcement had left little to be surprised about, but this was a new one.

Gillespie addressed the group in a congenial manner that smoothed over the tough, serious undercurrent in his voice. "Tell me again, who is this fella that's missing?"

Mike took a deep breath, looked at the sheriff squarely and answered, "One of our crew, Travis Walton." He paused, looking for some sign of how the sheriff was going to take what he was about to say.

With no change of expression the sheriff prompted, "Well, let's hear it from the start. What happened?"

The lawman listened carefully while the men explained. His sun-weath-ered Irish complexion wrinkled into a hard, inscrutable expression as he studied the men. He immediately noted the absence of any symptom of in-toxication among them.

"It's colder than hell out here," he said. "Mind if I get in there a minute while I ask you a few questions?" Gillespie walked around the truck and sat in the right front seat. He continued to question the men intently.

At length he shook his head. "You know, this whole thing sounds crazy, but I've got to admit—I've not seen anything to give me a reason to disbe-lieve you!"

Faith was restored for the crewmen. They were now sure that they had done the right thing in telling the truth and reporting their problem.

The sheriff had run into every sort of crackpot and con artist in his years as a law officer. By now he had a good feel for deception. None was apparent here. These men were sincere. And he knew—if he had ever seen it—that this was authentic shock on their faces.

The existence of UFOs was not so unheard-of to the lawman. He related to them an incident he had experienced years ago in this same county. The men were amazed to learn that Sheriff Marlin Gillespie himself had experienced a close encounter with a large glowing object!

"Okay, we've got to go out and see if we can find this guy," the sheriff concluded. "If this fellow is hurt, we need to find him as soon as possible."

"I ain't going back out there!" Steve declared emphatically. "No way." He was filled with dread at the prospect. The trauma of recent events had followed a long exhausting workday. John and Dwayne were equally firm in their resolution not to return to the forest.

"At least some of you are going to have to come along," Gillespie insisted.

Ken, Allen, and Mike agreed to accompany the lawmen back to the site of the encounter. Mike gave John permission to drive Steve and Dwayne home to Snowflake in the crew truck.

The three remaining men got into Deputy Ellison's car. Ken got in front and Allen and Mike climbed in the rear.

Gillespie drove down and got the owner of the Union 76 station out of bed. They filled the tanks of Deputy Ellison's car and the four-wheel-drive pickup, then headed up the dirt canyon road toward Turkey Springs. Ellison led the way with the directions supplied by the three tree-cutters. Gillespie and Coplan brought up the rear in the pickup.

The county car was designed for streets and highways, so the fifteen miles of rough dirt road were a little too much for it. In driving up the last steep hill before reaching the Rim Road, the muffler fell completely off the car. Ellison got out and put the muffler in the back of the pickup following. The car roared noisily on up the hill with the truck still behind.

When they reached the turnoff from the Rim Road to the contract, Ellison's car could go no farther. The thank-you-ma'ams were too high for its low ground clearance. Ellison, Allen, and Ken then climbed into the paddywagon-style camper on the back of the pickup. They sat on the two hard wooden benches of the "rolling cell" for the last quarter mile of the dark forest trail.

Mike rode in the front seat of the pickup with Sheriff Gillespie and Ken Coplan. The golden sliver of the moon which had earlier loomed in the western sky, had dropped below the horizon. It was pitch-dark. Gillespie shone the powerful beam of the truck's spotlight to the sides of the road as they drove.

As they neared the abduction site, everyone, including the officers, could not help feeling a bit uneasy. No one spoke. Only the sound of the engine and the tires scattering rocks could be heard as they broke into the clearing.

Mike said softly, "This is the place." The truck rolled to a stop. Coplan sent the spotlight scanning back and forth around the empty clearing. They slowly got out and stood in a circle in front of the headlights. Compulsively they all turned their eyes skyward. The woods were quiet. The ephemeral streak of a small meteorite silently crossed the star-studded void.

Gillespie cleared his throat. "Wounded animals usually travel downhill," he said. He discussed the possibility that I was hurt and had wandered away in the dark, perhaps delirious. It was likely that if I still had my senses about me, I would stay on the roads where help could find me. If I was very badly hurt, the chances were good that I had not gotten far.

They looked around with apprehension at the dark surrounding trees. With the temperature steadily lowering, they all desperately hoped they would find some sign of me soon.

"Ellison, you and Rogers take the truck and search the roads down below," the sheriff ordered. "The rest of us will use the flashlights and look around here."

The contract was riddled with old logging trails normally impassable with an ordinary vehicle. The big four-wheeler ambled over one rugged trail after another. Coplan sent the spotlight bouncing from left to right, the narrow shaft sweeping the roadsides. Mike and the deputy, an experienced tracker, kept a constant vigil for footprints. They stopped at intervals to check the dusty road for signs. There was no wind; any creature passing over that soft ground would leave distinct tracks. For another endless, bitter-cold hour, both parties continued to search without success. Not a single trace of anyone was found. The two groups gathered back at the clearing to exchange the grim news.

"I think we've done about all we can do here tonight," Gillespie announced. His statement gave the men a sinking feeling that they were afraid to put into words. Their thoughts were that if I was in the immediate area, they would have found me. I should have heard their calls if I was anywhere near. Unless I was lying unconscious in the nearby brush. Or perhaps I had simply started running and kept running until I collapsed. The chances of dying from exposure at this time of year were great. I had only a light jacket. I might also die from my injuries if I needed medical attention.

"We can only cover so much ground in the dark with the number of men we have," the sheriff continued. "I'm going to get more men out here first thing in the morning. We'll blanket the whole area. Right now we need to notify Walton's family. Who's his next of kin?"

"His mother, Mary Kellett," Mike replied. "She's staying in a cabin over east of Overgaard. Bear Springs is the place."

"Okay," Gillespie said. "You go with Coplan in the truck and notify Walton's mother. Ellison and I will take Dalis and Peterson back to Snowflake."

During the half-hour drive, Coplan remarked: "This whole thing sounds crazy as hell! If I didn't know Ken Peterson for so long, I'd have a heck of a time believin' the rest of you." He explained that he had gone to school with Ken Peterson's father and had known the family for years. "Ken just wouldn't lie about something like this," he said in conclusion.

It was shortly after one in the morning when they made the turn onto the last eighth of a mile to the house. It stood on the edge of a wide forest meadow and was overhung by grand old oaks.

Mom heard her lop-eared old hound dog start barking furiously as the pickup swung into the yard. She awoke and rushed to the window to see who could be arriving at her remote cabin at that hour. The truck pulled up and pointed its lights at the house. She could not recognize the vehicle through the blinding glare. She grabbed up her trusty Winchester from the corner. A woman alone could not be too careful.

The two men mounted the steps to the front porch. Mike felt weighed down by the responsibility of telling my mother what had happened to her son. He knew she was strong enough to have raised six children all by herself. He had seen her brave some pretty hard times in the eight years he had known our family. She was certainly a woman independent enough to spend her summers alone in this remote cabin. Not the sort of person to fly to pieces. But, under the circumstances, he did not know quite how she would take the news.

"That's far enough!" Mom said. She peered at them over the sight of the rifle barrel thrust through the partially opened door. Then, identifying Mike, she lowered the gun a little.

"Who's that with you?" she demanded.

She remained cautious until the man stepped out into the headlights of the truck. The man introduced himself as Navajo County Undersheriff Ken Coplan. At the sight of his badge her heart sank. She knew that something must be terribly wrong. This late-night visit could only mean one thing. She lowered the gun completely.

"What's wrong, Mike?" she asked, bracing herself for the worst.

"Could we come in and talk to you?" Mike began slowly.

"Who got hurt?" she asked, her voice rising slightly.

"Well, nobody got hurt, exactly. . . ." Mike tried to break it to her easily.

"Have you seen your son tonight, ma'am?" Coplan interjected. The officer knew it would have been impossible for me to find my way there on foot over those miles of rugged terrain, especially if I were in a dazed or injured condition. He was attempting to bring up the subject in a neutral manner.

"There's something wrong with Travis, then, isn't there?" she exclaimed. "Mike, he wouldn't bring you here if it wasn't Travis!"

"Well, we don't know if he's hurt. As far as we know he's just lost, but it's a long story, so let me explain," Mike began, as gently as he could.

Mom was struck by the look on Mike's face. She had never seen him look so badly upset. It made her very worried about what he had to tell her. She did not ask any more questions. She opened the door wide and asked them to come in and sit down. She leaned the rifle in a corner and went to put a robe on over the big flannel men's pajamas she wore on those cold mountain nights. The men groped their way into the darkened living room and found the couch.

She came back with a Coleman gas lantern. She threw a chunk of oak onto the dying embers in the old iron woodstove. They sat there in the dim light coming in the window from the pickup, while Mike began to break it to her, speaking with difficulty, groping for words that would not overly alarm her.

She managed to hold on to her composure on the surface, but while he talked, she continued vigorously pumping the handle of the lantern long after it was ready to be lit.

Mike broke from his narrative to suggest politely, "Uh, don't you think that's about enough?"

"Oh, yes. I guess so," she said, embarrassed. She struck a big stick-match and lit the lantern.

When Mike finished his incredible report, she asked him to repeat it, as though she could not quite grasp what he was saying. After he repeated the story, she asked the deputy: "Is this true?"

"I guess so, ma'am; we've been out there looking for him tonight," Coplan affirmed.

Then she threw Mike a hard look. "Do you mean to sit here and tell me that you just drove off and left him? You didn't try to help him?"

Mike looked away in shame. "Yeah," he admitted. "But when we saw what happened, we panicked . . . we just panicked! We thought it was after us, too! What else could we do? We did go back right away and look for him. . . ."

"We're going to resume the search at daybreak, Mrs. Kellett," Coplan interrupted. "We'll have search parties out there first thing."

"I'd better get dressed and go to town, and tell the rest of the family. I'll call Duane and get him up here." Duane is my brother. My father had died nearly three years before, and Mom had been divorced from him long before that. Duane had acted as father to the family in many ways in recent years.

Mom explained she had trouble with night blindness, and asked Mike to drive her into Taylor to my sister's. Mike agreed, although he figured her request had more to do with being too upset to drive and not wanting to be alone.

Deputy Coplan followed them in his pickup to Taylor, a small town outside Snowflake. The heater did not work in the old Chevy carryall. The twenty-mile ride in the old panel truck was miserably cold.

Mike got Mom to the home of my sister Alison and her husband, Grant, at twenty minutes to three. Coplan and Mike went in while Mom told her daughter and son-in-law, as calmly as she could, what Mike had told her. Alison was true to family character. Although her first reaction was naturally incredulous, she did not get hysterical or break down.

Mom reached Duane in Phoenix shortly before 3:00 A.M. "Duane, get up here right away! Something's happened to Travis. It looks like a *flying saucer* got him!"

The tone in her voice jerked him instantly awake. "A *what*? Now say that again?" When she finished explaining what had happened, he told her to stay at Alison's, that he was leaving immediately. It was nearly two hundred miles from Phoenix to Snowflake.

"Could you give me a ride over to Snowflake now?" Mike asked wearily.

"Sure, let's go," Coplan said. "That's about all we can do for tonight."

Duane and his wife, Carol, were already speeding north out of the desert city of Phoenix, where he worked as a farrier (horseshoer) and attended college. Duane had been a guiding force in the family since Mom's divorce from my father. To Mom, he was security itself. Duane is six feet two inches tall, nearly two hundred pounds of solid muscle. Twenty-six years old in 1975, he was an amateur boxer and rode bulls in rodeos. He was the sort of person who people listened to when he talked.

As he drove anxiously through the night, his brain clicked off the possibilities. Was I hurt? Could I actually have been abducted by alien beings? Maybe there had been a mistake. Mom had not been too clear on the phone about whether or not she was sure it had really happened. There might be a very simple explanation. The whole thing might be resolved when he got up to Snowflake. Perhaps I was really just out on a date or something, and someone had taken advantage of my absence to pull off an insane practical joke. If that was the case, there would be hell to pay if Duane caught the crazy bastard.

It was an exhausted, haggard Mike Rogers that Undersheriff Ken Coplan let off in front of Rogers' home at three o'clock that morning. Mike went in to a crowd of people in his front room. Ken had gone home to his wife, but Dwayne, John, and Allen were there, along with a few of Mike's relatives and even a neighbor.

Leaving the excited jabbering, Mike went to bed. He tossed fitfully as the guilt of abandoning his friend tormented him. Finally he sank into the reprieve of deep sleep shortly before dawn.

CHAPTER 5

Manhunt

Fear makes men ready to believe the worst.

—Quintus Curtius Rufus

No one rested well that night. Sleep for some was thwarted by dream images of shimmering metallic crafts blasting destructive rays in all directions. While morning refused to accelerate its arrival, the idea of a man's life hanging tenuously in the balance weighed too heavily for anyone to rest easy.

Mom did not sleep at all. After Mike had left Alison's with the undersheriff, Mom drove over to Snowflake where Don, my oldest brother, and his wife Maryanne lived with their two little girls.

When he heard the news, Don reacted with barely concealed skepticism. He immediately suspected that the story about the flying saucer was a cover-up for some kind of foul play.

He knew my friends and I were always practicing "them fancy fighting techniques" we learned in karate class. He thought that playful sparring might have flared into a serious battle. His own redheaded temper had gotten him into his share of fistfights. He knew how that sort of thing could get out of hand. He was careful not to express his suspicions to Mom, so as not to increase her anxiety. But his own worry over the possibility generated some hostility in his attitude toward the crew.

Mom remained at Don's house for a couple of hours, while he tried to reassure her. Nothing could be done until morning. Inaction increased the tension. The clock slowly ticked off the minutes as the night dragged on.

Sheriff Gillespie had managed a brief rest, but rose early to motivate his forces. By sunrise the Navajo County Search and Rescue Team had been alerted, the Heber Forest Service recruited.

Duane arrived at Alison's at seven that morning to find no one there. He drove on into Snowflake and found everyone at Don's. Mom had enlisted the help of a family friend with a Jeep capable of traveling rugged back country. With daylight, everyone embraced the relief of taking action. My family piled into the vehicles and left for Mike Rogers' house.

Duane arrived at Mike's first. The living room there was jammed with some of Mike's relatives and most of the men from his crew. Steve Pierce was the only crewman not present. The others had underestimated the severity of his condition the night before. He was still in a mild state of shock. Steve did not want to return to those woods again, ever. And, for then, he refused even to leave his house.

No one had wakened Mike yet. His wife, Katy, had asked that he not be disturbed any sooner than necessary because he had spent such a terrible, restless night. When Duane came in, Katy went to wake her husband.

While Mike dressed, Duane interrogated the other crewmen who were sitting around the fireplace. If they were up to something, he was damn sure going to find out. Heaven help them if they were covering up for darker deeds.

Mike came into the living room, puffy-eyed and wrung out.

"Why didn't you wake me up when everybody got here?" he asked Katy.

"You needed your sleep," she replied apologetically.

"We wanted to get back out there and look for Travis as early as we could," Mike said reproachfully. He eyed the early-morning sunlight already breaking through the tall trees across the street, pouring in the big front windows. His agitation increased. "Coplan said they'd be getting the search parties together in Heber at the crack of dawn!"

Mike looked at the clock. It was 7:10 A.M. Every minute they delayed could be reducing their chances of a successful rescue. "We've got to get moving right away!"

"We certainly do," Duane agreed. "But Ma and the rest of them will be here in a minute. So, Mike, I want you and the rest of these guys to tell me about what happened out there."

The men responded so openly to Duane's questions that his doubts began to waver. He considered himself a good judge of character, and his assessment was that these men were telling the truth. Nobody—and especially not these guys—could act that well. But Duane reserved judgment. He knew the coming search might turn up evidence of an entirely different sort.

During Don's drive to Mike's, the seeds of suspicion in his mind had sprouted and grown into full-blown conviction. He became certain the crew were covering up for a bloody chainsaw murder. He, too, had worked in the woods and knew what a chainsaw could do to human flesh. Ghastly images of my bloody, dismembered body tormented him as the horrible image grew more fixed in his mind.

Don was upset and irritable, having been awakened at three in the morning. Not knowing what was going on increased his irritation. Mom had been able to tell him only part of the story, and it seemed like no one else would tell him anything definite, either. Deputy Glen Flake had visited his house at nine the night before, asking where he thought I might be. Flake had been asked not to let out any details until the report was confirmed, so he only told Don to have me report to Deputy Ellison if I should show up. Don's temper was beginning to boil.

Don stomped up Mike's front steps and burst in the front door without knocking. Everyone stopped talking. He stood angrily surveying the group, his boots planted wide, his fists at his sides.

"All right, dammit. Let's have it!" he demanded furiously.

No one answered him. They just stared at him in surprise.

"I want to know what the hell is going on!" he raged. "I don't believe this flying-saucer crap for one damned minute! What did you do with Travis?"

Dwayne Smith flared. "It don't make any damn difference if you don't believe us! It happened just like we said!"

"You just keep quiet, *boy*!" Don pointed his finger threateningly at Dwayne Smith.

"Maybe you'd like to make something of it, *cowboy*!" Dwayne Smith countered testily. He slowly stood up, his six feet and seven inches towering over Don. They stood glaring into each other's eyes.

Everyone else sat in stunned silence at the outburst—except Duane, who was faintly amused.

"All right, you guys, that'll be enough!" Duane ordered. "Don, you'd better get on out of here and cool off!" Duane was more powerfully built than anyone in the room and his status as a boxer established his physical advantage as a given. But Don's anger would not be quelled.

"I ain't taking no orders from anybody!" Don shot back defiantly. He glowered at the crewmen. "I'll tell the rest of you guys one thing for damn sure," he stormed. "And each and every one of you better listen up real careful. If you guys have done something to Travis, I'm going to personally stomp a mudhole in the middle of every one of you!"

"Don, that's enough!" Duane interrupted. "You better just get on out of here and calm yourself down!" Duane stood up. "Come on, Don," he said quietly, heading for the door.

Don's anger wasn't completely spent, but he'd had his say. He followed Duane out.

Once outside, Duane said, "Don, I'm thinking some of the same things you are. But starting a ruckus right now isn't going to solve anything."

"Yeah," Don agreed. "But we'd better start getting some answers around here."

"If these guys have done away with Travis we're sure to find out," Duane pronounced ominously. "And if they did . . . they'll have hell to pay from both of us."

The others arrived and the group prepared to move. Mike got into the pickup with Duane and Mom. Don rode in the Jeep. The other crewmen left in Dwayne Smith's station wagon. The caravan set off for Heber.

By the time they arrived, the sheriff's posse, U.S. Forest Service men, and the Navajo County Search and Rescue Team had gathered in front of the Exxon station. Police cars and four-wheel-drives and green government pickup trucks crowded the big parking lot. Grim-faced men paced back and forth, gathering into tense, subdued huddles. A number of early risers were standing around watching. It was obvious to those civilians that something more than a simple lost-person search was afoot. That none of the searchers would talk to them about it only piqued their interest.

Duane pulled alongside a police car and asked a deputy: "How are you going to organize this thing?"

"There are some more men coming from Holbrook and in from some of the outlying areas. We've got to get everybody gassed up here and we'll meet out there. The sheriff will organize everybody and we'll move from there."

"Well, we're going to go on out there to see what we can find in the meantime."

Duane's pickup led my family and friends into the woods. One or two Forest Service trucks joined the mountain-bound brigade. The search party soon followed. When the vehicles arrived at Turkey Springs, a number of Forest Service trucks were parked under the pines at the turnoff to the contract. They drove on to the abduction site and found the Forest Service men already looking around.

Mike and the crewmen took Duane and Mom to where they had sighted the flying saucer. They showed them where the truck had stopped and went over the pattern of events to give a fairly clear picture of what had happened.

The caravan of search parties began to arrive. The growing crowd of vehicles parked near the site in a large clearing in the trees. Truck after truck of searchers gathered there. Over fifty men were present, almost all of them trained to handle emergencies. Sheriff Marlin Gillespie called the men together for briefing.

"Okay, attention everyone, gather around here. . . . What we're looking for is a man down, or wandering around dazed—possibly injured. The man is about six feet in height . . . one hundred sixty-five pounds . . . red hair. He was last seen wearing Levi's and a blue denim jacket. Look for articles of clothing that may have been discarded. Keep a close eye out for tracks or any other fresh signs. Look for blood or anything unusual, anything out of the ordinary. . . . If you should find anything at all, report back to me immediately." He surveyed the group. "Any questions?" Everyone apparently understood. "We're going to start up there at the Rim Road. We'll space ourselves out equally, staying within close sight of the man on either side at all times. When we get down to the lower road, we'll regroup and make another sweep. All right, men, let's go."

Mike was displeased when his suggestion of using tracking dogs appeared to be ignored. He, the other crewmen, and my family, were not asked to join the organized search, so they took up their own. The professionals knew their job, but help couldn't hurt.

Later that morning, a Forest Service man walked up to Dwayne Smith, grabbed his shirtfront and twisted it, pulling Dwayne's face close to his own. "All right," he snarled, "where'd ya hide the body?"

Dwayne protested: "What body? We didn't kill nobody. Dammit, there was a flying saucer here, just like we told you!"

My brother Duane walked up behind the burly forest ranger. "Hey you! Knock it off!" Some quality in that quiet voice left no doubt as to the wisest course of action. The man released his grip on Dwayne Smith's shirt and turned around, still defiant.

"You've got better things to do than stand around hassling people," Duane suggested. The man started to speak. Then, looking Duane up and down, he changed his mind. He turned and stalked off.

"We did *not* kill him," Dwayne Smith stated hotly. He looked at the small group of searchers standing about. "I'll even take a lie-detector test to prove it!"

"Yeah, we'll take lie-detector tests, truth serum, or any damn thing they want to throw at us, 'cause we're telling the truth!" John joined in. The other crew members chimed their agreement.

Meanwhile, my brother Don was conducting a very thorough search of his own. He was down on the piling strip where work had ended the night before. He rooted around in any soil that had been even slightly disturbed. He rolled over big rotting logs, dreading what he expected to find. Don looked into every hole and hollow log where even a *piece* of a corpse could be hidden. He dug into all the large slash-piles of dead wood, kicked apart all the smaller green piles that had been stacked in recent days. That strip of piling was certainly not going to pass Forest Service inspection.

Back up at the clearing, all the Forest Service men were bringing in armloads of litter. They were taking advantage of the sweep to clean up the woods. Now that's dedication!

They rounded up a disgusting amount of refuse for such a remote area. Old license plates, pieces of exhaust pipe, pop bottles, oil cans, even cigarette wrappers. They put the trash in the back of their trucks for disposal at the ranger station. They had found nearly every scrap of cast-off debris in that square mile, but had not found hide nor hair of anything that might indicate what had happened to me.

At the edge of the clearing, Mike noticed a man in a Forest Service uniform holding some sort of a small sensing device to the ground. The device was connected by a cord to a sophisticated-looking electronic instrument. Mike went over to see what was going on.

"Is that one of those radiation-checking things?" Mike asked.

"A Geiger counter, yes," the man curtly replied. "The sheriff requested it."

The man turned away. Mike followed him into the shade of the nearby pines. Allen, Duane, and a few others joined them.

"Is that thing finding any radiation?" Mike asked.

"No, there's no radiation here." The man passed the device along the ground, then put it up to some overhanging branches.

"Well, why are you checking here? If there was any radiation it would be over there where the thing was at," Mike suggested, pointing to the pile of logs across the clearing.

Without answering, the Forest Service man began checking the ground about halfway to the pile.

"Why don't you check right at the pile?" Duane asked, irritated by the man's uncooperative attitude. "Radiation would be strongest at the point nearest the source."

The Forest Service man continued to ignore the men's suggestions and began rolling up the cord of his instrument, putting it away.

"Hey," Mike proposed. "What about testing us?"

"Yeah!" Allen agreed. "See if we got any on us!"

The man began unrolling the cord again impatiently. He held the sensor up to Allen and Mike.

"See?" he said in an "I told you so" tone. "Nothing."

"Well, is that thing working? The dial says one and a half—what's that mean?" Mike questioned.

"That one and a half is *background* radiation. See, it registers that everywhere here." He waved the Geiger pickup around. "And yes, it's working, and this is the right setting," he added testily. "I've got it set as high as it will go just to pick up a background reading . . . look how it reads on a radium-dial watch." He held the pickup close to another Forest Service man's wrist. The widely spaced ticks came closer together as the needle swung up to a reading of three.

"Maybe we don't have any on us because we've taken baths and changed our clothes," Mike said. "Wouldn't that make a difference?"

"Maybe," he grunted indifferently.

"Well, our hats are the same as they were," Allen said, taking off his metal hard hat.

Mike removed his own hard hat, of orange plastic.

"Test these," Mike offered.

As the Geiger pickup moved closer to the first hat, the erratic ticking of the device increased—the needle swung all the way up to six! That reading was duplicated on the second hard hat.

The Forest Service man gave Allen and Mike a long, cynical stare. Abruptly he rolled up the cord of his Geiger counter and walked away.

"Hey, what about testing the truck?" Mike called to the man's retreating back.

The man kept walking, not even turning to look.

Up and down the ridges the searching sweeps went on. The search spread wider; still no trace of anything to raise hope. As the afternoon dragged past, someone brought a huge load of lunches out to the weary men. Footsore groups of searchers stopped by the clearing and rested their backs against the trees while they ate.

At the end of the day no one had found anything of significance. When the sheriff dismissed the searchers, they left under the dark cloud of a single, grim thought: If they found the man when the search resumed the next day, they would not find him alive. No one could survive two nights in those woods at near-zero temperatures.

My family and the crewmen spent the evening waiting, hoping that something would happen. The talk late that night resembled the mourning conversation carried on at a wake. No one knew what to do. All their hopes were pinned on the search still in progress.

The next day Mike and Duane went out early with a friend in his Jeep. Duane had ruined a tire in that rugged Turkey Springs area and left his truck in Snowflake.

The second day of the search was much like the first. Sweep after sweep made over the same ground. The only difference was the decline of enthusiasm in the searchers. They had not found anything the day before, increasing the chances that the second day would be the same.

Mom knew Mike well enough so that after she had a couple of days to think about it, she had few doubts about what the men had seen. She began to feel that searching further was worthless. It seemed obvious to her that if I had not been found right away in the immediate vicinity, it was not very likely I was there. That afternoon, she expressed her feelings to Sheriff Marlin Gillespie who told her he was beginning to feel the same way. That evening, after a second complete day of fruitless effort, the sheriff officially called off the search.

Family and friends went home with the heavy feeling that they would never see me again. The pressure and the sleepless nights had begun to catch up with everyone. Mike had finally succumbed, napping most of the day in the back of the bouncing Jeep.

That evening after they returned to town, Deputy Glen Flake paid Mike a visit.

"Heard you men volunteered for lie-detector tests," he began. "Is everyone still willing?"

"Yeah," Mike answered. "We're willing to take any test they want to give us. We'd like to prove that what some people are saying just isn't true!"

"Well, the sheriff heard that you guys offered and he's gonna take you up on it. He's arranged to give all you guys lie-detector tests."

"Good," Mike replied. "When are they going to be?"

"Eight o'clock Monday morning. You're supposed to show up at the courthouse in Holbrook," he said, getting up to leave. "Make sure nobody leaves town, all right?"

"Sure, nobody's planning to go anywhere as far as I know, but I'll tell 'em," Mike assured Deputy Flake as he left.

The visit made Mike feel a little less depressed. At least they'd have a chance to prove they hadn't killed me and that they *had* seen what they said they had seen. Ken, Allen, John, Steve, and Dwayne would sure be glad to hear about the lie-detector tests.

Members of my family got to talking things over that evening. They began to worry that perhaps the search had been called off prematurely. The possibility that I had only been injured, that I might still be alive, nagged at all of them. Even if I was lying dead out there somewhere, they would at least want me to have a proper burial, before the buzzards arrived. Prior to turning in for the night, they finally resolved to get a wider search going—even if they had to undertake it themselves.

Saturday morning Duane and Mike went to Holbrook to talk to Sheriff Gillespie. They pleaded with him to renew the search. "What if Travis is still out there?" they asked him. "We can't afford to lose the chance that we could still find him alive." They argued, perhaps more forcefully than politely, for another attempt to be made.

Finally the sheriff agreed. He could not very well refuse a request from the missing man's family. He picked up the telephone and by four o'clock that afternoon the returning search parties were joined by half a dozen men on horseback, a couple of expertly piloted turbine helicopters, and spotters in fixed-wing aircraft.

The widest, most intensive part of the search got under way.

Sheriff Gillespie had been cautious about releasing the report of the UFO abduction to the public. He realized the potential for panic, or false alarm, if I turned up. He had obtained the cooperation of the local radio stations in putting a lid on the news. The rumors that did leak out prompted telephone calls, fielded by radio stations and the sheriff's office with the response only that a search was on for a lost person.

Inevitably, however, the news escaped (probably via people listening to police scanner radios) to the larger television and radio stations. The media unearthed the story and, with electronic speed, the entire world was hearing the incredible report.

Along with the expanded search team came UFO investigators and reporters from as far away as London, England. Sightseers were underfoot everywhere. One UFO investigator, William Spaulding, of Ground Saucer Watch (GSW) of Phoenix, reported his group had taken some extraordinary electromagnetic readings at the slash-pile near where the craft had been and in the area above which the craft had hovered. Spaulding suggested it was indicative of the previous presence of a craft, possibly due to some kind of antigravity propulsion. He also reported finding residual traces of ozone in the area.

The release of the story to the media caused problems worse than sightseers getting in the way. The telephones at the sheriff's office and at my sister's home never ceased ringing. All day the calls kept coming in. Some callers were not mere curiosity seekers. My family's burden was increased by some people's insane concept of humor.

Some of the prank calls were just nonsense, and easily dismissed. Others caused the Sheriff's Department to expend valuable manpower in tracking down false reports. I was reported to have been seen strolling alone in a variety of places all over the county. One woman pretended to be Mrs. Travis Walton (at that time there was no such person), and said she'd received a message from her husband—he was safe on Mars. Very funny. Many UFO sightings were reported. It seemed as if everybody was out looking at the sky, reporting every little thing out of the ordinary.

Some calls were serious and well-meaning. Several calls verged on the ominous.

A retired CIA officer warned the family of possible covert government intervention. The man sounded sincere and left his name and address.

A nurse related an incident in which an elderly couple reportedly recovering from a UFO experience disappeared from a hospital where she was working. Their records also reportedly vanished and the top staff acted as if the incident had never occurred.

During those hectic days the telephone became the lifeline and the worst enemy of everyone involved.

Everybody was tired from sleeplessness and harassment. As if the searchers did not have enough problems, a horse bolted early Saturday evening, for no apparent reason, and could not be found.

All day Sunday the search widened. The men on horseback covered ridge after ridge. The helicopters circled wider and wider. Light planes crisscrossed the area. The quest was even broadened to cover the steep rugged terrain south of the Rim on the Apache Indian Reservation. The diligent rescue teams combed mile after square mile of that forested mountain country.

Finally, when the search was ended Sunday evening, there was no doubt in anyone's mind that I was definitely not lost in the forest wilderness. A massive four-day manhunt costing ten thousand dollars and involving over fifty men had been fruitless.

However, the search had not been totally useless. It served to establish one thing—where the missing man was *not*. That left the obvious question. Where *was* Travis Walton?

To Duane, the answer was now as obvious as the question. He sat with the group around the campfire at the site, musing over the days of searching. He sat with his back to the dark woods, staring into the dancing flames. He realized the rest of the family had come to believe that I was safe somewhere—out of desperate hope, the *need* to believe. He had flown high over the area in one of the helicopters, looking down with high-powered binoculars. The flight had been nothing new to him; he had often parachuted from helicopters in his army days. But the ride had brought home to him the futility of the search; also the reality of man and machine in flight. Pulling his collar up against the cold, Duane lay back and gazed up into the night sky.

"Could Travis be up there somewhere?" he wondered. "Yes—he must be up there." The idea appealed to Duane's adventurous nature. "If he is out there somewhere, he's probably having the experience of a lifetime."

CHAPTER 6

A Kidnapping . . . or a Killing?

Truth will come to light; murder cannot be hid long.
—Shakespeare, *The Merchant of Venice*

November 10, 1975. The day the final determination would be made in answer to the question of what really happened at Turkey Springs on the evening of November 5.

The unsuccessful search had left only two possibilities in the minds of the public and members of the Sheriff's Department. Either the men had indeed witnessed the abduction of their coworker by a UFO, or they were covering up for what could possibly be a gory chainsaw murder.

The crewmen were more eager than anyone to settle that question once and for all. Early that Monday morning they gathered at Mike Rogers' house, then piled into several cars, along with a few family members, heading for Holbrook.

When the men got out of their cars in the county courthouse parking lot, they were immediately thronged by newsmen. There were crowds of newspaper and magazine reporters, plus radio and television crews. The enthusiastic media men shoved microphones into their faces. The cameras followed them into the courthouse. The more persistent of the newsmen took up a daylong watch outside the Sheriff's Office building.

The crew and their group crowded into the small outer vestibule of the waiting room. The jailer/dispatcher, at his desk behind the glass, looked up with interest at their approach.

"We're here for the polygraph tests to be given today," they announced.

"Right. You're expected. The examiner isn't here yet," the deputy replied. "You'll just have to take a seat and wait. I'll tell the sheriff you're here."

The single bench in the little room was not nearly large enough for them all to "take a seat." The men's wives and mothers already filled the bench.

The space also served as a visitors' room for the prisoners who were kept on the other side of the heavy steel doors at the end of the room. The office had the tired look all twenty-four-hour offices acquire.

The smell of tobacco and despair wafted in from the cellblock, to mix with the odor of coffee and fatigue in the office. It was not going to be a pleasant wait.

After twenty-five minutes the men began to fidget. The standing-room-only conditions aggravated an already emotionally loaded situation. Newsmen kept trying to shoulder into the overcrowded room.

"Hey, are you guys the ones who think they saw the little green men?" one of the newsmen asked sarcastically.

"Stick it!" one of the crew called in return.

The men started grumbling among themselves. "I'm getting tired of this waiting business!" one of the men complained.

"I came down here to take a polygraph test," another joined in, "not to stand around."

"You know, like we were talking about this morning," Allen's mother began. "I've heard that the government tries to hush up UFO reports. You should be careful . . ."

"Hey!" somebody called to the deputy at the desk. "How long are we going to have to stand here?"

Just then, Sheriff Marlin Gillespie entered the office from the narrow hallway that led from the rear offices.

"Good morning," he greeted them perfunctorily. "I've been talking things over with the polygraph examiner. He's setting up his equipment in one of the back offices we'll be using for a testing room. You guys can come with me now." He led the men back the way he had entered, down the hallway and out into the sunshine at the rear of the building.

Behind the courthouse building was an unpaved compound enclosed by high stone walls and, on the opposite side, the jail kitchen. The sheriff and a deputy led the group across the courtyard to the kitchen.

The six crewmen, my brother Duane, Sheriff Gillespie, and his deputy jammed the kitchen. Seating themselves on tables and benches, they waited to hear what would happen next.

The sheriff spoke first. "I felt we needed to have a conference before we begin, to sort of let you know how the testing is going to be arranged. We've got certain rules you're going to have to follow. We can only test one person at a time. We want you all to remain back here and, as each one of you is tested, you are to remain here. However, we don't want the tested people associating with the untested people. So, when you're finished, stick around. But don't converse with the untested people. These tests are going to take all day, so . . ."

Everybody groaned. They were all under a lot of pressure from the reporters as well as from the accusations of suspicious people. The previous days had left them edgy. It looked as if it was going to be another hell of a day.

Gillespie continued: "We're going to require you to sign a consent/waiver form before testing. This statement gives us the right to test you and to use the results as evidence in a court of law. Just be sure you understand that when you sign. The examiner can explain it more fully to you if you have any questions." He paused briefly. "You need to work out an order between you. It doesn't matter which of you goes first. So—however you want to work it."

Just then a large, lean man with dark brown hair and a tanned, serious face entered the room.

"This is Mr. Cy Gilson," the sheriff introduced the man. "He's the Department of Public Safety polygraph examiner. He'll be the one testing all of you."

Allen spoke the thought that had been making them all uneasy. "How do we know we can trust this guy? We've heard that the government is always trying to hush these kinda things up. How do we know you're not gonna rig these lie-detector tests?"

The men began murmuring between themselves. They had nothing to lose if this guy was on the level, but if he was not, they could be tried for murder. The idea took hold and the grumbling increased.

Mr. Gilson snorted at the affront. "I'll guarantee you one thing. If you guys are telling the truth, those charts will show it. And if you're lying, I'll find that out, too."

"Your guarantee doesn't necessarily mean anything," Mike countered. "You would say that even if you've been bought off!"

Gilson was indignant. "What's your problem?" he shot back. "Are you lying?" He lightly popped Mike on the shoulder with the back of his fingers.

"Hell no, we're not lying!" Mike returned hotly. "We're really only worried that you've been bought off. It's not impossible, you know. We've heard that the government tries to keep these UFO things quiet."

Tempers flared and all of them began raising their voices. No one was more angry than Gilson at the insult to his integrity.

"You don't have a single thing to worry about—unless you're lying." As he spoke, Gilson again slapped Mike on the shoulder with the back of his hand.

"There's one way we can make sure these lie-detector tests are on the up-and-up," Duane interjected. "We can tape-record the tests. There was a UFO researcher out there at the site who told me he had access to this PSE computer thing, uh—a Psychological Stress Evaluation, he called it. We could run the tape through that computer to make sure the lie-detector tests were valid. PSE is supposed to be one-hundred-percent accurate."

Examiner Gilson was outraged. "I want to tell you men something about that PSE. I've seen a lot of research on the PSE. I've even done some research on it personally. The data shows that PSE is worse than worthless—it's downright dangerous. PSE is only twenty-percent accurate, whereas polygraph testing is consistently ninety-seven percent accurate!"

"You're just trying to get out of taping," Duane cut in. "If you didn't have something to hide, you'd allow taping!"

"I never allow taping of my tests," Gilson retorted. "There isn't a single method of lie detection available better than the polygraph. Why do you think it's the method used by law enforcement?"

"He's just trying to hide something," Dwayne Smith jeered. "Let's not take these damn tests!"

Everyone started yelling at once. The situation was getting out of control.

"All right," Gillespie broke in. "Hold on! Hold on, everybody!" His words were almost as effective as bullets fired into the air. The men respected Sheriff Gillespie because of his fair treatment of them in the woods, and the way he had handled the search. Everybody stopped talking and listened.

"Let's just calm down a minute here. You six men all came down here to take these lie-detector tests *voluntarily*," he reasoned. "If you decide not to take them, no one can stop you. If you want to pick up and leave, it's entirely up to you. But I'd like to point something out to you. A lot of people are thinking that you guys are guilty of murdering Walton. You haven't been arrested or anything yet, but things could become pretty hard for you if Walton never turns up—even if you're telling the truth. If you *are* telling the truth, then these tests are going to clear you. You don't have a thing to worry about from Mr. Gilson. I will give my personal guarantee that these tests will be conducted fairly."

The men were impressed by the sheriff's speech. Their misgivings were visibly mollified.

Mike said, "What do you guys think?"

The approving looks they exchanged expressed their unanimous vote.

"Okay, sir, if we have your guarantee, we'll go on and take the tests," Mike said to the sheriff. "Remember, it's in your hands, though."

Cy Gilson was still the picture of outraged indignation. His honesty had never been so insolently questioned in all his years in polygraphy. The examiner stalked from the room without another word.

"I'm going to go help Mr. Gilson prepare for testing," said Gillespie, striding out. He turned at the door and added, "You guys work out the order you want to be tested in. We'll be calling for the first one right away."

After he departed, the men drew straws to determine who would go in what order. Steve Pierce was first. After they worked out the sequence, the deputy came over from the courthouse and escorted Steve to the testing room.

Cy Gilson went over the questions with Steve, and explained the polygraph machine and procedure. Gilson then sat Steve down in a chair and wired him up. The examiner attached electrical pickups to Steve's hand and passed a flexible black rubber hose around his chest. Then the constricting band of the blood pressure cuff was tightened around the subject's left bicep. Steve started to feel like a guinea pig in an electric chair.

When Steve coughed or moved, the needles on the machine scratched wildly back and forth on the rolling chart of paper. The examiner told him to sit very still and relax. Every breath, every beat of his heart, his every reaction would trace itself neatly in colored ink. The tiniest fluctuation in his body responses would be precisely recorded for the examiner's expert analysis.

Steve's test lasted nearly two hours. At that rate it was going to be a long day of waiting for the man last in line.

Allen Dalis' test was second. He entered the examination room just before noon in a very suspicious and agitated state. He was the most excitable member of the group. The days of suspense, heckling by curious people and newsmen, and accusations from all quarters, had rattled him more than a little. Seeing the UFO had affected him more than any of the others, except possibly Steve Pierce.

After little more than an hour, Allen stormed out of the testing room. He loudly cursed the examiner and slammed the door behind him.

"I know that son of a bitch has been bought off!" he told the waiting men. "He keeps acting like he thinks I killed Travis. I'm damned sure not lying and if the bastard says I am, then I *know* he's the one who's lying."

"What makes you think he's been paid off, Allen?" Mike asked. "Did he tell you the results of your test?"

"No, it's just that he keeps acting like he don't believe us about the UFO!" Allen fumed.

"Well, Allen, if he didn't actually say you failed your test, why are you so mad? These guys are probably supposed to act like they don't believe us," Mike reasoned.

The other crew members started grumbling and talking about driving back to Snowflake.

"Hold on, everybody," Mike said. "There's no call to fly off the handle!" Mike, who had drawn the straw for fifth place, volunteered: "I'll go in next and have a talk with the guy. Maybe I can find out what's going on."

Mike went into the testing room and had a long talk with the examiner. He explained Allen's volatility as simply being one facet of his usual behavior, and that Allen was still overwrought from seeing the UFO. During his talk with Gilson Mike began to feel that he could trust the man. Mike's testing then began. A tedious hour and a half later, three or four separate tests were completed on Mike, as had been performed on the other two men.

When the examiner was through, he made no comment. While he was being released from the polygraph machine's sensitive black tentacles, Mike said, half defiantly: "I told you I was telling the truth." The poker-faced Gilson still wouldn't make any statement as to what he thought the charts showed. Mike, confident in the examiner and knowing he was telling the truth, didn't need to be told.

He went outside into the dirt courtyard and told the men that everything was all right and to go on with the testing. Ken Peterson, Dwayne Smith, and John Goulette each took their tests in turn.

The tested men hung around the courthouse waiting to see what happened. To fill the time, the men played basketball and sparred with boxing gloves—sports equipment kept in the kitchen for the prisoner trustees. Some of the men played cards. The day dragged on.

Newsmen, after interviewing the men at great length, found nothing better to do with their time than film the men at their games. Playful sparring and basketball did not seem to be the likely pastimes of men being tested for murder. Obviously the men were bored, not worried.

Finally, John Goulette came out. It had been a grueling thirteen hours for everyone. The crew had waited all day to hear the results of the tests. The other men waited in the kitchen area while my brother Duane and Mike went into the courthouse to hear what Gilson had to say.

Darkness had fallen; the swarm of reporters had long since drifted away. The wood-floored hallway to the testing room was deserted. The building was quiet except for the echoing coughs of a prisoner in the nearby cell-block.

They entered the testing room and found Cy Gilson standing behind the wooden desk, carefully putting away his polygraph instruments. There was a huge stack of paper charts on the desk—the test results of six men. The squiggly tracings of the jagged, colored ink lines were unreadable to the untrained eye.

"Well, what's the final verdict?" Duane asked.

The examiner seemed awed, or at least perplexed, as if he had unexpectedly uncovered something profound. But what? "I can't really say right now," he began quietly. "You'll have to wait until I make my final report." He turned his attention to carefully removing the slender needles of the ink-tracing pens.

Mike and Duane were frustrated. They had waited all day to hear the final word.

Mr. Gilson said, "Excuse me a minute, I've got to wash the ink out of these before they dry." He carried the thin chrome needles out the door. Duane and Mike followed him to the washroom at the end of the hall.

"We have a right to know the results of these tests," Duane began earnestly. "When is your report going to come out?"

Gilson finished rinsing the colored ink out of his instruments. "I have to go over these charts very closely first. That should only take a few days. I'll probably send the sheriff my report by the end of the week." He walked back to the testing room to finish packing his equipment. Mike and Duane doggedly pursued him.

"Couldn't you at least tell us—unofficially?" Mike persisted. "You must have some idea of how they turned out, from what you've seen of them so far."

Examiner Gilson stopped and looked at Duane and Mike. "I guess it wouldn't hurt anything to tell you—seeing the way the tests apparently came out. . . . Realize this, though—this is just a preliminary evaluation. I could go over these charts more closely and come up with an entirely different opinion. So keep this under your hat and don't tell any newsmen until after I make my official report." He cleared his throat. "From what I've been able to see from these charts, you men are apparently telling the truth!"

"Well, we'd like to apologize for this morning," Mike said, offering his hand. "It looks like we badly misjudged you."

Gilson's voice betrayed his amazement. "When I started testing you men this morning, I really expected to find that a murder had been committed. After all those hard words this morning, and the way Allen Davis reacted, I was even more sure of foul play. But none of the tests except Allen's showed anything like that. Allen was just too agitated to be tested at all. Even if his charts had been readable and showed foul play, he couldn't have committed a crime and made up a story about a UFO without involving five other men whose tests corroborate what they reported."

Cy Gilson shook his head soberly. He put his hand on the stack of lie-detector charts. "Incredible," he muttered.

CHAPTER 7

Return

Who never doubted never half believed;
Where doubt, the truth is—'tis her shadow.
                                                —P. J. Bailey

Apprehension had steadily grown in the Mogollon Rim area since that fateful forest encounter. Fear made some people prefer to believe that something as ominous as a UFO kidnapping could not happen in their quiet little community. But as time dragged on after the mysterious disappearance, many began to face the more obvious possibility in answer to the grim question, "Where is Travis Walton?"

It had been nearly five days and six hours since the beginning of my horrible ordeal.

I regained consciousness lying on my stomach, my head on my right forearm. Cold air brought me instantly awake. I looked up in time to see a light turn off on the bottom of a curved, gleaming hull. As I'd raised my head up, a white light caught my eye just before it blinked off. Either a light had been turned off or a hatch had closed, cutting off the light from inside. I only caught a glimpse as I raised my head; I could not be sure which it was.

Then I saw the mirrored outline of a rounded, silvery disc hovering four feet above the paved surface of the road. It must have been about forty feet in diameter because it extended several feet off the left side of the road. It was too large for the highway and it extended past the roadside to my left to clear a cutaway rock embankment on the other side of the highway. It appeared to be about fourteen feet high in the center.

For an instant it floated silently above the road, a dozen yards away. I could see the night sky, the surrounding trees, and the highway center line reflected in the curving mirror of its hull. I noticed a faint warmth radiating onto my face. Then, abruptly, it shot vertically into the sky, creating a strong breeze that stirred the nearby pine boughs and rustled the dry oak leaves that lay in the dry grass beside the road. It gave off no light; and it was almost instantly lost from sight.

The most striking thing about its departure was its quietness. It seemed impossible that something so large, moving through the atmosphere at such speed, would not have shrieked through the air, or even broken the sound barrier with a sonic boom. Yet it had been totally silent!

I scrambled shakily to my feet. My legs felt rubbery. I swayed, then caught my balance. I noticed the bluish white glowing dots of a couple of streetlights down the hill. I looked around and recognized the deserted stretch of curving road as the highway that wound down the canyon into Heber from the west.

I was overjoyed to be in familiar surroundings. It felt so good to have my feet back on the sweet earth. I still felt a little pain in my head and chest, a little weak, but otherwise I was physically intact. The memory of what had happened to me ran through my mind like a recurring nightmare. Struggling to grasp the thought that all this really had happened left me dazed and in a state of shock.

I ran wildly down the deserted highway, across the bridge into Heber, stopping at the new building across from the Union 76 service station. Smoke billowed from the chimney and lights blazed inside, but no one answered my desperate knocking. No cars passed by.

I ran on down the highway, over the second bridge, to the row of telephone booths at the Exxon station. I entered the first of the phone booths and frantically dialed the operator. (A dime was not required to reach an operator in our part of the country.) My panic grew with the discovery that the telephone was out of order! Nearly exhausted from my wild run, I staggered out of that phone booth and into the next, relieved to find this one functioning. I dialed the operator and panted out the number of my sister, Alison Neff. She was the only nearby relative with a telephone.

My brother-in-law Grant answered. It was 12:05 A.M.

I was in an incredible mental state, difficult to describe. As best I can remember, I shouted something like: "They brought me back!" Then I babbled, "I'm out here in Heber, please get somebody to come and get me!" My hand shook as I held the cold receiver.

Grant was not amused by the prank calls the family had been receiving.

He took this call to be another cruel joke. "Uh, I think you have the wrong number," he replied sarcastically, starting to hang up.

"Wait! It's me, Travis!" I screamed hysterically into the receiver.

"Where are you?" he asked, still suspicious of a joke.

"I'm at the Heber Exxon station."

"Okay," he replied, almost apologetically, yet still cautious of a prank. "Stay right there. I'll get Don or Duane and come and get you. Just hang on."

I remember hanging up and slumping down. Cradling my head on my knees, I hugged my shins. My nerves felt frayed; I was cold and weary. I waited in a sort of numb daze, or shock, for help to arrive.

Grant drove the three miles from Taylor over to Snowflake and found Duane at Mom's house. He told Duane about the call, and of his doubts it was really me. Duane, too, thought the call might have been yet another example of someone's idiotic concept of humor. But they decided they couldn't risk not investigating.

The rest of the family was overjoyed. Hope was rekindled. Grant and Duane cautioned them not to get their hopes up too high. Since they were not sure, they did not notify the authorities, but immediately set out for Heber, thirty-three miles away.

Lights suddenly shone into the phone booth. Relief flooded over me when I raised my head and saw the headlights of Duane's pickup. Duane and Grant got out and came to where I was still slumped in the phone booth. Duane opened the glass door of the booth and helped me to my feet.

"Easy, Travis, take it easy, man!" Duane soothed me as I haltingly tried to speak. "Don't try to talk now."

"Am I ever glad to see you!" Grant said.

Duane helped me into the warm truck and asked Grant to drive. On the way to Snowflake I tried to tell them about what happened to me, but I just couldn't get it all out.

"They were awful—white skin—great big eyes . . ." I sobbed in horror.

"Take it easy, Travis, you're all right now. They didn't harm you, did they?"

"No . . . but those eyes, those horrible eyes! They just kept *looking* at me!" I choked out in broken gasps.

"Just so you're okay, that's all that counts," Duane said. "Everyone has been worried sick about you."

"If it's already after midnight, I must have been unconscious for a couple of hours," I replied shakily. "Because I only remember about an hour or an hour and a half inside that thing."

Duane and Grant looked at me strangely.

"Travis, feel your face," Duane said.

"Good hell, I just shaved this morning and it feels like a week's growth!" I exclaimed, still not comprehending.

"Travis," Duane said gently, "you've been missing for *five days!*"

My mouth dropped open. I took a hard look at the date on my watch. "FIVE DAYS?" I screeched. "Good God! What has happened to me?" I ran my hand again over the heavy growth of rough stubble on my jaw. "Five days?" I repeated numbly. "Five days."

My mind reeled, trying to comprehend the staggering implications of this revelation. I muttered in wonder, "That means that . . . oh no . . . that can't be. . . ."

"As long as you're all right there's no need to talk. Just try to calm down for right now," Duane said. To Grant he said: "That crazy mob of reporters is not going to get ahold of this guy, I'll guarantee you that right now! He's not in any shape to be talking to anyone. If they wouldn't leave Mom alone in the shape she's in, it isn't likely they'll be any different with Travis." He put his arm protectively over my shoulders. I slumped down in the seat and gave up on trying to talk.

The ride back to Snowflake was an eerie one. Duane's work truck had an extremely loose steering mechanism and Grant was unaccustomed to driving it. The high speed caused the truck to veer wildly at every bump and groove in the pavement. There had been a lot of control burning of wood debris by the Forest Service to the south, and the wind carried the thick, pale gray smoke across the highway. It was like the weird ground fog you would see in the cemetery of some horror movie.

When we arrived at Mom's house, no one was there. Duane had sent his wife Carol with Mom over to Alison's to be near a telephone in case he had to call her from Heber. Grant went on over to Taylor in his own car to get Alison and Mom. While he was gone, Duane had me change into fresh clothes.

Duane had decided it was best not to tell anyone yet of my return. He could see I was a long way from being up to interviews. Newsmen and law enforcement officials would insist on launching a torrent of questioning immediately. Duane's memory was fresh with the hounding and questioning endured by the family in the preceding days; he knew it was certain to be even worse for me. I was not ready to go through that.

Duane's first priority was for me to see a doctor immediately, but to see a local doctor would mean getting mobbed by the curious. A local physician would mean waiting till morning anyway. By that time we could be in Phoenix, where I could see a doctor under confidential conditions. As the UFO investigator William Spaulding had advised, a complete physical check for radiation damage or other possible ill effects of my ordeal seemed the most sensible first step to take.

While I was changing my clothes in the bathroom, Duane noticed a single reddish dot on the inside of my right elbow. I told him I didn't know how I had received it. I didn't remember getting punctured or injected during my experience, but I told him that I might have been poked by thorns or something out at work. I didn't have any other major cuts, skin lesions, or bruises.

I weighed in on the bathroom scale at 154 pounds. I had lost over ten pounds in five days.

Duane had me put the work clothes that I'd removed in a paper sack for later examination. I had a little trouble standing, but it was probably from weakness rather than loss of equilibrium. I no longer felt dizzy. All the pain in my head and chest had disappeared. I sat down on the edge of the bathtub to finish changing.

I was terribly hungry and thirsty. I drank glass after glass of water. I was ravenous, but after stuffing some cookies in my mouth and eating some cottage cheese, I felt a little nauseated. I lay down in the bedroom for a while, but thoughts of those horrid creatures would not let me rest.

When my mother and sister arrived there was a tearful reunion, as though I had returned from the dead. I guess for them I had. It had been only a couple of hours for me, but for them it had been a week of worry and uncertainty that had slowly evolved into a half-mourning despair. In spite of my own condition, I was still very moved by their care and by the depth of their suffering. And this was just the first of many ways the aftermath of the incident would add, layer upon layer, to my burden of distress.

Duane had gone outside to siphon some gas from one of the other cars for the trip to Phoenix. There were no all-night service stations in Snowflake.

County Deputy Glen Flake came by the house and noticed the lights on. He saw Duane siphoning the gas and stopped to investigate. Flake did not reveal that Sheriff Gillespie had received a tip from someone at the telephone company that a call from Heber had been received at the Neff residence. Gillespie had ordered a couple of deputies out to dust the phone booths for fingerprints, and called Deputy Flake to ask him to go over and watch the highway from Heber. Flake had apparently not received the call in time, as he'd missed our return to town.

Flake got out of the car and asked Duane what he was doing. Duane explained truthfully that he was getting gas to return home to Phoenix. He kept his resolve to shield me and delay the news of my return. The warning calls received from well-wishers had planted seeds of caution. If such "engineered vanishings" were real, he was going to make sure his brother didn't experience one. Having trust in local officials was not sufficient, since such actions would come from beyond them, and irrespective of them.

Deputy Flake apparently dismissed the tip as another of the many crank calls local law enforcement agencies had been receiving over the previous five days. He didn't ask to enter the house and left without further comment.

Duane reassured my mother and sister (contradicting his own misgivings) that I was physically okay. We left for Phoenix. We arrived at Duane's house in the early morning. I went into the spare bedroom and tried to sleep. I tossed and turned, finally dozing off into a shallow sleep. My dreams were fraught with strange, chalk white faces and huge staring eyes, and I awoke with a start.

Duane came in. He told me that when I'd vanished, he had called William Spaulding, of a small Phoenix-based UFO research group, Ground Saucer Watch. Duane had met Spaulding at the abduction site in the forest. At that time Spaulding had told Duane to contact him if I should ever be returned and that his group would supply all the medical exams and research facilities necessary to assure my well-being and to assess the tremendous scientific implications of the incident. Mr. Spaulding seemed to be a competent researcher. He had already issued reports of his discovery of various physical traces left by the craft at the site.

Duane first attempted to call Bill Spaulding at seven that morning, but Spaulding's phone was unlisted. Duane finally reached him at work sometime after seven-thirty. Mr. Spaulding was employed by the industrial plant AIResearch.

Duane told Mr. Spaulding that I had been returned the night before and explained the need to prevent ourselves from being mobbed. Mr. Spaulding was eager to be involved, and inquired as to my condition. Duane told him that apparently nothing was seriously wrong with me but a thorough medical examination should be made anyway. Mr. Spaulding agreed enthusiastically. He directed us to a Ground Saucer Watch consultant, Dr. Lester Steward.

When I rose to use the restroom, Duane had me save the first voided specimen of urine for analysis. He had been advised by Mr. Spaulding to obtain a urine sample as early as possible for scientific testing. Spaulding had also been the one to suggest saving my clothing for forensic examination.

Those warning telephone calls made by different people during the search might have been entirely unfounded, but Duane was taking no chances. He loyally accompanied me everywhere as a bodyguard during the emotionally ravaging days following my return.

At about nine-fifteen that morning, Duane called Sheriff Gillespie and notified him of my return. However, in keeping with his desire to shield me, he said I had been taken to a Tucson hospital. Soon after that we left for Dr. Steward's office, taking along the urine specimen in a tightly sealed jar in a brown paper sack.

The first indication that something was amiss was the "office building" itself. It was a derelict, musty, nearly deserted downtown hotel. We later learned of the hotel's unsavory reputation. It did not seem a suitable place for a respectable doctor's office. We were not sure we were in the right place. But we found Dr. Steward's name on the room roster. Confused, we took the elevator up to his floor.

We were further perplexed by the sign on his office door: Dr. Lester Steward—Hypnotherapist. What? Mr. Spaulding had told us that Steward was an *M.D.* Our uneasiness grew, but we decided to go in, speculating that Dr. Steward might be an M.D. in addition to his hypnotherapy practice.

Upon entering we discovered a narrow one-room office that looked out over the roof of a wing of the building, with cheap furnishings and a pair of badly yellowed curtains covering the opened window. The window admitted enough fresh air to make the lack of air-conditioning bearable. It was still early, not yet excessively hot. Even in November, it can become uncomfortably warm during the middle of the day in the desert city of Phoenix.

Dr. Steward wasn't even expecting us! Bill Spaulding, director of Ground Saucer Watch, had not called his consultant to inform him we were coming. Duane asked him if he had heard about the UFO incident in the news. Steward said he had. Duane explained that we had been sent here for a medical examination by GSW. Steward reacted as if he had forgotten he was a member.

Seeing no professional volumes on the shelf nor an M.D. certificate on the wall, Duane asked Steward if he was a doctor. He replied that, yes, he was, but not licensed to practice in Arizona. When pressed on this point, he confessed he had been a medic in the Marine Corps. He reluctantly explained his rights to the title of "Doctor" with a vague reference to a degree he had received in school.

Duane asked him if he could still do the physical examination needed, suggesting blood tests and urinalysis. Duane handed Steward the jar containing my urine specimen. Steward handed it back with a distasteful expression. He said he could not do any of that sort of thing because he did not at present have access to laboratory facilities. He said he did, however, have a good friend and colleague who might be willing to do the exam.

Only Duane's extreme concern for my health and his desire for an immediate, thorough checkup caused him to stay at that point. I was exhausted from not sleeping the night before; my eyes were red and stinging. I sat down on a chair in front of the window, holding my head in my hands. I let Duane handle things. I was still feeling very dehydrated, and asked for a drink. Steward brought me a glass of water. I was still very thirsty and asked for another, in spite of the greasy fingerprints all over the glass.

Jets landing and taking off at the nearby airport continually passed low over the building. "Dr." Steward closed the window against the noise and telephoned his colleague. The phone call was almost funny in the way it further revealed Steward's phoniness. "Hello, Dr. So-and-so, this is Dr. Steward." A long pause. "Dr. Lester Steward, you remember me, don't you?" His so-called "friend and colleague" apparently did not remember him, and refused to do the examination! Needless to say, Duane extricated us as quickly as possible and we left.

I had not eaten that morning and I was very hungry. We stopped for a large breakfast on the way home.

When we arrived back at Duane's home, I again tried to sleep. The telephone rang again and again. Word had somehow gotten out that I had been returned, and people wanted to know where I was. Duane sent them on a wild-goose chase to protect me from harassment, telling them, as he had told Gillespie, that I was in a Tucson hospital. There were constant calls from the news media, curious people, and a couple of calls from "Dr." Steward. He had been in contact with Spaulding and was now very eager to reacquire our cooperation for GSW's investigation of the case. Duane politely declined.

Spaulding called later to suggest a meeting with Dr. J. Allen Hynek. Duane at first agreed, then changed his mind. I was still very seriously upset and did not want to have anything to do with anybody I believed associated with GSW. Contributing to our reservations was an earlier exchange with "Dr." Steward. In Steward's office Duane had told him that recently it had been suggested that Dr. James Harder and Dr. Hynek be brought in. Steward had exclaimed: "Oh, no. You want to keep your brother away from those two, they'd really put him through hell. They would really give him a pounding!" We wondered, Don't these GSW people get together on anything?

We knew so little at the time that we didn't even recognize Dr. Hynek as an astronomer who was one of the foremost investigators in the field of ufology. We also later learned that he was the head of the Center for UFO Studies, an independent research organization not directly affiliated with GSW.

Shortly after our rejection of GSW, Bill Spaulding suddenly began maligning me to the media. After publicizing his on-site recorded magnetic and ozone readings, he abruptly reversed his public stance without explaining his earlier endorsement of the case or offering new data to support his change in attitude. I don't know if this was motivated by wounded pride, or simply a continued desire to capitalize—one way or another—on the intense publicity surrounding the incident. "We're going to blow this story out today!" he declared to reporters. Their inaccurate assertions were exposed by the testing subsequently carried out by APRO, the Aerial Phenomena Research Organization, of Tucson.

Duane had also fended off the media by telling them I had been taken to a hospital in Tucson (although he called Sheriff Gillespie back and told him I was recovering in a private home in the Phoenix area). Coral Lorenzen, Secretary Treasurer of APRO, decided to try to track me down. She checked all the Tucson hospitals and found that no one answering my description had been admitted that morning. She then deduced that I was likely actually at Duane's house, so she called there.

Mrs. Lorenzen told Duane that my case was one of several others currently under investigation by APRO, and offered to provide anything possible that would be of help. Duane admitted I was there but asked her not to tell the media. Sympathetic to my condition, she agreed. He told her he thought it was important for me to be thoroughly examined by a physician as soon as possible. Mrs. Lorenzen assured him that APRO had the capacity to conduct a professional investigation and would be glad to provide an examination.

Coral Lorensen then called two reputable physicians in their Phoenix membership. One of them, Dr. Joseph Saults, was off-duty that day, so she left a message with his secretary for him to call back. She then reached the other doctor, Howard Kandell, at his clinic. He said he would be free at 3:30 P.M. and that he understood the need for confidentiality. She called Duane back and notified him that at least one doctor would arrive at his home shortly after three-thirty. Dr. Saults called Coral back right after that. She explained the situation to him and he agreed to make arrangements with Dr. Kandell to join him on the house call.

The doctors arrived on schedule. They agreed to Duane's requests to confine their questions to my health and not use the tape recorder and camera they had brought. An interview would require recalling some very upsetting memories, and I needed to calm down and collect myself.

They performed a thorough physical examination. The written report on the exam would be forwarded to APRO by Dr. Kandell. The doctors took the urine specimen with them for analysis. We made arrangements for the portion of the examination requiring laboratory tests to be performed the following morning, November 12, at Dr. Kandell's office.

That afternoon Sheriff Gillespie called Duane and requested a meeting with me. He was understandably upset with us for not having immediately notified him of my return. Duane explained that I had not been capable of being interviewed and was still too traumatized to be interrogated. Sheriff Gillespie insisted on meeting with me so that he could officially close his missing-person report. Duane agreed to have him come alone and see me that night. Duane asked him not to inform the media of my actual whereabouts. Gillespie agreed.

I was lying on the couch when he arrived late that evening. It was the first time I had related that much of my experience to anyone, including Duane. It was very upsetting. I struggled to keep from breaking down and made my answers short so that I would have to relive the nightmare as little as possible.

He did not react negatively or harshly and, except for a stern reminder of the consequences if my report were false, he seemed sympathetic to my emotionally fragile condition. I told Sheriff Gillespie I wanted to take a polygraph test, but that I did not want to be mobbed by curious people and reporters. He promised to arrange a polygraph test which the media would not know of until after it was completed and I had returned home. I thanked him. He left immediately for Holbrook.

I slept fitfully that night. I tossed and turned. Nightmares woke me several times during the night. I awoke the next morning feeling little better for the night's rest.

I arrived at Dr. Kandell's clinic very early. I weighed myself on his scales. They performed an EKG (electrocardiogram) and took X rays. Blood samples were taken. I was sent over to the renowned Barrows Neurological Center for an EEG (electroencephalogram), a register of brain-wave patterns. The testing dragged on, consuming the entire morning.

After returning home, I again tried to rest that afternoon. The telephone rang constantly. Gillespie may have kept his word about not informing the media of my whereabouts, but evidently someone had released the information. Reporters repeatedly came and knocked on the door. Duane's polite refusals necessarily grew testier as the harassment continued to build. The local papers reacted to these rebuffs by printing the only available comments—those from the very angry and vocal Bill Spaulding and Lester Steward.

APRO's Jim Lorenzen and other APRO scientific consultants (including the famous Dr. James Harder, Professor of Civil Engineering at the University of California at Berkeley, APRO's Director of Research) were on the *National Enquirer*'s Blue Ribbon Panel for UFOs. The *National Enquirer* first contacted APRO at about noon on November 11, asking their opinion of the case. APRO told them it appeared genuine so far.

The *Enquirer* does much reporting of UFO incidents and helps sponsor investigation of some cases. Mrs. Lorenzen told them I was in no emotional condition to confront the press and should be sequestered for testing. Privacy was rapidly becoming impossible at Duane's house. She told them that, although APRO could offer the services of its scientific consultants to conduct the needed tests, they could not assume financial responsibility for the hotel accommodations and other expenses necessary for sequestering me. The *Enquirer*'s representative agreed to underwrite that part of the project.

It was Paul Jenkins of the *National Enquirer* who first approached us on November 13 with the proposal. Duane at first took him for just another reporter and refused him. But Jenkins returned and explained the paper's association with APRO, saying that scientific testing would provide reassurance as to my condition while granting the opportunity for research. We agreed to go to the hotel for interviewing and testing. I hoped that an exclusive with the *Enquirer* would get me out of doing hundreds of interviews with other reporters.

Duane and I went to the hotel, the Scottsdale Sheraton Inn, that same evening. There we met the rest of the *Enquirer* reporters: Jeff Wells, Nick Longhurst, and Chris Fuller. Jim Lorenzen, the International Director of the Aerial Phenomena Research Organization, drove up from Tucson that night. He met Dr. James Harder's plane and the two proceeded to the hotel where Duane and I and the crew from the *National Enquirer* were waiting for them.

I had been extremely tense every waking moment since my return. When Jim Lorenzen and Dr. Harder entered the room, their first impression of me was of a "caged wildcat." Dr. Harder is a skilled hypnotist, but what he accomplished that evening was phenomenal. The longer Dr. Harder talked, the more my tension eased. I had been skeptical of hypnosis before, but his tremendous capacity to relax me deeply impressed me. He is a certified hypnotist of the respected La Crone school.

Dr. Harder did not attempt any deep hypnosis on me that night, as it was quite late and he did not wish to pressure me.

The next morning, November 14, Duane and I returned to his house for a change of clothes before heading for the Department of Public Safety headquarters, where Sheriff Gillespie had arranged for a polygraph test to be taken. The DPS (state police) examiner, Cy Gilson, had also done the tests on my six coworkers.

Just as we were leaving for the appointment, a reporter called and asked for an interview about the upcoming polygraph test. Duane hung up the phone and said angrily, "I smell a rat!" It appeared the sheriff had not kept his word.

"To hell with it, then! I told him I didn't want all those reporters sticking microphones in my face," I ranted shakily. Our agreement had been clear. If my one request hadn't been met, what else would I be in for? So, as I believe was perfectly understandable under those circumstances, I did not keep the appointment.

Later we saw Gilson on television, being interviewed by many reporters. Mention was made of my expected appearance. We didn't know it, but Sheriff Gillespie probably really had kept his word. The sheriff had asked

Cy Gilson to keep the tests as secret as possible, but the press had been tailing Gilson that morning. (Would they have surveiled him if they hadn't been tipped?) When Gilson noticed this, he left by the back door at headquarters, drove randomly around the streets and stopped for a while to make sure he lost them. But then he went directly to the appointed place—the same location where he usually gave the polygraph tests. One television station already had a crew and camera set up in an office window across the street. It seems the police had held a press conference that morning, supposedly concerning only Gilson's testing of the other six men, and word had leaked out from someone there about my scheduled test.

We returned to the hotel and related the turn of events. The *Enquirer* people were not unhappy. They preferred an exclusive story anyway. They said they would sponsor a polygraph test from a private firm.

Dr. Harder warned that any test taken now, so soon after such an ordeal was likely to come up inconclusive at best. Dr. Harder said a polygraph measures stress, not lies per se. The theory behind a lie detector is that people register stressful physiological responses when they lie. He noted that I was still extremely agitated when talking about my experience. He counseled that, if a test *was* performed, the results not be taken too seriously.

Despite his advice, arrangements were made for a test. Dr. Harder explained the situation to the examiner, who agreed to keep the results confidential if they turned out as Dr. Harder anticipated. The test yielded the predicted stressful tracings, so the researchers scrapped it.

Three psychiatrists brought in by the *Enquirer* that evening expressed the opinion that the test results were totally meaningless. Dr. Warren Gorman, Dr. Jean Rosenbaum (who has testified in court as an expert witness on the polygraph), and his wife, Dr. Beryl Rosenbaum, all concurred on that point. Other APRO consultants also later affirmed their conclusion.

After that polygraph experiment on November 15, Jean Rosenbaum stated in a press release to ABC-TV News 3 of Phoenix: "Our conclusion—which is absolute—is that this young man is not lying—that there is no collusion involved, no attempt to hoax . . . or collusion of the family or anyone else. There is a rumor around that there's contracts. There are no such contracts—no motivation for a lie. The results of tests show this is a person who has been going through a kind of life crisis like we all do; for example, a death or divorce or anything of that kind. The results of psychiatric tests and hypnosis show he really believes these things. He is not lying."

Question: "Any possibility of lying? There's no hoax as you see it?"

His answer: "None whatsoever, there's no way he could have gotten around these tests, that he could have gotten around in particular the hypnotic series that he was under."

A long session of regressive hypnosis had been performed by Dr. Harder the night before, concerning the details of my experience aboard the craft. The hypnosis was witnessed by Dr. Kandell, Dr. Saults, Dr. Jean Rosenbaum, Dr. Beryl Rosenbaum, long time associate Dr. Robert Ganelin, and also Duane and the *Enquirer* crew.

Dr. Rosenbaum later stated he had no doubt that the hypnosis had been performed correctly. He noted that all signs of anxiety (eye movement, respiration, muscle tension, sweat) had vanished as soon as I was put under and that all the appropriate tests for a deep trance checked out.

I did not recall any experiences under hypnosis that I could not remember before. Dr. Harder did, however, allow me to verbalize my experience in greater detail, without being overwhelmed by my heretofore clinging anxiety. It was the first time anyone had heard the entire account. Everyone in the room listened in silent amazement as the story of my horrible ordeal unfolded. . . .

CHAPTER 8

The Aliens

*Fear will drive men to any extreme; and the fear
inspired by a superior being is a mystery which cannot
be reasoned away.*

—George Bernard Shaw

(The account heard by the roomful of scientists and reporters during the hypnosis would only appear here as a long series of gentle, probing questions and terse responses. After I underwent the hypnoregression, I continued to be able to recall my experiences inside the craft with greatly reduced fear. Therefore, to avoid the tedium of question-and-answer form, I present the account in the form of a more detailed, smooth narrative.)

"Uhnng . . ." I moaned silently. My first glimmer of slowly returning consciousness brought with it the single overpowering sensation of pain.

"Oh, damn!" I gritted my teeth against the agony. The excruciating ache almost caused me to lose consciousness again. Tremendous swollen, tingling sensations, centered in my head and chest, diminished in intensity downward to my feet. I felt badly burned, all over, even inside me. Even worse than burned: It was as if I had been broken into a hundred pieces, had been literally crushed.

Oh, this damned pain! I don't know if I can stand it! I thought desperately. I've got to do something! But I didn't dare budge for fear of increasing the pain.

I was lying on my back. I didn't try to move or even to open my eyes at first. I was weak, so watery-weak, that I knew if I attempted to move even my arm I'd lapse back into unconsciousness. I was afraid I'd upset the balance of power in my inner battle with the excruciating pain. Desperately I summoned all I could muster of the mental pain-control I had learned in karate training. First managing to hold the sensations at bay, inch by inch, I gained ground against the tormenting ache.

That's better! I thought with relief. I managed to put most of the pain out of my mind. My head was clearer and I could think a little better, but I still needed most of my concentration to keep the pain blocked out.

A bitter, metallic taste covered my tongue. My mouth was dry and I was very thirsty. Oddly, the weakness in my muscles did not seem to come from hunger. The trembling felt odd, like a strange mixture of exertion and illness. I had never had a headache in my entire life. Something was terribly wrong.

God! What happened to me? I wondered fearfully. I tried to remember. My mind was still somewhat groggy. I could not recall anything.

I sluggishly dragged my eyelids open. I could not see anything. Then a blurred image began to coalesce. My eyes struggled against the agony. My sight shifted in and out of focus. My vision slowly became clearer. The hazy scintillations of light gradually solidified into an image. I could make out some kind of light source above me.

The fixture was a luminous rectangle about three feet by one and a half feet. The diffused light came from the flat, frosted surface of the rectangle. The direct light sent daggers of pain into my head. The fixture gave off a clear, soft white glow. It was not tremendously bright, but my eyes could not handle it. I winced and blinked, then shifted my gaze to the tolerable dimness beyond the glowing rectangle.

For an instant I could distinguish the brushed metal luster of a ceiling in the softer, reflected glow above the light. The fixture seemed to be suspended lower and closer to me than to the ceiling. I deduced from the nearness of the ceiling that the hard flat surface I was lying on was a raised table of some kind.

What's the matter with my eyes? I asked myself. The ceiling is all crooked. It's too small on this end and too large on that end! Were my eyes playing tricks on me? I closed them against the discomfort, but soon opened them again to ward off the feeling of vertigo that welled up in me. The odd-shaped ceiling was indeed as I had perceived it: generally triangular, with the base toward my feet.

What a weird place! I reflected wonderingly. I had been hurt. Yeah, that was it! . . . But what? I could remember straightening up and feeling as though somebody had whacked me with a baseball bat.

Suddenly, the memory of what happened before I'd blacked out came rushing back with stunning impact. I remembered standing in the clearing in the woods looking up at that glowing saucer! Good grief, what a sight! I had seen it move and heard its awesome sound. My approach had seemed to cause the thing to come alive. Then I recalled standing up and turning to get away from it. I had been hurt somehow. . . . Maybe that thing had hit me with something!

Where in hell am I? . . . Oh my God—the hospital! They brought me here to the hospital! I thought.

The implication gave me a sickening feeling deep down inside. Through the agonizing ache I could feel that I was at least still whole and in one piece. I needed to get up and find out what had happened, but I could not move. Trying only sapped what energy I had left. Next, I tried to call out. No sound came. I thought I had better relax and conserve my strength. I would let the doctors do all the worrying. I was safe for now.

It was very hot and humid. The heavy air was almost stifling. It smelled slightly stale and muggy. I was sweating; warm moisture beaded my temples. Feeling my jacket bunched up under my arms, I wondered why a nurse had not removed it. I still had all my work clothes on, even my boots, and the jacket was just too warm. I must be injured so bad there wasn't time to take off my coat, I thought. Maybe I was in an emergency room of some kind. Oh great, the emergency room! I must be hurt really bad! All I could do was hope for the best.

Then I felt something flat pressing down lightly on my chest. It felt cool and smooth. I looked down and managed to hold my eyes open long enough to see that my shirt and jacket were pushed up around my shoulders, exposing my chest and abdomen. A strange device curved across my body. It was about four or five inches thick and I could feel that it extended from my armpits to a few inches above my belt. It curved down to the middle of each side of my rib cage. It appeared to be made of shiny, dark gray metal or plastic.

I looked past the upper edge of the device. With the shift in distance my sight momentarily blurred again. I could discern the indistinct forms of people standing over me. One to the left of me, two on my right. I strained to bring them into clearer focus. My vision was getting better. I could see the blurry figures of the doctors, leaning over me with their white masks and caps. They were wearing unusual, orange-colored surgical gowns. I could not make out their faces clearly.

My body ached, but I could not feel the doctors cutting or sewing me. I wondered what they were doing and just how serious it was. I felt strong enough to move, but didn't, for fear of causing problems for the doctors.

Oh, no! I thought, my mind jumping briefly at the possibility of coming out of anesthesia in the middle of an operation. I felt no increase in pain and dismissed the thought. That kind of stuff probably only happened in the scare-stories people pass around. I decided to conserve my energy for recovery.

I had never been in a bad accident or hurt myself seriously. I had been pretty healthy throughout my life. I had not taken so much as a single aspirin in years. I was always careful to avoid injury of any kind. But here I had done something really stupid and it was too late to reconsider.

Why in hell did I have to get so close? That was so *dumb*. If I pull out of this one, I thought, I'll have learned my lesson about tempering curiosity with caution.

I looked again at the vague but reassuring forms of the doctors around me. Abruptly my vision cleared. The sudden horror of what I saw rocked me as I realized that I was definitely not in a hospital.

I was looking squarely into the face of a horrible creature!

My senses were instantly electrified to a new keenness. Everything clicked. The weird-shaped room, the strange device, the odd clothing, all added up to one inescapable conclusion: Good God! I must be inside that craft!

A creature was looking steadily back at me with huge, luminous brown eyes the size of quarters! I recoiled.

I looked frantically around me. There were three of them! Hysteria overcame me instantly. I struck out at the two on my right, hitting one with the back of my arm, knocking it into the other one. My swing was more of push than a blow, I was so weakened.

The one I touched felt soft through the cloth of its garment. The muscles of its puny physique yielded with a sponginess that was more like fat than sinew. The creature was light and had fallen back easily.

I heaved myself to a sitting position. The exertion caused beads of sweat to pop out on my forehead. I lunged unsteadily to my feet and staggered back. I fell against a utensil-arrayed bench that followed the curve of one wall. My arm sent some of the instruments clattering against the back of the shelf. I leaned there heavily, keeping my eyes riveted on those horrid entities.

My action had caused the device across my chest to crash to the floor. No wires or tubes connected it to me, or to anything else. It rocked back and forth on its upper side. The rocking sent shifting beams of greenish light out onto the floor, from the underside of the machine.

My aching body would not do what I told it to. My legs felt too weak to hold me up. I leaned heavily on the counter. The monstrous trio of humanoids started toward me. Their hands reached out at me.

With the superhuman effort of a cornered animal, I ground out the strength to defend myself. Fighting the splitting pain in my skull, I grabbed for something from the bench with which to fend them off. My hand seized on a thin transparent cylinder about eighteen inches long. It was too light to be an effective club. I needed something sharp. I tried to break the tip off the tube. I smashed the end of the glasslike wand down on the waist-high metal slab I had been lying on. It would not break.

I sprang into a fighting stance with my legs spread wide to brace for the attack. I lashed out with the weapon at the advancing creatures, screaming desperate, hysterical threats. "Get away from me! What are you?" I shouted wildly, shrinking away in revulsion.

The creatures slowed but continued toward me, their hands outstretched.

"Keep back, damn you!" I shrieked menacingly.

They halted. In a snarling crouch I held the tube threateningly back behind my head. I felt hopelessly trapped. I was surrounded, with my back to the wall.

There was a door beyond where the nightmarish beings stood. To get out I would have to go through them. It was a standoff. I crouched slightly on my trembling legs, the cold sweat pouring off me. My clammy grip on the rod was too feeble to lend me much reassurance, but I kept it drawn back in readiness. My mind was a whirling confusion of terror.

Silence hung heavily over the room. The taut emotions practically crackled in the air, like electricity. The creatures stood silently staring at me. I could hardly bear to look upon them, but I got my first good look.

They stood still, mutely. They were a little under five feet in height. They had a basic humanoid form: two legs, two arms, hands with five digits each, and a head with the normal human arrangement of features. But beyond the outline, any similarity to humans was terrifyingly absent.

Their thin bones were covered with white, marshmallowy-looking flesh. They had on single-piece coverall-type suits made of soft, suedelike material, orangish brown in color. I could not see any grain in the material, such as cloth has. In fact, their clothes did not appear even to have any seams. I saw no buttons, zippers, or snaps. They wore no belts. The loose billowy garments were gathered at the wrists and perhaps the ankles. They didn't have any kind of raised collar at the neck. They wore simple pinkish tan footwear. I could not make out the details of their shoes, but they had very small feet, about a size four by our measure.

When they extended their hands toward me, I noticed they had no fingernails. Their hands were small, delicate, without hair. Their thin round fingers looked soft and unwrinkled.

Their smooth skin was so pale that it looked chalky, like ivory. The skin was delicate and thin to the point of translucence. That subtle semitransparency made the life fluids just underneath the skin falsely suggest moistness of the surface, contrasting its actual dryness. The thin white membrane stretched over the curves of their small bodies, without wrinkles. The bends of their fingers and necks made very small, slightly rounded folds instead of sharp creases.

Their bald heads were disproportionately large for their puny bodies. They had bulging, oversized craniums, a small jaw structure, and an undeveloped appearance to their features that was almost infantile. Their thin-lipped mouths were narrow; I never saw them open. Lying close to their heads on either side were tiny crinkled lobes of ears. Their miniature rounded noses had small oval nostrils.

The only facial feature that didn't appear underdeveloped were those incredible eyes! Those glistening orbs had brown irises twice the size of those of a normal human eye's, nearly an inch in diameter! The iris was so large that even parts of the pupils were hidden by the lids, giving the eyes a certain catlike appearance. There was very little of the white part of the eye showing. They had no lashes and no eyebrows.

The occasional blink of their eyes was strikingly conspicuous. Their huge lids slid quickly down over the glassy bubbles of their eyes, then flipped open again like the release of roll-up windowshades. These huge, moist, lashless eyes and the milky translucence of their skin made their appearance slightly reminiscent of a cave salamander. But, strangely, in spite of my terror, I felt there was also something gentle and familiar about them. It hit me. Their overall look was disturbingly like that of a human fetus!

Their sharp gaze alternately darted about, then fixed me with an intense stare—a look so piercing it seemed they were seeing right through me. I felt naked and exposed under their scrutiny. I could not bear to meet their gaze, but I found my eyes continually returning to look into theirs. It was impossible to avoid their compelling stare. Those eyes were the creepiest, most frightening things I had seen in my entire life.

I've got to get out of here! My mind seized on that one driving, panicked thought. I had to get away from those awful monsters, away from those horrid eyes! I felt desperate to escape. Desperate to return to the open forest that I erroneously thought must be somewhere just outside this stifling place.

With all the screaming and the hysterical questions I had thrown at them, they never once said anything to me. I did not hear them speak to each other. Their mouths never made any kind of sound or motion. The only sounds I heard were those of movements, and of my own voice.

Those three silent beings were between me and the only apparent way out. With the instincts of a trapped beast, I gathered every ounce of energy I had, to fight for my life.

It looked as though those years of karate training were about to pay off. Although I couldn't for sure know what sort of adversary I was up against, there was nothing particularly formidable about the aliens in the sense of hand-to-hand combat. Still, I knew that an unknown opponent could hold many surprises.

What am I going to do? I thought wildly. I did not know what kind of combination of punching or kicking techniques to throw. My dilemma was like that of a woman needing to brush a huge hairy spider off her arm, but too loath to touch it to move.

If I can, I'll just push them out of the way and run past them . . . but the thought of touching them is so revolting! I groaned inwardly. I didn't have the slightest idea of what they were capable of doing to me—they could be carrying hidden weapons, or even be venomous, or something weird like that. I only knew I had to get out of there, and get away from them, at any cost, even though the prospect of battling my way past them was utterly terrifying.

Just as I girded myself to spring at them, they abruptly turned and scurried from the room! They went out the open door, turned right and disappeared. The anticlimax of their retreat was incredible. The extra adrenaline that had squirted into my bloodstream left me trembling uncontrollably. I collapsed back against the bench, struggling to slow my racing heart. I gulped the heavy air in ragged gasps.

Slowly I began to recover. Breathing deeply, I looked around me. I was in an irregular room with metal walls. The floor and ceiling were shaped like a slice of pie with the point bitten off. The ceiling was about seven feet high. Three of the walls were each about twelve feet in length. Two of these were straight with a concave one between. The two straight walls were not parallel but intersected another smaller, convexly curved wall, about eight feet wide, on the other end. In it an open doorway gaped, about three feet by six and a half feet.

The metal of the walls had a textured, gray matte appearance, dull and nonreflective. I saw no bolts, rivets, screws, or seams of any kind. The surfaces of the walls, floor, and ceiling curved into each other. Even the light fixture, the curving bench, and the table, simply curved into the surface to which they were attached. In fact, everything seemed to be molded out of a single, continuous piece of material!

The room was devoid of ornamentation or color. There were no windows or ventilation openings. I noticed no cupboards, closets, or other doors. I couldn't see any buttons, switches, or electrical receptacles on the walls. The small room contained only the light fixture, the table, the narrow counter I leaned on, and the device that had fallen off my chest.

The device had quit rocking back and forth by now. It lay next to the table. The odd glow still came from under its edges. It had hit the floor with a loud noise but, curiously, the floor had not clanged or rung with the impact. For a metal room, the acoustics seemed quite abnormal: flat and without echo. The floor and table only thudded deeply when I stepped on or struck the surfaces. The metal seemed to be very thick and dense.

The table I had been lying on was a slab, about an inch and a half thick and approximately three feet by six and a half feet in length. Its single round leg, about four inches in diameter, curved into the floor like a stem.

The light was similarly suspended by a single descending two-inch column that curved into the surfaces of the ceiling and the fixture like a stalactite formation.

Afraid of the aliens' return, I looked toward the door. No sign of anyone. I needed something better to defend myself with. I glanced around the room. I noticed an array of strange instruments lying on the bench. The bench was about eighteen inches wide and an inch and a half thick. Its edges were rounded off smoothly. It was made of that same odd gray metallic substance.

The instruments were arranged near the middle of the bench, leaving either end of it clear. There was nothing I recognized, but some of the chromelike objects reminded me of those in a laboratory or doctor's office. They were shiny strips, rippled, or twisted, formed into separate implements.

There was a variety of transparent tubes or cylinders in different sizes, similar to the one I was still clutching. There were also some black rectangular objects and something that looked like half of a slightly flattened, cream-colored handball with a sharp thin metal disc sticking out from the straight side. All the objects were too small to be effective as weapons. There was nothing that I could defend myself with. I was more afraid of *being hurt by* some of those instruments. I touched nothing more, throwing the clear tube I still held down on the floor.

Thinking I had heard a sound, I whirled, jerking my head around and riveting my eyes on the door. Again there was nothing.

Oh no! What if they come back here with weapons or reinforcements? I thought wildly. I'd better find a way out!

Stepping over the device that had been on my chest, I went around the table and stumbled to the door. I halted in the opening. I took a deep breath. I felt a little stronger, but pain still hammered relentlessly in my head, and especially in my chest. I was sweating; the heavy air was difficult to breathe.

I've got to get *out* of here, I thought frantically with a surge of determination.

There was a curving hallway about three feet wide outside the door. The ceiling of the hall gave off a faint, almost unnoticeable illumination. I looked to the right down the narrow, dimly lit passage in the direction the aliens had run. There was no one in sight.

Seeing nothing in the passage to my left, I began walking that way. I broke into a frightened run down the narrow corridor.

I have to find a way out of here, I thought again. My panic was almost claustrophobic.

The cramped hallway turned continuously in a tight curve to the right. I dashed past an open doorway on my left without looking in, only ten feet down the hall from the door I had just exited. I caught a glimpse of a room, but was afraid to stop.

Wait just a damn minute, Travis! I struggled to get a grip on my self-control. What if I'd missed a chance at that doorway to find a way out of this place? I still did not know for sure where in hell I was. I could be in a boat, a building, or a submarine for all I knew. I saw another doorway ten more feet ahead on my right. I slowed down to a walk as I neared it.

Maybe this would be my way out. . . .

CHAPTER 9

Human?

O, the difference of man and man!

—Shakespeare

The door was only a few feet ahead on my right, on the inside curve of the hallway. I slowed down, turned, and stopped in the opening.

I looked in cautiously. I saw a round room about sixteen feet across with a domed ceiling about ten feet high. Equally spaced around the room were three rectangular outlines resembling closed doorways.

No one there. The room was totally empty except for a single chair that faced away from me.

I looked behind me. The hallway was still empty. I slowly entered the room. I hesitated to approach the high-backed chair. There might be somebody sitting in it that I could not see from behind.

I circled, keeping my distance from the chair, checking to see if anyone was sitting in it. I followed the curve of the wall to get around to where I could see. I was ready to beat an instant retreat if I should see one of those hideous creatures again. I stopped every few steps to crane my neck over the back of the chair. Seeing nobody, I continued around to where I could ascertain, with much relief, that the chair was unoccupied.

It seemed to be made of the same dull gray metal was almost everything else. It had a single leg that curved into the floor like the leg of the table in the first room. The chair was angular, with rounded edges. There were some buttons and a strange lever on the arm of it.

Glancing apprehensively toward the open door, I slowly went toward the chair. As I gradually approached it, a very curious thing began to happen.

The closer I got to it, the darker the room became! Small points of light became visible on, or through, the walls, even the floor. I stepped back and the effect diminished. I stepped forward and it increased again, the points of light becoming brighter in contrast to the darkening background. It was like the stars coming into view in the evening, only very much faster. The matte gray of the metal wall just faded out to be replaced by the glinting, speckled deep-black of space.

I thought: Maybe this is a planetarium-type projection or . . . Good grief! What if this is actually some kind of a viewing screen showing where this thing I'm in *is*?

Space. Maybe it wasn't *like* the stars coming into view at night—maybe it *was* the stars, in the eternal void of space! I was suddenly gripped with the icy fear that even if I could find a way outside, I would die in the airlessness of space. My God, the sweet earth could be millions of miles away!

I could see no constellations I recognized among the myriad points of light. Even if I could find a door or a hatch, I might be trapped! . . . No. . . . *No!* I hoped and prayed it was not true. There just *had* to be a way out!

I looked at the controls on the chair. Maybe—just maybe—one of those buttons would open a door or something. I moved closer and studied the array of switches. On the left arm, there was a single short thick lever with an oddly molded handle atop some dark brown material. On the right arm, there was an illuminated, lime-green screen about five inches square. Under that, a square of approximately twenty-five colored buttons. I looked for symbols or written words and found none.

The screen had a lot of black lines on it that intersected each other at all angles. The lines had short little dashes intersecting them at regular intervals. On some of the lines, the dashes were widely spaced; on others, there were many closely-spaced dashes. The buttons below the screen were arranged in about five vertical rows, with one color for each row: red, yellow, green, blue, and violet. The colors were bright, lit faintly from within.

The experiment I was considering was risky, but I was desperate. I reached out, my finger hovering over one of the green buttons uncertainly. On impulse, I went ahead and pushed it. I looked around the room and listened carefully—nothing happened. When I pushed the button, I noticed that the segmented lines on the screen had moved.

I recklessly pushed another green one. The lines rapidly changed angles, slid down each other, then stopped. I pushed some of the other colored buttons. Nothing happened. Nothing moved and no sound could be heard.

Trembling, I sat down on the hard, slightly-curved surface of the chair. This put the short lever on my left. I put my hand onto its molded T-grip. The lever was about an inch in diameter. The chocolate-brown handle was slightly small for my hand. The whole chair seemed a little too small.

From where I sat, I could see stars all around me, even on the wall where I had just come through the door. The surfaces of the room were only faintly visible, but the doorway I had come through was as clear to see as ever.

I could see nebulous clouds of tiny stars and dust in a band like the Milky Way, only more distinct than I had ever seen it on a clear night in the woods. Except for the door, the effect was like sitting in a chair in the middle of space.

"Well, here goes," I said to myself. I rotated the handle of the lever forward, feeling the slow, even, fluid resistance of it. I felt suddenly disoriented as the stars began moving downward in front of me, in unison. Quickly I pulled my hand off the lever. The stars stopped moving. The handle slowly returned to its original position. The stars did not return to their original position, however, but remained where they were.

Damn! *Something* has to work! I clung to that one shred of hope like a drowning man.

Overcoming the momentary giddiness, I again grabbed the handle. Impulsively, I moved the handle in a series of different directions. The handle seemed to rotate independently of the lever when I rolled it forward or to the sides. The stars began whirling and changing directions wildly in response to the lever's movements. But the stars always retained the same pattern in their motions. I pulled my hand away from the lever and it returned to its original vertical position. The stars again regained the position they'd held when I released my grip on the handle.

If this thing is flying, I could crash it or throw it off course and get lost or something! I worried. What if it just exploded? I resolved not to tamper with those controls anymore. I might escalate a desperate situation into a fatal disaster.

I got out of the chair and walked to the edge of the room. As I did, the stars faded out and the surfaces of the wall, ceiling, and floor came into sight. I moved over to one of the rectangles resembling closed doors. I searched the edges for a sign of a switch or an opening mechanism. Seeing none, I ran my hands along the edges of the crack. I could not feel any draft through it. I put my eye to the crack; I could not see any light, either. I looked around for some kind of symbol or writing that would help me figure out where I was or how to get out of there. None.

I walked back to the chair and stood beside it, looking at the buttons. There were some I had not yet pushed. I was thinking about pushing some of them, when I heard a faint sound.

I whirled around and looked at the door. There, standing in the open doorway, was a *human* being!

I stood frozen to the spot. He was a man about six feet two inches tall. His helmeted head barely cleared the doorway. He was extremely muscular and evenly proportioned. He appeared to weigh about two hundred pounds. He wore a tight-fitting bright blue suit of soft material like velour. His feet were covered with black boots, a black band or belt wrapped around his middle. He carried no tools or weapons on his belt or in his hands; no insignia marked his clothing.

Wow! How did he get here? Is he from the air force? What's going on here? Maybe he's from NASA! I'm saved! Another human—one of my own kind! Relief flooded over me. Never before had I been so glad to see a total stranger.

The man gestured with his right hand for me to come toward him. He beckoned with his open hand.

I ran up to him, exclaiming, babbling all sorts of questions. "How did you get in here? Can you get me out of here? There were these horrible things in here. . . . What's going on? Who are you? Please, help me!"

The man remained silent throughout my verbal barrage. I was worried by his silence. I looked closely at his face through the helmet.

He had coarse, sandy-blond hair of medium length, covering his ears. He had a dark complexion, like a deep, even tan. He had no beard or mustache. In fact, I couldn't even see stubble or dark shadow of whiskers. He had slightly rugged, masculine features and strange eyes. They were a bright, golden hazel color—but there was something odd about those eyes besides their color that I could not quite identify.

His helmet was like a transparent sphere, slightly flattened. No tubes or hoses. Its wide black rim was set down close over the contour of his shoulder. The black rim had a small oval opening in it in the back. The helmet might have been lightly frosted on the back, or it might have been just the lighting that made it appear that way.

The man did not offer any acknowledgment of my questions. He only smiled kindly in a faintly tolerant manner. He didn't appear to even be attempting to reply. Then it hit me: That's it! Of course he can't answer with that helmet on. He probably can't even hear me!

He took me firmly but gently by the left arm and gestured for me to go with him. He seemed friendly enough. He probably just wanted to get someplace where he could remove his helmet. His need for the helmet made me somewhat uneasy. Maybe I'd better go with him, the sooner to get out of this air—which, even if it's not harmful, is stiflingly warm and humid. Anyway, he's too big to argue with. I was anxious to have all my questions answered, but I figured everything would be explained when we got to where we were going. For the moment, I was relieved merely to be in the company of a real human being. I knew one thing for sure: If I could get out of here and away from where those aliens lurked, I was going to cooperate.

He took me out of that room and hurried me down the narrow hallway, pulling me along behind him due to its narrowness. The hallway continued to curve to our right. He stopped in front of a closed doorway that slid open to his right, into the wall. I did not see what caused it to open.

The door opened into a bare room so small it was more like a foyer or section of hallway, although it was slightly wider than the hall we had just left. The door slid shut quickly and silently behind us. Again I attempted to talk to the man as we stood there.

"Where are we going?" I asked anxiously.

No answer.

We spent approximately two minutes in the metal cubicle, no more than seven by five by twelve feet. Then a doorway, the same size as the other door and directly opposite it, slid open, also to the right.

The brilliant warm light that came through the opening door into the airlock-like room was almost like daylight in color and brightness. Fresh, cool air wafted in, reminding me of springtime in the out-of-doors, making me realize just how dark and stifling that place had been. What a relief that fresh air was!

The side walls of the passage outside the door sloped down at a forty-five-degree angle to meet a ramp that continued its slope. While my eyes became accustomed to the bright light, I stood on the landing for a moment. The air moved around me in a softly fluctuating current. I stood and inhaled deeply the clean, cool breeze. The last twinges of the ache in my head and chest almost completely disappeared. I had nearly forgotten the discomfort that had been with me constantly since I had regained consciousness.

I looked around to discover that, although I was outside that dim, humid craft, I was not out-of-doors. I was in a huge room. The ceiling was sectioned into alternating rectangles of dark metal and those that gave off light like the sun shining through a translucent panel. The alternation of the light and dark panels reminded me of a checkerboard. The ceiling itself curved down to form one of the larger walls in the room. The room was shaped like one-quarter of a cylinder laid on its side.

I descended the short, steep ramp seven or eight feet to the floor. The ramp seemed as if it would be difficult to walk down at the angle it descended, but it turned out to be floored with a very sure gripping, rubber-like surface.

The outside of the craft we had just left was shaped like the one we had seen in the woods, like two pie pans placed lip to lip with a dome on top, but was very much larger, about sixty feet in diameter and sixteen feet high. It did not emit light; instead it had a surface of shiny brushed-metal luster. It seemed to radiate a faint heat from its hull. The craft either sat flat on its bottom or, if it had legs, they were only a few inches high. It sat nearly in the middle of the large room.

On my left, toward one end of the large room, there were two or three oval-shaped saucers, reflecting light like highly polished chrome. I saw beyond the edge of the brushed-metal craft a silvery reflection that could have been another shiny, rounded craft. I could see two of them very clearly, against the wall at the end of the hangarlike room. They were about forty or forty-five feet in diameter, quite a bit smaller than the angular vehicle I had just come out of. I saw no projections or breaks in the smooth, shiny, flattened spheres. They sat on very rounded bottoms and I could not see how they balanced that way. Perhaps they were braced or attached in some way to the wall behind them.

The man escorted me across the open floor to a door. The dull green floor seemed to be made of a springy, semihard rubbery pavement, somewhat similar to the material of an indoor track.

The doors opened silently and quickly from the middle outward. We were in a hallway about six feet wide, illuminated from the eight-foot-high ceiling, which was one long panel of softly diffused light. The walls were a pastel off-green, the floor was the same carpetlike soft pavement of the large room we had just left. The hallway was straight and perhaps eighty feet long. Closed double doors were distributed along the corridor.

"When do I get to go home?" I asked. "Where are we going now?"

No reply.

At the end of the hallway, another pair of double doors. I watched closely this time. I did not see him touch anything, but again the doors slid silently back from the middle. We entered a white room approximately fifteen feet square, with another eight-foot-high ceiling. The room had a table and a chair in it. But my interest was immediately focused on the three other humans!

Two men and a woman were standing around the table. They were all wearing velvety blue uniforms like the first man's, except that they had no helmets. The uniforms were cuffless and collarless. They fit very tightly on the upper body and upper legs, slightly looser on the lower legs. The pant legs tucked loosely into or were attached to the short boottops. The boots were made of a soft, dull black material. Neither the boots nor the band around the waist appeared to be made of leather. The boots did not have a hard sole; they were more like moccasins. A seam or a line in the material of their uniforms ran from the middle of the neckline down to the waist.

There was no buckle on the band around the middle, no weapons or tools on the band. They also wore no insignia.

The two men had the same muscularity and the same masculine good looks as the first man. The woman also had a face and figure that was the epitome of her gender. They were smooth-skinned and blemishless. No moles, freckles, wrinkles, or scars marked their skin. The striking good looks of the man I had first met became more obvious on seeing them all together. They shared a family-like resemblance, although they were not identical.

They all had the same coarse, brownish blond hair. The woman wore hers longer than the men, past her shoulders. She did not appear to be wearing makeup. They all seemed to be in their mid-twenties, perhaps older. All had those same intense, golden hazel eyes. Whether it was their brightness or some other quality, something was definitely odd about those eyes; but I could not pin down their disturbing nature. Their most encouraging feature, other than appearing human, was that they wore no helmets. Maybe *they* could hear me! Instantly I started talking to them, trying to get them to answer.

"Would somebody *please* tell me where I am?" I implored. I was still utterly shaken from my encounter with those awful other creatures. "What in hell is going on? What is this place?"

They didn't answer me. They only looked at me, though not unkindly. The helmeted man sat me down in a chair. He crossed the room to a door and, when it opened, went out. There was a corridor outside the door; he turned right.

The chair he had seated me in was soft and comfortable. It was upholstered with a close-grained, or weaveless, tan fabric. It was squared off, but the sides angled so that the bottom was smaller than the top. It had no legs; the back was rounded. It stood to the right of the door through which I had just entered.

The table was a shiny black slab with a single silvery leg about six inches in diameter. It stood midway across the room, was about seven feet by three and a half feet across, and two inches thick, with rounded edges and corners.

One man and the woman came around the table, approaching me. They stood on either side of the chair.

"What are you doing?" I asked.

Silently they each took me by an arm and led me toward the table. I didn't know why I should cooperate with them. They wouldn't even tell me anything. But I was in no position to argue, so I went along at first.

They lifted me easily onto the edge of the table. I became wary and started protesting. "Wait a minute. Just tell me what you are going to do!"

I began to resist them, but all three began pushing me gently backward down onto the table. I looked up at the ceiling, covered with panels of softly glowing white light with a faint blue cast.

I saw that the woman suddenly had an object in her hand from out of nowhere—it looked like one of those clear, soft plastic oxygen masks, only there were no tubes connected to it. The only thing attached to it was a small black golfball-sized sphere.

She pressed the mask down over my mouth and nose. I started to reach up to pull it away. Before I could complete the motion, I rapidly became weak. Everything started turning gray. Then there was nothing at all but black oblivion. . . .

Consciousness returned to me on the night I awoke to find myself on the cold pavement west of Heber, Arizona.

PART 2

Analysis

CHAPTER 10

A Question of Belief

Read not to contradict and confute, nor to believe and take for granted, but to weigh and consider.

—Sir Francis Bacon

In opening this book I included a discussion of bias and the need for an open mind in judging the validity of our (mine and my coworkers') experience with the UFO. Due to the unique and incredible nature of that experience, I feel that many of the questions asked are perfectly justifiable and appropriate. But when *answers* to those questions are arrived at without fair examination of all the evidence, I strenuously object. I maintain that if all the evidence had been analyzed with an open mind, none of the various wild accusations against my coworkers and me ever would have been made. Anyone unwilling to examine relevant evidence is really not justified in forming an opinion about *anything.*

While nearly everyone was prematurely making up their minds whether we were sane or crazy, truthful or lying, the Aerial Phenomena Research Organization (APRO) went quietly about its business of assessing the validity of the case from a scientific standpoint. APRO performed an extensive battery of medical, psychiatric, hypnotic, and polygraph examinations which, with other evidence and the physical facts of the case, expose all the accusations as unjustified.

When I step back and take a look at all the attacks made on the veracity of my incident over the years, I am disturbed by the simple fact that some of this stuff was ever judged fit to print. To be fair, I have encountered some excellent journalists, even some who were skeptical, who did their best to verify their facts and present an objective, balanced view; the ones who didn't just pretend to leave conclusions to the reader while actually making their own. Objectivity is the standard I have come to feel I should strive for.

I used to be offended, even outraged, not just at false "evidence," but at disbelief itself. I now realize that a certain degree of disbelief is perfectly understandable; after all, people are trying to judge a truly incredible report in what I frankly acknowledge is an absence of indisputable proof. Therefore, in reviewing these issues, I will play devil's advocate in places. Rather than say, "This ain't so 'cause I was there and I *know* how it really was," I will try to take what is (for someone in my place) the more difficult position: one that considers, rather than automatically dismisses, negative "evidence," at least for purposes of discussion. I'll try to present what is needed for an objective outsider to conduct an informed evaluation.

I enter this area of discussion with mixed feelings because here, in the midst of finally having my own say, I'm inadvertently providing an extended forum for statements by others that should never have been made in the first place.

There is a post-Watergate mentality that assumes that public denials (or even allegations alone) are in themselves evidence of wrongdoing. It's become so routine to hear trusted public officials make denials of things we later learn are true, that we have nearly come to treat denials as confessions. This situation leads many accused public figures to use the tactic of avoiding comment altogether, even when being truthful. Not me. I'm no longer going to let this litany of innuendo, this tissue of lies and ad hoc assumptions, dominate the floor unchallenged.

One thing I've learned about the media is that the retraction usually gets a smaller hearing than the original error, if the retraction gets heard at all. Besides wondering how such baseless attacks can make it into print, I am further annoyed at how things already disproved keep being recycled over the years. Not only were a lot of the allegations indisputably refuted long ago, they had been absurd right from the start. As I will demonstrate, a moment's thought would have immediately removed a lot of this stuff from consideration.

The credentials and credibility, methods and motives, of my advocates were microscopically scrutinized while those of my detractors went unchallenged. If even a fraction of the skepticism applied against me and my proponents had been applied to the naysayers, their campaign would have ended even as it began.

One misconception is so common it warrants being ranked as a classic logical fallacy: the belief that if there are so many different attacks heard so many times from so many different sources, there must be some validity to them. The truth, of course, is that a billion falsehoods told a billion times by a billion people are still false.

What makes this reasoning especially illogical is when the various allegations *starkly contradict* each other. The most fundamental test of validity is the law of contradiction—i.e., a thing cannot be both A and not A. It is irrational to take a collection of theories that are mutually exclusive and act as if they add up and give weight to each other. Yet my foremost critics do exactly that. One man even said that it was a hoax and a drug hallucination in one breath! Logically speaking, not only does a collection of incompatible accusations not have compounding strength, each cancels the others so that the collection has less merit than any one would have if made alone.

This observation is especially true when many disparate allegations are put forth by a single individual. Why? Because it becomes apparent that the accuser is not moved by the force of evidence for a specific theory, but instead by some motive *preceding* his flurry of tactics. Which brings up the question: Just what is his real motive?

Ironically, when one's foremost detractor makes an internally inconsistent scattergun assault, he is actually making a perverse sort of endorsement, because it is clear the detractor himself doesn't believe that any one of his attacks has sufficient merit to stand alone. He rather refutes his own position and impugns his own motives. Like the Bard says, "Methinks he doth protest too much."

But still, we have this hail of disparagement against what has otherwise been acclaimed by the top people in the field as the most proven, best documented case of alien abduction in the history of scientific ufology. So what is it about this incident that drew so much fire? Could it have simply been a natural reaction to the bizarreness of the report? I've seen my experience critically dissected in a magazine alongside a sympathetic, credulous report of bare claims of attacks by gigantic birds which offered no multiple witnesses, no polygraph tests, no physical evidence, virtually no documentation at all.

Don't misunderstand. There were many people who never doubted the reality of the story and many news reports gave unbiased accounts. But on the other hand, others put forth absolutely every conceivable alternative explanation. Attempts to explain it all away had a predictable, knee-jerk correlation to the naysayer's field of specialty. To lawmen our report was a cover story for murder. To some newsmen it was a publicity stunt. To a substance-abuse worker, the best way to dismiss it was an alcohol or drug hallucination. To a geologist, the craft became escaping underground gases or ball lightning generated by plate tectonics. To religious fanatics it had to be either Satan's minions in disguise or fiery chariots of the gods. To an atheist/humanist it was the result of quasireligious UFO fanaticism of "true believers." To astronomers the easy alternative was a misidentified planet. One psychiatrist explained it as childhood mental trauma culminating in a "transitory psychosis." And to a UFO "debunker," it was most of these simultaneously! (Readers will notice that I put "debunker" in quotation marks. That is because the people I refer to don't so much remove bunk as create it.) As I shall show, these various theories are at complete odds with each other and, more importantly, at complete odds with basic, easily verified facts.

It's almost as if people were saying, *Anything* but that! No matter how far-fetched, ad hoc, or poor-fitting the evidence—*anything but that*! What the heck was going on here? Could it have been backlash to what was seen as a challenge to an accustomed and comfortable worldview? Granted, the astounding nature of the incident could partially justify reactions, but the desperate grasping for alternative explanations which transpired really went beyond even that.

I believe I've isolated several contributing factors to why things turned so inexplicably negative. The causes comprise six main areas. I've already mentioned one: tenacious defense of long-held beliefs. The other five areas are ordinary fear (which need not be explained), ufologists' rivalry, media fallibility, human susceptibility, and the debunkers' obsession. Through these factors runs the common thread of conformity.

My ignorance of the field let me walk unsuspecting into the crossfire of a long-raging rivalry among ufologists. In November 1976 Jesse Kornbluth published an article, "The Ufologist Establishment," slamming the people and organizations in the field of UFO studies, using my experience as the football for his kickoff. Of my return he wrote:

> . . . Travis was abducted again, this time by the Ufologist Establishment . . . groups that have space-agey acronymic code names which read like NASA parodies . . . APRO . . . NICAP . . . MUFON . . . NUFONIN. And like the official space agency, the UFO Establishment has superstars: Dr. J. Allen Hynek, "the Pope of Ufology" who was for twenty years the Air Force consultant on UFOs, and physicist Stanton Friedman, "the Ralph Nader of UFOs" . . . Travis Walton never had a chance against this crew . . . he ended up getting devoured by these supposedly friendly forces. . . . Poor Travis. Nice kid but not too clever when it comes to the nitty-gritty of UFO politicking. . . . What Travis didn't realize, however, is that he was little more than a piece of prize booty in a bizarre intraorganizational war, and that flying saucers had nothing to do with it.

When I first read the article I was incensed by its untruths, its mockery of my experience. The loyalty I felt to APRO for all they had done for me increased my anger. I wrote a sizzling (but never-sent) letter of rebuttal. However I now realize there is some truth to the part I've quoted here, with two reservations: the inclusion of Stanton Friedman, and my belief that MUFON handled the situation pretty well, given the circumstances—lack of information from the media, and incorrect information from GSW.

I believe that mine would have been considered an exceptionally valid case by any one of those organizations—*if* that organization had been the one to get primary, or even better—exclusive—access to the investigation. However, whether deliberately, unconsciously, or unintentionally due to media misinformation, those more excluded tended to take the more skeptical stance.

That last sentence is a vast understatement in the case of GSW, Ground Saucer Watch. Spaulding had never even met me or any of the six witnesses. His pseudoscientific "bafflegab" was riddled with linguistic malapropisms and non sequiturs, but it was eagerly received by an information-starved press. I was declining all requests for interviews, and nature abhors a vacuum. The powerful vacuum generated by my silence had the unfortunate side effect of inflating a minor figure into the only available source regarding a major on-going news story.

The fourth cause of the negative reactions is media fallibility. In the competition for the "scoop" and the mad dash to meet deadlines, no time is allowed to check credentials or verify even basic facts—especially in the midst of a media feeding frenzy. And a little blood in the water can drastically transform a mild-mannered reporter. Once a negative treatment is adopted, many reporters succumb to a mob mentality, following in unison the swell of changing direction like a school of barracuda. To put it bluntly, they crib—copy each other. Instead of initiating their own inquiries, they unquestioningly use their colleagues' previous reports as foundation for their own. They read each other and call it research. People who just "go with the flow" should be more careful—someone may have just flushed the toilet.

The fifth factor causing the fallout, human susceptibility, refers to the behavior of people in and around the event. That event generated such intense emotional feelings in everyone involved that I am amazed so many skeptical theories were based upon observations of people acting at variance with what they expected would be "normal" behavior. In the midst of excitement so intense, pressure so high, a mix of variables so complex and circumstances so bizarre, how can anyone hold preconceived notions about what a natural reaction would be?

Being the focus of all this gives me a unique perspective, from which I can, in retrospect, venture an analysis of some common threads running through the motivations of people near the epicenter.

An earth-shaking event suddenly interrupts everyone's mundane lives, and, temporarily suspending ordinary concerns, creates a mixture of an "air of emergency" anxiety and a "school's out" carnival atmosphere. Combine simultaneously uncertainty and undeniability, stir in heaping measures of sudden shock, fear, strangeness, suspicion, and lost sleep, and the whole scene begins to take on an unreal quality. Anyone who doesn't live here might not be able to appreciate just how overwhelming all this upheaval was for such a serenely conservative little rural town where kids complain that "nothing ever happens."

Even more than this, though, is that when all this fervor is focused on one individual, when everyone is aware that everyone else's excitement and attention is concentrated on one person, one very distinct reaction results: People act almost compulsively somehow to find some way to thrust themselves into as direct of a connection as possible with that central person.

Such behavior is not confined to lone, star-obsessed late-twenties males or to screaming teenage rock groupies. This is a powerful phenomenon affecting every demographic group, professionals included. People you would never expect begin doing some very *un*expected things. And this "connection forging" can be negative or positive in nature, depending on where that person finds himself relative to the center of it all.

So I got people with whom I had a rather cool relationship claiming we were close friends, people I've never met claiming to know me personally as a scoundrel or a saint, a number of girls falsely claiming they were pregnant by me, a guy I once boxed claiming he knocked me out, people trying to take charge, exaggerate a genuine link, or even invent one altogether. Everyone became an instant expert on me and my experience.

Sometimes this inventing isn't really deliberate lying, in the usual sense. I think this phenomenon really bypasses conscious thought, coming from somewhere much deeper, something primal. And although some such claims were damaging (and difficult to counter when involving those close to me), I don't see this phenomenon as pathological. I think it's natural and probably nearly universal, given a strong enough stimulus.

For those less prone to this, all it takes to reach the threshold is for a TV crew to extend a microphone and ask a question. This is true not just of rural people—city people are just as prone. When heretofore bored people who have never even personally seen a "celebrity" are suddenly treated like one, being interviewed by a news team from some exotic place, in an atmosphere as intoxicatingly sensationalistic as the one here in November 1975, some very surprising remarks are certain to be made. Even the people making the remarks later seemed surprised when the spell lifted. Later on there was a lot of retraction, denial, backpedaling, apology, and just plain embarrassment.

For as long as anyone can remember, this problem has plagued every police investigation that has been the focus of much public attention. Exasperated investigators have had to contend with a parade of well-meaning "witnesses," each equally certain of his unique scenario but, often as not, each at odds with the unpublished facts of the case. Harassed officials just put them in line behind all the false confessors and copycat perpetrators. It wastes a lot of time and manpower, but they have to check them all out. Veterans learn to expect it, but rookies, eager to solve the case quickly, often get taken in.

Any skeptic who wants to stake his theory on quotes taken from this setting is being foolishly naive if he's sincere, or dishonestly opportunistic if he's not.

(An aside: After noting how so many people lose themselves being near the spotlight, one might wonder if I was even more affected; but I'm proud to say I don't believe that I ever succumbed. I'm confident those who know me best will vouch for that.)

The final area of discussion and a major factor instigating negative reaction was "the debunkers' obsession." The carriers of that affliction, while not ultimately effective, nevertheless have made quite an impact in the past on large groups who were affected by some of the other factors discussed here—especially, and ironically, the "Ufologist Establishment," when justification was needed for their sour-grapes reaction after APRO got the ball. In fact, the debunkers' obsession is deeply intertwined with every other factor involved in backlash to the incident, either by being part of their cause, taking advantage of them in their tactics, or even partly resulting from them. Therefore, the debunkers' obsession will serve as the framework and focus of extensive discussion in later analysis of attacks on the validity of the incident.

Conformity is one of humanity's most powerful motivators. The dozen or so countertheories "explaining" my case were picked up and mindlessly repeated.

Freewheeling, tradition-flaunting modern Americans are very fond of thinking of themselves as original, independent individuals. Not by a parsec, captain. The truth is, many people's desire to submerge their egos into the safe bosom of collective identity is so dominating that it permeates every aspect of their behavior. Especially when they are confronted with something strange and frightening that they perceive as a threat to their comfortable and accustomed worldview. Yet they believe they make up their own minds.

Even when they rebel, most people do it in lockstep. The tradition-defying sixties saw millions of "do your own thing" fashion clones, free spir-its chanting in unison a chorus of identical iconoclastic slogans fitting their group's exclusive version of political correctness.

Even when people actually do depart from what they perceive to be what "everyone else thinks," they often pretend to share views held by the ma-jority, even when no particular stigma or moral high ground is associated with either view. It seems that in the minds of far too many people, their desire to be right excuses itself when confronted with their terror of being different. So we have the social scientists scratching their heads over os-tensible conformity and examples of "faking good," when polls and actual voting differ, surveys and actual behavior are at odds.

We all could take a frank look at our own supposedly unique "taste" in clothes, music, books, movies, even politics, then ask ourselves if it's a co-incidence that millions of people share our taste and that in five years it will be all different from *this* but it'll still all be the same. Millions of people will have made their "individual choices" from an identical new menu. We might ask ourselves, Who writes that menu?

You may be thinking something like, Hey, if an entire herd of zebras all break and run at once, they aren't necessarily imitating each other, they might all have seen the same lion. And this analogy would illustrate a per-fectly acceptable justification, *if* all these disbelieving people were sub-scribing to a theory that made any sense.

However, you can be sure this analogy does not explain their reaction when the theory to which they flock is so patched together that its form bears distinct artifacts of its originator's unique needs. It's obvious those second-ing such a notion didn't come up with something so peculiarly custom-tailored on their own.

The best example of this is the theory stating that although my cowork-ers really saw me blasted through the air by a UFO, I instantly recovered physically, quickly gathered my wits, took this astounding event in stride, and then on the spur of the moment hatched a complex plan to take ad-vantage of it.

Yeah, right. With no warning I suddenly see the most shocking, awesome sight in my entire life. Then I'm hit with a tremendous bolt of energy, which sends me flying through the air. When I finally come to, I'm afoot miles from nowhere. But instead of being overcome with fear that the craft would fire again or, assuming it had left, that it would return, and instead of wanting to head straight to a hospital to see if I'm in serious need of immediate med-ical attention, I calmly think far into the future. A little lightbulb in a car-toonist's balloon blinks on over my head, and with a devious cackle, I say to myself, "Hey, this has the makings of a great book!" or, "I'll teach those guys a lesson for running out on me when I needed them." So instead of getting help, my first impulse is to (without a light, gun, or provisions) run off into the dark, somehow without leaving a single footprint (except those leading to the spot where I was hit), and hide in the forest with the idea of later claiming to have been aboard.

This absurd scenario doesn't help the archskeptics much, since it acknowledges the reality of the UFO, but it came to be put forth because it met the special needs of a very few people involved in the investigation. The first person to say it, probably Spaulding, had painted himself into a corner because of prior statements recorded in the media. He had already stated unequivocally many times that he believed the six witnesses had actually seen a UFO, and gave detailed reports of ozone and magnetic readings to back it up. Then, when GSW lost the case he made his angry vow to "blow this thing out today!"

What could he do then? How could he avoid making himself look suspect or foolish in his reversal?

This is what is known as ad hoc, meaning "for this case alone," special, an afterthought.

A second, absurdly incompatible idea was force-fit onto his original position. Ordinarily the evidence and reasoning that would justify belief in the initial part of the incident would naturally carry through the entire thing, and conversely, a disbeliever would ordinarily dismiss the entire incident. Which runs counter to Occam's Razor—*Non sunt multiplicanda entia praeter necessitatem* or: "Entities should not be multiplied beyond necessity."

Occam's Razor is a well-known (and often misunderstood) guideline in reasoning which says that the impulse to complicate theories needlessly and resort to unusual hypotheses in order to shore up an explanation ought not be indulged. Rather, it is observed that simpler, more common theories should first be pursued to a greater extent, as these are more frequently borne out as correct. It is not a "law," but simply an observation about the odds of success in various approaches to inquiry which boils down to say: The unusual is unlikely and the common is, well, more common.

"Skeptics" are fond of using this as if it meant that anything but a prosaic explanation for rare events should be disregarded, which as applied to this discussion amounts to saying UFO incidents don't happen. Or, more perversely, they act as if it means the popular view is always right (which is exactly the fallacy of *ad populem*). Ironic, and perhaps a measure of their extremism, that pro-rational principles actually could be distorted directly into logical fallacies. As I'll show, Occam's Razor cuts the other way in regard to the mismatched patchwork of desperately illogical alternative scenarios my critics rummaged together.

What really dismays me is that this odd "part true/part hoax" conglomeration was adopted by a couple of people involved in the investigation who are otherwise pretty levelheaded. But come to think of it, they were in a circumstance similar to Spaulding's, having made earlier endorsing statements and needing a convenient position to which to withdraw (perhaps for some of the reasons described next). To be fair, and to try to exhaust all possible rational explanations, it is possible that this kind of reasoning, where an incident can be *half* genuine, could come about like this:

They start out with, "No way, they killed him".

Then the polygraph tests disprove that, yet still no Travis. So they accept the crew's being innocent of murder and grudgingly concede the possibility of the abduction. But the evidence is mounting and they begin to anticipate the conclusion to which it's all leading—a conclusion with all the consequences described earlier. They panic; their minds begin resisting, grasping for a way to avoid a conclusion they do not want.

They can't deny the evidence so far; the facts have already forced them to accept it publicly, but to go further simply can't be accommodated in the conceptual framework of their minds.

For this group, this midstream bailout could be nothing more than a psychological defense mechanism. Even if they didn't formulate this scenario, hearing someone like Spaulding say it provides them with just what they were searching for.

That covers the six main areas (plus conformity) I feel best explain why there would be so much attack on the best-documented such incident ever. Enough generalities about where these allegations came from. Before getting down to the nitty-gritty of specific charges, let's take a quick review of the main points of the *supporting* evidence.

Seven men witnessed the event. Every one of them has stood by his story for over two decades. All passed polygraph tests concerning what they saw. There were simultaneous electrical outages in the nearest communities and various physical traces at the sight, all measured independently by persons hostile to the report. The principle witness has undergone not only positive lie-detector tests, but also voice-stress analysis, regressive hypnosis, and a battery of medical and psychological tests. The polygraph examiners have stood by their truthful verdicts to this day. And skeptics have been scratching around for all these years, keenly desirous of digging up anything that might remotely support their case and essentially coming up with nothing but the garbage refuted here.

Some people espoused multiple explanations simultaneously. But another reason there were so many alternative theories circulating was that as the current pet theory crumbled under the weight of undeniable evidence to the contrary, a new one was urgently needed to fill the breach.

For example, the first major charge, that my coworkers murdered me, hid my body, and in desperation came up with a wild cover story, came to an abrupt and permanent end when I was returned. This theory was seriously and widely held until the crew passed the state police lie-detector tests. Some people had doubts even *after* the tests (but before my return).

I shudder to think what might have become of my coworkers had I never been returned. (Of course, I shudder even more to think what would have become of me!) I believe they would have lived under a shadow of suspicion for the rest of their lives—despite their polygraphs—to satisfy the prejudice of some.

Dr. Harder has pointed out that six witnesses passing polygraph tests would have been more than sufficient evidence to have convicted a person of murder in an American court of law. It is alarming—chilling—to think that the level of evidence that can justify depriving a convicted man of his very life can be so casually dismissed just because it pointed to an undesired conclusion. And had I not been returned, the rejection of my coworkers' testimony would have been accompanied by their continuing to be suspected of that very charge—murder.

An early theory of law enforcement's, after the murder theory fell apart, was that since I had felt the beam as a "blow," maybe the crew had hit me on the head from behind, injected me with drugs, and put on masks or something, to in some way to make me perceive my "trip" as one on a spaceship. Medical exams showed no evidence of a blow to the head or drugs in my blood or urine. Like most of these imaginative scenarios, this just doesn't square with any of the easily verified facts of the situation.

One line of reasoning proposed that we didn't know what we saw, that we had misidentified the planet Jupiter, a plasma, ball lightning, papier-mâché, a weather balloon, a rubber raft, a hubcap someone had hung in a tree, or a sunlit cloud. The sheer variety of alternatives again points out that it wasn't force of evidence for any one idea motivating this thinking, but some belief prior to the casting about for explanations.

Plasmas and ball lightning are phenomena as rare and esoteric (if not more so) as UFOs. So much for Occam's Razor. The weather had been clear and dry. We hadn't seen the object indistinctly, from a distance. It wasn't papier-mâché hanging from a tree; it wasn't a point of light in the sky. We saw (and heard) a distinct, glowing, mechanical object hovering in midair at such close range that it was clear and unmistakable. No sincerely open-minded person could suggest such alternatives to explain our perception.

During the making of the film *Fire in The Sky,* Mike Rogers and I visited the Industrial Light and Magic complex and saw the special effects developed for the movie. It took dozens of highly specialized people months and millions of dollars to equal what we saw; and then only through the restricted and enhanced viewpoint of the camera.

One local elderly couple claimed to have seen me hitchhiking along the highway while the search was under way. They say that when I recognized them, I ran off into the woods and hid. They claimed to have seen me in an area that was literally crawling with people searching specifically for me, and where just about everyone would have an eye out. The sheriff had issued an all-points bulletin on me. And I'm supposedly standing out on a highway thumbing rides and this couple are the only ones to see me?

Town Marshal Sanford Flake, skeptical of the UFO report from the start, went over and interviewed the couple. They began arguing between themselves about whether it really had been me. Then they decided it had been me in disguise, but they still differed on major details. UFO doubter though he was, Marshal Flake had no recourse but to dismiss the matter.

Another example of human susceptibility is the "Kook Demands Airtime" story. Before my abduction, it was said, I had called a famous radio talk-show host and demanded to be put on the air to talk about UFOs. Rebuffed as a "kook," I allegedly called back after my return and said: "Now who's a kook?"

For a long time I believed that this story had been invented by the skeptical deputy, Coplan. It was he who first publicly suggested this scenario, but later denied doing so. Later, when another deputy was quoted, characterizing the story as "a bunch of bullshit, a rumor, it never happened," I figured that was the end of the matter. The Sheriff's Department must have looked into it and concluded there was nothing to it. They may have done the obvious—examined the studio tapes of the program. Supporting this impression was the fact that my foremost detractors dropped the issue like a hot rock—though their motive for keeping to themselves the reason for their retreat from the tale demonstrates the ethical shortcomings in the conduct of their entire campaign.

(However, in fairness to the deputy, I wondered if, by coincidence, before November 5 some crank did call a radio show about UFOs and get rebuffed. Then my incident hit the news, creating an opportunity for this person to call back and *impersonate* me in order to try to avenge his earlier treatment. Or perhaps the caller had only mentioned my recent incident as an example to show the ideas he'd expressed earlier weren't so far out after all. Then, like a child's game of gossip, it just grew with each person's hearing and retelling.)

I recently learned that this story originated when someone contacted the sheriff and claimed to have heard the *second* call at 2:45 A.M. on November 13. She never claimed to have heard the first call, in which the caller apparently never gave his name. So, unless there was error or deceit involved in her report itself, this fits my earlier speculation that impersonation was involved. At the precise date and time of the reported call I was sequestered at the Scottsdale Sheraton Inn, in terrible emotional condition and constantly surrounded by APRO personnel and a team of reporters. Any long-distance call from me would have had to pass through the hotel switchboard and would have appeared on the hotel bill. I certainly never made such a call, then or at any other time or place.

The Psychological Stress Evaluation (PSE) may be a dubious process, but voice-print analysis and identification is a very real and highly developed science. I later found out the sheriff *did* undertake to obtain the tapes of the show for an ID of the caller. I was unable to confirm or obtain documentation of what transpired then, but whatever it was led them to conclude it was "a rumor—it never happened."

Deputy Ken Coplan was also quoted in a variety of ways, some self-contradictory, concerning my mother's reaction when he and Mike went to give her the news. Apparently her failure to cry or lose control was not at all what Coplan expected. From the descriptions, it should be obvious that her reaction was just the sort you would expect from a strong woman independent enough to spend her summers alone in a remote mountain cabin. I'm not sure which, if any, are accurate as far as what Coplan really said, but he was quoted variously as saying my mother's first words were: "My son is with God on a UFO"; "Well, that's just the way these things happen"; "Well, I'm not the least bit surprised"; and a couple of other, equally unreal and ridiculous statements.

Since Mike had been present and knew these were *not* her words, he recently called Coplan to determine exactly what he more recently [1993] recalls about her reaction. Mike asked him if, in all his experience as an officer delivering bad news to relatives, families *always* reacted emotionally. Coplan answered that most of them did—which suggests that some didn't; but it also implies that he stands by his feeling she should have broken down and cried. However, when Mike said, ". . . I was just wondering how you felt. In my opinion she acted sort of numb, before she began to act like everything was basically—" Coplan then interjected: "Well, sure, you know she was, she was acting like a mother that was upset, you know, but that's normal." Finally! He'd acknowledged that, although she wasn't as emotional as *he* had expected, she did not appear unconcerned, and that he could see she really was upset.

Deputy Coplan was challenged by APRO (he recalls it was by the *Enquirer*) to take a polygraph test concerning this matter and a number of other assertions reported by the news media that he allegedly made about the case. He refused, however, saying he preferred to forget the whole thing.

Dr. William S. Bickel, physics professor at the University of Arizona, made some poorly informed criticisms of the state police polygraph examinations on my six coworkers, which were subsequently widely repeated. He claimed that the tests consisted of three questions: (1) Was any witness involved in foul play or angry at me? (2) Did any witness know if anyone else was involved in foul play? and (3) What did each witness see?

Bickel falsely claimed that the witnesses could pass the first two, fail the third, and still get a passing grade on the tests. *All* questions must be passed to pass: Allen Dalis earned an official "inconclusive" for walking out before his test was over. Moreover, Bickel's third question could never be on any polygraph test, since it can't be answered yes or no.

The fact is the official report listed four questions or question *areas*; three did seem to focus on the murder theory, and the fourth was worded on the report: "Did you tell the truth about actually seeing a UFO last Wednesday when Travis Walton disappeared?" So it might appear that the primary focus was on foul play. However, there were variations in the wording of the questions among the six witnesses. (There were not variations *within* the three or four runs through the charts on one individual. For purposes of comparison, wording must remain identical for each person's entire charts.)

The men later reported being asked variations of the wording in the four question areas each as asked. (I wasn't there; I'm going by what I've been told. There's a small possibility they confused test questions with pretest interview questions.) One reported variation of the UFO question was: "Do you believe that Travis Walton was actually taken aboard a UFO last Wednesday?" Also, one of the "foul play" questions—"Do you know if Travis Walton's body is buried or hidden somewhere in the Turkey Springs area?"—doubles as a question relative to the UFO hoax issue, especially in its variation; "Do you know if Travis Walton is hidden somewhere in the Turkey Springs area?"

One thing to be emphasized is that, in keeping with standard proper procedure, each man was interviewed by the examiner prior to being hooked to the machine, to make sure each man clearly understood his answers represented points drawn from what he had told the examiner and other authorities in the investigation. The examiner made sure the questions' meanings were unambiguous and in direct context to the pretest interview. Skilled examiners leave no room for mistaken interpretation or rationalization. (This in response to the uninformed speculation that the men could have

Travis: "Bathed in the yellow aura, I stared up at the unbelievably smooth, unblemished surface of the curving hull. I was filled with a tremendous sense of awe and curiosity as I pondered the incomprehensible mysteries..." The incredible object has been rendered in various progressively improved representations. Yet no art could ever do justice to the imposing grandeur of what the seven woodsmen witnessed.

Blind panic. The gut reaction to witnessing their fellow crewmen being hurled through the air by an awesome blast of unearthly energy sent six hardened woodsmen into reckless flight down that rough mountain road.

The monstrous trio of humanoids start- ed toward me . . . I sprang into a fight- ing stance with my legs spread wide to brace for the attack."

Burned into his memory, some of the most traumatic images Walton struggled to cope with were the huge dark eyes of his captors.

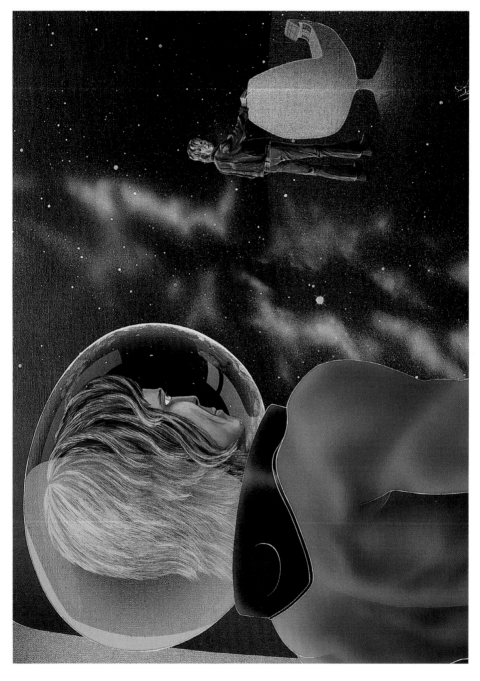

"From where I sat I could see stars all around me The effect was like sitting in a chair in the middle of space. Hearing a faint sound, I whirled around. There standing in the open doorway was what appeared to be a human being!"

Walton recalled
seeing two varieties
of disc shaped
craft inside a huge
enclosed structure
of unknown loca-
tion. A building, or
part of a larger
craft?

Before awakening on the roadway, Walton's last memory aboard the craft was of being forced down onto a table by large muscular, human-looking beings. "From out of nowhere the woman suddenly had an object in her hand that looked like one of those clear, soft-plastic ox-ygen masks.... she pressed the mask down over my mouth... then there was nothing at all but oblivious black-ness....

After being returned to the roadway outside Heber, Arizona, Travis Walton compre-hensive array of hypnotic, polygraphic, medical and psychiatric examinations to assess the validity of his extraordinary experience and to record its scientific value.

ond video is an exciting behind-the-scenes journey through the making of the movie, "Fire In The Sky" and their world promotional tour on behalf of Paramount Studios. Very colorful and entertaining.

Length of each: two hours approximate.
Specify **"A Personal Account"** or **"The Making Of Fire"**.
$29.00 per tape.

To order, send legible instructions along with the total for all items (include $4.00 Shipping & Handling per item) with check or money order to:

FIRE IN THE SKY Productions
P.O. Box 1072
Snowflake, AZ 85937

Please allow 2 to 6 weeks for delivery

seen only the planet Jupiter, then consciously tricked the examiner by think-ing of that while saying yes to having seen a UFO.)

Finally, the state police polygraph expert, Cy Gilson, obviously thought the questioning adequate in regard to the UFO, because he gave his opin-ion of its truth in his report to Sheriff Gillespie. He wrote, "These polygraph examinations prove that these five men did see some object they believe to be a UFO and that Travis Walton was not injured or murdered by any of these men on that Wednesday (5 November 1975)." He even elaborated on the UFO issue to refute law enforcement's hoax theory with the con-clusion that, "If an actual UFO did not exist and the UFO (incident) is a man-made hoax, five of these men had no prior knowledge of a hoax."

Notice Gilson mentioned the UFO before any reference to foul play. Also note the word "prove" was used, an unusually strong term for polygraph examiners. They usually use words like *indicate* or *show*, or write that the sub-ject "*believes*" such and such. He used such a definite term because consis-tent responses from such a large number of individuals on a single issue raises the statistical reliability to virtual certainty.

The test on one of the six witnesses, that of Allen Dalis, was officially ruled inconclusive. Possible explanations offered by experts included: (a) that Allen perhaps felt some guilt response to a question about hostility toward me because he may have had such feelings; (b) conceivably, at least in part, he had some guilt over recent unrelated misdeeds; or (c) that this was sim-ply because of Allen's extreme emotional volatility. The latter may have been exacerbated by his agitation after witnessing the incident. In any case, "inconclusive" means just that—no determination is possible either way.

I recently managed to get ahold of a copy of the original police report on the incident, which contained an interesting passage. On page three of Case-Number 23-75-56, Deputy Ellison wrote: "On Monday, November 10, the six men who were with Walton at the time of his disappearance, were subjected to polygraph tests at their own request, and of the six all of them passed the test with a positive reading. The fifth man was inconclusive on one phase of the test but it was stated that he 'had basically told the truth.' "

This quote also appeared in one news article back then, but wasn't given the attention it deserved.

Allen now admits to me that lingering bad feelings toward me caused him to know he was not going to come out clean on that phase of the test. He knew he was innocent of harming me, but felt his past misunderstandings with me might falsely brand him a murderer. This led to the blowup that ended with him walking out of the room before he had fully completed his test—a test on which his answer to the UFO question checked out. After the murder theory was conclusively disproved, it would have been nice if Allen's passing of the UFO question could have been made official. But polygraph procedure is strict: If he couldn't sit through all of his last run, the examiner was bound to officially rule it inconclusive. But again, "inconclusive" is a neutral verdict.

A long-standing assumption of UFO skeptics is that having prior knowledge or interest in the subject, and especially having a previous sighting, impeaches a person as a reliable witness. However, respected national polling organizations repeatedly find that over half the people in this country believe in the possibility of UFOs, and fourteen percent have seen them. Prior consideration of the question is nearly universal. Reputable people from every walk of life report distinct sightings, including astronauts and former U.S. presidents from both parties (and several of our local law officers, including the sheriff.) Yet skeptics seem to be saying that a report coming from a substantial percentage of the population should automatically be discounted!

Debunkers say the typical person who believes UFOs are real is a kook, a little old lady in tennis shoes, or some poorly educated farmer. On the contrary, the truth is that polls show that the older a person is, the less likely he is to accept the idea. Polls also show that the more educated a person is, the more likely they are to believe UFOs exist. Further, in 1979, when *Industrial Research and Development* magazine did a survey of its readership (predominantly high-tech, Ph.D. types at the very least), belief in the reality of UFOs went up to sixty one percent of respondents. Even higher percentages were obtained in a survey of the high-IQ association, Mensa, where the incidence of belief is sixty four percent—much higher than the general population. But in the archskeptics' typical reasoning pattern, this doesn't add credibility to the subject, it simply discredits the intelligentsia.

Odds are overwhelming that you have talked about UFOs at the dinner table, or commented in response to a show or news report on UFOs. How would you feel to be told that simply reading this book impeaches you, henceforth and forever, as a reliable witness if you were to sight such a craft? What the debunkers have with this criterion essentially is a "one size fits all" excuse to dismiss nearly *every* UFO case! So of course this criterion was heavily applied to mine. It was falsely claimed that the entire Walton family had been fanatical UFO buffs for years.

I do not assert that my family had never heard of the subject or spoken of it before. The mild degree of interest some family members exhibited is perfectly understandable in light of my brother's sighting twelve years prior to my incident. Duane has something in common with fourteen percent of the population. If the chances are one in seven of an individual having a sighting, it means that if an event as extraordinary as mine happened to anyone else at random, odds are overwhelming they would at least have a close associate or relative who had experienced a prior sighting. Most people have more than seven close friends or relatives. Whether considering a family of seven like mine, or our crew of seven, simple arithmetic proves that what some treated as a suspiciously unlikely coincidence was in fact a nearly inevitable likelihood!

I can see that true "repeaters," individuals who report sightings constantly or routinely, would violate statistical norms (even if constant sky-watching *could* measurably increase odds). But such frequency would be negatively significant only if it could first be established that sightings are indeed random and not concentrated in particular areas or on particular individuals due to some initiative on the part of the craft occupants. The combination of wide-open skies and seclusion of rural areas might contribute to greater frequency of sightings there, but I know of no studies demonstrating this. The more extreme of the "buff" claims asserted that not only did I come from a "UFO family," I came from a "UFO culture," an environment where almost everyone sees them all the time. In light of the community reaction to the incident, this charge is laughable. If someone had made a survey here before 1975, they would have discovered that this area was no more believing than the rest of the country, and probably considerably less so.

To illustrate that point: In late March of 1993, just after the release of the film *Fire in the Sky*, a huge glowing object passed over the Mogollon Rim area just after sunset. It was so large it was clearly visible by witnesses over eighty miles apart. It was so huge that from my perspective it subtended an angular span about a fourth that of a full moon, even though simultaneous observers eighteen miles away were telling me on the phone it was almost directly overhead. A local scanner buff told me he overheard police, some from way over in Apache County, asking each other, "Do you see what I think I see?"

Its shape was that of a sphere so flattened it appeared disclike; four thick, equally spaced, leglike appendages hung from the rim. I admit that when I first saw it I was pretty excited, perhaps even a little alarmed, and made a mad scramble for the video camera.

However, through powerful binoculars I was readily able to see detail sufficient to identify it correctly: a weather balloon. I could even make out a long cable hanging from the center with a shiny unit at its end. Apparently it was so high that it was bathed in sunlight from below the horizon, giving it an ethereal glow.

The police soon came to the same conclusion. At the local airport a report was relayed from a pilot who had just landed that he had seen a balloon he estimated (probably inaccurately) as nearly a quarter of a mile across. A second, similar balloon drifted across the sky at about the same time of evening on September 10, 1993, barely generating comment. They were spectacular sights, yet there was no rash of UFO reports in the local news. In fact, as far as I know, neither of these huge objects were even mentioned in the Arizona media. In spite of the recent release of the movie, people in the area exhibited no special predisposition to misidentify the object, but responded quite rationally.

The key problem with the "buff" question is the definition of the term. If my being a "buff" means ever having discussed the subject or seen something in the sky I couldn't identify, then the answer is yes, and I join a majority of people in the civilized world in being so labeled. However, if it means buying books and magazines on the subject, spending a lot of one's spare time thinking about it, going to UFO conferences, joining organizations, being knowledgeable about the subject, then I can say that I'm not even close to being a buff.

Before November 5, 1975, I had never seen anything I knew definitely to be a UFO. Other than my brother, no one else in the family has seen one. I have talked with him on a couple of occasions about the subject since then, but we've never had a disproportionate interest in the topic. None of us has ever subscribed to any UFO publications or joined any UFO groups. In fact, we had never heard of APRO, GSW, CUFOS, NICAP, MUFON, or any other research group (in spite of the fact that two of them were headquartered in Arizona) before all hell broke loose in November 1975.

Past activity on my part in the UFO community would have come to light when the UFO buff charge was very publicly debated. It's the sort of thing that is easily checked. "Debunkers" could have asked people who know me, checked membership files, publisher's sales records, subscription lists. I'll bet they *did* check and, when they came up empty, deliberately kept quiet about their discoveries. (More later on why I think this is true.)

I have a very wide set of interests and many are keen interests, but UFOs aren't one of the keen ones, even now! In the years since this happened I've got to know a number of individuals who would easily acknowledge fitting the second "buff" description given above. Ask any of *them* if they think it fits me, too. To this day my activity and knowledge in this area is minimal. And the skeptics know this.

If I *had* had prior UFO interest, I could have used the incident as a perfect excuse to display a newfound obsession with the subject. I (and my "avid buff" family as well) could have got out there and basked in the "UFO celebrity" limelight that the debunkers claim is a prime mover in such reports. We didn't. However, I don't believe such activity would discredit my case; I simply never had such an obsession in the first place.

The second definition of "UFO buff" given above is the one I think is reasonable, and it's the one I had in mind when I passed a polygraph answering no to the question "Were you a UFO buff?" The broad variety of my interests, my brother's sighting, and the subject's ubiquity in the media made it completely natural for the topic occasionally to come up in our many wide-ranging, on-the-job discussions—especially since current news reports were what brought it up. It would have been strange if we *hadn't* ever spoken of UFOs. Still, such talk was extremely rare overall, the tiniest fraction of our discussions.

Actually, the "buff" claim was magnified almost solely from some statements attributed to my mother and brother during a few of the most turbulent days following the incident. Remember, my family includes five other members. None of the others ever had any statements on this topic ascribed to them, except (negatively) Don, whose skepticism led him to tear into slash-piles looking for my corpse. While I was missing Duane tore the lock off the door to a room in my mother's house where I kept personal belongings, so evidently he was initially more skeptical then he had let on.

My mother's expression of belief that I was not on this earth, that I had been taken by a UFO, was not improper under those circumstances. This was *after* a thorough but unsuccessful search; *after* hearing sincere accounts from the crewmen, some of whom she knew very well. She placed great faith in Duane, and accepted his reassurances. However, beyond those factors, any concerned mother would prefer to believe her son was taken, with a chance of return, than to believe him murdered and buried somewhere. She was terribly upset and had to be sedated. With no corpse to finalize matters, it was only natural to hope against hope that I might be safe with non-hostile intelligences.

Duane's harsh criticism of one investigator for expressing doubt concerning chances of my return after so much time, his expression of confidence in my return, his saying that I was having "the experience of a lifetime," and repeating "they don't kill people" were remarks directed partially at bolstering my mother's morale. And, whether Duane wants to admit it or not, they were also aimed at convincing himself. But by no means does uttering such reassurances require any deep interest in or knowledge of the subject of UFOs.

My mother supposedly saying she had seen UFOs in the past was in contrast with her passing a polygraph test answering no to ever having seen "a flying saucer." If she did make the earlier-mentioned statements as immoderately as was claimed, she (if not the person retelling it) may have fallen prey to human susceptibility. Or perhaps both attributions are true. It's common for people to see unusual movement in distant points of light at night and think of these as UFOs, since, although potentially preternatural, they *are* unidentified. But the term "flying saucer" brings to mind a definite image of a disc-shaped spacecraft, which hardly could be considered unidentified, and implies much closer observation. My mother's polygraph test, in addition to addressing allegations of a hoax, included questions about being deeply involved with UFO phenomena. The examiner concluded that "Mrs. Mary Kellett has answered all the questions truthfully according to the best of her knowledge and beliefs."

At first I didn't believe Duane had made some of the remarks attributed to him; they didn't sound like Duane. I was surprised when I read tape transcripts of a tape made at the site during the search. When Duane volunteered these statements, the interviewer reportedly was irritated that Duane was interrupting an interview with someone else, describing Duane as "pushy," "hyped-up." You may be thinking that all this amounts to is Duane's having fallen prey to the human susceptibility discussed earlier. I can't deny this would account for some of Duane's behavior, because I don't believe anyone there was completely free from it. Frankly, there were major exaggerations in a few of his remarks. However, there was also—and more importantly—a core of truth in what he said. Duane had already grilled the crew; by then he didn't merely *believe* it had happened, he felt he *knew* it had happened. He *had* had his own sighting. But, I dimly remembered having a conversation with Duane, years before the Turkey Springs incident, about his sighting, in which I'd jokingly remarked out of bravado, "If they grab you, have 'em come back and get me, too." This offhand comment was blown completely out of proportion years later.

Like people in any area, those living out here in the Arizona mountains have their own unique characteristics. What some people viewed as Duane's lack of concern for me was something that was really jumped on. This is an example of judging by a standard of "normal reaction" that has no justification in reality. It doesn't take into account either the special circumstances or the uniqueness of the individuals involved.

And Duane Walton is an extraordinary individual. People sometimes commented on similarities between him and me, but we are very different in most respects. I've been called "wild" and "intense" in the past, but if you wanted to see "intense" in those days you would have had to meet Duane.

Duane always had a very striking effect on people. He had a strong "presence" about him. Some called him overbearing or pushy; he was the type of person who crackled with energy to the point that he seemed about to explode (not necessarily in the sense of anger). He maintained his massive body-weight on surprisingly little food. He kept up a work and training schedule that would have killed most men. In the midst of stimulating events, lack of sleep didn't slow him down a bit. Mike recalls that Duane nearly walked Mike's legs off during the search. Duane was attacked for saying he believed I was having "the adventure of a lifetime"; in a way, *he* was the one having the adventure of a lifetime, and he was irrepressible.

Investigators could have easily discovered, by asking anyone who knew him, Duane lived unswervingly by his own uncompromising code: No punches pulled. What you see is what you get. Take it or leave it. Let the chips fall where they may. He says what's on his mind, and was even more forthright back in 1975. But not everyone appreciates his bluntness as candor. I now believe some of the impetus for negative comments on Duane from Spaulding and a certain few lawmen arose from their having felt diminished by him.

Duane is an army vet, a skydiver. What attitude would you expect from a man who jumps out of airplanes, who straps himself to the back of fifteen hundred pounds of raging bull for the fun of it? Yet some thought it odd he wasn't wringing his hands and wailing about his missing brother. Duane was not one to display fear or weakness to anyone. I once saw a screaming, furious man point a loaded 44 Magnum at him and cock it. Duane didn't even flinch; he merely challenged the man to drop his gun and come get him, one on one.

I used to warn him about the risks of his lifestyle. He would say: "I'd rather live a day as a lion than a lifetime as a lamb." Duane has accumulated a few injuries now, and he's mellowed some, but he still skydives, and breaks and trains horses for a living. But he was a hell of an adventurer himself in those days; so why wouldn't he say he envied me "having the adventure of a lifetime"? How would *you* expect a man like him to react?

A number of things Duane said, which were taken as evidence of a previous preoccupation with the subject, were actually things he had only recently heard from ufologists and UFO buffs who sought him out at the site. They were quite eager to share their knowledge, giving everyone there, including Duane, a crash course in the subject. It would be only natural for him to have done *some* thinking on the subject after his sighting. But anyone who knew Duane then would vouch that he rarely, if ever, spoke on the subject prior to what happened to me.

What's really nonsensical here is that Duane's remarks were supposed to be some indication that he was party to a scheme acted out for public consumption. He's an intelligent man. If there was any truth to such suspicions, it would be hard to explain why he didn't tailor his remarks to simulate a more expected, acceptable reaction to my "disappearance."

I guess many people's concept of life is so mundane it can barely accommodate the fact that sometimes unusual things do happen. And they barely have room for the idea that the world outside their televisions might contain some extraordinary people. But when extraordinary things happen to extraordinary people, those people's minds go into overload.

The bottom line here: Duane passed two thorough series of polygraph test questions proving he had no knowledge of any hoax and had never been a UFO buff, and had not even read a book on the subject.

Later I offer additional disproof (as if it were needed) of the irrelevant "buff" innuendo, with the polygraph tests I passed. And it actually *is* irrelevant, simply because it ignores so many other forms of specific evidence which speak directly to the central issue—what we saw and what happened.

After my first meeting with Sheriff Gillespie I saw him quoted in the news media, concerning what I had told him of my experience. The report differed in a few details from what I had told Gillespie, but at the time I didn't think much of it because almost every news report concerning the episode contained errors. I figured that when subsequent accurate accounts were published, Gillespie, who was as familiar as anyone with media inaccuracy, would realize the discrepancy had been an error—either the reporter's or his own.

I found out later Gillespie takes pride in his reputation for recalling details. He chose to insist his retelling was accurate. I insist he is quite mistaken.

When Gillespie arrived at Duane's home in Phoenix, I was still in terrible shape from my ordeal, and Duane was fiercely protective. He asked Gillespie not to photograph or record his interview with me. Gillespie took no notes, although he claimed to have written it down afterward.

Gillespie heard a very condensed version of what happened to me at a time when I could barely bring myself to talk about it; with Duane standing over him, clearly displeased that the sheriff was making me relive the ordeal. Sheriff Gillespie had heard a lot of people talking about various other UFO cases for seven days—seven days during which he had been under tremendous pressure with very little sleep. Under such conditions, even persons with the best recall would naturally make more errors.

Understand that this isn't a case of me having said I saw a ten-foot jellyfish from Venus one day, then switching back to the real story the next. The problem is simply that Gillespie confused the two types of aliens and some other minor details. So in his version, among other minor discrepancies, he had me describing awakening to find tall, blue suited humanoids with helmets standing over me. It's one thing to misremember things related verbally, quite another to misremember events one personally experiences. I was in bad shape, but could *not* have confused events in that way.

However, I've been interviewed many times by reporters (another profession relying on accurate recall) who *did* take notes, and most of them made similar mistakes or worse—only I'd become wise enough to tape the interviews so I could prove *they* had erred. Duane agrees that Gillespie was mistaken. The sheriff's version was the only one that didn't agree with those heard by everyone else around me during those days and since that time he has not, to my knowledge, mentioned it again.

But Gillespie was an elected official, on the spot with that one. Gillespie's report was in the papers—what would people think if he acknowledged his error? I'm not saying he's consciously insincere, only that the embarrassment of the admission might have him prefer to stick by his account.

No one's memory is perfect. However, I do realize that the sheriff found himself in an awkward position several times throughout the whole affair. Comparing his actions to those of many other people involved, I have to say his performance was amazingly professional. I don't believe anyone else involved could have handled the situation as competently.

One development that brought a lot of negative press was my failure to appear for the polygraph test Sheriff Gillespie had set up for me. I had been returned on the morning of November 11. Gillespie saw me on the 13th and set up the test for the following morning. I had gotten almost no sleep and was still in terrible shape when Gillespie interviewed me, but, being ignorant of polygraph testing, agreed to take one as soon as possible. I subsequently learned the hard way that taking a test so soon, when I was still in such emotional upheaval, virtually guaranteed stressful tracings.

The big question in skeptical minds was, Why didn't I show? The question that didn't seem to occur to anyone was: If I had something to hide, why did *I* request the test in the first place? I was not under arrest or charged with any crime. This was all strictly voluntary. I was simply eager to prove myself.

I was in no condition to get mobbed by reporters and had requested there be no publicity about the test. Gillespie had promised that there would be none. When we were preparing to leave for the test, a reporter telephoned and wanted to know details about the upcoming "secret" test. Then, on television, we saw many reporters at the testing location. The polygraph examiner was shown next to his machine, evidently inside the testing room.

Yet Gillespie insisted he had kept our agreement. He (at the appointed time, two hundred miles away in his office in Holbrook) strenuously denied the media had been there. "There was not one TV camera, there was not one newspaper man, not one, at the place where I told you to go." He even denied that he had personally announced the upcoming test. But a November 14, 1975, Associated Press newspaper story stated: "The sheriff said

Walton will take a polygraph test today as a step toward proving or disproving his story." Hal Starr, APRO's director of public relations, spoke with one of those reporters who had been there and confirmed that many reporters had awaited my arrival. Even Cy Gilson admits knowing of cameras set up in office windows across the street. (On March 12, 1993, Phoenix local TV station KPHO Channel 5's Larry Martel spoke scathingly of that day: "You recall at several staged events at where he was to appear, he did not appear." Cohost: "That's right, one of them being the time he was supposed to take a lie detector applied by a DPS polygrapher and never showed up." Larry Martel: "And reporters swarmed around there and waited and waited and waited, but no Travis.")

Gillespie later tried to use the excuse that even if there had been media present, they would not have been allowed inside the testing building while the tests were actually being conducted, and that we could have gotten into the building through a side or rear entrance. Since Gillespie wasn't there maybe he really believed there were no media present. Maybe those news quotes of the sheriff's announcement were mis-attributions of statements by someone else in his office or at DPS. Perhaps it could be claimed his was a legitimate misunderstanding of what "no media" means. But it certainly didn't square with what I understood as our agreement. What little trust we had had was gone.

One of the long-established beliefs concerning UFOs in the minds of the American public is that the government tries to suppress public knowledge and acceptance of this phenomenon. The thought had occurred to Duane immediately after my return that if he were to put me in the hands of authorities, it could be the last he'd ever see of me alive. The previous uproar over this issue at the crew's polygraph test and APRO's comments did nothing to lessen our distrust of a government-sponsored test. In fact, as stated in APRO's November 14, 1975, press release, APRO specifically recommended against a polygraph as too soon after the trauma and because of fear of a possible government coverup. In looking back, I wonder if perhaps maintaining exclusivity of the investigation and of all test results may have also been a factor in the minds of those advising me.

Gillespie set up a second test I never even learned of until I read it reported in the newspaper. The Sheriff's Department had already issued a November 14, 1975, press release saying ". . . as of now, this office and the Department of Public Safety will not be conducting any further examinations in this matter . . . any further testing of Walton will now be up to Walton and a private examiner." I had no advance knowledge of any second test, and probably wouldn't have agreed to it anyway, because it had been publicized, and because my faith had already been breached. And I was beginning to feel more apprehensive about the government-conspiracy angle myself. Nevertheless, here again was another unfair situation I held absolutely no responsibility for, resulting in another round of negative reports.

What I was focused on at that time was the medical testing. Was I okay? Was I going to suffer horribly, perhaps die, from the effects of breathing some toxic atmosphere, or radiation sickness, or some bizarre infection unknown to medical science? Had the blue beam of energy done any permanent damage? These questions obviously have long since been resolved, but at that time I was terrified.

Even that terror was nothing compared to the shock I was desperately struggling with. I was barely coping with the psychological impact of what I had been through. I was hanging by a thread, desperately clinging to my senses, on the verge of disintegrating.

I think it's pretty unrealistic for anyone to visualize themselves in my situation, in that condition, and imagine that my number-one top priority would be a polygraph test. *I* knew what had really happened, and I was confident of proving it in good time. A test sponsored by APRO would help ensure (I naively believed) a fair outcome.

Earlier in this story I described the day of the sighting as a typical workday; which it was, except for my being asleep when the truck got to the job site. Most of the guys had done this at least once. Allen had had a sick hangover three or four days before and had stayed in the truck all morning.

At that time I was not about to tell Mike I'd been out late with his sister the night before, not after taking a day of sick leave. In *The Walton Experience* I was trying to show readers what a typical workday was like; being tired in the morning wasn't typical. I omitted that embarrassing detail, not thinking it had any significance to the sighting and subsequent events; but, since a question has been raised, here's the straight of it.

An attempt was made to buy Steve Pierce's testimony to deny the reality of the sighting, which never came about, as he had nothing to sell (and the suborner probably had no intention of actually paying). However, he did claim in his conversations with the person relaying the offer that I had not worked at all that day, was gone most of the day, and that Mike Rogers had disappeared for hours that morning.

I don't know if Steve sticks by this claim since I haven't spoken to or seen him in years. None of the other six of us supports Steve's claim. You might be thinking that I shouldn't bother to go into this since Steve said it only after an attempt at *paid* testimony, but I've set out to cover them all.

When we do fuel break, as opposed to when we do regular thinning, we have to stay in a tight group because the pilers have to stack the slash. If the sawyers don't complete the cutting in any given spot before moving on, our pile spacing would be off; the trees cut later would knock piles over and there would inevitably be material overlooked that needed to be cut. As is usual, the road paralleled the piling strip. Since I'm too tall to lie in the truck seat comfortably with the door shut, the door was open, facing the guys who were always making trips back to the truck for water, gas, saw tools, or parts.

I spent less than two hours resting. Otherwise I put in as long and hard a day as the others. Mike retorted: "I was not gone from the job that day, or any other day, not for two hours or any other amount of time. Travis had been sick the day before, and he spent some time that morning lying in the truck. But he spent the rest of the day working with the crew."

Here's what John Goulette had to say about it:

"The truck is never very far away, usually not even out of sight. They move it up, keep it close to the crew. We keep all our lunches and stuff in it. That day I think we took two breaks—one halfway through the morning, and one halfway through the afternoon.

"Nobody left the work site. We were cutting pretty well all along the line. The pilers come up right behind us. They pile right behind us. You know, if you're out working, working pretty hard, and you see somebody else goofing off, you kind of notice if they're not there. You think they're out messing around. Nobody's going to put up with that, if you're sweating away and somebody else is goofing off.

"Nobody was gone that day. It's not true that Travis and Mike took off, or something, and then came back a couple of hours later together."

More later about the attempt to pay Steve for false testimony.

All a publicity stunt, a way to get attention? Nonsense. Had I been seeking publicity, I would have jumped in, center stage, when all the reporters were clamoring for an interview, and grabbed every inch of print and minute of airtime possible. I would not have remained sequestered in the face of such active interest expressed by the media. My silence shifted more attention to my detractors and generated much negative reporting. (Another bit of media wisdom: Refusal to comment nearly always brings about a negative slant.)

My cooperation with APRO's *Enquirer*-financed testing has been denounced as a contradiction to my other efforts to avoid the media. But a single interview, monitored by APRO officials in a subdued and controlled setting, was completely in keeping with my stated objective to avoid being mobbed and forced to field a barrage of insensitive questions. I never received the money offered by the *Enquirer* for my exclusive story. We were taken completely by surprise when the publication's annual prize for the best UFO story of the year was awarded to us.

I turned down many offers from writers and movie producers. I avoided more interviews than I gave, and in every case it was *they* who sought me out. I never even reported the incident in the first place. That was out of my hands. To this day, I have never sought an interview. Media presence kept me from that polygraph-test appointment. No, if I were a headline grabber I certainly would not have remained silent so long. All I wanted after my return was to be left alone to think things over and adjust. I maintained that stance for years.

I found myself in a "damned if I do, damned if I don't" dilemma. If I gave interviews, it proved me a publicity seeker. If I rejected a public forum, I was unwilling to face my detractors. One so-called debunker even excused his actions in publishing a false charge he was later forced to retract by saying that he had published it long ago and I hadn't immediately rebutted it. In other words, if I ignore my critics, they interpret it as conceding the truth of their charges. They're going to wish I had remained retired.

My attackers dug up a number of "witnesses" to attempt to discredit me. Here are a couple more classic examples of the human susceptibility problem. These "charges" easily could have been exposed with the simplest attempt to check them out, but those doing the reporting were not so disposed.

A man who owns one of the local motels was quoted at the time of the incident as saying: "Bullshit! Long before this happened I thought he and Duane were big bullshitters. They exaggerated everything. I don't trust them as far as I can throw them. . . . Bullshit! I don't believe it."

This guy has never spoken with Duane Walton in his life. I'll bet he never knew I had a third brother before November 1975; I wouldn't be surprised to learn he never knew I existed before then. Duane did not live in Snowflake, and when he came up to visit on rare occasions he always stayed at Mom's. I hadn't seen Duane in weeks when the UFO incident happened. I did not know who this guy was at that time, and although I know who he is now—I see him downtown occasionally—I have never confronted him. He and I both already know the truth concerning his remarks. But how in the world could I have ever "bullshitted" or "exaggerated" *anything* to this guy when to this day I have never spoken with him? Unless the guilty party is whoever first quoted—or misquoted—him, I say *he* is the big bullshitter. Over the years countless investigators, journalists, and film crews have come to see me in Snowflake, and I've always known where *not* to send them for accommodations.

Another man heard William Spaulding attacking me on the radio and came forward to tell Spaulding's field man he had known me since 1969 (human susceptibility again), and that Allen Dalis and I had always been together, heavily into drugs, burglary, car theft, and other unsavory activities. I supposedly lived in west Phoenix, attended—with Allen *and* the "witness"—Carl Hayden High School there, earned below-average grades, etc. Spaulding's field man told this man he'd sure appreciate him calling with more of "whatever we can find in addition to this, to rate it kind of down, why this we're very much interested in." This from Spaulding's same field man who later in the same conversation said: "It's amazing how gullible John Q. Public really is."

Who's being gullible here? They took this guy at his word, when he volunteered from out of nowhere, failed to ask even a single skeptical question, and did no later checking of his tale. A perfect example of selective suspicion—question everything against your position, blindly accept all that supports it.

I never even knew Allen Dalis until he came to Snowflake to work for Mike. I had exceptionally high grades. I went to high school at Payson and Snowflake only. I have never met the "witness" Spaulding's field man interviewed. I hadn't attended a Phoenix school or lived there since right after I finished the fifth grade at age eleven. What could be easier to verify than residence and school attendance? Spaulding could have made simple checks and found out it was slanderous garbage, but instead he circulated it widely. We finally found out about it when we were sent a copy from Texas. We then sent a certified letter of rebuttal, but never heard whether they dropped that one, or if retractions followed.

Spaulding invested over a year trying to discredit me. He published reprints of the writings of anti-UFO debunkers who attacked me. He gathered irrelevant letters and tapes he hoped would incite legal prosecution, sending them to Sheriff Gillespie with a letter urging charges be filed against me, absurdly attempting to point to a legal precedent by comparing my case to one in which the lone female survivor of a plane crash in the forest was prosecuted for setting a signal fire that got out of control.

Even though I've mentioned William Spaulding and Ground Saucer Watch (GSW) before this, I've delayed making a complete rebuttal of Spaulding's attacks. I place this rebuttal right before my final topic, "debunkers," because Spaulding had joined forces with a so-called debunker in his efforts, and several debunker claims relied on Spaulding's inconsistent reports. I may repeat a few things said earlier, but if I can show that debunkers rely on statements and expertise from people who can be shown to be without credibility, so goes their case, too. (In making my case, I make no personal attack on anyone. I here address only statements and credentials directly related to the issue.)

Sheriff Gillespie states unequivocally that GSW and William Spaulding were *not* called in to the investigation by law enforcement agencies, as GSW claimed in the February 1976 issue of *Flying Saucer Review*. On the contrary, on November 10, 1975, Spaulding sent a letter to Gillespie: "GSW offers its complete investigation staff at your disposal, [*sic*] if you feel we can assist you." Spaulding was asked by Dr. J. Allen Hynek to relay information to him. Hynek later told me: "I guess I sent the wrong man in on this one." Hynek also later wrote to Spaulding, chastising him for his character-assassination tactics against me. Two other GSW people from New Mexico preceded him to the site; Spaulding did not arrive on the site until November 9, the fourth and last day of the search (the day *before* he offered his services; it's obvious he wasn't "called in" by the sherriff.).

Spaulding made a detailed grid map of the site on which he plotted out some extraordinary readings of residual magnetism, which according to theory is consistent with the recent presence of extraterrestrial vehicles powered by antigravity engines. His charts, which he sent to APRO, showed +8 Gauss at the slash-pile near where the craft hovered, and +10 to +12 Gauss in the area directly behind that (opposite the direction of its departure). Normal readings of the surrounding ground and trees ranged from +1 to −2. But on the side of the clearing across from where the craft hovered (in the direction it departed), Spaulding reported recording a whopping −15 Gauss. ANIS TM Gaussmeters, model numbers 25 and 20B were used, but it's not certain whether Spaulding or his two field people made the measurements and follow-ups a week later, which showed the anomalous readings had dissipated to normal. I do not know what equipment was used to take the ozone readings.

Spaulding never spoke to any of the six crewmen, yet claimed in the press, "We have uncovered some more data in the form of the medical condition of the six witnesses. There was nausea, loss of acuteness, which is temporary blindness, and a body rash." None of the men reported these symptoms directly to Spaulding. To my knowledge none ever met Spaulding. Nevertheless, he made many positive statements ("We found some interesting things up there. If this is a hoax, it's one of the best I've ever seen.") to the press concerning the case, right up until the moment he realized he had lost my cooperation in investigating the case.

He abruptly switched to attacking the case with vague references to "some holes in the story" and "some questions" and other "factors" that caused him to have "doubts." From the *Tucson Daily Citizen*: "William Spaulding, head of Ground Saucer Watch, a Phoenix-based UFO investigation group, said he had information leading him to disbelieve Walton's story. Spaulding did not reveal the information, but said a statement from his group was forthcoming."

I believe he didn't "reveal the information" because he didn't *have* any new information. But the media were pressing him for something specific to explain his switch. At first all he and Steward could come up with was accusations of "noncooperation" and "refusal to undergo scientific testing." But of course I *was* undergoing examination—but with their rival, APRO. They needed some better argument.

Spaulding made one last-ditch attempt to reacquire the investigation, coming to Duane's house with more substantial corroboration for the case— a small, clear plastic pill bottle containing some unusual-looking fragments. Spaulding claimed he had picked them up at the site, from the ground over which the UFO had hovered.

Duane was suspicious. The sheriff's men had made a careful forensic search of the area without finding any similar fragments in the four days before Spaulding arrived. No one had seen Spaulding pick them up. And he hadn't said a word about them to anyone before this, even though he had reported other evidence of the UFO. Although it was possible the fragments were genuine, Duane was not persuaded; he made it clear that APRO was in and GSW out. Duane kept the mystery sample, probably much to Spaulding's dismay. His apologies about "misquotes in the press" fell on deaf ears. He left angry.

Spaulding offered another batch of vague charges to the media, adding the angry threat: "We're going to blow this story out today!" But he needed a charge against us. Even though GSW's initial attack hadn't mentioned "drug hallucination," all of a sudden "Dr." Steward "remembered" details of our visit. (Since Steward claimed to "teach drug abuse [*sic*] at Maricopa Tech," this was the logical charge.) He told the news media: "The story is an absolute hoax; [Walton's] been out hallucinating on some drug, probably LSD." What garbage.

For all Spaulding's failings, he had seemed almost clairvoyant in giving Duane advice concerning what to do in the event of my return (an event not in any way certain at that point): save the first voided urine specimen, and bag my clothing for forensic analysis. The urine sample, Spaulding had said, would be needed to counter what he anticipated would be accusations of a drug hallucination. Why would he think this likely? Perhaps because people were still recovering from the late sixties and early seventies when every time something really bizarre hit the news it was explained away by "drugs." But it was from Spaulding's organization that this accusation soon came. Coincidence?

Later, after hearing about the mark on my arm, Steward claimed to have seen it during our visit. Then when it was proved I had worn long sleeves to his office, he falsely claimed that due to the heat I had them rolled all the way up above the elbow. He claimed to recognize the mark as an injection, yet a genuine physician had noted that it was not over any major blood vessel. Steward claimed to be able to tell I was still heavily under the influence from a five-day binge of hallucinogens while in his office, yet blood and urine samples tested a few hours later by the Maricopa County Medical Examiner's drug screen showed no trace of any drug. Steward then claimed all traces could vanish from the body that quickly. It's now common knowledge, because of widespread workplace testing, that evidence of drug use can be detected weeks or months later. Drug expert indeed.

Readers may wish to refer to the descriptions of these events in chapter 7 in evaluating this part. Recall that when Duane renewed contact with Mr. Spaulding, who directed us to GSW consultant, "Dr." Lester Steward, it was for *medical help.*

Spaulding and Steward went on to claim variously that we "hurriedly" left Steward's office in alarm at hearing that Steward was a drug expert, or, in another version, because we were afraid of hypnosis: "They can't lie through hypnosis." Then, apparently to counter the medical credentials issue, they claimed the whole reason we had come to Steward's office in the first place was for "hypnosis experiments."

How could we be going there *for* hypnosis while being scared off *by* hypnosis? If I was so scared of hypnosis, why did I undergo hypnosis with APRO only hours later? Spaulding claimed I had been "interrogated" at GSW "headquarters" for hours. Totally untrue; the timetable is documented with a call to the sheriff before we left and one from Coral Lorenzen after our return. I said almost nothing in the brief time I was in Steward's office. Spaulding's stationery gives his *home* address as GSW Headquarters', where I have never been in my life. (He really could get pretentious, putting on airs with important-sounding language. He told the press that "GSW headquarters had ordered him to drop the case." Spaulding *was* GSW headquarters!)

Why didn't the press ask the obvious questions? "How can it be a hoax and a hallucination at the same time?" "How can six other men have identical hallucinations, down to the last detail?" "How can a hoax, which would have to be planned, be part of a drug hallucination, which no one can control?"

Pressed about his claim to medical and doctoral degrees, Steward eventually had to back off "doctor" and "psychologist," but continued to boast no less than three Ph.D.s, in "health science, psychology, and physiology," from California Western University of Santa Ana, California.

APRO checked it out. No California academics in the APRO membership had ever heard of the school. When it was located by telephone, APRO's caller got an answering service. APRO sent someone down there. No campus, no catalog, no accreditation, a claimed faculty of twelve, and a very evasive spokesman. This "university" was only two years old in 1975. How did Steward get three Ph.D.s from a school only two years old? All three "degrees" were based on a single research paper that was called "freshman level" by individuals described by APRO as qualified academics who read it. Some expert.

Bill Spaulding had been billed as an "aerospace engineer." Everyone accepted it because he worked for AIResearch, a high-tech aerospace company. But by now he had really overhyped himself, as this letter from ufologist and nuclear physicist Stanton T. Friedman makes damningly clear.

Mr. William Spaulding
(address)
Phoenix, AZ   September 10, 1979

Dear Bill:

This is one of the more difficult letters I have ever written, but please bear with me.

1. As you know, I have admired your dynamic approach to ufology, your willingness to speak out and to *not* be a closet ufologist or an apologist ufologist. I am also all for a scientific approach to evaluation of UFO photographs.

2. I have had several concerns, however, about your activities that led me to question whether or not you do indeed have a scientific background:

    A. Your reasoning and activities in the Haflin picture evaluation and the Walton case struck me as not being like those of any of the many engineers with whom I have worked over the years.
    B. There seems to be frequent exaggeration in your public commentary. I don't believe that there are five hundred professional people associated with your group, for example.
    C. I can't understand how no college was associated with you in the background in the 1977 MUFON Symposium volume but Bowling Green is mentioned in 1979 and then you told me and others that you have a B.S. from BG. Why wasn't it mentioned before? How come when I asked for the year, you said 1961–62? When I asked for the major you mentioned a list of subjects. It has been my experience that everybody remembers the year of their first college degree and that nobody who has one gives a course list as a major.

3. For the above reasons and others—such as your not giving adequate credit to others for the CAUS suit and apparently taking credit for the release of documents not part of that suit, I decided to do some checking to evaluate my suspicion.

4. Here are my findings:

    A. According to your employer your job title is that of a high-level technician and in no way implies an engineering degree or background.
    B. According to your employer the only post high school education

you have is a one-year certificate in electronics from Griswold Technical Institute in Cleveland.

C. According to Griswold you attended a twelve-hour-per-week electronics course from March to May 1961, for seven weeks, but did not complete the course and did not receive a grade or certificate.

D. According to Bowling Green University you have not received any degrees from them and have not completed any courses at any of their campuses.

5. Please correct any of the above findings if they are in error. Please also understand that I do not believe it is necessary to have a college degree to be a competent UFO researcher. One of the best bosses of research I have ever had had only a high-school diploma and yet directed many people with Ph.D.s. The point is that apparently you have seriously misrepresented your background. I don't believe that fraud should have any place in dealings with the public, the media, or colleagues. I think you should seriously consider setting the record straight and should henceforth cease and desist from making any claims that are not totally accurate. I have no present plans to make my findings public but will consider doing so should you continue the misrepresentation.

Anticipating your response and writing in sorrow,

Stan Friedman

CC: Walt Andrus, Dr. Bruce Maccabee, Brad Sparks, Dr. J. Allen Hynek, Travis Walton, Jim Lorenzen, Idabel Epperson, Robert Pratt

Spaulding never responded. Ultimately, even the photo analysis Friedman complimented Spaulding on was discredited. A devastating critique of Spaulding's work written by Jan Herr was published in the June 1977 *APRO Bulletin*.

The "mystery metal" fragments Spaulding supposedly recovered from the site of the incident looked like small chips of shiny, silvery, grayish black obsidian, and would have noticeably contrasted with the drab tan earth at the site. They supposedly turned out, upon analysis, to be some kind of high-temperature silicone—such as one might find at a place like AIResearch.

Spaulding then reportedly suggested that "someone" might have dropped them at the site (again, with no one else finding them in four days of forensic examination before Spaulding had even arrived). Yeah, and they might never have been at the site. Who knows? It's surprising how little interest this "physical evidence" stimulated in either UFO proponents or debunkers.

Speaking of debunkers, although one debunker with whom Spaulding had joined forces was hands-off regarding dubious credentials and assertions concerning Spaulding or Steward, it was not out of gratitude for the help. It was only to avoid undercutting his own stacked deck against the case. In fact, this debunker was undeterred in publishing a September 1978 "white paper" claiming to expose the claimed credentials of Spaulding's right-hand man, Todd Zechel, GSW Director of Research. Supposedly Zechel claimed to have worked for the CIA and NSA for ten years, but the debunker claimed he had discovered that Zechel had instead spent three years in ordinary army service; six years at a small factory in Baraboo, Wisconsin, as a carpenter and fireman; then worked in a "sex shop" and pornographic bookstore.

Not long after these revelations GSW, William Spaulding, his director Zechel, and "Dr." Steward virtually disappeared from the UFO scene. Both they and their vicious attacks had been thoroughly discredited. But the damage they did to me remained. Why? Partly because the media rarely backtracks, and partly because the debunkers worked hard at keeping those false claims alive.

Which brings us to the debunker's obsession; the last of the six factors in my analysis of why what ufologists came to regard as the best case on record also became the most attacked.

For many years a number of individuals have been yapping and biting around the edges of ufology. Their position: Without any doubt there has never been a genuine UFO sighting by anyone anywhere on Planet Earth in all of human history, and there never will be, and anyone who says otherwise is either mentally aberrant, foolishly deluded, or deliberately deceptive—maybe all three. These people presume to title themselves "debunkers" or skeptics. I will show that their actions fail to justify either term. Readers will notice that I put "debunker" in quotation marks. That is because the people I refer to don't so much remove bunk as create it.

Media people are fond of trotting these people out in the name of "balance." Often, when a UFO researcher appears, journalists feel obligated to "counterbalance" particulars *within* an issue by giving a forum to people who dismiss the *entire* issue. Some are of the grudging opinion that debunkers are a necessary evil, like hyenas trailing a herd to weed out the inferior animals.

In this model the ufologist and debunker are viewed as opposites, with the journalist in the middle. Actually, the better ufologists are in the *middle*, with the debunker on one side, scoffing a priori at *every* case, and the UFO cultist on the other side, blindly accepting every UFO claim he hears. Blind disbelief isn't a whit better than blind belief. Top ufologists do their own quality control, with their competitive peers providing a further check. For example, the late, great Dr. J. Allen Hynek at times resolved upward of 90 percent of received UFO reports his organization investigated, reclassifying them as IFOs—identified flying objects (the sightings having been explained in prosaic terms).

Debunkers promote a myth of ufologist gullibility so extreme that those listening only to their claims would be amazed to learn ufologists discover prosaic explanations for any of the cases they investigate, let alone *most* of them.

The journalist's stated aim would be better served by including ufologist peers of opposing opinion in a given case or issue. Even so, debunkers or so-called skeptics would have a legitimate place in the discussion if they would adhere to the principles to which they give lip service. They don't, as I shall illustrate.

One debunker is our chief detractor and author of the worst charges leveled against us. I embark here on the most thorough analysis ever put forth in rebuttal of his allegations. I will name this self-proclaimed debunker and take each of his charges head-on: his shameless character attacks, his concocted Forest Service Contract Theory attacks, and the entire gamut of his distortions of our polygraph evidence. Documented facts (most never before made public) will undo his case. Nothing will be left standing.

Although he is promoted as a most objective and scientific investigator, I will fully unmask his motivation and methods for the biased and unscientific sham they are. I make some startling revelations concerning him and those in league with him. I will document his misrepresentations and concealment of positive evidence. Moreover, I will provide *proof* of his outright falsehoods and his scandalous misuse of documents and tape transcripts presented as evidence.

This is far more than a routine refutation of a passing article by some misguided reporter. It is a detailed exposé of a massive, multifronted campaign of calculated disinformation perpetrated by a dedicated specialist over a span of decades. Dealing with his endless convolutions and devious tricks has been like wrestling with a stringy mass of tar. In a war of words there is an intrinsic unfairness and inequality between the positions of attack and defense. It's the principle I express as follows: "It takes thirty seconds to falsely claim that which requires thirty minutes to completely refute." A vast understatement in the case of this particular person. To untangle all his insidious minutia comprehensively would have made it necessary to expend exponentially more ink than the flood he unleashed against us. But even this measured counterwork has become truly prodigious.

Which presents a dilemma. Such a thorough accounting requires space greatly disproportionate to the rest of this book. Yet I didn't undertake this work merely to tell my story yet another time. I was motivated to the task by several factors, one of which was to have nothing less than opportunity to answer every major charge against us.

Therefore the remainder of the material on this topic begins on page 283 in what has become an extraordinarily lengthy appendix. Make no mistake, this analysis is not presented for entertainment purposes. It is a mountain of detailed evidence. Faced with a passage of such depth, the casual reader could be forgiven for skimming through it. But in order fully to comprehend my experience it is essential to stay with me through the entire odyssey.

I highly recommend reading the appendix before continuing with the remaining six chapters. Full appreciation of those chapters (especially chapters 13 and 16) is made possible by important information contained in the appendix. Some surprising rewards await the reader there.

CHAPTER 11

The Final "Questions of Belief"—and Conclusive Answers

Veritatem dies aperit.
("Time discovers truth.")

—Seneca

After shooting began on *Fire in the Sky*, I received a call from Tracy Torme, asking me if I had heard of a UFO investigator named Jerry Black. I told him no, but that, since I don't keep up with the field, he might or might not be prominent.

Tracy told me he'd been receiving a series of phone calls from Black. Tracy described Black's approach as initially courteous, explaining that he was calling to provide Mr. Torme with certain facts of which Mr. Torme evidently must not be aware, but his tone gradually grew more strident. After he'd read that *Fire in the Sky* was in production, Black had hastened to advise Tracy of his folly.

Why in the world, Black wanted to know, would Torme want to make a feature film about the Turkey Springs incident, when that case had long ago been proven a hoax?

Tracy wanted to know what made him believe that was the case. Black responded with great vehemence and certainty, proffering as evidence some of the misinformation clarified in the appendix of this book.

Tracy had researched the whole case, including all the old allegations, and was therefore well aware of the truth of the matter. I can almost hear his exasperated sigh as he refuted Black's charges point by point. Although

Black remained staunchly unconvinced of the veracity of my experience, he gradually began to realize that it was *he* who was proceeding on incorrect or incomplete data.

I told Tracy that Black's skeptical litany sounded a whole lot like Spaulding's and PJK's line of nonsense. It turned out that, indeed, Black had been a past associate of Bill Spaulding and GSW. Apparently PJK had been a major source of misinformation—Mr. Black had even cooperated with him on another recent case that together they had branded a hoax.

Although at first Black's basic conviction concerning our incident remained unchanged, this initial contact led to a series of long and sometimes heated phone conversations between himself and Tracy. However, unlike other so-called investigators, Jerry Black did something comparatively radical—he checked the facts for himself. After all these years, a *qualified* investigator had reopened the case.

Mr. Black went back to the key sources of information. He spoke with former sheriff Gillespie, Cy Gilson, McCarthy, Ezell, Mike Rogers, and the Forest Service. He discovered for himself that the Contract Theory (See appendix) was so full of holes it wouldn't hold a drop of water. Other "theories" crumbled as well. Valiantly defending his skepticism, he even temporarily considered of all things, Spaulding's half real/half hoax scenario. But he kept pushing and looking, and what he was gradually discovering all on his own was just how much the "true facts" had been obscured. His doubts began to waiver.

Still, Black returned to harp on certain points, emphasizing the oft-repeated distortions of the polygraph evidence. Tracy's exasperation eventually turned to real annoyance. He told Jerry that if he couldn't come up with a plausible alternative scenario, a series of hypothetical events that would fully account for everything they both knew to be fact, there wasn't any point in continuing their discussions. Mr. Black said, "Sure, that's easy." He tried a couple of scenarios that Tracy immediately was able to demonstrate were ridiculously out of sync with the indisputable facts of the case.

Not long after first phoning me about this new investigator, Tracy asked me to participate in a three-way conference call with him and Jerry Black. During the conversation Black took issue with some errors in my first book. One was the "typical day" I'd written of to help illustrate the nature of our work. Another was my error in reporting that Cy Gilson rather than another polygraph expert (see appendix) had perused Pfiefer's charts, unofficially concurring with his conclusion.

Black also took issue with my assertion that the six witnesses had been given UFO questions of varied wording rather than all being asked identically worded questions. I emphasized that, whatever Gilson remembered, all I could do was accurately report what I had been told by the six crewmen, since I had not been present. We went through some points about the McCarthy test invalidity. Black basically agreed the test was not credible; but he felt strongly, as a former APRO affiliate, that keeping it confidential had been a major misstep of the investigation. He then proceeded to the old "dictated questions" nonsense. I countered that this objection had been unequivocally discounted by Pfiefer himself. Black came back with Ezell's "unofficial disavowal" of the Pfiefer test. I told him I believed Ezell's real motive was to defend against a public perception which he believed would harm his business reputation. I predicted that Ezell would decline to test anyone concerning UFOs, on the basis of the subject alone, and challenged Black to test my prediction. (My assessment was subsequently borne out.)

Jerry Black places much stock in the polygraph aspect of any case he investigates. His remaining suspicion of my case came down to the tests involved. His gentlemanly attack culminated, during that telephone conference call, when Black asked me if I would be willing to take an all-new polygraph test.

I asked him why I should take another test when I'd already passed one. He criticized the validity of the Pfiefer test; I defended it. I acknowledged that misinformation might interfere with an investigator's *perception* of the test, but that if he would check, he'd find out I was right about the disputed points.

Black persisted. What would be the harm in a new test? All it could do was strengthen my position. I retorted that if I agreed to new testing, archskeptics would attack anew; then another test would be deemed "necessary" to defend the previous one, and so on. Why open the door to that? Besides, a new test would amount to an implicit admission that the test I had already passed had been somehow insufficient. Why should I make such a concession to my critics, when nothing would ever satisfy them anyway?

I had nothing to gain. I would pass, but if the smallest thing went wrong with the way the test was conducted, it would be jumped on and magnified by my critics. Even if the test was flawless, it really would add nothing to my credibility in their minds.

Jerry Black remained insistent. He said he didn't like it at all when the subjects of his investigation are unwilling to take a polygraph. Their mere willingness or unwillingness is a big factor in his judgment of a case. I told him I did not wish my life to become one long cross-examination. A point is reached where one says: There it is, take it or leave it. I felt I had reached that point.

My answers didn't seem to satisfy Jerry Black, but I ended the call with a repeat of my challenge for him to verify what I was saying about the Pfiefer test. He didn't take me up on the part of my challenge that Ezell's problem was with the UFO subject, not the test results themselves, and that asking Ezell to administer a new test would prove that. Black said that, judging from his talks with Ezell, that wasn't really all that implausible anyway. But he did take me up on verifying my explanations about the Pfiefer test with Pfiefer himself. After our call he did some sleuthing around and was finally able to locate George Pfiefer, who did indeed, Jerry told Tracy, personally verify what I had said about how his tests were conducted.

Even so, Jerry Black pursued further polygraph testing, switching his efforts to Mike Rogers. Mike at first resisted on grounds similar to mine. Wouldn't a new test imply that the original tests of the six crewmen somehow had been faulty? Such a doubt would open the door to retesting all six. What if someone couldn't be found, or didn't want to bother? I too was initially against new testing for anyone.

But Jerry persuaded Mike that at the very least, retesting Allen Dalis would do the old tests no damage. The only one among the nine people previously tested who had not officially passed, his test would serve as a benchmark to confirm the adequacy of the UFO question in the earlier testing.

Jerry Black selected Cy Gilson as the examiner. I agreed that he was the best logical choice to test Allen. Allen's passing a test with the same examiner would resolve his original inconclusive test and complete the series—all six witnesses would have passed with the same examiner.

Cy Gilson was now one of the top examiners in the nation—*the* top examiner in Arizona, by virtue of his twenty-two continuous years of experience, sixteen of those years spent on criminal testing for the Department of Public Safety (the state police). Even after he entered private practice, most of his work was in the area of criminal examinations; because of his reputation and experience, prosecutors, lawyers, and police throughout the state still came to him for important work. Criminal polygraph work entails one's recognition in court as an expert witness and is considered the high-status end of the field, as opposed to self-employed storefront operators performing mostly routine preemployment and marital fidelity tests. In addition, *all* of Cy Gilson's experience was with modern Control Question Tests (CQT), state-of-the-art methodology.

When I told Tracy we were considering retesting Allen Dalis, his response was less than enthusiastic. "Like you told Jerry Black, what if it turns out to be one of those few percent of tests that falsely accuse? What if Allen got nervous? You know how emotionally hyper he gets." Tracy recommended against testing for anyone involved. The movie was to be released soon. He believed, at this point, there was little to gain, much to lose.

His point was valid, as far as it went; but Gilson's credentials were impeccable. If anyone could properly test Allen, he could. So I didn't raise the subject again with Tracy, and never said anything to Paramount. Plans went ahead, with great caution exercised in every aspect of the arrangements. The only point in doing this was if absolutely everything was beyond reproach.

Self-sponsored tests are not as highly regarded as independently sponsored tests. Those sponsored by skeptical third parties rate highest of all. In exercising his right as sponsor of the test, Jerry Black formulated a series of airtight question areas for Allen's test, with specific wording to be worked out by Cy Gilson—open, of course, to possible refinement with Allen, but nonetheless subject to Gilson's final approval.

It was left to Mike Rogers to persuade Allen Dalis to submit to retesting. After considerable trouble I had located Allen some months earlier for Paramount; but other than that brief phone call, Mike's call was the first contact we'd had with him in many years. But Allen didn't need much coaxing. He knew what he'd seen, and felt he'd been unfairly judged as the only "inconclusive." He welcomed the chance to vindicate himself.

Throughout the arrangements, Jerry Black was pushing to include others in a retest. Mike had been considering this for himself. Mike was gradually persuaded in principle, but still resisted, wary of appearing to devalue the original tests on the crew. He eventually offered to undergo retesting if Gilson would agree to comment in his report that the test was *supplemental* to the earlier testing. Gilson flatly refused, saying nobody tells him how to conduct his tests, and nobody tells him what to write in his report. Mike finally settled for a letter, under separate cover, reaffirming Gilson's final opinion of his earlier testing of the six:

30 January 1993

Mr. Michael H. Rogers
(Address)
Show Low, Arizona

Dear Mr. Rogers,

This letter is in regard to the polygraph examinations I administered to you and five other men in November of 1975, about the disappearance of Travis Walton and the UFO incident.
The results of the examinations I administered in 1975 determined you and four of the other men were being truthful to the four relevant questions asked during that examination. The sixth man's examination was

inconclusive, in that his chart tracings were such that no determination of truth or deception could be made.

Today, in 1993, I am still of the same opinion that they were valid examinations and the results were conclusive on the five. Even though there was only one question asked that related to the UFO sighting, it was a valid question and the results proved none of you were lying when stating you saw an object that you believe was a UFO.

The other three relevant questions asked during that examination were to determine if any of you had caused the death of Travis Walton. Again the results of the five examinations were conclusive and that none of you did anything nor saw anyone do anything to injure or kill Travis Walton. The results of these three relevant questions were positively verified when Mr. Walton reappeared about a week after these polygraph examinations were administered.

I hope this letter will satisfy you, and anyone else, that my beliefs in the results of those examinations, are the same today as they were in 1975.

Sincerely,

Cy Gilson

At Jerry Black's urging, Mike tried to talk me into joining him and Allen in being retested. I held firm, repeating my reasoning. But once Mike had been persuaded to commit himself to being retested, he became an avid proponent of broadening participation. He wouldn't let up on me. He enthusiastically ticked off Cy Gilson's credentials and the improvements in sensitivity and reliability of modern equipment. I agreed that Cy Gilson was the top examiner; it was virtually certain we'd get an accurate test. My concerns were with getting dragged into defending against a new round of unfair attacks. I still felt I had nothing to gain. I reasoned that if only one test in three hundred gave inaccurate results, that it would be the equivalent of playing Russian roulette. If there was *any* possibility of destroying yourself, with nothing to gain, why would any sane person play? Even if there were two hundred ninety-nine empty cylinders instead of five, there was still that one live round.

Mike and Jerry would confer, then Mike would come back at me. His reasoning had a gradual effect on me. But what really clinched it for me, at the last moment, was when Mike told me that Cy Gilson had expressed his opinion that both the McCarthy test *and* the Pfiefer test were inconclusive, for the same reason—their same, obsolete methodology. I'd never before realized that Pfiefer had been using the same method for which McCarthy's test had been invalidated. Pfiefer had used a few newer refinements, making his test seem different from McCarthy's. All I'd known was that McCarthy's had been called "an old military method."

I now know that the validity of Pfiefer's test can still be justifiably defended, because the methodology's inaccuracy in virtually all cases leans in
the direction of false positives. But at the time the thought that I hadn't yet
taken an unassailable test gave me pause.

I finally agreed to undergo reexamination by polygraph. I had other business in Phoenix anyway. Before arriving at his office complex that day, I'd
never seen or spoken to Cy Gilson. I pulled up a chair and we got down to
business.

We resolved a few minor issues, then I told him I wanted to take a drug
test both before and after my test. Gilson said that wasn't necessary. I insisted, saying that I would pay the additional cost myself. Gilson said that
since it wasn't ever needed he didn't know how to go about having such
tests done. (Years before, PJK had made drug tests a part of our polygraph
retest challenge, so I'd thought they were necessary for an airtight test.)
Gilson explained that the belief that drugs could help a liar pass a polygraph
test was a myth. Research had proven no drug could ever neutralize a subject's autonomic nervous reactions to deception on relevant questions, while
simultaneously having no effect on reactions to "known lie" and "directed
lie" questions. That was one of the tremendous advantages of modern
CQT methodology.

I said I wanted to be absolutely certain that no one could ever claim *any*
basis to attack this test for any reason. Gilson assured me, the lack of drug
influence was well established. Since some misinformed subjects had
thought this would work, he'd seen such attempts—he could easily spot a
drugged reaction chart—and the result is as far from a passed test in appearance as would be intense stress reactions to relevant questions. No
drug effect can be repeatedly turned on and off in a matter of seconds. Many
years of research had been done, and if there was any way chemicals could
defeat a test, drug tests would have become a standard part of the procedure. Critics wouldn't get too far with such an attack if no knowledgeable
polygraph expert would substantiate their underlying premise. I finally re-
lented—Gilson's logic was unassailable.

We had a lengthy pretest interview. I went through a description of my
experience. He took notes, and asked many questions. His questions weren't
in the nature of a cross-examination. They rather appeared to be directed
at establishing a mutual understanding of the facts as I stated them to be.
He showed neither belief nor disbelief, only concern with my being clear
about the truth of what I was saying.

Cy Gilson formulated in his own words questions based on Jerry Black's
guidelines. I exercised great care never to suggest specific changes in their
wording, but raised one or two minor points on which a given question ex-

hibited ambiguity to me, but left them entirely up to the examiner to re-solve however he saw fit.

We went through the other standard procedures, then took a short break before I was strapped into the chair. It seemed like hours before my testing was complete.

No hint of what he'd read on my charts showed in his face. Not that I needed to be told, assuming there were no glitches. It probably took less than an hour, as he scanned the charts and computer readouts, but it seemed longer as I silently waited for his preliminary conclusion. Finally, he told me with no trace of emotion what I already knew was nearly cer-tain. Although subject to continued evaluation as to exact scores, my charts were clearly within the upper range of truthfulness.

We broke for lunch and returned for more testing. I'd been disappointed to learn that modern methodology considered only four questions to be op-timum. I had other areas I wished to cover. My first test that day had cov-ered the incident comprehensively, but I wanted to address specific allega-tions by my critics which couldn't be perfectly refuted in any other way. Mike had wanted his Forest Service Contract Theory stuff specifically cov-ered in a second test. I pointed out that all those questions had been fully addressed in the questionnaire Maurice Marchbanks (see appendix) was an-swering. I'd argued that if Jerry Black's budget would only cover one per-son getting a second test, then as the person at the center of all the allega-tions I ought to be that one.

Cy Gilson really didn't see any necessity for either of us to have a second test. In his opinion, no subissue could elude the four interlocking relevant questions we had each already answered. We simply could not pass those and be lying about any of the other issues. In fact, one reason recom-mended procedure focused on only four questions was that almost any issue could be completely addressed by four properly worded questions. Nevertheless, it ultimately was agreed that I would undergo a second test.

When we began my second pretest interview, I enumerated a half dozen areas I wanted covered. Gilson deleted a couple as either already covered by some of the other questions or not central to the issue. Again, I was very careful to suggest changes only in the most general fashion. And again Cy Gilson formulated the questions according to his own judgment and proper principles of practice. And finally, again, when it was all over he gave me his favorable preliminary verdict for my second test.

You can imagine my feelings as I headed home. It occurred to me that ultimately I'd kept my appointment for a polygraph test with Gilson, though not very punctually.

Allen's and Mike's testing had been conducted without any problems on February 1, 1993. Great care was exercised to avoid even the appearance of any possible impropriety. Mike had stayed overnight in Phoenix to pick up his own polygraph report. Therefore he had been unable to attend a surprise birthday party thrown for me at my home. (My wife, Dana, had called me from the college where she taught aerobics to tell me she couldn't get the car started. I headed over there and the guests moved into the house as soon as I rounded the corner. She got me. I never expected a thing. It was great.) Coincidentally, my test with Pfiefer also had been right after my birthday, seventeen years earlier.

Allen had already completed his test when Mike arrived at Gilson's office. They'd spoken on the phone in getting the tests arranged, but it was the first time they'd laid eyes on each other in many years. Allen had showed up at the agreed time, and evidently conducted himself properly on this occasion, because everything went well. His new test and the one he took back in 1975 were the only polygraph tests Allen had ever taken. Mike's test was routine and naturally, reflecting the truth as well as his first test had, more than seventeen years earlier.

Before long, I had copies of all three completed official polygraph reports in my hand. They don't come any better than this. Here's what I read:

1 February 1993

Mr. Jerry Black
(Address)
Blanchester, Ohio

Dear Mr. Black,

On February 1, 1993, a polygraph examination was administered to Mr. Allen Dalis. The purpose of this examination was to determine whether or not Mr. Dalis was being truthful in his statement about witnessing a UFO-like object in the forest near Heber, Arizona, on November 5, 1975. The object will be referred to in the balance of this report as a UFO.

During the pretest interview, Mr. Dalis related the following events that occurred on that day. Mr. Dalis said they had finished work for the day and were heading home. It was almost dark. He saw a glow coming from among the trees ahead of them. As they came to a clearing, he saw the object he called a UFO. Mr. Rogers was slowing the truck down to stop as Travis Walton exited the truck and began to advance towards the UFO in a brisk walk. Before reaching the UFO Mr. Walton slowed to a normal walk.

Mr. Dalis described the UFO as being a yellowish white in color. He said the light emitting from it was not bright but a glow that gave off light all around itself. He equated it to the glowing light you get from a lamp with the shade on and the light shining all around.

Mr. Dalis saw Walton reach the UFO, stop and look up at it. He said it looked as if Walton was standing there, slightly bent over, with his hands in his pockets. Mr. Dalis said the UFO began to wobble or rock slightly and he began to become afraid. He put his head down towards his knees. As he did so, a bright light flashed that lit up the area, even the inside of the truck. He immediately looked towards the UFO. He saw a silhouette of Walton. Mr. Walton had his arms up in the air. Mr. Dalis cannot be sure if Walton was off of the ground at that time.

Mr. Dalis turned towards Mr. Rogers who was in the driver's seat and yelled for him to "get the hell out of here." They drove to the main forest road and stopped. He believes some of the crew got out of the truck and others stayed in it. They talked about what they had witnessed and the concern for Walton. It was decided to return to the area and help Walton.

When they arrived at the scene, Mr. Walton was nowhere to be found. [Mr. Dalis] said all of the crew got out of the truck and walked shoulder to shoulder towards the area where the UFO was seen. They could not find Mr. Walton nor any sign of him. They then drove to town and reported the incident to the Sheriff's Office.

During the review of the questions, Mr. Dalis understood all of the questions. He understood #R3 to mean any conversation with Walton either by telephone or in person and any visual contact, even if they did not speak to each other.

The relevant questions asked and the answers given are as follows:

Question #R1:
    On November 5, 1975, in the forest near Heber, did you see an object that you believe was a UFO?
        Answer: YES.

Question #R2:
    Did you conspire with the Walton brothers or anyone else to perpetrate a hoax about that UFO sighting in 1975?
        Answer: NO.

Question #R3:
    Between November 5 and 10 of 1975, when Travis Walton was missing, did you have any verbal or personal contact with him?
        Answer: NO.

Question #R4:
    In the past seventeen years, has anything occurred to cause you to now believe that UFO incident was a hoax?
        Answer: NO.

Mr. Dalis' physiological responses were monitored during the presentation of these questions by means of a Scientific Assessment Technology's Computer, Model CAPS 700. The following responses were recorded on this instrument's strip chart: relative blood pressure; skin conductance; thoracic and abdominal respiration. Data from three presentations of these questions were obtained and subject to numerical scoring and computer-based analysis.

The numerical score after three charts was +22. In the system of numerical scoring developed and validated at the University of Utah, total numerical scoring of +6 or more is considered indications of truthfulness. The computer-based analysis returned a posterior probability of truthfulness of .993, indicating that charts like these produced by Mr. Dalis, are produced by truthful examinees 99% of the time.

Based on the numerical score of the polygraph charts and the computer-based analysis, it is the opinion of this examiner that Mr. Dalis was being truthful when he answered these relevant questions.

Sincerely,

Cy Gilson

1 February 1993

Mr. Jerry Black
(Address)
Blanchester, Ohio

Dear Mr. Black,

On February 1, 1993, a polygraph examination was administered to Mr. Michael Rogers. The purpose of this examination was to determine whether or not Mr. Rogers was being truthful in his statement about witnessing a UFO-like object in the forest near Heber, Arizona, on November 5, 1975.

During the pretest interview, Mr. Rogers related the following events that occurred on that day. He and his crew of six men had worked late on that day. It was after sundown as they were driving back to town. Nearing a clearing to the right of the truck, they saw an object that is commonly referred to as a UFO. This object will be referred to during the balance of this report as a UFO. As the truck neared the clearing, Mr. Rogers slowed the truck to a stop. Mr. Travis Walton exited the truck and walked fast towards the object. Mr. Rogers was on the opposite side of the truck from the UFO. He had to bend over slightly to view it in its entirety through the truck windows.

He described the UFO to be glowing a yellowish tan color. He could not say if the light emanated from within the UFO or was a lighting system outside, that lit up the UFO. He did say he could see the shadows of the trees on the ground, around the UFO. He said it was round and about 20 feet in diameter. He said the UFO was about 75 to 100 feet from the truck.

He saw Walton walk near to the UFO, stop near some logs and brush and was standing there looking up at it. At this time Mr. Rogers decided to move the truck due to the fact they were becoming frightened. As Mr. Rogers started to move the truck a brilliant flash of light lit up the entire area, even inside the truck. It was described as a prolonged strobe flash. He did not see a beam of light emit from the UFO and hit Walton.

As the flash occurred, Mr. Rogers turned around in his seat to look at the UFO again and saw Mr. Walton being hurled through the air in a backwards motion, falling on the ground, on his back. At this time, Mr. Dalis and someone else yelled to get the hell out of here. Mr. Rogers drove the truck along the secondary road until he came to the main forest road where he stopped. A brief discussion took place and it was decided to return to the area to help Mr. Walton.

Upon returning to the same place, they all exited the truck and advanced towards the place where they had seen the UFO. There was no sign of Walton nor any indication of Walton being injured, such as blood on the ground. There were no burns of the vegetation in the area where the UFO hovered. Not being able to find Walton with the aid of a few flashlights, they decided to go to Heber and notify the Sheriff's Office of what had just occurred.

During the review of the questions, Mr. Rogers understood the content of all the relevant questions and in particular, that question #R3 meant any type of conversation either in person or by telephone and any visual contact with Walton even if they did not speak. He understood "conspire" to mean any planning or his knowledge of any planning to perpetrate a UFO hoax.

The relevant questions asked and the answers given are as follows:

Question #R1:

On November 5, 1975, in the forest area called Turkey Springs, did you see a large, glowing object hovering in the air below the treetops about 100 feet from you?

Answer: YES.

Question #R2:

After the bright flash of light did you see Travis Walton propelled backwards through the air?

Answer: YES.

Question #R3:

Between November 5 and 10 of 1975, when Travis Walton was reported missing, did you have any verbal or personal contact with him?

Answer: NO.

Question #R4:

Did you conspire with the Walton brothers or anyone else to perpetrate a hoax about that UFO sighting in 1975?

Answer: NO.

Mr. Rogers' physiological responses were monitored during the presentation of these questions by means of a Scientific Assessment Technology's Computer, Model CAPS 700. The following responses were recorded on this instrument's strip chart: relative blood pressure; skin conductance; thoracic and abdominal respiration. Data from three presentations of these questions were obtained and subject to numerical scoring and computer-based analysis.

The numerical score after three charts was +31. In the system of numerical scoring developed and validated at the University of Utah, total numerical scoring of +6 or more is considered indications of truthfulness.

The computer-based analysis returned a posterior probability of truthfulness of .990, indicating that charts like these produced by Mr.

Rogers, are produced by truthful examinees 99% of the time.

Based on the numerical score of the polygraph charts and the computer-based analysis, it is the opinion of this examiner that Mr. Rogers was being truthful when he answered these relevant questions.

The truthful outcome of this examination tends to validate the truthful results of the single question I asked, regarding this incident, during the original examination of Mr. Rogers in 1975.

Sincerely,

Cy Gilson

4 February 1993

Mr. Jerry Black
(Address)
Blanchester, Ohio

Dear Mr. Black,

On February 4, 1993, a polygraph examination was administered to Mr. Travis Walton. The purpose of this examination was to determine whether or not Mr. Walton was being truthful in his statement about seeing a UFO and being abducted by the UFO plus other facts surrounding the abduction.

During the pretest interview, Mr. Walton said he had worked for Mike Rogers intermittently for about six years on a seasonal basis. He never socialized with any of the crew.

On November 5, 1975, they had worked a little later than usual trying to meet the contract commitment. By the time they were driving back to town, the sun had gone down but there was some light, like twilight.

As they were driving, he could see a glimmer of light in the trees ahead. At first he thought it may be a downed airplane. The light was unusual. As they neared a clearing he saw the object he called a UFO. This object will be referred to as a UFO throughout this report.

As the truck came to a stop, Mr. Walton got out. Believing it may take off, he walked briskly towards the UFO but slowed his pace before reaching it. He described it as being round and hovering about 20 feet above the ground. He did not go underneath it but stood there looking up at it. He said the UFO started to wobble slightly and make a noise. Mr. Walton said the noise was like a low rumble that developed into a higher pitch that seemed to increase in frequency. At this point he became afraid and decided to go back to the truck. He recalls being hit with an electrifying type of shock that stunned him, leaving him unconscious.

He recalls he slowly regained consciousness. He found himself in a small room that was damp or humid. He had pain throughout his body but mostly in his chest and head. He then saw three creatures he described as being about four feet tall with large, dark eyes. He was lying on some type of table. As these creatures approached him he got off the table. There was some type of shelf near the wall where he found a straight pipe-like object lying on it. He describes it as being round like a piece of pipe but lightweight. He cannot recall if it was solid or hollow. He picked it up and started to lash out at the creatures to keep them at bay. The creatures left the room by an open doorway, turning right.

Mr. Walton walked to that doorway, looked down a hall and he went left. He walked into another room, trying to find an exit from this enclosure. He did not know if he was in a spaceship or a building. A human-like creature came into the room, took him by the arm, leading him to another very large room where several more human-like creatures were. By this time most of the pain was gone. He was forced down on a table and had a mask, similar to an oxygen mask, put on his face. He does not remember anything else until he awoke next to the road, just outside Heber. As he regained consciousness, he looked up, seeing the UFO or one similar to the original one, hovering overhead. As he looked up at it, the UFO sped off into the sky.

Mr. Walton said his story is true. He said accusations made about him are lies. He had not been on any drugs of any kind. He was not hiding out somewhere on the Gibson ranch. He urinated in a jar and this sample was given to Dr. Kandell later that same day. Mr. Walton denies he conspired with Mr. Rogers to perpetrate a hoax to help him get out of the Turkey Springs contract with the Forestry Service.

Two series of questions were asked to cover all the areas we believe were important.

The relevant questions asked and the answers given are as follows:

Series #1:

Question #R1:
> On November 5, 1975, in the forest area called Turkey Springs, did you see a large glowing object hovering in the air?
> Answer: YES.

Question #R2:
> While you were standing near that UFO-like object, did you believe you were struck by an energy source emitted from that large object?
> Answer: YES.

Question #R3:
> After regaining consciousness in a small, humid room, did you see nonhuman creatures with large dark eyes?
> Answer: YES.

Question #R4:
> Did you conspire with your brother Duane or anyone else or act alone to stage a hoax about your UFO abduction?
> Answer: NO.

Series #2:

Question #R1:
> Between November 1 and 11, 1975, did you use any drugs, either legal or illegal?
> Answer: NO.

Question #R2:
    Between November 5 and 10, 1975, were you hiding anywhere on the Gibson ranch?
        Answer: NO.
Question #R3:
    Was the urine sample given to Dr. Kandell on November 11, 1975, your first voided specimen following your UFO experience?
        Answer: YES.
Question #R4:
    Was this UFO incident a conspiracy to help Mike Rogers get out of his Turkey Springs contract?
        Answer: NO.

Mr. Walton's physiological responses were monitored during the presentation of these questions by means of a Scientific Assessment Technology's Computer, Model CAPS 700. The following responses were recorded on this instrument's strip chart: relative blood pressure; skin conductance; thoracic and abdominal respiration. Data from three presentations of these questions were obtained for each series, and were subject to numerical scoring and computer-based analysis.

The numerical score of Series #1 was +34. The numerical score of Series #2 was +26. In the system of numerical scoring developed and validated at the University of Utah, total numerical scoring of +6 or more is considered indications of truthfulness.

The computer-based analysis returned a posterior probability of truthfulness of .964 in the first series, and a .961 in the second series. These indicating that charts like these produced in each series, by Mr. Walton, are produced by truthful examinees 96% of the time.

Based on the numerical score of the polygraph charts and the computer-based analysis, it is the opinion of this examiner that Mr. Walton was being truthful when he answered these relevant questions.

                                        Sincerely,

                                        Cy Gilson

Thank you, Jerry Black! These examinations clear the air with a thoroughness, an utter finality, which can't be refuted. Cy Gilson used a widely practiced, extremely accurate, state-of-the-art method developed and perfected at the University of Utah. This involves a computerized monitoring and analysis of the tracings along with a point-scoring system of the charts applied by the examiner.

In summary: The computer put all three of us near the top of the range designated as conclusively truthful (almost no one ever achieves the theoretical maximum of 1.00), with me at .964 and .961, Mike at .990, and Allen at .993. On the numerical score I was first with +34 and +26 points, Mike had +31 points and Allen had +22 points. Since +6 and up is considered truthful, the minor scoring differences between the three of us are of no meaningful significance because they are less than the difference you could get from two identical tests on the same person in the same day.

It's unlikely my critics will be bragging up Cy Gilson's years of experience, but the fact is, he had more experience when he tested me than McCarthy (his claims notwithstanding) actually had at the time he tested me. Gilson was probably the best examiner in the state even in 1975, but now no one can dispute, by *any* criteria, his being the top examiner in the state of Arizona. If debunkers surrender their credibility and dare to attack these tests, we can expect that suddenly years of experience won't be the crucial factor in a polygrapher's credentials to them. The truth is, there is absolutely *nothing* critics could say that wouldn't be barefaced hypocrisy at this point. They've painted themselves tightly into a corner.

Cy Gilson is a top-notch examiner of impeccable integrity and credentials. No critic ever made a personal attack on his credentials or conduct relative to my case. His objectivity can't be doubted. To this day, I've not been able to figure out where Gilson stands in regard to the UFO issue in general. I know he was a complete skeptic before November 11, 1975, though the results of our tests must have had some effect on him. None of us really asked him, because, since he's as professional as they come, his personal opinions outside of his test reports were kept out of it. I might have been spared much aggravation had the situation worked out so that my first—and only—test had been from him. However, I'm happy that at long last I had the opportunity to set the record straight once and for all.

I had waited to tell anyone at Paramount about the tests until they were complete because I wanted to head off any possible suggestions from my critics that the studio, because of its financial stake in the movie, had exerted any influence on the results. But the next day I fired off a letter with the news to the publicity department. It had a more dramatic impact than I had expected. Apparently some of the old, skeptical claims had been affecting attitudes more negatively than I'd known. Needless to say, everyone was pleased.

His investigative experience with us, culminating in our triumphant polygraphs, has made a changed man of Jerry Black—at least regarding his opinion of the Turkey Springs incident. But he didn't lose, he *won*—in a big way. Unlike my other critics, he came by his new understanding the "old-fashioned" way—he earned it. Unusual indeed is the man with the objectivity and intellectual honesty not only to seek the truth in opposition to a strongly-held opinion but—rarer still—to face it when he meets it. All those he questioned—Ezell, McCarthy, Torme, Pfiefer, Gillespie, the Forest Service officials—can attest to his skepticism when he entered the investigation. His reversal not only confers credibility on our incident, but it attests to his own credibility as an investigator.

Jerry Black admits his new understanding of the Turkey Springs incident came gradually, but that one of the key points of conviction for him was my decision to undergo new testing by polygraph. He said: "There's no question in my mind that the clincher, as far as Travis Walton himself is concerned, was his agreeability to take the polygraph in the face of realizing that he had really nothing to gain and everything to lose at this late point and date. The film was already made, he had his money; if he was really lying he would have been a fool, under the circumstances, to take the test with nothing to gain and everything to lose. [This] showed me that he had nothing to fear, that in his mind he knew, he *had to know* that in his mind he was telling the truth as he knew it. He knew full well that it was going to become public record. The questions were tight. Everything in the polygraph just confirmed my total investigation."

Well, that's it. I know I'm done. I'll never again undergo testing on this issue. But I have been mulling over the idea of a reunion with the rest of the crew, and perhaps getting the rest of them re-polygraphed. The logistics are a little daunting, but we'll see. However, the bottom line is we've *already* proven ourselves, nearly to the limit of what's possible.

Look at the case presented by our detractors. Then look at the evidence we provide. It's all there on the table. You decide.

To obtain an expert opinion on what conclusions could be drawn from the polygraph tests in the Travis Walton case we interviewed Edward Gelb, President of the American Polygraph Association: "Hundreds of police departments and corporations throughout the world utilize the polygraph to separate truth from deception. The 94-percent accuracy of the polygraph has been well documented, not only in real-life situations as we've discussed here, but in laboratory and university studies that have been conducted throughout the world. The odds against six people successfully deceiving a trained polygraph examiner on a single issue are over a million to one."

—Courtesy of Brandon Chase's video, *UFOs Are Real,* 1979

CHAPTER 12

Speculations

Men love to wonder and that is the seed of our science.

—Emerson

In writing of the events of my abduction, I've tried very hard to stick strictly to describing the events as I *experienced* them, not as I *interpreted* them. I've remained as objective and factual as possible, refraining from any embellishments or assumptions of detail, so as not to contaminate the scientific value of my experience.

However, what occurred inside the craft and the events surrounding my capture and return are not in the least self-explanatory. In fact, in the absence of conjecture or further data, these events do not seem to make much sense.

I've been asked countless questions by those keenly desirous of understanding not only the physical events themselves, but the wider implications, the overall *meaning*, of my experience and therefore possibly to gain clues to the mysteries of the phenomenon in general. Who? What? Why? Where? The uniform answer is that I do not know. Many of these same questions have continually nagged my own mind since that November day in 1975.

While almost nothing is definitely explained by the events themselves, endless ideas can be inferred from them. The scientific presentation of facts has had its place. Here is the place for speculations.

I do not know which, if any, of the possible scenarios considered here best corresponds to reality. The *potential* for a rough matchup is maintained by sticking to extrapolation of the known facts. However, without more data, the *likelihood* of its actually being one of them is probably low. Nevertheless, it is both fascinating and somewhat constructive to try to piece it all together.

The questions that arise from the events are obvious; nor can I claim originality in formulating most of the theoretical explanations. Naturally, I have done much thinking in the search for meaning in my experience. But newsmen, researchers, family, and friends have also advanced many intriguing questions, and suggested still more fascinating answers.

Who are these beings? What do they want? Where are they from? Exactly how much can we deduce regarding them with the data we have?

It's logical to concentrate first on particulars of my own experience before attempting to address the broader questions. Why did they pick the seven of us? Was our being chosen even deliberate? What form of energy did that beam consist of? Why did it strike me? What were the craft's occupants doing with me? Why were there two types of beings? Why do I remember only two hours out of five days? The questions are endless, but let us explore a few. I want to reemphasize however, that at this point it is *purely* speculation.

First of all, why us? Why pick seven ordinary tree-cutters, instead of a world-renowned scientist or national leader? Or, was our contact only a fluke, entirely unintended beforehand?

It's possible we were singled out. They could have seen us working from high above the ground and waited near the path by which they knew we would leave. If they did actually *choose* us from six billion earth people, why? Possibly they do not recognize the kinds of distinctions between persons that we make or consider such criteria relevant to their purposes. It has occurred to me that they may have been attracted to us by somehow overhearing or monitoring our conversations on the job. It might seem presumptuous to think that anything we might say could be of any interest to them, but we did philosophize on an incredibly wide array of topics during the months out there in the forest—even a brief conversation or two about UFOs. So it's not inconceivable that we inadvertently attracted unwelcome interest.

It doesn't seem to me a biological examination could really be of all that great use to them, especially if they have already done so on other humans, but who could fathom the purposes of such a totally strange civilization? It could be that they are instituting a "conditioning" program to prepare the people of earth for the social impact of open contact with other worlds. They have not completely disguised their presence. If they have the powers of motion and memory-erasing that some claim they have, they could easily keep their presence (or visits) *completely* unknown.

Perhaps the growing number of UFO reports characterized by increasing believability is intended to accustom us to what the future holds in store. It almost seems as if UFO occupants control the specific degree of provableness of reports in terms of the number of witnesses and the amount of evidence left behind. The growing acceptance of reports may be deliberately engineered.

This could explain the grassroots level of their selection of contactees. To make brazen contact by landing on the White House lawn or descending into the Kennedy Space Center would be too sudden. Such a jolt of irrefutable evidence might generate widespread panic, or other unpredictable and negative reactions. Societies might abruptly abandon stable patterns for activities focussing on the new knowledge. New "cargo cult" sorts of belief systems might be formed. Humankind might focus on prematurely achieving spacefaring sorts of goals, diverting energies best applied elsewhere for now. UFO occupants might want to avoid this for their own good or for ours (or both).

One radio announcer I met theorized that aliens might be selectively altering human genetic makeup to change the course of human evolution! After the incident, the entire crew experienced an acute increase in their interest in the opposite sex. But only one of us was abducted, so this is likely only the result of a psychological release of nervous tension. A couple of the men attempted regressive hypnosis but were unsuccessful at getting into a trance state. None of the men noticed any time loss on the evening of November 5, 1975, that would indicate hypnotic repression of events they might have experienced but could not recall. If their memories had been blocked, then why were not theirs as well as mine *completely* blocked, so that no one would know the difference? If the aliens are attempting to manipulate the inherited traits of man, for purposes of improvement or otherwise, one would think they would somehow do it on a larger scale. There has been growing support of this theory idea among researchers.

What if the contact was entirely accidental? We could have simply stumbled upon their craft hovering over the clearing. They could have been temporarily incapacitated, stopped for repairs or adjustments. The area was covered with visually alert deer hunters; they should have been aware they were taking chances of being shot at, or being seen by people other than us, if they were there deliberately. But then, if they are closer to omniscient than that, they could have had instruments or other ways of locating every nearby being. They could use such knowledge in coordination with tree cover, clouds, and high-speed maneuvering to make themselves visible (or invisible) to whomever they choose.

Maybe the *contact* was deliberate, but the *abduction* was accidental. My somewhat foolhardy approach to that craft could not have been a readily anticipated reaction. They may have decided on the spur of the moment to kidnap this oddball to see what makes him tick. My sudden approach could have caused them to fire at me in the mistaken impression that I was attacking them. Or an automatic defense mechanism might have fired the beam.

Could what these men saw zap Travis Walton actually be the result of phenomena formed by shifting in the earth's crust? The Mogollon Rim is a gigantic fault line; perhaps movement deep in the earth released gases that somehow ignited or became electrically charged. (Shades of swamp gas.) "Earthquake lights" are widely reported in association with underground tremors. These are speculated to be a sort of piezoelectric effect—electrical charges generated by stresses in the crystalline structure of rock or changes in ground-water flow related to underground pressure.

Dr. Michael Persinger, a professor at Laurentian University of Sudbury, Ontario, Canada, and John Derr, a geophysicist with the U.S. Geological Survey in Albuquerque, New Mexico, say they have a strong statistical analysis showing a link between UFO sightings and quakes.

What about ball lightning? A Forest Service expert says the Mogollon Rim area has the highest number of lightning strikes per year of any area in the United States except the Florida Everglades. For example, in the three days between June 13 and June 16 of 1993 there were twenty-seven lightning-caused fires in the Sitgreaves National Forest—and the stormy rainy season doesn't even begin until July. If there's more lightning, maybe there's also more of the rare ball form.

What about plasmas? Plasmas are gasses in a highly energized state—so energized they radiate intense light. Maybe ball lightning is a sort of plasma. In the basic theory, whichever of the three types of energized balls were actually the UFO, they're saying Travis Walton could have inadvertently narrowed the gap between it and the ground with his body, acting as a sort of lightning rod by providing a grounding path for the charge. They believe this could perhaps create bizarre neurological effects like a five-day blackout replete with hallucinations.

My experience made me a lightning rod all right, but only in the metaphorical sense. In the first place, the earth is pretty well networked with seismic detectors, and as far as I know no tremors were reported. Second, lightning season was over and the weather was clear and dry—the least likely conditions to generate or sustain these kinds of atmospheric phenomena. The statistical analysis linking UFO reports and earthquakes was criticized because supposedly large time lags and distance allowances were thrown in to help make a link more likely. Also, all these phenomena are as exotic and even more rarely reported than UFOs. Remember Occam's Razor. One doesn't explain away an anomaly by invoking an anomaly.

How in the world could I be wandering around the woods in an electrically induced hallucination for five days and not freeze to death or be found by searchers? People get struck by lightning every year in this area and when they survive they bear unmistakable signs: the hair on their bodies is all singed off, clothes burned, paramedics have trouble getting vital signs because their veins are all blown out, and they often have large exit wounds in the bottom of their feet. I exhibited none of these effects.

How could such a transient phenomenon possess sufficient energy to hover and move around for minutes, discharge through me without dissipating or leaving the area, then ten minutes later rise up and streak off into the cloudless night sky? And it made a tremendous mechanical sound, which doesn't fit. The bottom line is, as stated elsewhere, what we seven saw had a clearly visible, perfect mechanical structure. What we saw was definitely not a nebulous fireball or glowing cloud of gas.

What struck me might have been some sort of electrical static discharge, not an offensive or defensive weapon. The effect of dry, autumn air moving at tremendous speed over the surface of the craft's metal hull could have caused a buildup of static electricity. Buildups like this are common in airplanes, so that a grounding wire is always clamped to the plane during refueling to prevent the discharging sparks of electricity from igniting the gasoline. Nearly everyone has experienced the shock of touching a grounded metal object after shuffling across a carpet on a dry day. My close approach could have caused a similar static charge, only on a gigantic scale.

A static charge also could have resulted as a side effect of the propulsion unit that powers the craft. A charge might have developed merely by the craft's hovering. Or the craft might have suddenly developed a charge—I remember hearing a surge in sound from the craft, like the start-up of powerful engines, just before I was struck and blacked out. The occupants of the craft could have been increasing the power of their driving unit(s), preparing to leave in response to my approach.

That beam behaved in some ways like a bolt of lightning or electricity, but it might have been some other form of energy entirely. The beam also could have been fired to keep me from getting too close to the craft, from actually touching it. The motive might have been to prevent me from being burned by heat, radiation, or some other unknown danger. Or it might have been to prevent me from seeing or learning something.

Any of those possibilities could also serve to explain my being taken aboard. If harm had accidentally befallen me as a result of their presence, they might have felt responsible for repairing the damage. Even if taking me aboard had been planned, perhaps they underestimated the damage of the stunning ray. This might explain why I was taken for five days, instead of the few hours usually reported, as Coral Lorenzen has suggested.

Miracles of advanced medical technology might have been performed on me in those five days, if not to repair damage, perhaps for some other purpose. Did the aliens leave that mark on the inside of my right elbow? Perhaps a needle did not pierce me, but some other instrument. A terminal for some electronic device? It is also entirely possible that the mark was a minor injury I received at work *before* I was abducted.

My weight loss is another mystery. I weighed myself on my own scale the very night I was returned (1:00 A.M., November 11), revealing a loss of over ten pounds since leaving for work the morning of November 5. My scale was later compared for accuracy to the physician's scale in Dr. Kandell's office and found to register correct weight (unusual for a common bathroom scale).

However, Dr. Kandell insists that if a weight-loss is caused by starvation, it results in the presence of ketones (acetones) in the urine. Ketones were not present in my first voided sample, subjected to analysis. But are ketones *always* found in the absence of feeding? Or could there be exceptions to this, based on the patient's prior body reserves, or perhaps an extremely high or low ambient temperature? Could virtual immobility in a humid environment further reduce ketone production? I have not yet sought expert medical advice in regard to this question.

What else could have happened to cause the weight loss? Perhaps my captors did not know enough of human physiology to provide me with sufficient moisture. Is it possible to lose as much as ten pounds solely from dehydration? I did have many symptoms of dehydration; but ten pounds of water amounts to over a gallon. I did drink at least that much between my first and second weighings, but normal losses of body-water stores would have continued to some degree. But if not starvation or dehydration, what was the caused of my weight loss?

One obvious question that very often springs to mind, and is asked with some embarrassment: What about the body's processes of elimination? I was conscious for less than two hours of those five days; I do not recall either using toilet facilities or eating in that time. Let's exercise a little clinical objectivity here. My underclothes were clean when I returned. My bowel habits are usually very regular, but I did not void urine for approximately ten hours after my return, and had no bowel movement for nearly twenty-four hours. Could I have used a toilet on the craft and not remembered doing so? I don't recall my bladder pressure during my brief conscious period, but that isn't the sort of thing that captures one's awareness in dangerous situations.

Maybe I was fed intravenously while unconscious. Perhaps my body's metabolic processes were somehow lowered to a very slow rate, so that my body experienced the five days as only a few hours . . . possibly as a result of a state of suspended animation, or some mysterious space-travel time contraction? If so, then why, upon my return, did my face have five days' growth of beard?

My six coworkers missed seeing me taken aboard the craft due to their panicked flight. I lost consciousness when the beam struck me, so how the remainder of my abduction was accomplished remains a mystery. Sheriff Gillespie and his men carefully searched the ground at the site immediately after the abduction. They found no burn marks, pad impressions, or alien footprints. No footprints led from the spot where I was struck. The ground on that ridgetop was dry and rocky, so there exists a possibility that the craft *landed* to take me aboard.

They also could have hovered close and low, reaching out through an opening in the craft to pull me inside. Perhaps a mechanical device extended from the craft to me on the ground; maybe even something as unearthly as a levitating or dematerializing beam. Perhaps instead the occupants left the craft by some sort of individual floating or flying method to manually carry me aboard. The means could have been something as unsensationally low-tech as a lasso of rope. Was my unconsciousness during both my entry into and exit from the craft a coincidence? Were they trying to hide something? What?

My experiences inside the craft seem so much to be fragments of something more, that the number of things that could explain them are of endless variety.

When I awoke inside the craft, I assumed I was in a hospital. Possibly nothing more than my sensation of overwhelming pain inspired that deduction. Maybe an odor in the atmosphere suggestive of a hospital didn't consciously register; I don't recall specific supraliminal awareness of smells while I was conscious. Perhaps I was injured in a way that temporarily impaired my olfactory sense. The walls, resembling stainless steel, might have lent the impression of a hospital; most trips I have made to a hospital have been as visitor, not patient, but I have noticed an extensive use of stainless steel in those facilities. However, I do not recall entire rooms so constructed. Perhaps the impressions formed by the pain, the overhead light, and the stainless steel–like walls *combined* to create the mental association with a hospital.

The false image of being in an earthbound hospital might have been planted in my mind, a hypnotic suggestion to inspire confidence—in case I regained consciousness during whatever procedure they were performing. Even if my regaining consciousness was part of their plan, it would have been useful for them to give me some posthypnotic suggestion, to pacify me with reassuring thoughts.

Why *did* I regain consciousness? If they had expected I would react so violently, wouldn't I have been restrained somehow? Maybe unfamiliarity with human physiology made them fail to anticipate my regaining consciousness.

The shock and pain accompanying my awakening should adequately explain my negative reaction and hysteria. To those disappointed that I didn't control myself and try to learn more, I can but say my reaction was only natural for me under the circumstances.

Why was I kept for five days? And why unconscious? Did my fighting reaction delay my return by worsening medical problems, or could my behavior have caused some other difficulty for them? What did they do with me during the long period I was knocked out?

For that matter, what had been the reason for my unconsciousness? Did my awakening occur soon after being struck by the ray, or sometime later during the five days? If it was later, did the effect of the beam keep me blacked out so long? Or did the beings perpetuate my unconsciousness by other means? If so, why? For medical treatment, tests of some kind, or some other purpose? Was my muscular weakness and stiffness upon regaining consciousness the effect of having been unconscious and immobile for an extended period? Or did that effect have some other cause?

Most often my questioners are first interested in communication. "Did they talk to you?" No, they did not. I screamed at them, yelled at them, threw a veritable flurry of questions at them. They made no answer. I might have chosen and presented my questions in a more effective manner. But why were they silent? Were they ignoring me because of my emotional display? Are they not vocal beings?

I know I would have heard them had they spoken, because I could hear my own voice, as well as the sound of their movements and of objects in the room. I did not see their mouths move at any time. I did not even see teeth exposed, if they had any. Perhaps their voices were of a frequency to which my ears are not sensitive. They could be telepathic. What if they did not want an accent of some sort to be detected that would suggest something of their origin? They might simply not been able to speak or comprehend my language.

Did they even have mouths at all? Perhaps they were wearing masks, for disguise, so as not to give away clues to their true origin. Or perhaps their real faces were even more horrid than the mask, so awful I could not have stood it. Maybe they wore masks, not for disguise, but perhaps in an entire body shield for protection from the environment or radiation. I remember seeing no fingernails on their hands, which might indicate they were wearing gloves, as part of such an entire body covering. This might explain their rubbery, marshmallowy apperance: a technologically advanced surgical mask/suit perhaps—either to protect me from their microbes or themselves from mine (or both).

Then again, even the human-looking creatures did not speak to me. At first I had believed that the first man I encountered could not hear me through his helmet. But when I encountered the other three human-looking individuals, who wore no helmets, they also were noncommunicative, despite my desperate efforts.

Although they appeared human in nearly every way, there was something that didn't seem right about their eyes, something very strange. I've never been able to figure out what that was. Perhaps it was something communicated by expression or subtle movements which do not match our eye functions; maybe something structural like pupil shape, size, proportion of subparts, coloring, or light reflectivity; perhaps an artificial covering, a sort of whole-eye contact lens. If the latter, why? Something to enhance sight? To protect the eye? To hide something?

I failed to notice the presence or absence of normal breathing in any of the creatures I encountered; but the helmet might have been related to the stifling atmosphere inside the first craft—unless my perception of that air as hot and humid was a physiological reaction of my own, rather than an actual condition. But if it was a subjective perception on my part, why did the air seem so good and pure immediately on leaving the craft?

Maybe the air was not "hot and humid" as in earth's atmosphere, but an alien atmosphere of different gas compounds that caused a physiological response that made me feel hot and sweaty. This also might have been the source of my muscular weakness, to some extent, though I recovered somewhat as time passed. Perhaps heavier or lighter gravity was in some way a factor.

Dr. Robert J. Hudek of Toronto, Canada, an APRO consultant on biological sciences, advanced some speculations on the apparent structure of the aliens, commenting specifically on the significance of the aliens' apparent "human fetal" resemblance.

Dr. Hudek noted consistencies in their structure with ours in terms of current understanding of human anthropology and anatomy. If humanoid creatures have such extreme similarity to mankind that they exhibit common basic form, it is strongly indicative of very similar environmental origins. In other words—separate but parallel evolution! The extent of resemblance is nothing short of phenomenal even in the case of the more alien entities. If the human-looking creatures did not originate here on earth, their similarity to human form is mind-boggling and sobering in its implications.

The significance of the human fetal appearance of the aliens lies in the present apparent course of man's own evolutionary development. The longer man has been in possession of an intelligent brain, the more time he has had to influence his development by controlling his environment. By his elimination of hostile conditions, he atrophies in his ability to deal with those conditions. He becomes less rugged and coarse in his structure. Lack of exposure to cold and the elements eliminates the need for a hairy body covering or larger musculature. Only his brain need increase in size.

An infant human is the most helpless of creatures. Man's initial helplessness as an infant is proportionately the longest period of infancy of any animal. Yet, when grown, his brain makes him the most formidable animal. Early fetal stages of apes and man exhibit great similarity. But the rugged qualities developed in the ape reduce the need for intelligence; the developing brain of the human makes the rugged qualities of the ape less necessary to survival.

Thus, the further man advances in his brain structure, the less his remaining structure develops from the more fetal, or physically helpless, stage. Dr. Hudek's theory sounds very logical, *if* you believe man is evolving, which is sometimes a highly debatable issue in itself. The ideas expressed by Dr. Hudek are in agreement with "accepted" or relatively undisputed modern scientific thought. Whether they are valid in terms of accepted religious beliefs is another matter.

The director of APRO noted that the structure of the aliens, particularly their faces, might indicate origins on a planet with high atmospheric density. Sound would travel well; hence small ears. Oxygen density would require less chest volume, and give rise to the small nostrils. The dense atmosphere would limit solar light penetration, requiring the oversized eyes.

The horror I experienced in witnessing those aliens is a curious thing. The fear was not really caused by any appearance of threat. They were smaller than I, carried no weapons, showed no claws or fangs. Perhaps it was simply their strangeness which caused my reaction. But then why don't I, or we as humans, experience fear and revulsion at the first visual encounter with odd earth animals?

I am beginning to believe this anomaly is due to mankind's "monster fixation." The very *similarity* to man is the key to horror. The popular monsters in the movies are all based on an underlying man-form. This is not simply a low special-effects budget, "man in a suit" problem. The fear factor lies in the monster's deviation from the human. The link to human form is important because if the similarity is reduced too much, other fear factors, such as gigantic size, are needed to enhance the effect of terror. This effect is evident in most of man's imagined "man-beast" monsters of the old legends and myths handed down through the centuries in various cultural heritages.

The near identical appearance of the three alien beings, and the odd "family resemblance" of the four human-type individuals, led to speculation about them being robots, their similarity an artifact of assembly-line mass production.

Did they "look like" robots? It seems to me that any technology advanced enough to create a robot that could function as an organic being would also be sufficiently advanced to create one with no visible mechanical distinctions. So there's no way I could have been able to tell if they were indeed machines rather than organic creatures. Both entities moved with a natural fluidity, arms in time with legs. Any movements less natural would have been immediately apparent. The small beings were expressionless, but their faces weren't frozen. I didn't register specific facial movement, but the organic impression must have been communicated to me as such minute functions as subtle flaring of the nostrils or narrowing of the eyes.

Many find amazing the presence of the "alien" creatures and the human-looking ones *together*. Some people's idea of flying-saucer occupants does not leave room for nonhuman types; perhaps they are simply repelled by the idea of the existence of alien creatures. So they try to explain them away by saying they were really robots. For others, human-looking individuals do not fit their particular preconception. So the robot theory was offered to explain the presence of one type or the other. If one type were robots, why were the robots and their makers of differing forms? This could be explained by alien creatures using human robots in order to relate to me better, or the human-type entities using alien robots in order to confuse our efforts to know more about them.

Robot theory aside, some have suggested only one type of being was there! They say maybe the aliens left and returned in a more human form in order to calm me. That would be a remarkable disguise! Over a one-foot difference in height and almost a hundred pounds in weight! They would have had to have an almost magical ability to transform themselves.

Another reason offered for their carbon-copy look was that one or the other type were *clones*. Cloning is a process where a single cell taken from an adult animal is grown into an identical twin (only younger) of the original cell-donating animal. Hundreds of duplicates of one animal can be generated this way. One race of beings could have produced clones of another race to act as slaves to fulfill functions their own form is less able to, or even *incapable* of.

The aliens could have appeared to me to resemble each other more closely than they actually did, due to their strangeness. The aliens might have possessed differences that are quite apparent to them, but too subtle for me to have noticed. These even could have included gender differences, which I did not discern. The human type, being more similar to my kind, seemed somewhat less than identical, though evincing that strong "family resemblance." This could have been due to the group of characteristics that differentiated them from my human race. It could also have been an actual family resemblance. (Speaking of resemblance, just for fun, compare the countenance of the human-looking male in Mike's rendering [see illustrations] with the "Mars face" photo NASA released years after Mike's work.)

Who was cooperating with whom? I saw nothing to indicate the answer to that question. In fact, I never saw the two types together in one place at the same time. Nothing indicated one type was a bred-up slave of the other. Nothing positively indicated friendly cooperation, either. Some people are of the strong opinion that the human-type individuals captured the alien craft for breaking some interplanetary law in kidnapping me. They believe the human types act as guardians for this planet.

The aliens and the human-looking creatures might have cooperated in my abduction—or they might not have. There might or might not exist an interaction and cooperation of all intelligent life forms in space. If there does, what would their goals be?

Possibly the aliens took me to the human-looking beings (or vice versa) because the aliens lacked medical knowledge specific to my physiology. They might have needed advice or instruments they were not equipped with, due to the difference between my form and theirs—this assuming I was injured by that ray, which is only conjecture in itself.

If I was *not* injured, what *were* they doing with me? What was that device across my chest? Was it an instrument of treatment for my chest? The crewmen did say the beam struck me mostly in the head and chest. Maybe it was some sort of X-ray viewer or fluoroscope. If so, were they looking inside my chest cavity for injury? Perhaps I was not hurt at all and it was part of an examination.

I underwent comprehensive chest X rays from APRO physicians immediately after my return. The X rays showed only normal, uninjured structures. And the X rays showed what appeared to be a tiny calcified granuloma in my upper left lung. Dr. Kandell told me that a granuloma is a deposit of minerals caused by an injury or infection of the lung tissue. Such deposits can be temporary and normally occur in greater incidence in all people as they grow older. If repairs were made on my body during those five days, they apparently didn't make everything so perfect as to remove that fleck.

There was one speculation that I might have had a transmitter planted somewhere in my body! That I had been tagged for later retrieval, or become an indetectable, mobile spy device for the aliens. Unpleasant concepts. Theoretically every sensory input to my brain—sight, sound, touch, smell, and taste—would be automatically transferred to an alien craft high above the earth. Ha! Speculation can reach extremes at times. APRO scientists asked for permission to X-ray my head. I refused because I don't believe there is anything there but my brain, and radiation is harmful to living tissue. The brain is the *most* essential part of the body, so I didn't find sufficient justification in speculation to risk my health.

Some of the following speculations may seem more like concepts best discussed in the chapter 11. But since "the demon question," like the "electrically induced delusion" theory, weren't major elements in the archskeptic's attacks, and because they are so speculative, I have placed them here.

Were these creatures Satan's minions or chariot drivers of the gods? As I've stated elsewhere, this is not necessarily a religious matter—no more than the question of simple life existing on Mars is a religious matter. However, maybe it's natural this is so often suggested. After all, don't both religion and ufology deal with central questions about the universe, who we are, and our place in that universe? In fairness to all religions, the supreme being or beings are, by definition, over and above all that there is. The UFO phenomenon is just a part of all that there is. So, no contradiction of any religion is necessarily implied. I know of no religion with scripture specifically stating that humankind are the only sentient creatures in the universe.

Did the first type of alien act like demons, the other like angels? I did not see anything whatsoever that would fit my understanding of anything remotely linking this concept with what I experienced. Others may disagree, if they wish to disregard my impressions here, thinking I've been duped or was insufficiently attuned. Who wouldn't prefer to believe they had spent time in the hands of angels? But I don't see evidence to justify such a conclusion.

Could the UFO incident at Turkey Springs be an effect of the UFO fanaticism of "true believers"? This is strange logic. Unless they're claiming that this could generate a mass hallucination, they're implying that when a person believes something so very intensely, that when it satisfies all the needs that religion would satisfy for that person, they are then most likely to falsify the very thing they worship. Ridiculous. This is like saying that those who most believe in the Second Coming are most likely to simulate it with an antichrist. In other words they're saying that the most religious commit the greatest sacrilege. Another theory more incomprehensible than what it purports to explain, to say nothing of the fact that no one involved in the incident felt this way about the subject of UFOs. However, it does suggest the possibility that some of those who are attacking with such frenzy are doing so because *they* see religion, UFOs, etc., as manifestations of what they believe to be the same human shortcomings.

The variety of spacecraft I saw generates unanswered questions. Which type of craft belonged to which type of being? Why do the craft vary in appearance if they are designed for the same function? How are they made? What powers them?

When I awoke in the first craft I was in the presence of the aliens. Did the first craft belong to the aliens? Or was it owned by the human type, with the aliens present in the craft only for the purpose of their activities with me? Was there a forceful capture of the first craft by the human-type people before the "man" came in?

Was the planetarium-like view of the stars an elaborate three-dimensional star map, or an actual view of the surrounding stars? If it was an actual, outside view, had the craft been brought into the large hangar structure while I was being led down the hallway and kept waiting in the airlock-like room? Or was the star view visible inside the first craft in spite of the surrounding, larger structure?

What happened when I pushed those buttons in that room? Was the motion of the stars the turning of a star map or of the entire craft? I did not feel motion when the stars moved. In fact, I did not feel motion of the craft at any time during my experience. (Neither did I become aware of any definite background noise.) However, it has been theorized that flying-saucer occupants have overcome the effects of inertia. This would allow them to accelerate instantaneously without being crushed from the g force. If the craft was somewhere outside, far away from the hangar structure, when I pushed those buttons, then possibly my unskilled button-punching could have caused the craft automatically to return to a home base.

Those controls might not have been pilot controls; someone else may have been steering the ship from another area. And even if those buttons *were* controls, an override system elsewhere in the craft or even at a main base may have functioned. If the craft did not enter the hangar structure at that point, how did the "man" get there? Maybe he was there all the time.

What was the purpose of the green screen on the chair? What was the significance of the black lines and their relative motions? Why were there no numbers or other denotations accompanying them? Perhaps the lines were some sort of calculation concerning operation or powering of the ship itself. Maybe they were navigational computations. Rather than lines *lacking* numbers or words, they might have even *been* the aliens' way of expressing numbers or words.

The lever on the arm of the chair was on the left, which may be a clue as to the "handedness" of their species, unless they don't possess this neurological feature. The buttons on the right would still require some dexterity. Perhaps they are ambidextrous.

The craft we saw in the woods was only about twenty feet in diameter, while the first craft in which I awoke appeared to be sixty feet in diameter, when I left it. It is doubtful that seven witnesses could have so badly estimated the size. They must have been two different crafts of identical configuration. (Unless they can shrink living beings!) The humanlike creature who took me out of there could have been the pilot of the smaller first craft, which he could have flown from the ground to a rendezvous with the second craft in space. The first craft was of a size that would fit within the lower part of the larger one.

Why the simplicity of the internal features of that second craft? Was it newly made, as yet unfinished? Or were the makers simply extremely practical and undecorative by nature? One person speculated that the strength of the *material* of the ship was unimportant as long as there was a *continuous connection of matter* in its construction. This could be because the strength of the substance would rely on a bonding field of energy that holds it together indestructibly. The continuity of the structure would be necessary for the bonding field to act upon the matter. This idea would explain the lack of visible seams, welds, bolts, or rivets in that craft. For whatever purpose, the craft might have been either machined from (or cast as) a huge single piece of metal, or made from a process involving both casting and machining. What gigantic molds and lathes that would require!

I have heard and learned a few things about UFOs since my experience. There is an odd consistency that runs through nearly all descriptions of UFOs: most are circular in at least one geometrical dimension. A disc, a sphere, and a cylinder all are round or circular in at least one view. Is this one of the factors to which their construction is limited, or can they design them in any shape (aesthetically preferring the round) that pleases them?

Why, in all the consistency of flying-disc descriptions, is there so much variety of the finer particulars? They are as alike and also as different from each other as snowflakes. Could the circular factor be necessitated by limitations imposed by their power sources and functions? But then, why the variety? Can it be accounted for entirely by witnesses' discrepancy from fact? It is quite common for a dozen people witnessing a traffic accident each to report a different version of the incident. Maybe everyone is really seeing basically the same thing, only reporting it differently. But I saw two designs myself; and there seems to be far too much variety in the descriptions to defend the notion of a single design.

Maybe the differences are simply a matter of style, as is the case with our automobiles. Russian spacecraft appear different from ours, but the function is the same. Maybe the differences in shape are due to differences in function, as with a motorcycle, a luxury car, and a dump truck.

The craft in which I regained consciousness was angular, of a dull finish, and sat flat on the surface it was parked upon. The other craft in that larger room were rounded, highly reflective, and seemed to balance on their rounded bottoms. They could have had some sort of magnetic or gyroscopic mechanism holding them up. Or they might have been heavier on the bottom, thereby enabled to balance. They might also have been mechanically supported by attachment to the floor or the wall. Such attachment also could have been the means of entry to the craft, since no hatches were visible. Or the surface might only have appeared unbroken, the edges of a doorway unnoticeable when closed.

What was that hangarlike room in which I saw those crafts? *Where* was it? Was it part of a craft, shaped like a giant cigar, such as sometimes is reported in UFO sightings?

That large hangarlike structure also could have been a building on a planet somewhere! Perhaps here on earth as part of a base, or on one of the planets of our own solar system? Maybe on a planet that no man of earth has ever seen. To look out at the stars at night and think: Which one? If I *was* taken to a place outside the earth, which one of those stars could have a planet revolving around it that I might have actually been taken to?

I actually cannot gain the slightest idea where I was taken to. I have used the terms "human-type" and "human-looking" in referring to one class of beings I encountered. I have variously called the other group beings, creatures, entities, aliens, and humanoids. Actually both types would be properly described as humanoid, having the basic form of a man in terms of arrangement of arms, legs, and facial features. But by "alien" I didn't necessarily mean "extraterrestrial." Nothing positively indicated those crafts or their occupants came from outer space. A number of other theories have been advanced as to their origin. Dr. J. Allen Hynek advanced a hypothesis of an otherdimensional origin. Some people believe that these objects come to us through time! Visitors arriving from the past or future? Perhaps—if time travel is physically possible.

There are also a variety of theories to explain these crafts as of earthly origin. One variation has it that some present earth government, most likely our own, is responsible. This theory has our "black budget" scientists making extraordinary advances far beyond what is generally known, or perhaps successfully deciphering the technology of a crashed craft. In this scenario the crash of an extraterrestrial visitor would be an extremely rare event, perhaps a singularity, with most modern sightings actually being our own earthly creations. In keeping with this premise, all or most "alien" encounters are with robots, actors in special-effects makeup, or the result of hypnotic manipulation by the ordinary humans actually responsible.

This idea has great appeal to many for manifold reasons. Some people view aliens as an impossibility within their own religious cosmology. Some merely don't feel at ease believing in such "monsters." Many view modern science as so complete that current pronouncements on the limitations of speed and distance, as we understand them, they regard as inviolable. There are conspiracy buffs, who like the idea of vast secrecies in matters cosmic as well as mundane. And there may be some who know something we don't.

A few things in my experience lead me to be interested in this theory, too. I admit I would find such an explanation easier to cope with than the alternative. The presence of those human-looking individuals strikes me as out of sync with purely extraterrestrial activity. The odds against such a coincidence of appearance makes me suspicious. Certain things have happened since then to suggest powerful human influence behind the scenes.

Why are the human-looking beings conspicuously absent from my nightmares and flashbacks about the incident? Perhaps my entire conscious memory of what happened during the five days is an implanted memory and not what happened at all. A subsequent event involving military intelligence, which I'll not describe yet, also fits such a scenario.

This is all conjecture, but we can further speculate that perhaps one reason that the Pentagon's internal newspaper, *Pentagram*, gave *Fire in the Sky* a four-star review and called it a "must-see" is because they have a more-than-passing interest in it. Maybe my whole experience is an enormous inside joke to certain people there. I don't know, maybe I'm reaching a bit here. But, it's something I speculate about.

On a recent episode of Dr. Dean Edell's syndicated TV show I saw a magician demonstrate how some con men simulate psychic surgery. Rolling up his sleeves, he displayed his empty hands. After miraculously producing a bloody "tumor" extracted from his volunteer "patient," he revealed how it was done. He'd had the blood and tumor (chicken viscera) hidden inside a false fifth finger. I'd considered myself pretty observant, but I'd not noticed the extra digit inserted in between his other fingers when he had displayed his "empty" hands so openly at the start. I shouldn't feel so taken in—no one in the studio audience had noticed, either, and they were up close and live. The lesson I see in that little demonstration is that we need to scrutinize more than just those parts of our memories which seem hazy or uncertain. Sometimes feeling certain is not a dependable indicator of the reliability of our beliefs.

Another variation of the earth-origin theory is that the alien pilots are the returning explorers of an ancient technological civilization now extinct.

Still another refers to the fact that frequency of modern-day sightings rose dramatically with the end of World War II. This is supposed to suggest that the secretly surviving remnants of a group of Nazi mad scientists have slowly rebuilt their might for the day when their hordes will swoop upon us for the final coup—with Hitler himself in command, no doubt. Good grief!

In the various earth-origin theories of UFOs, their bases are built at the bottom of the oceans, underground, inside a "hollow earth," or on the moon and other planets in this solar system. Could that hangarlike structure actually have been in one of these places?

Almost the first instrument-checking anyone thought of doing was radiation testing. The radiation check made out at Turkey Springs was actually of limited use because it was so belated and incomplete. The prior presence of a strong radiation source might not necessarily result in higher radioactivity of the surroundings once that source is no longer present, unless some quantity of "hot" matter is left behind. The readings on the crewmen's hard hats worn during the sighting remain unexplained. The question is open either way as to whether radiation was present at the site. On the other hand, the electromagnetic readings recorded by Bill Spaulding may—surprisingly—have some validity, since the actual measurements may have been taken by associates of his that may have greater reliability.

The question is, however, why radiation? There seems to be a general, immediate assumption of a nuclear power source for these craft. This might not necessarily be true. Just because nuclear power is our own newest developed source of energy does not mean an advanced technology has not discovered something superior. The presence of radiation at some UFO sightings may mean that at least some of these craft have a nuclear power source. Or it could mean that other functions of the craft are atomically fueled, while the main drive depends on an unknown energy source.

It has been suggested that if these craft require atomic energy in some form, that fact might explain their presence at Turkey Springs. The Mogollon Rim is a big crack in the earth exposing many layers of geological strata. Uranium has been discovered in numerous places on the Colorado Plateau, of which the Rim is a part. The aliens may have been secretly engaged in prospecting or mining of radioactive minerals. But then again, their presence on the Rim may reflect merely the characteristic preference of UFOs for activity in remote areas.

Exactly what *is* their power source? If we could discover it, we too would gain the freedom they might possess to traverse the universe!

While our speculations are running so far afield, consider the interesting observation Mike made during a return to the site we made in 1993. He noticed that the trees nearest where the craft had hovered seemed to have grown *far* more than would have been natural in the intervening seventeen years. Intrigued, Mike went there again after the snow melted to investigate further. His long forest career made him aware that the thinning process alone can induce accelerated growth. But these trees are in the clearing, so no competing trees had been removed from near them. He also noted that, since they grow near the crest of the ridge, their enhanced growth couldn't have been caused by increased rain runoff from a thinned area uphill from them. So he cut down one of the trees in question, selecting one which would have qualified for removal under normal TSI specifications. Examining the pattern of growth rings in the resulting stump, Mike was amazed. Carefully counting back seventeen annual layers, he found that after 1975 the thickness of growth abruptly jumped to four or five times that of any of the tree's previous years!

At the time the craft neared it, the tree, though small, had been fifty-seven years old, but had more than doubled in diameter and nearly tripled in height by the time it was cut. Using the formula ($v = \pi \times r^2 \times h \div 3$) that gives you the volume of a cone (a trunk tapers—it's actually a tall cone rather than a cylinder), Mike calculated an average yearly total increase in wood mass more than thirty-six *times* the average for the fifty-seven rings formed *prior* to 1975. Other trees, located in similar conditions but farther from where the craft descended, showed no phenomenal growth change.

Mike wondered if there might be another explanation. He considered consulting a forestry expert to confirm his observation and calculations. Where could anyone be found who was sufficiently objective, and willing to take the consequences of passing official judgment on such a question? Obviously, pursuing it would be futile. However, the stump and other trees are still there.

With all the upset and hassle and other life-changing experiences I have gone through since November 5, 1975, I have paused to ponder in retrospect the wisdom of my decision to approach that UFO. Those first fateful steps began it all. The one last question the interviewers nearly always ask is: "If you had it all to do over again, would you be so eager to run up close to one of those craft?"

Hindsight is useless. What is done is done. I cannot change it. I have had some pretty rough experiences as a result of that choice, but I have also benefited from the lessons I have learned.

"Well," they persist, "if the exact same circumstances were to present themselves again, would you approach the craft?"

In the past, I've been undecided and given varying replies to this question. However, in my present frame of mind, the answer is a flat *no!* I took a very foolish chance in approaching something so completely unknown. I could have been killed, but I lived to deeply regret it.

"Well, you seem to be fine now. Do you think they had bad intentions?" they ask.

I perceived the entire experience as infinitely terrifying and threatening while it was happening. Yet in hindsight I must say that their intentions seemed at worst neutral, if not exactly benevolent. I was returned safely, when they did not have to return me at all. When I was returned, I was put down close to town, and not left lying in the middle of the road. I was returned when there was no traffic on the road (so I could not flag down a passing motorist for help), but that was probably due to their efforts at concealment. They probably could see from very high up that no headlights were coming from either direction on the highway. My head was placed on my arm with my face turned away from the craft. This could have been a protective measure for me, or they might not have wanted me to see them leave, for some reason. The placing of my body might also have been mere chance.

Although I was psychologically traumatized, I have no conscious memory of being harmed or treated cruelly during my experience. The shock of suddenly seeing such creatures, coupled with my pain, the suffocating sensations, and the perception of being trapped, combined to create an extremely negative reaction. I have no better reason to ascribe to them bad intentions.

However, the absence of evident bad intentions does not necessarily mean they had good intentions. There was a certain degree of high-handedness in their taking me in the first place. I did not exactly ask to go. They may have been merely *presenting* a harmless image. They may actually have sinister intentions in regard to Planet Earth. I am *not* saying that they are definitely bad; it is only a possibility. But a possibility is all there needs to be, in order to advise caution. I would strongly recommend against anyone approaching an alien spacecraft at this stage in knowledge of ufology. Since, without more data, almost anything is possible, they could intend anything—even war or cannibalism!

Many people are predicting greater activity of UFOs in the near future. The trend of increasing reported incidents supports this prediction. I believe that serious large-scale research effort on UFOs is urgently needed. Whether their intentions are good, bad or indifferent, we should not be caught unprepared. Let's take our eyes off the ground and prepare for whatever the future brings. Who knows?—it may also prove greatly rewarding.

Until the publication of my first book, I avoided mentioning something that came out under the hypnosis performed by Dr. James Harder. The reason for my silence was fear. I delayed revealing it while I wrestled with the relative values and dangers involved.

This information came out while I was under a particularly deep segment of the hypnoregressive series. I retained no memory afterward of what happened during that session, and my brother Duane delayed telling me of it because of the potential emotional impact. Later, when I could handle it better, he told me, for my own safety. With the knowledge came his advice to refuse *any* further hypnotic regression.

After Dr. Harder first caused me to relive in greater detail the two hours I consciously remembered, he probed deeper, trying to discover if I had experienced more during the five days than I had recalled.

Duane told me that after a difficult series of psychological maneuvers, Dr. Harder arrived at a mental block in me, enforced by a subconscious warning—or threat—that I would die if regression continued any deeper! I had wondered why those witnessing the session looked at me so oddly after I was brought out of the trance.

Dr. Harder could not precisely determine whether the block is an actual warning, meaning that I would really die, or only a false threat designed to discourage efforts at uncovering blocked memories. Dr. Harder also considered it possible the mental block was the result of my own deep subconscious fears, and not actually the result of an implanted posthypnotic suggestion. So I learned that it was possible that more to my experience existed than I could then recall.

That knowledge weighed upon me in the aftermath of November 5, 1975, perhaps more than any other aspect of the entire experience. The infinite variety of possibilities of what could have happened in those five days really worried me. What if my entire conscious memory was a false implant? Could my nightmares actually contain fragments of surfacing memories? I had had enough struggles in adjusting to the short span I could already consciously recall. I worried what sort of deeply emotional or frightening experiences I would be forced to cope with if I were to suddenly recall everything.

Dr. Harder did not even attempt to continue to probe the nature of the block, let alone try to penetrate it. Dr. Harder and other APRO officials were most considerate of my welfare in this regard. After I learned of it, I asked them not to publicize it, as I felt I would be in danger if it were to become known. Some of them felt I might be overestimating the danger, but nonetheless agreed to confidentiality.

The danger of people knowing about that part of the hypnosis lay in some men's insatiable greed and lust for power. What greater physical power can there be in the universe than the power of interstellar flight? If such men were to believe that I might have hidden knowledge of propulsion or weaponry developed by a superior technology, they might well stop at nothing to get at it—even if I should die in the attempt.

Why then did I finally reveal the fact? It seemed unlikely that such intelligences would ever allow that sort of knowledge to fall into our hands; so they would not have allowed me to learn it in the first place. Even if I had been exposed to the workings of their greatest technological achievements, what would I have gained? If I could lift the hood of my automobile and show the engine to a caveman, could he possibly go home and build one?

But the greatest reason for revealing the deep-trance discovery was the safety doing so automatically brought. There are always a few who learn of the most carefully kept secrets. A state of semisecrecy would have allowed the unscrupulous a freer rein to engage in covert activities. If *everyone* knows about it, it is that much more difficult for an illegal act against me to go unnoticed.

I took steps to ensure my personal safety, but maybe it wasn't really necessary. No one can be hypnotized against his will. I could not even be hypnotized by anyone I did not trust.

I once thought that someday I might get up enough nerve to try hypnosis again. I thought I would initially deal only with the *nature* of the block; to determine the extent of the danger without going too far. That missing time bothered me, because, as Leonard Nimoy said in reference to my experience: ". . . the implications are *enormous.*" Regression seemed the only way to get rid of that feeling. I considered self-hypnosis. But after all these years I have never felt sufficiently moved to go under again. In any event, from the lessons learned in the aftermath of my experience, I think if I actually did uncover previously blocked memories, either by self-hypnosis or spontaneously, it would probably be best never to reveal them publicly.

"Are you afraid they will come back to get you?" Yes and no. I'm not possessed of any mind-consuming phobia that it might happen again. But for a while, when I stood out on my porch on a quiet evening, gazing up at the stars, I would feel a little uneasy and cast an apprehensive glance or two into the shadows.

What I dreaded more than anything was seeing those awful, huge, staring eyes set in those bulging pale-skinned domes. A verbal description or a drawing just cannot duplicate what you would feel if you actually saw one of them. No amount of rationalizing my fear, in realizing its source or telling myself there is no objective reason for it, can neutralize that terror. If you think: "What's so scary about that?" I can only say, just wait until you meet one face-to-face.

I don't mean to give cause for alarm. If anyone is extremely worried about it I could offer advice, tongue in cheek, to carry a camera—that should keep them away. To all appearances, there is little or no danger. It's just that I don't want to be responsible for the consequences if I reassure everyone of harmlessness, and I turn out to be wrong.

Just that one word of caution. However, don't let these doubts overly affect your attitude. Be ready to greet people of other worlds with friendliness, if they ever make open contact with us. They could have much to offer. In the meantime, we need to support better research to find out exactly what we should do to get ready. Should we try to have a stronger defense—or a warmer handshake? Who knows.

Who knows any of the answers to the questions discussed in this chapter. I have probably raised more questions than I have answered with these speculations. Don't forget that they *are* merely speculations—pure conjecture.

Right now we don't have any solid answers. Will we ever?

One of the most frequent questions: What sort of a person was Travis Walton to be the only crewman to get out of the truck and recklessly approach such a dangerous unknown? At that time, exactly that sort.

Michael Rogers, crew-boss said in 1975: "I've been working these woods for over ten years and this is the damnedest thing that ever happened to me!" In 1995 he added: "I've been working these woods for over 30 years and this is <u>still</u> the damnedest thing that ever happened to me!"

Travis Walton: "If I had to do it over again I wouldn't get out of the truck."

Kenneth Peterson: "I saw a bluish light come from the machine and Travis went flying—like he'd touched a live wire!"

First to spot the object was Allen Dalis. "We couldn't believe what was happening. The horror was unreal."

Dwayne Smith: "The UFO was smooth and was giving off a yellowish-orange light."

"That ray was the brightest thing I've ever seen in my whole life!" declares Steve Pierce.

John Goulette states emphatically, "I know what I saw—and it wasn't anything from this earth!"

"I gotta say they passed the (lie detector) tests." When asked about the possibility of the crewmen being intoxicated, Sheriff Marlin Gillespie replied, "I sat in their truck a short time after it happened and talked to each one for a long time. I sure didn't spot anything—and I was looking."

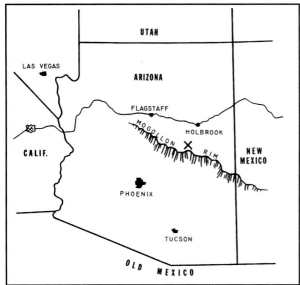

Map of Arizona (X marks abduction site).

This helicopter, along with other aircraft, crisscrossed the rugged Mogollon mountain area as part of a massive manhunt for the missing woodsman.

Arizona Department of Public Safety (state police) polygraph examiner Cy Gilson's report to the Holbrook Sheriff's Office stated, "These polygraph examinations prove that these five men did see some object they believe to be a UFO...." Now in private practice and the top polygraph expert in the state, Gilson later retested several of the crew, including Walton. "Based on the

numerical score of the polygraph charts and the computer based analysis, it is the opinion of this examiner that Mr. (Dalis, Rogers, Walton) was being truthful when he answered these relevant questions."

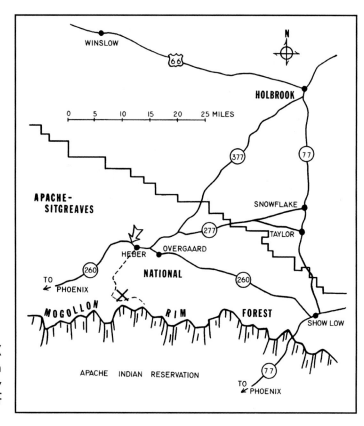

Map of area (X marks abduction site and arrow marks site of return).

Travis Walton and the late L.J. Lorenzen, International Director of the Aerial Phenomena Research Organization and chief field investigator of the Walton case.

Dr. James Harder, then Director of Research for APRO, made it possible through regressive hypnosis for Walton to relive his experiences without undue stress, and was present in the research group to first hear the entire account of Walton's amazing ordeal.

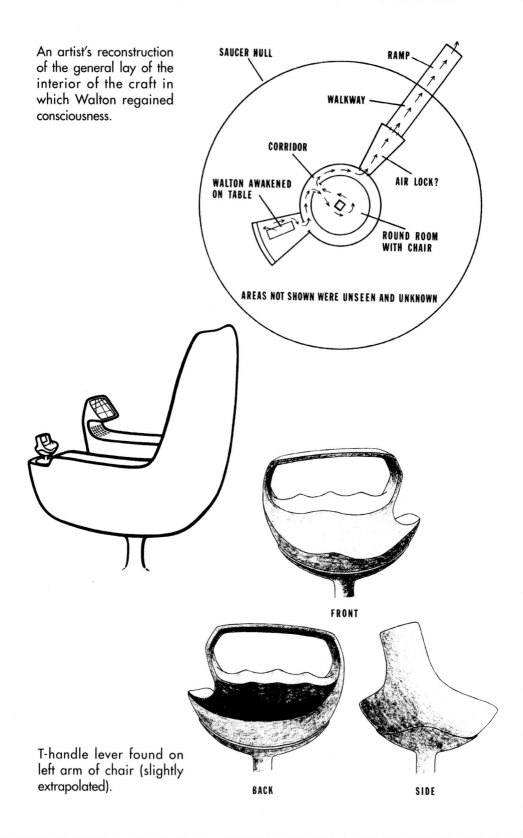

An artist's reconstruction of the general lay of the interior of the craft in which Walton regained consciousness.

SAUCER HULL

RAMP

WALKWAY

CORRIDOR

WALTON AWAKENED ON TABLE

AIR LOCK?

ROUND ROOM WITH CHAIR

AREAS NOT SHOWN WERE UNSEEN AND UNKNOWN

FRONT

BACK

SIDE

T-handle lever found on left arm of chair (slightly extrapolated).

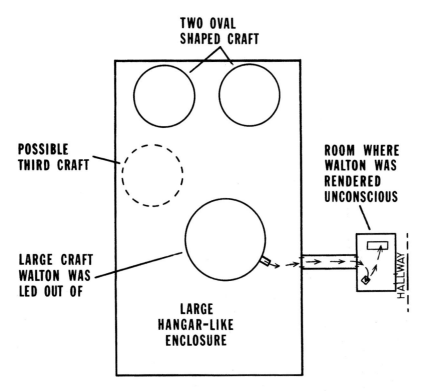

TWO OVAL
SHAPED CRAFT

POSSIBLE
THIRD CRAFT

ROOM WHERE
WALTON WAS
RENDERED
UNCONSCIOUS

LARGE CRAFT
WALTON WAS
LED OUT OF

HALLWAY

LARGE
HANGAR-LIKE
ENCLOSURE

ALL AREAS SURROUNDING WERE UNSEEN AND UNKNOWN

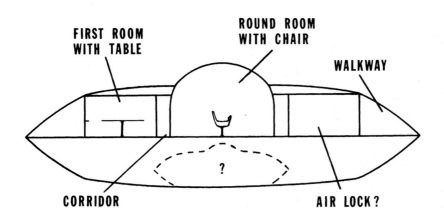

FIRST ROOM
WITH TABLE

ROUND ROOM
WITH CHAIR

WALKWAY

CORRIDOR

AIR LOCK?

?

Saucer cutaway illustrating speculated position of smaller craft.

Dr. R. Leo Sprinkle, APRO's consultant in psychology and Director of Counseling and Testing at the University of Wyoming, interviewed Walton and reviewed the results of psychiatric examinations taken by him. Dr. Sprinkle spoke of "indications of normality" and described a "picture of a healthy young man, with a good sense of self-awareness, a tendency toward skepticism, and an inner strength or emotional stability."

The incident eventually led to a rift between two best friends which lasted for several years.

Dr. J. Allen Hynek, astronomer and prominent ufologist, told newsmen after meeting with Walton that he believes Walton is "not hoaxing" and that, "He has been made the subject of a lot of unnecessary and unfounded accusations."

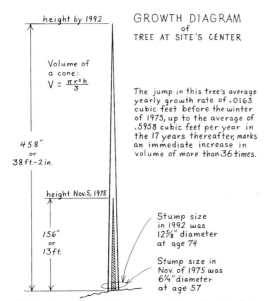

GROWTH DIAGRAM
of
TREE AT SITE'S CENTER

height by 1992

Volume of
a cone:
$$V = \frac{\pi r^2 h}{3}$$

The jump in this tree's average
yearly growth rate of .0163
cubic feet before the winter
of 1975, up to the average of
.5958 cubic feet per year in
the 17 years thereafter, marks
an immediate increase in
volume of more than 36 times.

458"
or
38 ft.-2 in.

height Nov. 5, 1975

156"
or
13 ft.

Stump size
in 1992 was
12⅝" diameter
at age 74

Stump size in
Nov. of 1975 was
6¼" diameter
at age 57

Total volume of first 57 years growth = .93 cubic feet
Average yearly growth rate first 57 years =.0163 cubic feet
  (after subtracting first 57 years growth from total):
Total volume of next 17 years growth = 10.13 cubic feet
Average yearly growth rate next 17 years =.5958 cubic feet

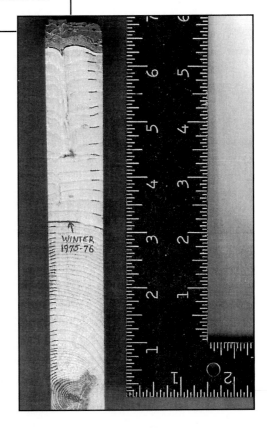

WINTER
1975-76

From left to right: Travis, DB Sweeney, Georgia Emelin and Dana, at dinner on location in Oregon.

The reception Travis and Dana received on the set warmed quickly as the cast and crew came to know them.

James Garner, Dana and Travis on the set of *Fire in the Sky*. Garner is as likeable off screen as on.

Rome. *Fire in the Sky* was well received by audiences all over the world.

Travis Walton: "All I ask is for an objective considera-tion of all the evidence. Anyone who won't do that isn't really entitled to an opinion."

DB Sweeney, after varied rolls in films such as "Eight Men Out" and "The Cutting Edge", plays the philosophi-cal but overly curious Travis Walton in *"Fire in the Sky"*.

Mike Rogers, logging on the north Kaibab above the Grand Canyon.

Robert Patrick's portrayal of the liquid metal cyborg assassin opposite Arnold Schwarzenegger's *Terminator* was indelible but, not to be type-cast, his warm interpretation of salt-of-the-earth crewboss and family man, Mike Rogers, was every bit as convincing.

Travis Walton, Leonard Nimoy and L.J. Lorenzen on the set at Wolper Studios for filming of the series pilot, *The Unexplained*. One of the most impressive accounts he has heard to date comes from Travis Walton, Nimoy said. "It's a bizarre story, but after speaking with him over a period of several hours, I felt he was being truthful."

Polygraph examiner and former Miami Police detective-sergeant George Pfiefer administered a test to Travis Walton. "After a very careful analysis of the polygrams produced, there are no areas left unresolved and it is the opinion of this examiner that Travis Walton has answered all questions in a manner that he himself is firmly convinced to be truthful regarding the incident commencing 11/5/75."

PART 3

Latter Days

CHAPTER 13

Aftermath

Mente tamen, quae sola loco non exulat.
("The mind alone cannot be exiled.")

—Ovid

What happens in the wake of events as extraordinary and profound as those of November 1975? After such an intense period of nonstop assault on the sensibilities, can life *ever* be as it was before?

At first, I was in perpetual doubt as to whether or not I was even going to get through it. I lived each day, each hour, from minute to minute. It was burden enough to cope with that by itself, without looking beyond.

One sunny fall day I was a young, single, devil-may-care guy full of plans, relishing the prospect of tomorrow. The next thing I knew, everything was in doubt: my future, prior relationships, people I'd thought I could count on, institutions I'd taken for granted, my place in society, and, right at the beginning, even the reality of my own perceptions.

Day and night I was wired tight. Adrenaline surged constantly. The images of those recent traumatic events were constantly in my mind's eye, waking and sleeping. When I *could* sleep, vivid but chaotic dreams woke me nightly. I had a tremendous amount of inner processing, sorting, confronting, accepting, and adjusting to do. To do that, one needs enough time and peace, enough space and sleep.

And I wasn't getting it. The spectrum of reactions to what happened— good, bad, or indifferent—kept me constantly off balance. There was a constant torrent of things to deal with. I had so much coming at me so fast, that coping with this overwhelming cacophony took everything I had. It seemed as if almost everyone wanted a piece of me—sometimes literally.

I was afraid of what I couldn't remember. And I was afraid it would happen again. Or maybe government agents would come and take me and subject me to mental, maybe even physical, dissection. What if I came down with some bizarre infection unknown to human medical science? What if I began suffering weird effects from breathing that strange atmosphere? What if I started exhibiting symptoms of severe radiation damage? What if I just couldn't cope with all of this?

I can laugh at such fears now. But at the time, that natural faith we carry, that the familiar and conventional will naturally be there the next time we look, had for me been severely shaken. Fortunately, years of thinking and living in a more normal world have restored that confidence to me.

Adding to the pressures on me was my strategy of trying to present the outward appearance of being in control. Going on as if nothing was wrong did have a steadying effect, but it also led many people who might have been more helpful to assume I was already on my way to recovery.

In spite of the fact that it all seemed to be nearly too much for me, I went it alone. I navigated that whole period without professional help or counseling of any kind. Why? Partly because my family are a pretty self-reliant bunch. Partly because I didn't believe there was anyone in the counseling or psychiatric field who had anything in the standard framework of their training or experience that would remotely equip them to handle something so extraordinary. An example illustrating this was Dr. Jean Rosenbaum's conclusions. He was more disposed to perceive the matter as fitting into a standard category with which he was familiar, than to try to apply his experience and knowledge to something outside his paradigm. There was nowhere to turn. So, internally, I was on my own.

However, I can't say there was no help at all around me. My family stood by me. And so did some of my friends, but most of all there was my sweet Dana. She didn't have any answers to the profound questions, she didn't have any special psychological insight. I'm sure she often felt at a loss to know what to say and do. Perhaps at times she even felt pushed into the background by the incident, from the way some people approached us. But she was there for me, with her loving understanding, centeredness, and warm support. Her grandmother's simple, earthy, caring, small-town ways had their echo in her. So she became my anchor, my one rock in that sea of chaos.

I went back to church for a while. But rather than finding spiritual answers there, I encountered a microcosm of my situation within the wider community. So again I was on my own. As vast and mysterious as the cosmos is, ultimate religious truth lies far above any of this—or the world in which it happened. I am not saying the event lies *outside* of religious considerations, but that it's just one more element within the grand scheme of things. That which encompasses and supersedes everything, must naturally do so to truly *everything*. People too often make exclusively religious interpretations of things of this nature. I suppose this has a lot to do with their previous orientation to life in general. I did a lot of very deep searching in the religious area, but my earlier outlook had emphasized more of a scientific or philosophical approach. So that's the kind of sense I tried to make of this experience to a great extent.

Popular wisdom has it that denial is not a good coping strategy; but as a temporary measure it worked for me. I pushed the experience and its aftermath into the background. I boxed it up, put it aside and went on with my life. As time went on, I pulled things out of that box one at a time, dealing with them at my own pace. Eventually I worked up to returning to work in the woods. I spent a lot of time alone, laboring under the sun with ax or chainsaw in hand. The work itself didn't demand a lot of concentration, so my mind was free to ponder and reflect, accept and adjust.

There were no stages or definite turning points for me, except the initial hypnosis session. My recovery was a long, gradual process—so evenly evolving and natural that I realize it most resembles the changes which come with life, simply living, the personal growth of maturity. And like that sort of growth, it continues to this day.

In my earlier account I tried to pass off, to minimize the negative reaction I was experiencing; I was still in the middle of it and I hoped to avoid making worse what was already bad enough. During the peak of the feeding frenzy, the press had gone for the kill. Once the tone was set it became a free-for-all. It's a familiar aspect of human nature that such a pattern determines the fate of certain unfortunates in school and work situations. I didn't want to create an atmosphere in which the dimmer minds among those around me would be incited to such a mob mentality.

One of the strategies I use most to get a handle on complex matters is to step outside myself and the situation mentally, then try to take an objective overview. When I do this concerning everything involving the UFO incident, I continually think I have arrived, that I can finally see it for itself without distortion by personal referents. I do this only to find I need to step back again. And again. Each time seeing more, realizing a wider perspective, but each time coming to sense the existence of a larger frame of reference.

It's like the reverse of one of those pictures on the wall, which is a picture of the whole scene including the picture on the wall . . . and so on. If we look first at one in the series, we ask, when can we finally see the whole? This is like the converse of widened perspective—deepened introspection. I, however, of course believe this apparent paradox arises from the nature of consciousness and growth, rather than anything unique to the incident of 1975.

I was adjusting to more than the experience itself. I was adjusting to people's reactions to the incident and their altered perceptions of me—everybody's—or so it seemed from what the world news media presented. It's no exaggeration to say that the human reaction gave me as much to cope with as the incident itself. Which is saying a good deal more than most people realize.

There were ironic parallels between the incident and its aftermath. In both I felt powerless to control my destiny, to affect my condition. In both I felt victimized. In both I felt inspected, on display, like a bug in a jar. I couldn't go anywhere without the stares, the pointing, the smirks, and the whispers. I often felt singled out, made to feel like some kind of sideshow freak. Expectation of seeing something bizarre was so strong I would hear of people who didn't know me reinterpreting some perfectly normal behavior of mine. People would walk up and talk to me, and as they talked, seemed to be looking for something, scanning for who knows what. They seemed to study me with a distracted air, as if thinking of something other than the conversation.

If they expected to find a pair of antennae sprouting from my head or perhaps some odd green patches showing through on my skin, they were disappointed. I'm not sure what artifact or thrill was anticipated, but they didn't seem satisfied.

People see what they want to see. Introducing anyone to an average group primed with stories arbitrarily attributing various characteristics to the newcomer is certain to result in that person being perceived as amply confirming those preconceptions. Regardless of their actual behavior or traits, the tendency would be for them to be seen as hostile, friendly, nerdy, cool, dumb, smart, or whatever was earlier described.

I was aware that it was only human nature, but that didn't make me like it any better. So, for someone used to living by his own concepts and standards, it was especially demeaning to be put in the ironic position of having to make sure my every public act was more normal than "normal."

Although people were serious in inquiring whether my experience had left me with any impairments or enhanced abilities, in that environment it was very important to do nothing to confirm notions of being anything but straight down the middle of the road, bland, neutral, boring, *normal*. Anything less might get me carried off by a torch-carrying mob wielding pitchforks, to be stoned, dissected, or burned at the stake. Well, at least metaphorically speaking.

My determination to ignore it all and continue on with a normal life was continually challenged. Whenever my detachment lulled me into believing for a moment that I could blend back in, someone would walk up and, with what they must have imagined was marvelous cleverness, ask some sly, insinuating question I'd heard a dozen times before.

Occasionally people would say something like: "Well, I heard that they proved [some baseless charge or typical rumor]." I'd turn and ask, "Just exactly what do you personally know about it that you could be sure of? Anything at all you'd feel safe to call a fact?" Their stammering admissions were all the demonstration I needed to make my point. Opportunities for repartees were rare, though. Usually I heard about such comments secondhand, after the fact.

That's okay. Those scenes revealed the measure of those people, not me. I won't say that thought gave enough consolation to make their attitudes not matter. But I could take it. What would really enrage me was something like that directed at Dana or one of my kids. The kids weren't even born before the incident. To this day, a dig at them in that vein will elicit from me a quick and decidedly non-passive reply.

For the most part I became inured to it. I withdrew to a detached existence, a life apart. I suppose you could say I was "alienated." Later on, I wasn't so affected that I couldn't see the humor in some of the situations arising from the Turkey Springs incident. One joke made the rounds: "You hear they proved Travis was telling the truth? When he came back they found a Mars bar in his pocket." There was also the obvious "Milky Way" variation. School kids chanted a singsong on the playground: *"Flying saucers, UFO, where did Travis Walton go?"* That was embellished to: *"Travis Walton, UFO. Where did all the spaceships go? Travis ate 'em, now he's back. Now he has to take a spaceship crap!"*

Great humor, eh? Actually the big motivator for such reactions, humor included, is fear. People often resort to humor regarding things they fear, especially when it's something over which they have little control. Witness the topics of the standup comic: crime, the boss, death and taxes. For soldiers, the enemy, who might end their life, is a principal butt of jokes.

Another dimension to fear is the fear of ridicule. The irony of bigoted thinking is that the put-downs directed at the out-group are really a nervous attempt at a hollow sort of self-validation. Foment derision to divert it, lest someone make you an object of it.

Related to that insight, and particularly disappointing, was how some people, who treated us with normal friendliness and respect in private, became cool and distant (if they didn't pretend not to see us altogether) when we encountered them in public.

And there were a couple of matters when I had good reason to believe certain authorities didn't act with objectivity because I was involved, even though my role in the situation was clearly on the side of justice. In one case I stopped a grown man who was beating a third-grade boy bloody for taunting his children on the way home from school. Authorities had the boy's testimony, his wounds, and my testimony. Imagine my feelings when the investigating officer couldn't get her superiors to do anything about it—and we all knew why.

Then there were those who, in the normal, day-to-day course of human interactions, would occasionally perceive themselves at odds with me over some unrelated issue. So, of course, they would immediately bring up the UFO incident as their ad hominem trump card, behind my back, of course.

It would be easy for someone in my position to blame all life's little setbacks on such discrimination. But to do so would be a cop-out, making unjustified excuses for one's own natural shortcomings, or ordinary bad luck. Under the circumstances I believe I've done well not to fall for using such a perpetually ready excuse. Although there were times I didn't get the job when I was the more qualified, you can't assume. It's inevitable that not everything will go one's way.

Reactions weren't all negative; but even positive reactions could present problems. I would get calls at odd hours of the night, from people who simply felt it monumentally important—they weren't sure why—to relate to me a sighting they had made ten years earlier of a strange, moving point of light in the night sky. Perfect strangers would call in the middle of dinner and expect me to let it get cold while I gave them a detailed account of my experience—apparently merely for their private entertainment. A number of calls were more than a little strange.

On the other hand, many individuals called whom I was glad to come to know. Some are good friends still. And to be contacted by old friends with whom I'd lost contact was yet another small recompense, a lighter thread in the lining of that dark cloud hovering over my days. My life was not without happiness; some aspects have been richly rewarding.

Nevertheless, calls became a big problem. I still felt it was very important to get the truth out, but to try to do so one person at a time would've burned me out without ever accomplishing it. I had the phone disconnected, went without one for years. My sense of community was reduced further still.

Every time Mike Rogers was interviewed, and sometimes when asked about it by people he knew, the question was raised: "How could you just drive off and leave your best friend to his fate at the mercy of such a threat?" Certain members of my family made known their strong feelings about it.

Mike was having a big load of guilt dumped on him. Plus, it was obvious he was being hard on himself about it. He became overly sensitive to criticism from me on unrelated matters. He kept saying I was "accusing" him. I think that in his mind he was projecting onto me the reproach he was getting from others. I personally don't remember ever verbalizing such blame. In fact, I got the strong impression that he blamed me for many of the troubles that came his way because of the incident. "If you weren't so reckless, if you hadn't gotten out of the truck, if you'd come back when everyone yelled at you to, none of this would be happening."

Admittedly there was some truth to that, but I didn't take kindly to the manner in which the point was made. Things deteriorated between me and my best friend of many years—my wife's brother. There was a blowup. We hardly spoke to each other for a number of years.

I don't know if it was solely to avoid me, but Mike started not showing up for family gatherings. Mike's family has always been much closer to each other emotionally than mine; they regularly get together for birthdays and holidays. But Mike started to withdraw, to become an emotional hermit. One more major brick in my growing wall of isolation—and one for him.

In 1977 I wrote my first book, for its therapeutic effect and with an eye toward accomplishing in a single effort more than I ever could with thousands of interviews.

For a long time the media kept up a steady stream of inquiries. Curious people would seek me out. Snowflake is a bit off the beaten path, but that didn't seem to slow them. Day after day, mail from around the world poured in. The phone only stopped ringing when I had it taken out.

When I finally consented to interviews, I began to feel like a broken record, I repeated the same words so many times. Most people were understanding of my need to get away from all that, apologizing profusely, thanking me for my time. But they still kept coming. "Just one more."

They didn't seem to realize that for me, retelling it was like reliving it. No matter how many times I went through the memory, it never failed to knot my gut, cause me to break into a cold sweat. I would feel wrung-out afterward. I felt it important that the world be made aware of some things. But I often wondered if it was worth the price.

I wasn't very sophisticated about the media. Before November 1975 I didn't know the meaning of "tabloid," "ambush interview," "green room," or "trial by media." My naiveté destined me for some exploitation and a few hatchet jobs. I learned about "ventriloqual attacks," where, to preserve the illusion of neutrality, journalists in a face-to-face interview express their own accusations as coming from a vague "they."

A few media pros, like Richard Robertson or Sam Lowe of the *Phoenix Gazette* or many others I should name, had the integrity even when they took a skeptical stance to present the facts as fairly and objectively as they could.

Then there were other persons who hit the lows of journalistic ethics. Those who, in the name of "balance," merely listed some of my critics' charges, without printing the solid refutation of which they were perfectly aware.

That was mild compared to some behavior of media people I could name. People who made false promises just to get cooperation. People who looked me straight in the eye and promised there would be no slant, no last-minute intercutting of "sniper" viewpoints, in their interviews. People who would include surprise guests to attack me. People who would pretend to be completely sympathetic and in agreement with my statements, then turn right around and write attacks they *knew* to be false because I had shown them the proof. People who use "monster lighting" and photos taken so close, with a specific lens, there was actually a pronounced parabolic "fish-eye" distortion to the pictures, where the nearest features of the face appear to bulge huge, the periphery shrunken. Such photos appeared only in the "hatchet job" articles, so it was no accident.

These people managed to transform my naive openness into cynical wariness. If such laxity wasn't their habit, perhaps the subject matter made them feel they could abandon their usual journalistic standards. Perhaps mainstream media people, viewing the topic as one for the tabloids, felt justified in behaving like tabloid writers. For a time I refused to give interviews. One more addition to my feelings of isolation and estrangement.

As I wrote the foregoing passage, an incident occurred to really drive home to me how powerfully people's predispositions dominate their perceptions. After a discussion with a visitor to our home about always telling the truth, my children were asked to summarize the message and tell why lying is so destructive. After their remarks, with my usual abstract conceptualizing I added something like, "Yes, you should never speak untrue things because it can go out into the world, maybe far, far away, and you can never reach everyone who might have heard it. And you can never know how the lie might change people before they hear the truth, if they ever do." Our visitor's pause, his sidelong glance from under arched brows, accompanied by a deeply drawn breath—the "ahem" look—momentarily puzzled me. Then I realized he thought I had unconsciously "slipped," that I was speaking of myself, not my detractors and the media! How can one reply to the unspoken? Confused, I groped unsuccessfully for words, then realized in frustration there was nothing I could say which wouldn't deepen his conviction. I'm sure my expression only further confirmed to him his assumption.

One community might have welcomed me with open arms: the UFO community. I was repeatedly invited to attend their gatherings, but I rarely accepted. That wasn't a put-down of those people. It's just that I'd had enough of the controversy, the reaction, the subject. My best coping strategy was simply to try to get on with my life and live it as normally as possible.

I sold off my hot cars and my Chevy Nomad ("the Wanderer"—my first name comes from an ancient word for *traveler*). I kept a modest four-door sedan with a six-cylinder, a Mercury Comet. (Now come on, lots of cars have such names, and most of the cars I've owned have come to me by chance circumstance rather than conscious choice.)

I became quite conservative in my conduct. No motorcycles. No more risky stuff. The car doesn't move till everyone is buckled up. My driving record in the last twenty years has been perfect—how many people can say that? I am one of the very few fathers who has never missed a parent-teacher meeting. Even when I have had to take off work to attend, I've almost never missed one of my kids' play or performance. I really turned inward in the sense of focusing myself on family, home, yard, and my personal studies (which *haven't* included ufology).

If I had had any illusions it would all go away if I ignored it long enough, it was a futile effort. I found out that when I turned down requests for interviews; often it didn't kill the project, it merely changed it for the worse. There would be many more errors and a much more negative slant than if I had simply agreed.

I consented to several television appearances where I met a few famous people. What with finding our names all through the media, one might expect the whole business would go to our heads, that we'd start acting different and putting on airs. So what effect did becoming famous (or notorious in some eyes) have on us personally? The surprising answer is—almost none. All seven of us were too totally blown away by the impact of the experience itself to be much starstruck by the sudden worldwide interest.

I've been so proud that none of it had changed me in that way, but heck, it didn't have much apparent effect on the other six, either. Of course, they haven't had nearly the experience I did, but I have to hand it to those guys. They eventually got on with their lives pretty much as if Turkey Springs had never happened. So why should I act as if it had made *me* special? The extraordinary thing was the event itself. I'm only the man it happened to.

Although it didn't confer on me an exaggerated sense of myself, to travel to a big-city television station and see some of those famous persons was a novel experience. Meeting the hosts was something quite by itself—but knowing how any other ordinary red-blooded American male would have felt to be asked to sit in the very same chair that seconds earlier had been warmed by Raquel Welch—well, maybe you can see why I was proud to have remained unaffected. I met soccer star Pele in the green room at *Good Morning, America*. I met some child stars whose mixture of precociousness and a saccharine, typically-adorable-kid act seemed a little incongruous. All this was long before *Fire in the Sky*.

It was particularly intriguing to me that a couple of stars I had occasion to spend time with were persons who had special meaning to me. Of all the hundreds of celebrities I might have encountered, why did I meet those whose work had made such a difference to me? I had dinner and spent an evening with Cliff Robertson, whose Oscar-winning performance in the movie *Charly* and role as J.W. Coop constituted only part of his significance to me. His principled stand on certain real-life issues was the main basis of my great respect for him.

Then there was Leonard Nimoy. I was never a Trekkie (oops, excuse me, I mean Trekk*er*) and, believe it or not, I'm probably one of the few Americans who has yet to see every last episode of the perpetually syndicated and rerun original television series, *Star Trek*.

But Nimoy's characterization of the eminently logical Mr. Spock was something I believe made a positive mark on an entire culture. It gave embodiment (largely lacking elsewhere) to a respectable role model for young people with an interest in logic and reason. Only my boyhood reading of the Sherlock Holmes stories compares in personifying those ideals for me. What could a culture such as ours need more for the upcoming generation than popular paragons of the intellect, charismatic mentors of the mind? It is said that one of the most telling measures of a society is who it chooses for its heroes.

Because of our work together on the set of *The Unexplained*, I had a chance to talk awhile with Nimoy, which was quite (forgive me) fascinating. He doesn't remotely resemble the emotionless being of his alter ego. (I later learned that besides his success as a director of some heartfelt movies, Nimoy is the author of a number of volumes of exquisitely sensitive verse.)

I suppose our meeting made more of an impression on him than I expected. Over two years later, after hosting a program that included many episodes concerning UFO incidents, he was interviewed concerning his views on UFOs. He was quoted as saying that mine was one of the most impressive accounts he'd ever heard. "It's a bizarre story, but after speaking with him over a period of several hours, I felt he was being truthful."

Subsequent to her being taken into custody, I received a postcard with a brief greeting signed, *Patty Hearst*. After hearing of some supposed connection between her and basketball star Bill Walton (no known relation to me), and the fact that the card came postmarked from where she was at the time, I didn't think it too improbable that it was genuine. However, I've never had the handwriting authenticated.

When world heavyweight boxing champion Muhammad Ali moved his training camp to this area nine months after the UFO incident, most locals bought the explanation he was trying to get away from the crowds of gawkers and hustlers hanging around his Michigan facility. The gregarious, exhibitionistic, microphone-devouring, camera-mugging, "most-recognized face on the planet" Ali, seeking to get away from all the attention? If you believe that, there's a bridge you'd probably buy.

Perhaps Ali, master of media, was wise enough not to tell reporters what really brought him here. Of all the places in the world to train (and he could afford to go literally *anywhere*), would he choose the Mogollon Rim area solely for its fresh air and scenery? Maybe so. This is the place, out of any, where *I* choose to live.

One place he showed up a few months before he arrived here was Phoenix—at the boxing gym where my brother Duane trained—looking for sparring partners. Ali wanted somebody quick and with a style similar to his upcoming opponent, Jimmy Young. If you wanted quick, Duane was the man to see—or try to see. He could literally jab twice in less time than most men took trying to block the first one. But Duane was astounded at Ali's stamina. He'd spar Duane, then each of the others in the gym, and get back around to Duane—over and over—none the worse for wear. On April 30, 1976, in Landover, Maryland, naturally Jimmy Young lost a unanimous decision to Ali.

In August Ali came here, set up his training facilities at the Show Low Airport (in the very airplane hangar where I had worked to pay for my private-pilot training), and began training there for his September 28, 1976, match with Ken Norton.

I later learned Muhammad Ali had been deeply into UFOs for years, and that he'd had distinct sightings, which others had witnessed, prior to each of his major fights. He told reporter Timothy Becklay he'd seen UFOs eighteen times. One of his most sensational sightings was over his mountaintop training camp in Pennsylvania, as he prepared for a bout with George Foreman. Another of his better sightings was in the mid-sixties, while driving along the New Jersey Turnpike, when an enormous UFO with glowing portholes buzzed his car. He said: "The thing was so huge that I could see its shadow on the highway—it covered both lanes."

Ali's famous Central Park sighting was reported in one newspaper account to have occurred in 1971, and 1967 in a television account (unless there were two sightings). The sighting was witnessed by his entire entourage. His trainer, Angelo Dundee, was quoted as saying, "It was a real big sucker." Sports reporter Bill Verigan: "We all saw them. There were several of them up in the sky . . . they were objects . . . they were lights. . . . It hovered for what seemed like a very long time, which was perhaps a minute or less and then just, whoosh, disappeared behind the buildings. Ali was *extremely* excited. He started screaming, I can remember, he kept yelling, 'It's the Mothership! It's the Mothership!' "

Angelo Dundee confirmed separately: "Muhammad was *deep* into the Mothership routine, because I heard it many, many times, many, many places." Angelo Dundee was a close enough friend to be able to joke about it, but not *too* much. "I said, 'Muhammad, when those guys come down, please let me meet 'em, I want to manage one of those, train one of those guys'—'cause it would of been a first. So, we made a little joke out of it and my own *little* one. But he was *serious*. Forget about joke, he felt and *believed* something was following him."

Reporter Bill Verigan said: "He apparently believed that this was perhaps the coming of a messenger in one of these spacecrafts."

Ali believed if he remained faithful and humble he would continue to be blessed as one chosen to use his status to achieve his earthly missions, that Allah would continue to smile upon his victories.

Muhammad Ali was quoted saying: "The late Elijah Muhammad, my religious leader, said the first reference ever made about UFOs was Ezekiel's biblical description of a wheel within a wheel. He also says there is a ship known as the Mother of Planes that is a half-mile long. I think this is what I observed over my training camp."

A few things happened while he was here that don't warrant mention here, but maybe living for a few weeks in accommodations far less luxurious than he was accustomed to, and training in an old airplane hangar, were worth being able to jog through this remote forest for some fresh air and scenery. And, oh yes, getting away from those pesky crowds. But then, he was continuously thronged throughout his stay, and the sociable champ seemed to enjoy every minute of it.

Now, I know I've said I didn't see a necessary connection between religion and UFOs, but apparently Ali does. Who am I to say? Maybe Ali knows something I don't. After all, he won that September 28, 1976, fight against Ken Norton, too.

Not all contact with celebrities was positive. I was scathingly snubbed by one particular prime-time macho television star. I never even spoke to him, but he refused to share a green room with me and demanded that his seg-ment of the show be moved to precede rather than follow mine. *C'est la vie.*

In the makeup room on another show, a certain beautiful young televi-sion starlet gushed easy friendliness, adoringly held my baby son Cliff, and gave us an autographed publicity photo of herself. Later, back at my hotel, I stepped into an elevator. I hadn't known where she was staying, so I was surprised when I glanced over and saw her with her publicist. We were the only ones in there, but, having heard how stars hate to be bothered during their off hours, I didn't stare, and said nothing. When we exited the eleva-tor, I let them go first. As we headed toward the lobby, I heard her warble the *Twilight Zone* theme music to her companion, glancing back at me with a mocking laugh. Ouch.

The fact that I can bring myself to relate such incidents is a measure of how far I've come. I used to get really depressed after some of the worse ones.

People who did know me well weren't a problem. I don't want to seem boastful, but actually the people who know me best make it clear they view me as an exceptionally rational person. They seek my opinion on their most difficult problems. Time after time, people who get to know the real me, end up telling me they were really surprised I was nothing like what they had expected. Also, again and again, journalists who do an in-depth inter-view say the same thing—not at all what they expected.

In fact, I don't recall a single person getting to know me and going away *less* believing than before. This is often the case when the subject isn't even discussed (I never bring it up on my own). Even when it is discussed, I never try to convince anyone: I just lay it on the table for them to take or leave as they see fit. I do vigorously rebut all false charges of my critics if they are brought up, but that is another matter. Biding is not ceding. Neutrality is not passivity.

Such people need not specify what they mean by "what they expected." I already know only too well. To a great extent I've come to terms with dis-belief itself. After all, this is amazing stuff. Why shouldn't people initially have difficulty accepting it?

An unexpected side effect of disbelief, and even of belief, is one of my biggest troubles. It might surprise people to learn that one thing that has brought a lot of frustration and pain into my life since 1975, is that the in-cident has essentially made the real me invisible.

How can the subject of so much media attention possibly feel unseen? Well, I certainly don't mean in the public sense, because I avoided most media requests. In that sense, I'm a private type of person who would cer-tainly have felt more comfortable with much *less* of that sort of interest.

What I mean by becoming invisible is being unable to get through to people as an ordinary guy on a personal level. My first contact with each new person is completely dominated by their perception of the incident, filtered through the distorting lens of their beliefs about what happened to me as a young man.

Positive reactions have this effect as much as negative ones. The incident could have happened to *anyone*. I haven't done anything special or heroic. I don't want to be regarded as a hero or celebrity for this, any more than I want to be viewed as a deceiving rascal or some crackpot space-cadet. I want to be judged on the basis of what I *am*, not what's happened to me.

This was the final dimension to my isolation. I really simply gave up on forming positive new relationships with people, not because I didn't yearn for such contact, but because it was futile. The pain of estrangement was less than the pain of seeing someone who could have became a friend not become one, only because he couldn't see the real me. I fell back on the vague hope that "maybe someday things will be different."

For one who was told all his life he could become just about anything, who once felt the whole world was open to him, it was particularly crushing finally to come to the stark realization that, on account of a single decision, certain avenues of life were forever closed to me.

However, it's always best to look for the positive in whatever negatives we might encounter in life. Even in the worst circumstances, with no apparent good in the events themselves, one can at least look for the lesson to be learned. So, unexpectedly, I've grown gradually to see some positive aspects in the aftermath. I've mentioned the insight into humanity I've gained. I've broadened my perspective, looking at small events more in terms of the overall scheme of things.

All those benefits are, it bears repeating, an outgrowth of the immense isolation—the feeling of being set apart—I've endured all these years. I suppose it's only natural I would take this view of the matter, because I've always used a similar mental technique in trying to make sense of complex problems. As I described earlier, "stepping outside" is a way of getting a clearer picture of things. It's like stepping between two mirrors hung directly opposite each other, and seeing—ahead and behind—two series of identical, regressing images vanishing into an infinite series of successively smaller likenesses. The key landmark, we come to realize, is ourselves, the very self I had sought to momentarily step outside of.

In the struggle to survive and adapt, my isolation became a gigantic, not-so-temporary version of my earlier reasoning strategy. I believe that being on the outside looking in has given me exceptional opportunities to see from a more objective, realistic perspective—and, more importantly, the crucial capacity to comprehend the pricelessness of such insight.

I'm the only one of the seven who still lives in Snowflake. Most of them left for far-flung places almost immediately after the incident. People have often asked why, in the face of such reactions, didn't Dana and I move away? The answer is that, in the first place, I don't think the reaction here in Snowflake was much different from what it would have been anywhere in the nation. And secondly, even if it would have been easier elsewhere, I'm not inclined to run from difficulty. It's usually better to confront things and let the chips fall where they may. Not that we didn't seriously consider the option a few times. But my wife's roots run pretty deep here; and I could never live with the feeling I'd run out with my tail down.

What about the other guys? Has the incident's aftermath had similar effects on them? Most of the guys say they've been ribbed about it on occasion, but were basically able to get on with their lives without too much negative impact.

I recently saw Allen Dalis face-to-face for the first time since right after it happened. Allen had reached the culmination of his life's problems, unrelated to the incident, and wound up serving a couple of years of a five-year sentence for robbery. Detractors tried to make the most of this turn of events with a contemptible shot at "guilt by association," which recoiled on them. But it was Allen who turned himself in. He knew he needed help for his personal problems, so as part of his rehabilitation he came clean, confessed to everything he'd ever done. (By the way, if our story had been false, he'd have confessed that, too.) Allen's counselors reported he'd made very good progress, and he earned early release. Allen says he's changed his ways and hasn't had any major trouble since. He emphasizes that he's paid his debt to society, it's a thing of the past. He wishes everyone would simply forget it.

In fairness and common sense, if we don't give people another chance, we remove the motivation for them to reform. Allen is at present over in western Arizona, back working in the woods for part of the season and as an auto mechanic the rest of the year. He says he's settled down and is finally considering marriage in the near future. Something else surprising: Allen has displayed a remarkable talent for art! I'm not talking about merely drawing well. His work is actually of professional caliber. None of us had any idea Allen had that in him.

Before I continue with what's been happening over the years to the rest of the crew, I'd like to pause here to commend my coworkers on their courage in returning to the site of the incident to search for me. It's totally understandable to me that they argued about whether they should go back. Many people would have just kept going. If they *had* continued into town to get help, many people would not have done more.

No one can fairly criticize them for their emotional breaks, nor for their initial action of fleeing the craft. I would challenge the bravest man to react differently under the same conditions. They had no weapons. What could they do? Get out of the pickup and throw rocks at the craft? From what they describe they had good reason to believe me dead; to attempt a rescue at that point wouldn't have been sensible. Any other course of action would have seemed not courageous, but suicidal.

I can only thank them for their concern and the disregard for their own personal safety they displayed in returning. All six of these men deserve respect, not criticism, for how they behaved under extreme circumstances.

John, Dwayne, and Steve refusing to return that night with the sheriff's search party in no way diminishes their courage earlier that evening. However, I would like to extend an extra measure of thanks to the other three for going back again, so soon, in the dark.

Allen Dalis might have seemed to be one of the most terrified as the crew fled. But overcoming his fear to volunteer to return with the lawmen makes that much greater of an impression. Ken Peterson and Mike seem to have acted most consistently with what they felt they had to do. But this is also to be expected, since they were the oldest, most responsible men on the crew.

Steve Pierce has withdrawn from the whole issue more than the others, but that may have been the wisest course anyway. He doesn't like to talk about it, and I think I know where he's coming from. His first marriage broke up over difficulties typical of couples who marry young. (But he's remarried and seems to have his life on track.) Financial difficulties add to the pressure on any marriage, no matter the main source of trouble. Right after the incident and after we'd lost our forest jobs, Steve was offered ten thousand dollars to deny his UFO experience. Steve was tempted, but, at bottom, was too honest to perjure his testimony. So he refused the offer and went into the army shortly thereafter.

John Goulette's marriage at the time of the incident also broke up, but he soon remarried, remaining with the same woman all these years. He's also remained at the same job, operating farm machinery and tending to all the usual duties of a ranch hand, on a spread owned by his wife's family. He's on a pretty even-keeled course, apparently.

Ken Peterson has remained Ken Peterson. He's continued quietly to pursue his spiritual leanings with various inquiries, but nothing all-consuming or fanatical: only a restless questing for growth which he's periodically renewed over the years. He's remained a steady worker in a variety of construction-related trades—drywall, building maintenance, house painting—as well as some social work. He's recently divorced, but a devoted family man who likes to spend time with his sons.

I was finally able to locate Dwayne Smith after all these years, and reached him by telephone. He has returned to his home turf in Oklahoma, where he's worked as an electrician for the last ten years. He has two sons and a daughter. He says he always has handled the ribbing with good humor. "I've always, and still today, when things are thick, when the air is really thick with crap, I try to make light of it, you know. And now I'm even better at it, now I do it where I pretty much try not to hurt anybody." I think Dwayne meant hurting others' *feelings*, even though being so big undoubtedly encourages people to avoid aggravating him at any rate. He's put on nearly a hundred pounds since 1975. I haven't actually seen him since then, but imagine him with his Hulk Hogan mustache, his six-foot-seven frame, up on western boots with a cowboy hat on top, weighing over 250 pounds. Combine that picture with his positive attitude, and one can see why he's never felt much negative energy from the aftermath of Turkey Springs.

Compared to the rest of the crew, I know a bit more about Mike Rogers' life over the intervening years. He had been my best friend, and I'm married to his sister. So even when we weren't speaking, I heard all about him from his family.

Like most of the other guys, Mike endured a divorce in the wake of the incident. I know how this must look, but I don't think any of these divorces were directly caused by the incident. I believe they're simply a symptom of social problems in general. It's everywhere. Society seems to have opted for an array of conditions which place enormous pressure on the nuclear family.

Not only do I *not* see the incident as a wedge between these couples, it seemed that nearly every one of us sought the arms of a woman in our readjustment to life. John, Steve, and Dwayne—all three of them—married within a few months after the incident. All three of them soon fathered new babies. The two men who were already married, Mike and Ken, both conceived with their wives within a few months after their experience; each had a son. I, too, married, and our first child was a son. All our children have been perfectly normal and healthy in every respect. Mike has always been big on his kids (of which there are now many). When his marriage ended he received primary custody, although the children have lived with both parents at times.

Mike has appeared to me pretty depressed in his outlook on life since the sighting. I don't think he would ever attribute his subdued spirits to his marital breakup, but I personally think it was a factor. But only one factor out of many, including changes in his relationships—not only with me, but everybody important to him, and many people unimportant to him. Another factor, of which I don't think he is aware, is the consequence of some philosophical turns in his thinking, which have led him into what I consider positions out of sync with his true needs.

One way he describes the feeling he is left with—something all the guys felt at first, but got past—is with a phrase I used in my first book, *The Walton Experience:* that of a "stripped ego," which I'll explain once more in my conclusion in chapter 15.

Mike used to be Mr. Ego as much as either my brother Duane or I, but now a bit of the edge is gone. Maybe for all of us. I could write off that change as an effect of general maturity, if it hadn't coincided so exactly with the incident. On the other hand, there was much about those days which demanded instant maturity. Sink or swim.

In any event, like all of us, Mike has adjusted. "Fall back and regroup" is the military term. Reconcile, amend, revise, and carry on.

And carry on he has. Mike returned to work in the woods for a while, built some houses, put his artistic talents to use in designing and painting signs for outdoor advertising. I joined him in some of those projects. One accomplishment which particularly impressed the Forest Service was coming up with a way to mechanize with heavy equipment much of the work we had been doing by hand and with chainsaws.

In the area of traditional logging, there is no more prestigious work to woodsmen in the Southwest than cutting timber on the North Rim of the Grand Canyon. Just as with the Sitgreaves National Forest, most of the world is unaware of the lush timberlands just north of the Canyon. The usual photographs of the area give the impression of desert. But some of the biggest and best fir timber in the state grows there.

Loggers here consider work up there to be (to borrow a phrase) "not just a job but an adventure." Only the best get on and Mike was hired immediately. This was his hermit phase. During one of his seasons up there he lived alone in a cabin. Part of the time he camped in a tent. One campsite was out on a place called Fire Point: golden sunlight glowing on huge trees growing impossibly dense next to a sheer cliff thousands of feet straight down, and beauty so wild descriptions sound like a fairy tale.

Logging up there is a society to itself, but Mike did well there right off the bat. Performance is closely monitored with complex scorecards measuring board feet and a variety of detailed specifications. Mike's scores were higher than those of many of the more experienced sawyers. To be able to work so rapidly and accurately, yet remain uninjured in an occupation so dangerous, requires extraordinary ability. Mike received only one minor injury to his ankle.

We've seen a number of men we knew killed over the years. Logging is the number-one most hazardous line of work in the United States, with the highest number of work-related injuries and deaths of any industry, including mining and agriculture. That point is emphasized by the 1993 nationwide news report of the logger forced to save his own life by using his pocketknife to cut off his own mangled leg. Freeing himself from the fallen tree which had him pinned so that he would have bled to death otherwise, he tied off the stump of his leg, crawled a great distance to his log skidder, drove that to his pickup, then drove himself to get help. They retrieved his leg, but I never heard whether surgeons were able to reattach it. Hard work, hard men.

In his first year of competition Mike entered every loggers' contest held in Arizona and every time placed first, second, or third against a dozen, two dozen, or more experienced, seasoned competitors. This is a serious sport to many of the world's hardiest men and there are national and world competitions. In some of these contests the overall winner gets the title of "Logger of the Year." There are three main categories of competition: ax, saw, and physical. In the ax category there are a variety of chopping events and (the most popular event of the whole contest) ax throwing. Mike did very well at this.

In the saw category there is quite a variety of events measuring skill, speed, and accuracy. It's much more than super equipment. Some events don't even allow the use of competitor-owned saws. You have events that combine speed and accuracy to an astonishing degree. Using heavy, powerful saws that plow through tough logs like butter, they make cuts where winning scores are measured in fractions of both inches and seconds. One event they had at the Angelfire, New Mexico, contest was accuracy felling, which is the ability to control the direction the tree falls by cut alone—no push allowed.

The physical events emphasize strength and endurance but still require a considerable component of skill. There are events involving throwing green logs so heavy they're hard to lift, let alone throw. The log toss, not the same as the log throw, involves timed hurling of a number of smaller (though still heavy) logs onto a pile. Log rolling is a timed event in which massive green logs are moved across a certain distance and back with a cant hook on a pole. But the woodsman has to pass the ends of the log (which is tapered, making it veer) through the narrow gap between two pegs and arrive at the goal with his log centered enough to hit two pegs which are only slightly closer together than the length of his log. Then he must return the same way.

Mike came in without ever having even *watched* these events and surprised everyone with his performance against men who'd been doing it for years, and some of these guys were much larger than Mike.

Writing this book makes me look back over the years for perspective on all the changes that have occurred, both personal and global. Who would have predicted the breakup of the Soviet Union? After adjusting our thinking to such far-reaching realignment of world affairs, we must now hope it doesn't turn out to be less of a blessing than it first seemed.

Earlier, in March 1982, came the death of Ayn Rand. Her inevitable passing was in a sense less of a tragedy than the manner in which news of her death was handled in the media. A few mentions, nothing remotely commensurate with her accomplishments and with her "contributions" (a word to which she might take exception in its literal sense) to human understanding. At the same time, news of the self-destructive death of a bloated, drug-saturated nihilistic comic was everywhere, which the enthralled media endlessly bewailed and examined, eulogized and dissected, in fascinated detail. The spectacle was dragged out morbidly for months, while the passing of Ayn Rand, one of the most phenomenal minds of modern times, generated a few brief mentions and was quickly forgotten.

Much has happened, but 1986 was a particularly significant year to me. Beginning in January, we witnessed the fiery, midflight explosion of the space shuttle *Challenger.* Nothing I can say here could add to what's been said about that heartrending catastrophe. I watched it on live television along with the rest of the world. The meaning of that moment extended beyond words, beyond the immeasurable loss of the crew, beyond the staggering financial loss of mere hardware, beyond the effect on the U.S. space program, beyond the political fallout, beyond the endless analysis and recriminations. It contained a monumental symbolism best understood without words, and a particular dimension of personal significance I could never communicate.

Then in April 1986 (two days before the meltdown and explosion at Chernobyl), the world-renowned astronomer and ufologist, Dr. J. Allen Hynek, died. The brain tumor which was the ultimate cause of his death had first interfered with his speech. His embarrassment at that loss caused him to refuse to see most people. When I spoke with him near the end, it was saddening to see this once articulate man stop in mid-sentence to grope for the simplest words. I believe I had sensed a genuine warmth from him in our relationship.

In 1910, when J. Allen Hynek was a newborn infant only five days old, his father carried him up onto their roof to see the glowing plume of earth's most famous celestial nomad—Halley's Comet. This was a touching scene—it recalls for me the moment in *Roots* where the father holds his baby up to the night sky and says, "Behold, the only thing greater than yourself!"—and a prophetic one. He grew up to become one of the best-known modern astronomers. As Chair Professor of Astronomy at Chicago's Northwestern University, he often told his students of Halley's Comet: "I hope to see it again before I go out." It was another of life's twists that just before he died he did see Halley's Comet return on schedule, to blaze a path across the skies of the Northern Hemisphere. (It is illogical to attach undue significance to coincidence. With an orbital period so close to an average human life-span, it is inevitable that known figures might have birth and death dates so coincide. Mark Twain is one example.)

His legacy contributed greatly to the adoption of a scientific approach to a field sometimes dismally lacking in science. He leaves behind a massive body of work, and the two organizations he founded: the Center for UFO Studies (CUFOS) in Chicago, Illinois, and the International Center for UFO Research (ICUFOR) in Scottsdale, Arizona. His contributions to ufology are too numerous to list. However, regarding my association with him, I can only express my appreciation for his honest curiosity, circumspect fairness, and his courage to call it as he saw it.

A few months later, on August 28, 1986, Jim Lorenzen, international director and cofounder of APRO, died at age sixty-four. Jim and his wife Coral started APRO in 1952 and published the *APRO Bulletin* continuously for over thirty years. Jim Lorenzen and Allen Hynek had been colleagues, with a mild rivalry, over the years. Hynek didn't found CUFOS until twenty years after APRO. Also, his position on UFOs had been pretty skeptical all through his years as a consultant for the U.S. Air Force on Project Blue Book. Hynek's beliefs gradually shifted during his last years with the air force (which probably contributed to their decision to terminate his consulting contract). The turning point for Hynek seemed to come in the wake of public reaction to his infamous "swamp gas" verdict on a case he investigated in the mid-1960s. Jim, and especially Coral, viewed APRO as the original UFO investigation group, and later groups like CUFOS as territorial infringers, with this particular upstart's (Hynek's) previous anti-UFO stance making the interloper undeserving of addressing the material.

Jim and Coral Lorenzen did more for me in the aftermath of my experience, by far, than any other agency I came in contact with. Their approach was nonexploitative, scientific and objective. Something which really drove home to me the true objectivity with which Jim Lorenzen approached my case was an exchange we had while en route to a television program on which we were to appear together. We were sitting in an airport waiting for a connecting flight. I took the opportunity to thank him for standing by me when so many people were down on my case. He turned, looked me in the eye, and spoke with an unexpected sternness I never heard before or after. He said evenly: "Don't thank me for that. Because if I thought for one minute that your case wasn't genuine, I'd say so."

Early in our association I'd referred to Jim as "Dr." Lorenzen. He hastened to correct my error, but it was an easy mistake to make. Jim Loren-zen was a very intelligent man. Some of the inventions he was working on in optics, electronics, and music were amazingly ingenious. It's regrettable that he never had funds to pursue them to fruition. His work on the Kitt Peak telescope was highly skilled and spoke well for his scientific compe-tence. He was well versed in proper research procedure, with a broad un-derstanding of basic science, though never one to put on airs. He looked the part of a scientist, too. He'd had his beard, he told me, before Hynek's, when I commented on their physical resemblance.

What is really ironic is that these two men, so prominent in the same field, should both fall prey to the same disease (prostate cancer, which had spread), and that, even though neither knew of the other's illness at first, both died within a few months of each other.

What's become of the lawmen involved? After more than twenty-eight years of service, Town Marshal Sanford "Sank" Flake left office under a cloud, with the DPS coming to investigate how he had conducted his of-fice. Although a few minor deficiencies were noted when his procedures were compared with those used in big-city police departments, no major offense was ever publicly cited. It looked as if they had come looking for an excuse to justify their actions and cited things which seemed kind of silly to me. I don't know many of the details of what went on there, because local newspaper accounts were a little cryptic, but it looked to me as if he'd been railroaded. He and his wife then left to do overseas church missionary work.

Some writers and reporters tried to portray Sanford Flake as a dumb, sadistic, rednecked hick, a caricature of the small-town southern sheriff. This was highly unfair and highly inaccurate. Sank can sing and play the guitar well, and has painted many works of western art of respectable quality. I still take exception to misguided innuendos he made concerning my mother, but I'll call a spade a spade: Sank's slow western drawl belies his quick wit.

After losing an election bid for sheriff, Undersheriff (Chief Deputy) Ken Coplan left law enforcement for good. Last I heard, he was driving a gas truck in another part of the state.

Glen Flake was one of the county sheriff's deputies back in November 1975, but had been sheriff twice before that, and was elected sheriff again when Marlin Gillespie retired. After a law enforcement career that spanned over twenty-nine years, Glen's last day as the Navajo County Sheriff seemed uneventful. He'd turned in his county car, checked out at the main office and gone home. On New Year's Eve 1988, four and a half hours before his third term would be officially over, his dispatcher called to tell him one of his deputies had been shot. Accompanied by another officer, he immediately left for the scene running "code"—fast, lights and siren on. After all those years without a single officer fatality, Glen Flake's deputy, Bob Varner (himself due to retire soon), had made a routine traffic stop when a maniac with a companion jumped out of a car and put a burst of automatic-weapons fire into Varner's chest.

When they arrived at the scene they found another officer pinned under machine-gun fire. Flake and his men set out in pursuit of the two gunmen, who continued to stop at intervals to shoot back at the lawmen. The cars of the law enforcement men were riddled with bullets. In the darkness the gunmen drove their car off into a concrete-lined ditch. SWAT teams surrounded the car, only to discover the pair had escaped on foot. They reached a farmhouse where they tied up the couple who lived there, stealing their car. One of the gunmen shot himself to death just before capture; the other escaped, and was later captured without any shooting. Quite a last day on the job for Glen Flake.

Marlin Gillespie completed a long career in law enforcement December 31, 1984. After four years in the navy he'd joined the Sheriff's Department in 1957. (He'd been chief deputy during Glen Flake's 1984 term as sheriff.) Even after more than twenty-seven years in the Sheriff's Department, the last decade as Sheriff, Gillespie didn't actually retire. He was elected to the county board of supervisors, where he's actively served ever since.

I didn't know it at the time, but Gillespie shared my interest in motorcycling. (An interest to which I've begun to return . . . indication of how much I've recovered?) He and his wife have logged an astounding number of miles on two wheels, covering nearly the entire United States. Since Gillespie was also a good family man, they also often went on weekend backcountry camp-outs, each family member on his or her own bike. Their youngest son was fatally injured in a motorcycle accident in 1975. Dealing with that personal tragedy in the middle of the Turkey Springs uproar must have made things much harder for him, but he performed as professionally as ever. It makes you wonder how he finds time for it all, since he's always been active in a variety of community services. He was a very popular sheriff, a hard thing to be in a position where, inevitably, your every action is sure to offend *someone*.

When, in preretirement interviews for the local papers, Gillespie was asked what were some of the most outstanding investigations of his career, he cited two. One was the murder of Freddie Jensen. Jensen's body was found by two Apache Indians on horseback, about twenty-five miles from Whiteriver on the reservation, facedown, dead for several days, no identification. In spite of initial difficulty identifying the victim, an intensive investigation by Gillespie's department led to solving the crime. The complexity of the case, the quality of the sleuthing, and the bizarreness of some of the clues (the victim was one of those rare individuals whose internal organs are reversed from normal arrangement, right for left) led to the case being written up in the national magazine *Inside Detective*.

The other case he cited was ours. *The Herald* wrote: "The most baffling was the Travis Walton UFO incident. 'For a month I had telephones growing out of both ears,' the sheriff said. This was another case that was reported across the nation and all over the world. It never was proved true or untrue that the people involved had seen something. But it still puzzles him, as well as others who might recall the incident."

What with all the comings and goings, deaths and divorces, it seemed everyone was changing but me. While my phone was disconnected and I was avoiding interviews, the controversy raged on in my absence. Skeptics and ufologists continued to debate the merits of the case. Even in the absence of much of the data included in this book, a general consensus emerged.

When journalists came seeking interviews, they would tell me they'd checked with the experts in the field. Whether they'd asked for the most interesting, most witnessed, most controversial, best-known or best-documented case, the answer they received was always the incident at Turkey Springs in 1975. It is the only abduction case with witnesses, and the only one ever reported to authorities while the person was still missing.

So they came to me, with their self-contradictory approach: "Give me the top UFO story so that my [article, documentary, book, movie] will make me a success." But: "Of course, I know you really wouldn't want to be paid much, if at all, because, since your experience is real, you couldn't care at all about money."

Accepting their hypocritical messages, I was embarrassed by any payment I received for various appearances, although rarely if ever did it do more than cover my expenses. I was afraid if I accepted the opportunities—I certainly *had* to accept the liabilities—resulting from the incident, my credibility would be damaged. The writers were right to that degree: I *did* value credibility more than I did fair compensation. I started turning down almost all offers without waiting to hear the entire pitch. No way was I going to "sell out."

Friends hastened to advise me otherwise. "You've a perfect right to those opportunities," they reasoned. "It couldn't even begin to make up for what it's cost you. It's no different from anyone telling of an unusual life experience." They said, "It's like people accusing the guys who survived that plane crash in the wilderness, of deliberately downing their plane and enduring the hell of cannibalism just so they could sell their story. It doesn't matter what your detractors say, they'd suspect you in any case." They told me to get out there and make the most of my experience.

But I didn't care about that. I felt, as the line ran in one of the songs about our experience, "Leave me alone and give me time to think." At that time I would have preferred to have it all forgotten.

CHAPTER 14

The Making of *Fire*

Who teach the mind its proper face to scan,
And hold the faithful mirror up to man.

—Robert Lloyd, from *The Actor*

After a number of years, things began to quiet down a little. Letters came less frequently. People didn't seek me out so often—especially reporters. As always, there were programs and articles produced by journalists who didn't do any firsthand research (which of course were the least accurate) but even these were fewer and farther between.

It seemed safe to have a telephone reinstalled. At one point the disadvantages of having one had heavily outweighed the advantages, but those advantages were considerable. In today's world it's really hard to conduct your normal day-to-day affairs without a telephone.

If problems developed, I could always have it taken out again, or have the police order the installation of another line trap by the phone company. The police investigation of that early series of sick threats had put an abrupt halt to it. (Caller ID hadn't been developed at that time.)

So, I took the plunge. Welcome back to the twentieth century. What a labor-saving device the telephone is. A one-minute call spared me a twenty-minute trip. Job-related questions were quickly resolved. It was much easier to stay in touch with friends and relatives. And I was glad to relieve some of the isolation Dana had been enduring. Everything seemed great.

But then, right off the bat I received a call from this guy named Tracy

Torme. He wanted to make a movie. I'd heard it all before. A writer, director, or producer would call, write, or come to Snowflake, to try to persuade me to grant rights for a movie to be made. I listened to some of those people, but eventually the same message filtered through. The two things that put me off were (1) failing to convince me the material would not receive a sensationalistic, exploitive treatment; and (2) no one could show me how I could avoid being perceived as "selling out" without being taken advantage of.

I couldn't see any way the net result would not be negative. My life had settled some. I had inched forward toward being accepted for myself in a few relationships. What could a movie bring to my life? Stir up all the old controversies, animosities, and ridicule? Wouldn't a movie, the accompanying research and promotion, result in further public dissection of me and my life? Wouldn't it only put the bug back in the jar—this time under a spotlight?

I told Mr. Torme I wasn't interested. Still, I sensed something different in his approach. He seemed better informed on the facts and details of the incident than any of the others. So, when he persisted, wanting me to wait to make a final decision until after he had come to Snowflake for a face-to-face meeting, I agreed. His interest in a personal meeting wasn't especially persuasive; others had met me face-to-face.

When he arrived at my house after a hectic drive through some crazy weather, his father, Mel Torme, called. Tracy seemed embarrassed his dad was checking on the safety of his grown son. I thought it was neat. Neat that I got to speak to Mel Torme himself, and neat that even in Hollywood, fathers could still act like dads.

I was impressed with Tracy's sincerity when he emphasized his intent to stay true to the material. There didn't seem to be any sense in his paying such close attention to the details of the incident if he didn't plan to stay true to those details. During his stay he continued to investigate the incident closely and impartially. I took his objectivity in that regard as a sign of how he would treat a dramatic interpretation of the story. But the factor that persuaded me more than anything was something he said.

We were sitting in a booth at the doughnut shop across from the post office, watching the local traffic come and go outside the window. I remarked on how few of those people seemed to base their opinions concerning the incident on the facts; their opinions seemed to be mostly derived from their prejudices and emotions.

Tracy responded that a movie would induce people to experience the sighting and its aftermath for themselves and open up their thinking about it. That viewpoint immediately clicked for me. In my first book I'd expressed the desire "to put readers where we were when it happened," because it was the only approach I thought capable of removing the prejudices preventing objective analysis of the facts.

It hadn't really dawned on me there were better ways than a book to achieve that. Tracy's comment made me immediately realize that nothing in current existence could equal the power of film to impart vicarious experience. People might be moved to reexamine the facts, perhaps even to seek out more complete information.

To get people thinking: One could reach for more, but that in itself was no modest goal.

That prospect clinched it for me. I would have an opportunity to be understood, to be seen for what I really am. I'd have a chance to correct published misconceptions about myself. So I signed.

I don't know whether they thought I was simply foolish, or if they finally understood why, but every time it came to signing papers, they were surprised that the points I negotiated most earnestly were matters unconnected with the money.

One thing I wanted, but soon realized was out of the question, was the right to maintain some say over the story's treatment. Almost no writers, not even top-name authors, get creative control. I came to understand why that is so.

Creativity is an individual thing. On such a project, to share the creative control (in films, normally the director's perogative) would lead to inevitable dissension, with no built-in means of resolution. To give complete creative control to a writer would be the equivalent of making him the director. What studio would stake the outcome of a project in which it invests tens of millions of dollars, on the judgment of someone who might not know the first thing about the various considerations to which a studio gives priority (chiefly, commercial success), to say nothing of technical understanding of the filmmaking process?

So I knew the minute I signed on that dotted line I was essentially relying on my trust in the scriptwriter, Tracy Torme, to stick by our understanding.

Part of my agreement was to assist in gathering permission signatures from others involved in the story. I pursued this diligently, putting Torme in touch with a number of the principals. I ran into some problems, however. Steve Pierce's family weren't anxious to help me locate him. We ran out of leads in our search for Dwayne Smith. And Ken Peterson simply refused to sign. It wasn't the money. He felt some personal principle would be violated by his signing. We never figured out what it was, but his decision was final.

Faced with these roadblocks, I wondered how the project could go forward. How could anyone have rights to his own life story, if telling it required getting signatures from everyone in your life? The answer came back. Permission wasn't necessary, but was sought anyway just for good measure. Studio lawyers are a cagey lot.

I finally spoke with Steve Pierce and he gave his verbal okay. Tracy would have to fly to Texas for a meeting. Since Tracy already realized two other characters were unlikely to be signed on, he said, "Forget it." Anyone not on board at this point would simply lose his chance at a little extra cash. To appease lawyers, those persons would be replaced with fictional characters. That news didn't budge Kenny; so that's how we left it.

I was uneasy about fictionalizing. Would this open the floodgates to more departures from the original story? Tracy assured me it would not.

As an interesting aside, the transformation books, including real-life stories, undergo in translation to the screen is legendary. People routinely compare the book and the movie, expressing preference for one or the other, the fact that they often differ greatly not drawing comment. That situation with film leads people to assume that, in publishing, authors routinely turn in manuscripts which the publishers then substantially alter through massive "editing" so extensive it amounts to quasi ghostwriting.

I don't think that is so common as believed; it certainly hasn't been the case with me. Except for proofreading sorts of errors, and a certain passage my editor suggested, correctly, would be best presented in an earlier chapter, my first book was published virtually word-for-word as I submitted it.

(And for the record, there's been no effort to bring this account into line with what the film did with the story. The greater insight and understanding I have gained since then did allow me to do more than correct errors; I've added things I've since remembered or discovered, and generally refined some of that earlier material.)

Signing an agreement with a writer/producer, as I had, does not automatically mean a movie will be made. As I was to learn, the chances are astronomical against any particular script actually becoming a feature film up on the big screen.

In terms of numbers alone, the odds are overwhelming, because only a tiny fraction of available scripts can possibly be produced. There are only so many development dollars, and ultimately only so many theater tickets that will be bought in a given time. Only a few dozen major new movies are made per year, and only some of those are successful. Meanwhile there are nearly a hundred thousand scripts circulating on the market at any one time, with over forty thousand new ones registered every year.

However, there's no shortage of hopefuls trying to generate interest in their particular project. The odds against us weren't merely a matter of numbers. It would be bad enough if the playing field were level, but it's far from that. The competition's first line of advantage is held by the many writers and directors with "standing"—hugely successful track records and established connections. (Theoretically there are enough of these to fill every available slot.) There are those who get a hearing through extraordinary manipulation: contrived coincidental meetings, friend-of-a-friend connections, return of a favor, casting couch, extortion, and signature at knifepoint. (Just kidding!) Then there are the trend-followers: projects cloned from the last crop of successes, for which insecure decision-makers always have a compulsive attraction.

This is not to imply writer/producer Tracy Torme was completely without track record and connections. He was certainly averse to invoking his famous father's name to open doors, and bristled at occasionally being introduced as "Mel Torme's son." He had no need of nepotism. He had written the MGM occult thriller *Spellbinder*, which starred Tim Daly and Kelly Preston. He'd been a successful writer for Canada's award-winning *SCTV*, writer/filmmaker for *Saturday Night Live*, and executive story-editor and creative consultant for *Star Trek: The Next Generation*. He wrote six episodes for the series, among them the Peabody Award–winning "The Big Goodbye."

However, now he had his work cut out for him. Hollywood is famous for the euphemistic decline. Refusals are routine, but rarely does anyone utter the "N word" outright. A simple no would actually save a lot of wasted time for all concerned, so why not? Partly because it is difficult to descend from Tinseltown hype, in which every project is "wonderful," "tremendous," "fantastic," and "maaarvelous." No one ever just "likes" something, they love it, they adore it, or they are intensely excited by it. So by this inflated currency, everything becomes artificially elevated.

You're lucky to get a response as direct as, "We love it, and except for the fact that [we're already doing a similar project; the only star we'd consider for it is totally booked this year; I love it but my partner or boss doesn't; or, my housekeeper is ill] we'd take this project on in a minute." Often they just stall.

If they don't want it, why don't they just say so? I don't know; maybe because, in Hollywood, no one is sure of anything. If they can keep stringing you along, they have a greater range of possibilities: what they're "considering" won't be taken by someone else; they can feel important and sought after. And since the business favors those with good contacts, and no one can predict which supplicant will be tomorrow's Tinseltown god, it's wise not to offend carelessly. While no one wants to be the guy who turned down someone else's megahit, studio executives never get fired for being wrong when they say no; only when they say yes.

We had many false alarms. Tracy reported each glimmer of hope accurately; going by what he was told, time and again, we had every reason to believe we were about to get a movie made. And time and again it wound up a near miss.

I started getting pretty cynical in my reactions to the news. I didn't come out and say so, but I came to expect false alarms. I knew Tracy wasn't exaggerating the prospects; in fact, as time went on, he downplayed them. Even so, those considering the project perpetually made its acceptance look imminent.

I vacillated in my feelings. There were times when things had gone so well for me for a while that I didn't want any form of media to come back and stir things up again. And there were times I wanted it to happen so as to get it over with, so I could get past the feeling of being on hold and get on with my life.

At one point my agreement with Tracy and his associates expired. I agreed to let them go on trying to market the script for free, with no contract, for quite some time, because such an arrangement left me free to decline the whole thing, should I feel so inclined when a deal was ready to be made. I wrestled with very mixed feelings all the way along.

Even though a friendship had begun to grow between us, I'm sure Tracy thought I was too wary and unenthused. But once burned, twice shy.

As the script took shape, I initially had misgivings about any departure whatsoever from my own perspective on the incident, let alone any material fictionalizations. I had a lot to learn.

I learned there are an indefinite number of perspectives, or "takes," on any real-life series of events. For example, a war story can focus on the protagonist's love interest back home, his relationship to his fellow soldiers, an historical perspective, a geopolitical perspective, or combat, either as horror or heroism. Or any number of other aspects—all of which are the story as much as any other.

Tracy could have chosen to weave his "take" from any of a variety of threads and still had a movie about the incident. The story could have been told from the point of view of any of several minor characters. It could have been done as a psychological study. It could even have been told from an archskeptic's point of view! The natural tendency, judging from previous offers I'd received, was to focus on the more visually lurid aspects of aliens and spaceships.

After some wrangling back and forth, I was made to understand that major studios don't set out to make films for the purpose of providing scholarly expositions or a soapbox for one person's views. Their bottom line is—well, the bottom line.

Their goal is to entertain as wide a cross-section of the population as possible. Commercial considerations aren't the narrow, crass, materialistic, *irrelevant* factors some people represent them to be. Without such considerations, a movie of *any* perspective would quickly become impossible to bring into existence. Nothing is free; you can't get something for nothing.

Ultimately, however, I knew that only a script focused on the human story would satisfy the goal I had in mind when I finally agreed to permit a movie to be made. The best way to get people to feel what we had felt would be to have them in effect living it for themselves.

However, to the disappointment of some, our story was not to receive the obvious, FX-driven, UFO-focused treatment. Instead, it emphasized the human story. Tracy: ". . . a study of how a single event can alter your life forever just by your being in the wrong place at the wrong time. *Fire in the Sky* is also about friendship and betrayal—and forgiveness." Producer Joe Wizan: "This is a story that speaks to human character and behavior—about our inclination to presume the worst in someone before considering ideas that challenge our own skepticism."

Tracy Torme was true to his word in working closely with me in writing the script. I found him an open, decent sort of person, very imaginative and intelligent, loyal to his friends—a very centered, balanced, likable personality. Most of those in Hollywood have egos too big (or actually too small, if ego equals self-esteem) to allow anyone like me to comment on or contribute suggestions to their work. I was given the opportunity to read what he had written as we went along, and he would listen to my reactions. He frequently solicited information from me. I was asked for details about the way things really had been, minor things never before important enough to bring up. I was able to offer insight into the characters of people I knew, as to how given individuals might react in a given situation.

The script gradually metamorphosed. The process wasn't perfectly smooth, however. One by one, and sometimes two by two, departures from reality crept in. Sometimes I could see the reason immediately, especially when the change was covered by the rationale which had justified an earlier alteration. But sometimes a change didn't make any sense to me at all; when the events that had actually occurred were every bit as interesting, and as functional, for the script (if not more so).

We cooperated; at times we argued. Throughout these exchanges, I was ever aware that I had no contractual power to approve or veto anything. But Tracy never pulled that trump card on me. Nevertheless, even though I won on a few points, I usually wound up giving in; sometimes because I was persuaded the fictionalization was justified, sometimes because I realized there was no way I could win my point without undue long-term cost: if I built up a "concession debt" to Tracy, I might be overdrawn when an issue arose which was really vital to me.

As Tracy cast about for that just-right title for the movie, I tossed out a few ideas. I have no doubt that if I had suggested one which really nailed it, Tracy wouldn't have hesitated to accept it. However, my suggestions didn't remotely compare with the bull's-eye Tracy quickly scored—*Fire in the Sky*.

Since the script was to focus so much on the human drama and events surrounding the incident, I wasn't much bothered by the temporary absence from the script of the short segment depicting the time period aboard; it reflected my treatment of it in my life: encapsulated and set aside for the moment.

One nearly insurmountable obstacle to getting a major studio interested in the project was the subject matter. As conventional wisdom has it, UFOs aren't an acceptable topic for major movies. Never mind that they are continually the subject of best-selling books. Never mind that the majority of top movies in the previous decade have had space and aliens as subject matter: Spielberg's *Close Encounters of the Third Kind,* or his all-time box-office champ, *E.T.: The Extraterrestrial.*

The studios would counter that no major theatrical film had ever been made about a real-life UFO incident, and the fictional version (*Close Encounters*) had already been done. Space and aliens were possible subject matter, but UFOs were regarded as an entirely distinct category. In the insecure, imitative, bandwagon world of Hollywood, if it hasn't been done, there must be a good reason why not. The requirement of external validation leads to the convention of "high concept," pitching projects by describing them in terms of a marriage of prior hits. *Fire in the Sky* has been described as *Close Encounters* paired with, variously, *Bad Day at Black Rock, The Last Picture Show, The Ox-Bow Incident, River's Edge,* and, mockingly, as "*E.T.* meets *Deliverance.*"

Perhaps those cheesy old black-and-white movies of saucer invasions of earth, or the excesses of modern tabloids, have invested the topic with an air of the ridiculous. For whatever reason, the subject matter is very off-putting; the film was a hard sell over a six-year period. One strategy was to avoid the baggage attached to the term "UFO" simply by emphasizing descriptions of story elements without use of the stigmatizing acronym.

I didn't know it then, but the project's difficulties weren't any worse than those encountered in the long prehistory of many other successful movies. Eight- and ten-year concept-to-screen time spans are common. On the other hand, Tracy had been accustomed to quick sells with his other projects. But for all we know, he may eventually discover he'd been having an unusually long run of unusually easily marketed scripts. Also, at times he became completely preoccupied with other work and wasn't able to push as vigorously on *Fire* as he would if he'd been able to give it 100 percent of his time.

As I wrote earlier, during those six years there were times I wrote off the project as something that would never be—sometimes with mild disappointment, more often with great relief. This was especially true toward the end. In fact, when we first heard Paramount might take the film under consideration, my wife and I went for an evening walk and firmly resolved that if it didn't go this time, that would be the end of it. We would part as friends with Tracy, but would agree to cease to entertain any future offerings.

We continued to get word of increasingly positive signs from Paramount, but we'd seen that before. We'd long been schooled to wait until we'd gotten what's called the "green light" from the studio. My skepticism was such that I was inclined to disregard the green light until all final contracts were signed. Better yet, until the cameras actually began rolling. I held off telling people I knew until I was certain, because I didn't want to pay the price of stirring up buried memories in the community if there was a chance nothing would come of it after all.

Even when it came time for me to fulfill one of my obligations, to furnish the current addresses of all of those who had signed releases for the film, I wasn't fully convinced. And I emphasized the film wasn't a certainty. Nevertheless, I went ahead and gathered them, but again not without some difficulty.

The hardest to reach was Allen Dalis. None of the old phone numbers or addresses for Allen panned out. Former associates couldn't be found themselves, or had lost contact with him. His father, too, had moved. I managed to find the right office in the big corporation where Allen's father had spent his career, but they had no active employee file on him. The overworked secretary was finally able to locate current data in another file of retirees, but she wasn't permitted to release either his phone or address. I barely persuaded her to allow me to send her a stamped letter for Allen's dad, which she kindly forwarded. Allen's father called me, relayed my message, and Allen finally returned my call.

Those were pretty anxious days for me, not knowing what to do. My job required almost all my time and energies, but if the movie was really going to be made, there was a great deal I should be doing. I agonized over the wisdom of my decision to grant movie rights.

The scale and finality of the Paramount contract caused all the myriad implications of my decision abruptly to dawn clear to me. I suddenly felt—déjà vu—that my life was barreling forward in the grip of enormous forces I was powerless to control.

I had been leading a very conservative life, defined by control and predictability. That way of living had been my anchor in the aftermath of November 1975, but I was again adrift. Things started happening too fast. My coping strategy was obvious when faced with the inevitable: simply to affect what I could, resign myself to the remainder, and take it as it came.

As part of the process of judging the project, Tracy made plans to accompany Rob Lieberman, who was eventually signed on as director, to Arizona to meet me and scout possible locations. Even this was not sufficient to convince me that the movie would become a reality.

We went to dinner at the Longhorn Restaurant, a rustic, frontier-style place built by Snowflake town marshal Sanford Flake and his brother, Navajo County deputy Glen Flake. We talked and got to know a little about each other.

When Tracy had been pitching the project to Paramount, he'd asked me to send a dozen or so photos that would give a cross-section view of my character. Lieberman had directed Robert Conrad in the made-for-television movie, *Will,* about G. Gordon Liddy. He spoke with scathing contempt concerning the machismo of the actor and his real-life counterpart. His remarks were so doctrinaire, anti-ego politically correct, that I realized a couple of photos of my karate and boxing must have made a very negative impression on him. ("Uh oh," I thought. "If this wimpy, less-macho-than-thou übermensch is irreversibly attached to this project, we're screwed!" This wuss was going to take the teeth and grit out of this crew of woodsmen to the point that we'd all wind up looking like choirboys. Within the facade of those infected with anti-ego disease are some of the most vain, arrogant, conceited prima donnas one can imagine. I asked myself: How is anyone going to be able to work and get along with this "Wonder of the World"?)

Dana and I expressed a desire to visit the set and, for the fun of it, to appear as extras, perhaps in a crowd scene somewhere. The director was friendly and assured us he would be delighted to have us. Dinner was nice, the western decor and weathered lumber of the restaurant's interior adding a warm country atmosphere.

After we had eaten, we went out through the wooden bat-wing doors, across the boardwalk on the front of the building to the cars. I'd felt a little self-conscious talking in front of inquisitive customers and waitresses. We went on back over to my house for further discussion.

It went downhill from there. Soon we reached a point where the director expressed some skepticism about my experience. Maybe I was reading too much into the situation, but it felt to me he had contrived a scenario, in which I was expected to stand up, pound the table, look everyone in the eye and tell 'em how certain I was I'd had a real experience. I didn't care how it affected anyone's opinion, I felt antagonized by the situation and refused to rise to the bait.

To top off our initial meeting, the next day we headed out to the site in a four-wheel-drive vehicle, piloted by their guide for location scouting—a representative from the Arizona Film Commission. We never made it to the site. We had almost reached it when we got stuck, burying that four-wheel-drive in a snowdrift. We spent a number of miserable hours digging ourselves out, without gloves, snowboots, or tools.

When we were finally free the director said: "Let's go back to Heber. I got us out twice and I don't feel like making it a third time." What? *He* got us out? All that struggle and work the rest of us did was apparently only ineffectual bumbling while the real man saved our incompetent asses. We finally made it back to Heber, wet, cold feet, starved. We wolfed some lunch, then said good-bye so they could head off with their guide to scout locations around Arizona. As I walked to my van I mentally wagered the director would never choose to shoot locally.

Most people would expect a great feeling of elation and celebration to accompany the news that a part of their life was going to be turned into a major motion picture. No such toasting occurred with us. The fact that at no clear-cut, abrupt point did I believe a movie would actually be made, created uncertainty beyond the ambivalence I felt about doing it at all. A portion of my mixed feelings one can probably understand from imagining oneself in my place; but the remainder is made up of things most people wouldn't be likely to understand. As Tracy said of me in a character sketch in an earlier script: "Still waters run deep."

Naturally the script was again being modified to meet the desires of its new owner. Too many creative minds pulling one way then another can really distort something so complex. People coming in so late in the game can very easily overlook factors only the original creator is completely aware of.

Every line of a well-written script has tendrils and links and synergism with the rest throughout. Adding to and subtracting from something so intertwined is very difficult for a newcomer to do without inadvertently severing nerves and arteries he didn't know were there. A short-necked, four-legged chicken with no wings has more meat on it, but it begins to look a lot less like a chicken. We're all familiar with the definition of a camel as being a horse designed and built by committee.

Tracy himself was commissioned to effect the requested changes. Even though his position in the production would be listed as writer/coproducer, most of Tracy's power to enforce his judgment likewise vanished when he signed his contract. When I learned that, it hit me with more than a little apprehension. Were the understandings and the trust with which I'd entered the project now moot—neutralized? Was the story now to become wildly altered?

Fortunately, Tracy Torme's opinions were still respected. I felt I had an ally in the thick of things. But Tracy was coming under pressure to do some outrageous things to the story. But Tracy knew his material inside out, and since he's a very well spoken, convincing person, he was able to get the more absurd suggestions quickly set aside.

Still, I knew from my recent perusal of movie-industry literature that what are called "creative differences" eventually come up in nearly every single movie production. Would an accumulation of such confrontations eventually weaken Tracy's influence on the process? I had to rely on Tracy's strong likability and his past friendship with the others.

In keeping with my rapport with Tracy Torme, I received copies of each new rewrite of the script. During preproduction I received one of the more final versions. Many of the changes were clearly for the better, but I was concerned about aspects of the script which had evolved, and broached the subject with Tracy. But unlike before, without hearing me out, Tracy said decisions were no longer his to make unilaterally. He suggested I speak to him, the director, and producers as a group, in a conference call. It was late in the process for changes to be made very easily. I was leery of being taken wrong, of distancing anyone. So I suggested I first write a letter to them, more carefully explaining my viewpoint:

Dear Tracy, Rob, Joe & Tod,

I have read the current version of the script and I have a comment that I feel is urgent that you consider.

First, so as not to be misunderstood (being misunderstood has been a major theme in my life) I want to say enthusiastically that overall this version is great! Much improved over an already absorbing perspective of my experience. I was very moved by parts that express so well things I have felt. Dana was actually brought to tears at the part where I am returned. Neither of us could put it down. Not just because we're in it, but because it's such a gripping telling of it that everyone is going to react the same way.

But I say this with certain qualifiers. Throughout the years of my association with Tracy I have consistently expressed my reservations concerning any departures from reality my story might take in the process of translation to the screen. Tracy has given me a number of logical explanations for the necessity of such changes. Not as just so much gratuitous artistic license but as clarifying, condensing devices and as tactics in avoidance of rights problems. Of course there are the concerns of keeping it all (wince) commercially appealing. And I can see and agree that the intrinsic limits of film in communicating detail result in the need to represent some things not so much documentarily but in a broadly symbolic fashion . . . in "essences" of reality. I can concede the validity of these explanations in principle, only limited by the question of whether one of these rationales was actually the reason for any particular change.

Specifically, my central complaint is about what has gradually happened to the representation of me in successive versions of the script. It may be possible for me to come to terms with a wide variety of omissions or alterations of actual places or events where warranted by the reasons above. But I find it much harder to reconcile changes made to the most central *characters.* I mean, after all, what is this movie *about,* if not the people it happened to?

The two most persuasive points Tracy used in getting me to agree to grant rights for a movie to be made were: (1) he would do his best to stay true to the facts; and (2) I would have an opportunity to become *understood,* to be seen for what I really am, a chance to correct misconceptions that have been publicized about me.

In earlier versions of the script there were scenes and dialogue that displayed the more philosophical, thinking side of my personality. I went along with magnification and focus on some (presently embarrassing) risk-taking acts of mine because of the counterbalance provided by the "intellectual side" scenes.

But now, with all the chopping and shuffling involved in rewrites, a critical factor has slipped away. Inadvertent though it may have been, in this script I have become not much more than a *one-dimensional character, a wild, irresponsible risk seeker.*

It was with some difficulty I managed to open up one night to [Tracy's secretary and research assistant] Leslie and reveal more to her about how I moved from Payson where I had the nickname "the Professor," to Snowflake where I was then determined to get out of that pigeonhole I had been placed in. I had been called "mad scientist," "Einstein," and such. I was unfairly cast as nothing more than a sensitive goody-goody, a wimpy egghead nerd. So I guess that all that boxing, biker, karate, bull-riding, hell-raising stuff was a struggle of my psyche to break out of a prison of other people's perceptions. The irony is that all I succeeded in doing was moving from one pigeonhole to the next. At least, to most people in this town. Certain teachers saw through it, as well as those who were close to me. Polysyllabic vocabulary and lofty references had a way of sometimes slipping out. And at my recent twenty-year high-school reunion the story was recounted to the group of how I would never take a book home, cut classes all week, and come roaring up to school on test day and ace the test. At least now they could feel a little amused at the consternation experienced by our disapproving, conservative town fathers in viewing this refutation of a major tenet of their ethic.

Even this dichotomy of character is an enormous oversimplification of my makeup, but that's okay because after all, this movie isn't exactly a character study.

An important consideration from your viewpoint is that, as you know, the better actors are going to have greater interest in playing a more complex character. Contrasting, contradictory, even paradoxical traits put meat in the part for them. Audiences, too, prefer more depth. "One-dimensional clichés" are common criticisms of lesser movies.

Obviously, since I'm approving inclusion of unflattering traits, I shouldn't be accused of seeking to gold-plate my character. I'm just looking for a little more balance and authenticity. And authenticity is something that must also be a high priority with you or you wouldn't buy rights to a true story. You'd just invent the entire thing out of whole cloth, and there would be no value in beginning the movie with, "This is a true story."

I do not drink. I objected earlier to the scene of my receiving a gift of alcohol from Dalis and it was removed; now it's back. One of the things he had against me was that I supposedly thought I was too good to drink with him (or drink like him). You could save this scene by using a different gift, or have me turning around and giving it away, or something like Allen saying, "I know you don't drink anymore but with what you've just come through, I thought you could use a little something anyway." I find this one real difficult to accept as is, especially since some people tried to dismiss my whole experience as an alcohol-induced delusion. I was very into healthy eating (considered far-out here at that time) and so even that scene of me being the one who ordered the butterscotch-grape twist would be seen by anyone who knows me as 180 degrees off. One article that came out even tried to paint me as real unconventional because I ate whole-wheat bread! The doughnut scene is a useful story device, but could be changed to agree with reality and not lose a thing.

On page 13 there is reference to my not worrying about tomorrow. If it means not worrying in the sense of being confident, it's fine as is. If it means I only lived for the moment, it's not. I was full of plans, so many that I was often accused of being *too* focused on the future. My brother (the boxer/bullrider) was always saying, "I'd rather live a day as a lion than a lifetime as a lamb." I would counter with, "Why not live so as to have a lifetime as a lion?" My major failing in this area is that I still took that attitude of immortality that was held by so many of us at that stage of life. So it was not, "I take risks as if there is no tomorrow," but more like, "I can risk because I am *certain* of tomorrow."

Speaking of plans, the story device of "the dream plan" being a motorcycle dealership carries the biker angle too far and isn't based in fact. A better "dream plan" might be the infinite-ratio transmission I told Leslie about. I invented this thing in high school, and Mike and I talked about forming a company called "Transpectrum" or something like that, to develop and market it to the big auto manufacturers.

I'd like to again emphasize that I feel that Tracy's script is well done and that his ability to capture the likeness of people has been good. It's just that when you see yourself being sort of summed up to the entire world, it's quite reasonable to pay a little extra attention to whether or not that representation resembles you. I doubt that anyone would be any less concerned in this regard than I am if it were them.

Regardless of the extent of Paramount's plans for me to help with promotion, it is inevitable that I will be doing a very great number of interviews concerning the film. It would be very embarrassing to field questions, or do a bunch of disclaiming sorts of explanations about things excluded or included that I feel strongly about. I really want this movie to be something I can put my wholehearted support behind.

Earlier, when Tracy was researching with me for material for the scenes depicting my philosophical, intellectual side he asked me for an appropriate title for a book to be used as one of my favorites and asked also for a quotation representative of ideas I was then exploring. So I put together a short list of such titles and quotes I would like to offer again as possibilities for use in putting those things back in the script. I have a few suggestions for where and how these things can fit in in a way that I think only helps in the original intent.

At your earliest convenience I would like to get together in a conference call and discuss this with you.

I sincerely hope that you will take a good look at this from my perspective and perhaps be able to understand my concern. I think it is a reasonable request and I offer it in a spirit of cooperation.

Sincerely,

Travis Walton

I didn't broach the subject of the abduction sequence because it had been left out of versions of the script I was given.

Tracy received his copy of the letter at the office provided him by Paramount at the studio. He contacted the others and arranged for our conference call. Over the next several weeks the conference was postponed three times, then dropped altogether. The message was relayed that my letter had been read and not to worry, I'd like the end product.

This felt like a pat on the head and "Run along now." I remained deferential and undemanding. There was certainly no reason anyone should listen to me; heck, I was only the guy it had happened to. I heard later that in a meeting with the actors and producers, Lieberman quoted my letter and referred to my comment on the butterscotch-grape twist, rolling his eyes derisively.

Nevertheless, I made phone calls and wrote other letters trying to influence certain minor parts of the script, all to little effect. I grew a little exasperated. I wrote: "The earliest version of the script said, 'This is a true story.' Now it's become 'Based on a true story.' What's next, 'Loosely inspired by a true story'?"

I wasn't trying to make major changes. I knew better than that. I wasn't trying to get creative or meddle in anything stylistic, only to set straight factual things about the way myself and others, my town and the church, were portrayed. Small things from their point of view, big things only from the perspective of the people depicted. Most of my requests went unheeded.

Tracy Torme had fought valiantly for the integrity of his work. True to my prediction, the director vetoed a fistfight scene, saying no one was ever going to hit anyone in his films, so the physical tension peaks with a couple of shoving matches, with cocked fists, punches never thrown. Some of Tracy's battles were waged over issues specifically directed at keeping his word with me. I'm very grateful to Tracy, because I know it cost him in his ability to maintain a working relationship with the others. Eventually it came to pass that Tracy ceased to have any input and no longer visited the set.

Toward the end of it, Tracy bowed out of rewrites, citing other commitments. After filming was under way, another writer was brought in to work (uncredited) on the script, mostly on minor dialogue changes. The director himself was responsible for more departures from reality than anyone else.

I felt I'd done all I could. The contract was clear. I had no legal power whatsoever to change one word.

Not to worry. The story behind *Fire in the Sky* will ultimately transcend any of the vagaries of its interpretation. There was nothing to be gained by pushing further, estranging everyone from me. I recalled the opening quote in the script: "Chance makes a plaything of a man's life" (Seneca). I thought wryly: "Hollywood makes a plaything of a man's life" (Cynica).

I brooded deeply for a little while, but I thought it all over and resolved, not another word about how I felt it ought to be. When confronted with the inevitable, it is wisest simply to face reality and change course. From this point forward I was going to be a team player and do whatever I could to help. Emotions aside, "Let's make lemonade."

Paramount Studios. There wasn't a better place on the planet to make this movie. The studio had held the largest market share over other studios in recent years, the springboard of numerous blockbuster megahits. They shared with a couple of other studios the services of United Pictures International (UPI), the largest exhibitor (movie theater) distribution network in the world. Owned by the conglomerate Gulf-Western, Paramount Communications is a multimedia company with far more development capital available today than any other moviemaking entity.

Casting the movie was a fascinating process. It was really funny sometimes to picture certain actors as portraying Mike Rogers or me or some of the others. I figured there was no way they were going to get anyone very similar to the real people. Since these weren't people whose characters and likenesses were already widely established in the public mind, they were actually free to choose anyone who'd fit well with the story.

I was in for a real surprise. Some of the casting was uncanny in the actors' physical resemblance to the actual persons. Coincidentally, some of the best-nailed likenesses were of less central characters, for whom, as far as I knew, they didn't even have photos or descriptions. There was, however, a passable likeness between the Mike Rogers of 1975 and the actor who ultimately played him.

The actors considered for *Fire in the Sky* read like a Who's Who of known names in Hollywood. It is best not to list names here concerning who was considered for what roles, and why they wound up not getting those roles. It certainly wasn't because I vetoed anyone. I didn't even try.

Very often actors are thought of in terms of their looks or the roles they've played, rather than their ability to project, in conjunction with their natural look and personality, various emotions and characters. Some actors, however intensely appealing and popular, are always really just playing themselves in a new situation. Others astound by their ability to transform themselves completely, literally *becoming* starkly different people, sometimes almost unrecognizable as that actor. On the other hand, very often the former type receives as much, if not more, adulation as the latter, because people can only identify with an appeal that remains consistent long enough for them to feel they've come to know a personal friend.

Naturally I was most keenly interested in who would be chosen to play me. Many people fantasize being played by actors who are nothing like them. I think I was pretty realistic on that point. Still, there were actors whose names came up that I fervently hoped would not be cast, I didn't care how big their names were. My curiosity was not to be soon satisfied; my part was one of the very last to be cast. Since I wasn't a regular movie-goer, I wasn't sufficiently familiar with some of the actors to be able to see how very aptly they'd been cast.

Craig Sheffer was cast as Allen Dalis. When it opened, I ran out and saw *A River Runs Through It*, watching to try to see him as Allen. I was very impressed with the range and subtlety of his performance, but I couldn't see him as Allen Dalis. Was I ever in for a shock. Compare his performance in *A River Runs Through It* to that in *Fire in the Sky*. You'll be asking yourself, is this even the same guy? Same thing with his other films.

Craig Sheffer played Allen Dalis in a manner that even Allen is proud of, and justifiably so. He added nuances and ad-libs that dang near stole his scenes. That parting look and shrug he gave as the other crewmen left the polygraph tests is an example. If some even better parts of his performance had been used, he just might have run off with the whole show.

There is always far more film shot for any movie than the audience will ever see. Most movies could be made two, three, or even four times longer than they end up by using all the footage shot. The extra isn't error, it's insurance. Having more raw material gives the editors more range, something to work with to solve technical problems, and occasionally, to correct story-flow problems. A good editor has to be prepared to exclude outstanding scenes if they don't fit in a way that maximizes the progression of the overall story.

Conventional wisdom places the optimum length of a movie at 95 to 105 minutes. The question has been extensively researched and measured. People tire, not only of sitting, but of responding intensely. Modern life makes people so busy, many people can't budget more time than that. Actually, they've found a large percent of the audience believes they would be pleased with just a little greater length. But exhibitors (the movie theaters) have a good deal of input into the equations. So the net effect of their tradeoff of overall attendance versus the number of showings they can get into a given time span, contributes to pushing back running times.

Most people are like me. When they like a movie, they wish there could have been more. Which is exactly what moviemakers want. Leave 'em just a little hungry for more, even when a sequel is out of the question, as with *Fire in the Sky*. When the final credits roll, filmmakers certainly wouldn't want moviegoers feeling they've had their fill. The most favorable reactions (those which stay with audiences long enough for them to recommend the movie to friends) are those which keep people thinking about it long after leaving the theater. I noticed many thoughtful expressions on the faces of people leaving *Fire in the Sky*.

More than forty actors were considered for the part of Sheriff Frank Watters, a composite character developed to embody the skeptical viewpoint. Among these were Gary Busey, Scott Glenn, Peter Strauss, James Caan—even Richard Dean Anderson. I suggested Cliff Robertson.

There are many reasons why an actor might end up losing a certain role. The two obvious reasons—either the actor or casting gives a thumbs-down—are probably neither one the most frequent. Scheduling conflicts and prior commitments are probably the biggest reasons. Financial mismatches—in either direction—are probably second. Salaries must reflect the budget. Some actors often don't even learn they had been considered for a role, aren't even sent a script, because casting eliminates them out-of-hand on the basis of factors they discover early, like unavailability.

Talks with James Caan broke off over a number of things, mainly his desire to have the script rewritten to greatly enlarge the part of Frank Watters. When James Garner was suggested, I was privately a little doubtful. I liked Garner a lot, but, to me, that was the problem. He was so enormously well liked I wondered if audiences would read his character's embodiment of hostile skepticism too sympathetically. I thought he seemed too kind to be hard, too cuddly to be crusty. I was wrong again. James Garner brought to the role *precisely* the exact mix of hostility and sympathy to convey the essence of our real-life situation. Also, his western image and country charm were just right for hereabouts. All the lawmen who were combined into his role were pleased to identify themselves with him.

For myself, it went beyond his absolute appropriateness as Watters. I had great admiration for his much-publicized gutsy stand against those few in the Hollywood establishment who had not given him his financial due from *The Rockford Files*. His was a moral victory which cleared the way for better treatment for others in his profession who lacked his clout. I'm not an actor, but my respect comes from his willingness to undergo huge personal sacrifice and risk great monetary loss in order to stand on principle. Too few people today do anything purely on principle.

I'd heard a lot of impressive names tossed back and forth for the role of Mike Rogers: Nicholas Cage, Mark Harmon, Johnny Depp, and Tim Robbins. When Robert Patrick was suggested for an audition, everyone's reaction was, "Huh?" Robert Patrick's rendition of the liquid-metal man disguised as a cop, the T-1000, was indelible. This portrayal of the second terminator opposite Arnold Schwarzenegger in *Terminator II: Judgment Day* was so riveting, so coldly, threateningly, precisely convincing, people had trouble envisioning him as anything else. This is one of the mixed blessings to befall new actors who deliver too powerful a performance in a breakthrough role.

The man who showed up at the audition was no slicked-back, lean, fixated homicidal cyborg. This guy was fuller, bearded, long-haired, with humanity and character radiating from every pore. He read the emotion-packed scene where Mike confronts the congregation (the townsfolk gathered in the church to demand that local officials "do something") with such intensity and such a wide range of upwelling feeling that he blew them away. Hollywood types can sometimes get pretty cynical, but that group was genuinely moved. And it was just an audition.

They continued to hold readings for the part of Mike Rogers, but from then on they were just going through the motions. No one said so, but I, always one to try to reserve judgment, was certain Robert Patrick would play Mike Rogers.

Robert Patrick didn't know that—yet—but was nevertheless sufficiently interested in *Fire*, out of all the scripts he'd been offered, to pay a visit to Snowflake, Arizona. He was out driving with his wife on vacation and without a word to anyone at Paramount, toured the area—Pinetop, Lakeside,

Show Low—and spent a night in town. He obtained my address and cruised by my house while I was out raking my yard. His wife persuaded him it would be too much of an intrusion to stop in, so he didn't. Drat! I would have loved to have invited him in and taken him on a tour of the site at Heber, the point of my return, etc.

After shooting began I got a phone message to call him on location. I spoke with him and one or two of the other actors who happened to be in his room. I wasn't as familiar with their work but they seemed like a great bunch of guys, especially Pete Berg.

Robert Patrick was very interested in reality-based research to increase his understanding of the role of Mike Rogers. I answered his questions, which were full of insight. I put him in touch with Mike. They talked for hours about the work, the town, the incident, and other things directed at filling in the larger blanks in Robert Patrick's concept of Mike's character in 1975.

I didn't have clearance to share my copy of the script, so I sat under the crab-apple tree in my front yard one afternoon and read the entire thing to Mike. A real workout for the vocal cords, but I wanted to see his reactions, and to comment myself as we went along.

Since Mike hadn't know the movie was coming, he hadn't had the gradual education I'd had about the cinematic facts-of-life and commercial realities of the industry. The departures from reality the script took hit Mike all at once. I explained it to him, but it took awhile for him to assimilate. He got much more upset than I had but, in a few weeks he came around. Time, and talking with me, did it, but talking with Robert Patrick helped a bunch. It wasn't long before he was also an enthusiastic supporter of the making of *Fire in the Sky*.

All the guys suggested for the part of Travis Walton had considerable popularity and were big box-office draws. But, although I never once made any outright demand, I kept hoping they would come up with somebody who fit my own self-concept better.

It was a hard part to fill. Some of the preliminary filming had already begun, with my part the only one remaining to be cast. I was a little alarmed; there was a shooting schedule to keep. But the producers didn't seem overly concerned. Perhaps they knew something I didn't, perhaps negotiations were under way with a number of actors.

Finally, it was official. I would be played by D. B. Sweeney. My unfamiliarity with his work was quickly remedied. I rented videos of almost everything he'd ever done. He'd starred in *The Cutting Edge*, *Memphis Belle*, *Eight Men Out*, *Gardens of Stone*, and *No Man's Land*. On television he'd played Dish on the Emmy-winning miniseries, *Lonesome Dove*, and starred in the NBC movie *Miss Rose White*, which won three Emmys in 1992, including

Best Made-for-Television Movie. We had a little D. B. Sweeney film festival at my house. I was impressed and relieved. D. B. Sweeney wasn't the biggest name of the contenders, but he was hands-down my favorite out of those I'd heard mentioned. He didn't resemble me in appearance and he didn't match my present sense of myself, but he was perfect for *Fire in the Sky*'s take on the Travis Walton of 1975.

The movie was being filmed in a place called Oakland, Oregon, population 700. Why there, everyone asks, and not in Snowflake, Arizona? Snowflake and Heber were the first towns scouted, and the movie trade publication *Variety* ran an early article based on press leaks that *Fire in the Sky* would "lens in Arizona." So we were definitely considered. Many other Arizona towns were also personally scouted by the writer and the director. So were Silverton, Colorado, and Paris, Idaho, among others. All were rejected for one reason or another. One town had some minor event scheduled that they were decorating for, and which they didn't want interfered with. And so, in their wisdom, they passed up the enormous financial benefits the town would have received. Another town was visually right, but too inaccessible in terms of transportation. The logistics of moving great numbers of people and equipment back and forth makes having major highways and a good-sized airport nearby a major plus. A related factor is sufficient infrastructure to provide food, housing, entertainment, etc., to several hundred members of the cast and crew. Any such shortcomings can be (and have been for other films) overcome with greater budgetary allowances when justifiable. But anytime it's possible, finding places already equipped is preferred.

Snowflake would have been hard for potential audiences to perceive as heavily involved in forest product–related industries, because it is actually physically located just outside the forest. The producers wanted a town that could send this message visually by being surrounded by forest. Snowflake had nearly doubled in size since 1975, so it was said to be "too grown-up and modern to pass for seventeen years ago." No one said so, but perhaps they also thought local controversy about the incident might cause problems for the production.

Anything a movie can *show* as background is one less thing to be communicated in dialogue. They wanted not just a small town, but a small-town *look*. A place where Main Street fits into a single camera shot.

They ultimately found the answer to those considerations in Oakland, Oregon. The town was founded in the mid-1800s by two (fortunate) dropouts from the ill-fated Donner Party. The original center of Oakland still contains numerous buildings in excellent condition, built back in the town's beginnings. I can find in Snowflake a near twin for almost every building in Oakland: the only problem is, these buildings are not adjoining and therefore could not be filmed together as a town with the desired look. Oakland is surrounded by forest resembling that which can be found in our area. Oakland, Oregon, possessed the idyllic small-town country charm of 1970s Snowflake the director was searching for.

The production's ground transport could be trucked north directly up the freeway from L.A. The nearby city of Roseburg was big enough for a base of operations (lodging, offices, etc.). The airport at Eugene was still a fair drive away, but at least it was freeway all the way.

Five weeks of a planned seven-week shoot had elapsed before Dana and I finally got to go. Seems the director tried, but couldn't come up with justification to renege on his promises; good old producer Joe Wizan prevailed. We flew up to Oregon for a week of visiting the set. It was quite an adventure.

When we got off the plane in Eugene we were met by one of Paramount's drivers, a pleasant young fellow who'd emigrated from England during his high-school days. On the seventy-mile drive to our hotel in Roseburg, we chatted about how filming had been going so far, and about the differences between America and England. In regard to a passing mention of the word *billion*, I remarked that a billion is equal to a thousand million here (and in France), while in England and Germany the term *billion* denotes a million million. Since he was a transplant with quite a number of years in both countries, I thought such a curiosity would be a safe bet for light conversation. One of the painful lessons I've learned since 1975 is to *never* share knowledge of little-known facts or surprising oddities with people whose beliefs about the incident are uncertain or unknown (and therefore possibly skeptical). These people regard such statements as confirmation of their suspicion that I'm a colossal liar. I could tell he thought I was just indulging in what he diagnosed as my usual fact inventing habit. I shrugged it off. Nothing new in my being misperceived and misjudged.

Even though the area was supposedly in the middle of a drought, the countryside was lush and verdant. Trees grew densely, wild berry bushes everywhere. Our hotel was one of the two best in town, across the highway from each other. All the actors and the more important crew members stayed in those two, while others stayed in some smaller hotels around the area. The director and producers rented houses. Perks of the job.

When we arrived, there was a gift-wrapped bottle of wine from the crew and a welcome note waiting for us in our room. Though we don't drink, it was a pleasing gesture. The area is a famous wine-growing region, so it made an appropriate souvenir.

We'd only been there a few minutes when the phone rang. It was producer Joe Wizan. He welcomed us, inquired as to our needs, and told us about the cheese and wine festival going on over in Oakland. (Filming finished there just in time for the production designer's crew to return the town to normal for the annual celebration. Most of the remainder of the Oregon production would be filmed in nearby Sutherlin.) It was Saturday afternoon and production was shut down for the weekend, Joe told us. He invited us to dinner that evening. He said we'd be on our own for the rest of the weekend to relax, have a look around, and attend the festival. Joe Wizan was the key person responsible for bringing us to Oregon and a most gracious host throughout our stay.

(Joe Wizan knows the business. He is the former president of Twentieth-Century Fox Studios. Before leaving the studio to form his own company, he presided over the production of such box-office successes as *Alien*, the remake of *The Fly*, *Romancing the Stone*, *Jewel of the Nile*, and *Cocoon*. Wizan's first independent production was *Jeremiah Johnson* with Robert Redford. He was producer of, in no particular order, *Tough Guys* (Kirk Douglas, Burt Lancaster), ... *And Justice For All* (Al Pacino), *Unfaithfully Yours* (Dudley Moore, Nastassja Kinski), *Best Friends* (Goldie Hawn, Burt Reynolds), *Two of a Kind* (Olivia Newton-John, John Travolta), *Voices* (Amy Irving), *Iron Eagles* (Lou Gossett, Jr.), *Junior Bonner* (Steve McQueen), *Prime Cut* (Lee Marvin, Gene Hackman), and *Stop or My Mom Will Shoot* (Sylvester Stallone), as well as *Audrey Rose*, *Wrestling Ernest Hemingway*, HBO's *El Diablo*, the Disney Channel's *Perfect Harmony*, and Tracy Torme's *Spellbinder*. In all he has six television films and over twenty feature films to his credit. He's worked with most of the top directors in the business, including Norman Jewison, Michael Ritchie, and Sam Peckinpah. His partner in production for *Fire in the Sky*, Todd Black, worked with him on the production of a number of the films listed here. *Fire in the Sky* was the very first film to be packaged by his newly organized company, Wizan Film Properties.)

Before he hung up, Joe told us there were shuttle buses making regular runs to the Umpqua Valley Wine and Jazz Festival. One of their regular hourly pickup points was right outside our hotel.

That evening at dinner Joe told us he'd planned to have dinner with the cast in honor of our visit, but that some of them had needed to make quick trips, back to L.A. and elsewhere, during the weekend break. However, most of the main cast members would join us for dinner the next day, Sunday evening. Dana and I were thrilled at the prospect.

The weather that Sunday morning was beautiful. Since we'd been told filming in Oakland was completed, going to the festival would likely be our only opportunity to visit the town. The main street shown in the movie was filled with many colorful tents and booths of the various exhibitors and concessions.

The good sense in the director's choice of Oakland was plain, except for one thing: it looks *too* perfect. I could see why they had to "dress down" the buildings for the movie. In real life these restored hundred-year-old buildings look too new. The town hardly looks lived in—just a little too clean, too much like some fake 1950s TV soundstage. It was ironic enough that *Snowflake* didn't look enough like Snowflake, but when they found a town that did look enough like Snowflake, it looked too much like a movie set to look natural in a movie!

There was a bandstand set up nearby, where not only jazz, but also groups playing other musical styles, entertained. A number of local wineries and cheesemakers offered taste samples. Local artists displayed and offered their work for sale. We respected the requests of the Native American artists that we not photograph them with their work. It was because of a religious belief, we were told. It was strange to see store chains like Coast-To-Coast, which we were used to seeing packaged modern-style, housed in such antique buildings.

We went to Rae's Cafe and "the Sheriff's Office" (actually the fire station) where the polygraph tests were filmed. No one recognized us. Everyone was friendly, with that small-town openness and sense of community that gives America its underappreciated infrastructure, its backbone. Yes, Oakland could stand in for our mountain community, no problem.

We caught the shuttle bus back to the hotel in plenty of time to rest and get ready for our dinner meeting with the cast. We met with Joe Wizan in the restaurant and waited for the others to arrive. They were, naturally, fashionably late to just the right tantalizing degree, but not unpleasantly so. We eventually got together with the rest of the primary cast. However, James Garner, Henry Thomas, and Craig Sheffer wouldn't be coming. The current filming didn't involve these three, so they were elsewhere. Garner was at home; Henry Thomas had accompanied his girlfriend back to Los Angeles; Craig Sheffer was back East somewhere doing promotional work for *A River Runs Through It*.

I don't know who was most curious—them about us, or us about them—but that evening is one we'll always remember. Bradley Gregg, his wife, and a very well behaved, red-haired baby son were there. Bradley had appeared with D. B. Sweeney in *Lonesome Dove*. Other television-film work included the CBS Hallmark Special, *O Pioneers!*—starring Jessica Lange. And he was a regular in the TV series *The Marshall Chronicles* and *My Two Dads*. His feature-film work was notable: *The Fisher King*, *Eye of the Storm*, *Indiana Jones and the Last Crusade*, and *Stand by Me*. His pleasant wife bore an amazing resemblance to a girl I knew from Snowflake.

Georgia Emelin, who was playing the part of Dana, was one of the first to arrive. They'd said she was beautiful, and they were right. While we were at the festival she'd spent the morning on a nature hike in nearby Cougar Canyon—alone. Now *there's* a lady with independent spirit. She had been chosen partly on the basis of a credible family resemblance to Mike Rogers; it was therefore no stretch to note features she and Dana held alike. As Joe Wizan had told me, Georgia had a sweetness about her like Dana's. Not surprisingly, she and Dana hit it off right away.

Fire in the Sky was Georgia's motion-picture debut. She'd been born in New York, raised in Colorado and California. She'd played the lead in stage productions of *Fifth of July*, *Rude Awakening*, *Fractions*, and (understandably) *Beauty and the Beast*. In television she'd made guest appearances in *Murder, She Wrote*, *Quantum Leap*, and *The Young Riders*. She starred in the made-for-television movies *Siege at Alta View*, *Leap of Faith*, *Deadly Relations*, and the miniseries *Common Ground*.

Peter Berg (who played David Whitlock, a crewman created to replace the real life crewman from whom movie rights were not obtained) was a real character. He was a quick wit who kept everybody laughing. That is, socially. When it comes to work he is a very serious and hardworking actor who puts every bit of himself into his role, doing whatever he can to bring out the most in the characters he plays.

Pete seemed to be right in the middle of the close camaraderie that developed within the cast. That group chemistry was fortunate but very real. Some genuine friendships were formed during the making of *Fire in the Sky*. They all—especially the guys playing the logging crew—played golf together constantly during their off-hours in Oregon. But having played the second buddy in both *Fire in the Sky* and *Aspen Extreme* shouldn't give casting people tunnel vision about Pete. Because (something he may not know till he reads this) he had been the first name on one early list I saw of potential candidates for the lead—number-one buddy Mike Rogers. Peter Berg's other movie credits are: *Crooked Hearts*, *Late for Dinner*, *A Midnight Clear*, *Race for Glory*, *Heart of Dixie*, *Never on Tuesday*, *Tehachapi*, and, for USA TV, *Key Evidence*.

Scott McDonald played my brothers Don and Duane rolled into one person named Dan. Scott is a likable fellow and did a good job—although he's not as intimidating as my real brothers.

It may surprise some that we weren't so distracted that we didn't eat our dinner, but the atmosphere was pretty casual and we thoroughly enjoyed our time.

Once more I picked up on the fact that we'd turned out not to be the far-out specimens they had anticipated meeting. I believe that had been a factor in D. B. Sweeny's earlier reluctance to make contact by phone. In fact, he later told me he'd been concerned: What if he met me and then didn't believe me? That would have seriously interfered with his ability to give his all to his performance. Putting myself in his shoes, I could appreciate his thinking.

Later, after some of the people conversing started to divide into sub-groups, Sweeney called me over, and we sat and talked awhile. He apologized for not getting in touch sooner, but I told him I understood. I also got a little insight into his psyche. His status as a young single actor with a high quotient of appeal to female fans, and with regard to some of his extracurricular activities, have given him a bit of a wild, bad-boy reputation off-screen. But those stories paint a very incomplete picture. He's a man of far greater depth and intelligence than any of his roles have given him the opportunity to display.

Sweeney's frequent casting as characters with roguish, daring qualities may stem from some of his offscreen activities. He says he's lately begun to curb his natural instinct to take risks, on and off camera. As he told *DramaLogue:* "I'm trying to cut back a little bit, because statistically speaking, I've dodged a few bullets. I recently passed on an offer to bungee-jump, but I still want to skydive. I do a lot of scuba diving, and I really enjoy that, but I'm not as reckless as I was. I used to be really reckless—now, I'm just sort of moderately adventurous." . . . Sort of parallels some of the changes I've been through.

During this whole movie episode I picked up a lot of juicy gossip about the cast, crew, director, producer, etc., but you won't be hearing any of that here. For that sort of stuff you'll have to go to the tabloids.

The pleasant weather held for our first day on the set at nearby Sutherlin. Buildings there represented the motel, the church, and the homes of my mother, Mike, and the crew. Work on a film begins early. We were surprised at how chilly the mid-September mornings dawned, but wardrobe kindly lent us some jackets.

The film crew seemed naturally curious, but didn't quite know how to react to us at first. But it wasn't long before I got that old familiar, "Wow, you're not at all the flake I expected you'd be." That reaction was also true of a few of the extras, but many of them were very friendly from the start.

Right away we met executive producer Wolfgang Glattis, an extremely nice man we didn't really get to know well until after our Oregon trip. He had just picked up breakfast from the food-service wagon that fed everyone on the set (including all the extras). He invited us to grab something to eat, too. He sent someone to take us over there who, to our embarrassment, put us at the head of a long line of people waiting there. "Unlike you, they aren't needed till later," he explained, "and they don't have anything better to do while they wait around here."

After eating our breakfast in the local men's club, rented to the production, we checked out the vehicles used in the movie. Parked out back was my motorcycle—or both of them, I should say. In no production paying out costs of around fifteen thousand dollars per minute can only a single item of any key piece of mechanical equipment appearing on camera be considered sufficient. The expense of a schedule delay caused by a few minutes' mechanical difficulty makes paying for doubles of all the vehicles a very cost-effective insurance.

In the case of our crew truck, *four* identical trucks were readied. Three of these were prepared with all-new running gear. Unlike Mike's real truck, mechanical breakdowns were very unlikely. Every detail was duplicated. All the papers, tools, and grubby work-gloves that normally cluttered the dash of Mike's work-truck were duplicated and glued into identical positions. Four sets of identical brand-new seat covers were artificially aged with the same assortment of stains and worn spots. They'd done their homework well, producing very authentic work-trucks.

Apparently the team who produced the quadruplets and the team who added the finishing touches were not the same; four trucks with nice, new white paint jobs had been the starting material, but identical dents, scrapes, and battle scars had been added. What appeared even at close range to be dust, mud splashes, scraped-off paint, and even gasoline drip stains under the tank-filler cap were all, upon very close inspection, actually paint or lumps of plastic applied *over* the underneath coat. It was amazingly authentic—insurance that the matches wouldn't be ruined, rubbing off with contact with clothing or washing off in the rain.

One of the trucks was built without any engine or running gear at all. It was specially prepared for the cab to be split apart right between the front and back seats. It had special brackets to attach steel casters underneath to support the unwheeled ends of the halves after they were separated. The whole thing could be put back together with bolts.

No, this wasn't done for some bizarre special effect depicting a crash, laser blast, or such. It was simply a way to allow access for a large cluster of camera, crew, and soundman to film toward the back seat from the point of view of those in the front seat and vice versa—to allow filming of the view from the back seat and over the shoulders of those in the front seat. The latter was done mostly with stand-in doubles for the actors. The dash lights were operable and the speedometer was rigged to read speed. Road movement was simulated by rocking the truck.

In order for the driver to move the steering wheel in a free and natural way, as if the truck were actually moving, the steering wheel was disconnected from the front wheels. This made the front half difficult to maneuver when it was off the trailer. For night scenes there was no need for a darkened building, or to wait for night. A special lightproof black tent was quickly framed up and placed over the whole unit—truck, dollies, film and sound equipment, and operators.

The black-tent trick was also used to cover the exterior doors and windows of buildings used in interior nighttime filming, as in the motel office scene. But for exterior night shots, real, 100-percent-natural, unadulterated night was employed. The same thing with the scenes out on the contract—real trees, real chainsaws.

These were some of the first scenes shot in Oregon. Local loggers were hired to train the actors playing the crew of woodsmen. They were taught how to handle chainsaws, how to fell trees. They discovered that felling a tree accurately is no simple thing. Robert Patrick related an amusing incident, when he was supposed to fell a tree on a particular spot, and wound up sending a film crew scrambling in all directions when the tree didn't—as they say in director's lingo—"hit its mark."

It was a good thing the forest scenes up on Boomer Hill were shot first because they were some of the most difficult. The weather held on to the last of the summer heat. The steep, narrow, mountain dirt-road up to the set was the only way in or out. Big trucks of equipment and supplies went back and forth with barely room to get by each other, dust boiling up and reducing visibility to a few feet ahead. It was a nightmare of logistics because *everything* had to be brought in, including toilets. Anything not on-hand would take hours to get. People often got lost trying to find the place. Tempers grew short. There were a number of incidents. Some strained working relationships never recovered. On top of this, much of the footage was filmed at night.

The crew gave me some of the *Fire in the Sky* hats they had made up, with "Boomer Hill Gang" added to the front, and, on the back, "Boned again, again and again." I was told to be glad I'd missed that time on the set, but I still wished I could have visited then.

The set in Sutherlin consisted of several streets barricaded with orange traffic cones. This one small area was wisely chosen so as to put everything to be filmed within convenient distance. Uniformed local off-duty police hired by the production as security officers kept throngs of fans and local sightseers behind yellow plastic ribbon strung up around the perimeter.

The men's lodge and its adjacent vacant lot (now filled with trailers) served as base of operations. Wardrobe was across the street from that, with the church next door. The "Chaparral Motel" was on the street behind, while its manager's office was actually mocked up in someone's carport on another street a block away, across from the church. Residences used in the movie were on nearby side streets.

The first scene we saw filmed was that of "Mike Rogers" leaving his motel room as he and David Whitlock are ambushed by a television news team. Dozens of people standing around displayed great discipline when the call "Stand by to roll!" went up. People standing on crunchy gravel simply froze for many minutes at a time. You could have heard a pin drop. The rest of the signal ritual was a bit different from what I'd seen in movies about movies being made, but still ended with "Action!" The director, Rob Lieberman, busy and stressed-out as he was, took time to welcome us with cold drinks from his personal cooler, explained a few things, and let us sit in his chair and watch the scenes unfold just as the camera saw them. The modern equipment they were using had a dual video-monitor setup so that the director could sit apart from two separate cameras and see exactly what each camera is filming.

Pete Berg as David Whitlock was waiting for "Mike" (Robert Patrick) on the porch outside his motel room. When Mike comes out, shaking sleep off, the reporters rush him; Mike snaps back at them and David Whitlock throws out a few defensive, defiant remarks; then they drive off. Pete Berg is so ambitious in trying to fill out his role's full potential that sometimes he works too hard, getting off his mark and into shots not planned to involve him.

In one take of this scene, the director yelled "Cut!" and everyone looked at each other, as if to say, *"I didn't see any problem, what went wrong with that one?"* Rob Leiberman said, good-naturedly, "I don't remember David Whitlock having that many lines in this scene!" Everybody laughed. The director was one of those wise enough to tolerate actors ad-libbing lines, because some very good ones came through in the final product.

Also filmed outside "Mike's motel room" was a scene where a couple of Japanese reporters (among the various foreign journalists who descended on Snowflake) walk by chattering in their native language. What most of the audience was unaware of, since it was not translated with subtitles, was that they joked about the availability of a sushi bar in a place like Snowflake. We had a nice talk with those two actors, one of whom had been a samurai in the *Ninja Turtles* movie.

To the regulars on a movie set it's supposed to be very boring, all the waiting and repetition. But it was all so new to us, everything was continually exciting. We met a lot of nice people. The crowds hanging around on the other side of the yellow tape barriers didn't seem to tire of waiting for a chance to glimpse a celebrity, get an autograph or maybe even get to take a picture with one of the stars.

We were also the targets of attention, after they found out who we were, which evoked a kind of "Who, me?" reaction from us. There was a very stabilizing—though not intended as such—reminder from a kid who, *after* he got our autograph, asked, "Are you guys anybody?" We loved it. Nothing like a guileless youngster to help you keep things in perspective.

The extras (people without lines hired to be crowds, passersby, etc.) were a really great bunch. There were some great people on the crew, too. Hank Garfield, the sound mixer, told me about an article about *Fire in the Sky* in the *Hollywood Reporter* (a movie-industry trade publication) and, when I expressed curiosity about it, promised to let me see his copy, which he hadn't brought with him. I've had many such promises from people I've met in connection with the incident, and never gave it another thought.

Much to my surprise, days later, our driver delivered Hank's copy of the publication to us as we left. I was impressed by things like that. It's easy to be nice to someone's face and then forget it. It really means something when someone remembers and goes out of his way to keep his word later.

The crowds really gathered when Robert Patrick appeared. Everyone wanted to see the T-1000 from *Terminator II.* He was very good natured about it and didn't mind giving a few minutes to the people who ultimately pay to put stars where they are. That rascal D. B. Sweeney didn't care much for contact with his fans, but he sure had a different gorgeous lady on his arm each time I saw him. Robert Patrick's wife, also an actress, wasn't on the set, but he kept a big picture of her prominently displayed in his trailer.

A lady who owned a local card-and-memorabilia shop had Robert Patrick signing cards for her. When Dana expressed eagerness to get a few of those *Terminator II: Judgment Day* trading cards for our kids, Robert Patrick bought, out of his own pocket, a whole case from the shop owner, and sat down and autographed every one of them for us. That sort of kindness has real meaning.

I had thought Robert Patrick and D. B. Sweeney drew a big crowd until James Garner finally showed up on the set. *That* man can pull in a crowd—and from every age group. Here again was somebody who didn't merely *understand* who buttered his bread, but seemed to have a genuine liking for his fans. There was nothing self-centered about him.

One incident illustrating that fact to me occurred as a group of people crowded around James Garner on the second landing of the high steps to the church, listening to him tell an interesting story. He was seated comfortably in his special western-style chair, a gift presented to him years past. It was a director's-style folding chair of hand-tooled leather, with saddlebags engraved with his initials, and padded with sheep's wool. In the midst of all that comfort and attention, James Garner abruptly got up and waded through the crowd to assist a frail old man. The elderly gentleman was over ninety, an extra in the church scene, unsteadily trying to make his way down the long, steep stairway.

No one else had even noticed. People leaned obliviously against both handrails, so the old fellow had nothing with which to steady himself. But James Garner, no self-absorbed star basking in the admiration of his fans, was the only person to come to the rescue. This was only one of several incidents I observed that demonstrated his sensitivity to the needs of others around him as a natural part of his personality.

Yes, I did run into one or two of those archetypal insecure, ego-driven, spoiled-brat prima donnas, but I was surprised at how few "Hollywood types" I encountered on the set of *Fire in the Sky*. I know plenty exist, but I ran into more of them incarnated as production *office people* than as actors.

There was unusually fine casting, just about perfect, for *Fire in the Sky*. The chemistry of that group was phenomenal, on and off camera. All those upcoming young actors on the logging crew looked upon James Garner as a mentor, from whom they learned much. About golf, too! Sweeney says Garner kicked their greenhorn tails out on the golf course.

I don't want anyone to think I'm fawning over or being ingratiating about these people. I don't think I was very starstruck at all. Most people think I'm just a little bit cynical in my judgment of others (as if events in my life hadn't encouraged worse!). I pride myself on looking past exteriors and superficial judgments, because I've too often been a victim of such bias. I really believe that cast was an unusually decent bunch. I've run into a number of celebrities over the years with whom I was not so impressed. It is amazing to find such good people surviving among the sharks and jealous mega-egos of that business. What quality could they possess to permit that survival? Talent. The beasts won't devour those golden geese because they *need* them.

I did an interview while I was there with Doug Lewellyn, the "People's Court" commentator, who also does "The Making of . . ." videos for different movies. After we went back out into the street, he was engaged in some other filming of the goings-on, when he came over and asked one last question as an afterthought: "Look at all this commotion going on here, all those people asking for your autograph, all these actors, crew, equipment. All this is on account of you. How does that make you feel?"

I shrugged and without thinking gave some half-intelligible answer which didn't fully express what I felt. I could tell he couldn't believe anyone wouldn't be starstruck by all that. What I wanted to say is that basically, it's a wash. I don't regard as positive all aspects of my movie experience, even those most people would so regard. It would take one hell of a lot of positive to counterbalance all the negative I'd lived through for so many years. Also, the same philosophy which insulated me from the negative insulates me from the so-called "positive" attention. The shell that protects an animal also prevents its feeling being petted. On both extremes, it only stems from the ideas that people who don't know the real me hold in their minds. I had to face it. The facts are what they are. An inaccurate perception, whether positive or negative, must be disregarded. If one is irrelevant, then so is the other.

Dana and I were going to get to watch the filming of one of the more emotionally intense scenes of the movie, in which Mike Rogers confronts those assembled for a town meeting concerning the incident. In fact, we were going to be *in* it. Golly gee, this was going to be my big break into instant superstardom! Joe Wizan's idea was to have us in the crowd, verbally attacking "Mike" with suspicions of foul play. When someone called out in an accusing tone, "Well, then, where is he?" I was to stand up and say with heavy suspicion: "Yeah, Mike, where *is* Travis!?" A nice ironic twist for a cameo appearance.

Getting a speaking line required me to join SAG, the Screen Actors Guild union. We had to go to wardrobe for mid-seventies garb, and Dana had to go to the makeup trailer to have her normally full curls combed down into a style appropriate for the time. She felt really funny wearing bell bottoms again.

We sat there in the crowd all day for two days. Periodically the smoke machine would pump in some more (cough) "atmosphere." There was a light rain the first afternoon and second morning. But rain or shine, early or late, it was always a sunny afternoon inside the church. Thanks to the stained glass, sunshine was easy to simulate by setting up powerful lights outside each of the west windows. "Sunlight" streamed in at the same angle throughout shooting.

Robert Patrick's performance was incredibly powerful. When he confronted and chastised the people for their behavior, his words were so intense, his emotions so strong and real, that the roomful of extras didn't have to act. Everyone was visibly affected and many said they actually felt ashamed of what they'd "done." Me too. It was amazing. Several of the women, Dana included, were actually moved to tears. No wonder he blew them away with his audition of this scene.

There was take after take. Again, they weren't mistakes. The director wanted many angles on this one, as well as different intensities. Time after time Robert Patrick went out and came back in and delivered another torrent of varied emotions.

Without pause he had to run the gamut of had-it-up-to-here, can't-take-it-anymore anger. Then a fervent rupturing of overflowing sadness, dismay, anger, and disappointment at betrayal. And finally he had to shift quickly to a defiant challenge. Each time, he shook with anger, poured out tears, and then hardened into steely, straightforward defiance.

From where was he dredging this incredible energy? He literally stunned the crowd. One thing he shattered permanently was his typecasting as a bloodless, unfeeling cyborg. Most people wouldn't recognize him in person from his previous role anyway. But to see him as Mike Rogers playing with his laughing little daughters, forever evaporates the knee-jerk tendency to see in him a sinister air of hidden menace (although he can still do that as no one else can).

I did quite a number of takes of my little spoken line, too. Only, my repetitions probably were due to not getting it right, because the director ordered the line cut from the movie very early in the editing process. Inexplicably, the director picked one of Robert Patrick's milder renditions of that scene. A lot of Robert Patrick's best stuff, as with the other actors, was cut out. But for the actors the cuts were for technical reasons like pacing, context, to keep the length within limits, or merely the director's artistic preference; my bit was chopped so early, it must have been pretty bad.

However, there's a positive way of looking at my part being cut. Every one of the actors was moved from a somewhat skeptical attitude about the incident, to a much more believing position after meeting and speaking with me. Actors are professional simulators of reality and therefore, it seems, would be much more capable of detecting "acting" (lying, if you will) than the average person. Juxtapose this with my failure to act well enough to win even a tiny spot in my own movie. Together those facts should say quite a bit for my credibility, if nothing for my thespian talents.

Peter Berg's big moment in *Fire in the Sky*, from an actor's viewpoint, was when he finally had a long, intense scene, alone on camera and in close-up, when he goes to the deserted church and prays for forgiveness—forgiveness for failing to attempt an immediate rescue of me, not for having committed my murder, but the audience is supposed to be left wondering.

Peter Berg's buddies, Robert Patrick and D. B. Sweeney, got together with the director and planned a practical joke. Pete was about to get his comeuppance for his earlier scene-stealing. The director went through a number of takes as usual to make sure Pete's best was in the can (and it *was* very good, intense emotion; they could have used more of it, had there been time).

I stood back in the corner with my video camera and taped the whole thing. When they were sure they had his performance, the director told him he needed one more take. As with the previous takes, this shot would begin with the camera on the stained-glass window in the rear. The camera would back down the aisle to take in the front of the first pew, where it would then pan over to Peter Berg, facing forward, praying aloud while the camera came in for a close-up. Only this time, at a prearranged signal, Robert and D.B., whom Pete believed had left hours ago, came up from the rear stairwell and followed the Steadicam down the aisle, slipping quietly into the pew behind Peter Berg. As the camera came in on Peter Berg for what was supposed to be his solo close-up, there on either side of his face were the mugging faces of Robert and D.B., leaning forward into frame, stealing *his* scene!

As the shot ended the guys behind sniggered a little to let Pete know he wasn't alone. When he turned and saw them, everyone roared with laughter. In spite of being wrung-out from his earlier outpouring, Pete took it well. He joked that since they'd intruded on his best take, it would be necessary to get those two matted out of that scene so it still could be used.

I have a prediction. Watch those three, because I believe they are really going somewhere in their profession.

It was a pleasure meeting Henry Thomas, who played Greg Hayes, another crewman character created in absence of contracts with all real life crew members. Part of the reason he was cast was because of his prior role in the blockbuster *E.T.—The ExtraTerrestrial*. That fact had the unintended effect of inviting some unwarranted comparisons between *E.T.* and *Fire in the Sky*. Henry Thomas, like many actors in his situation, has had his own share of difficulty getting people to see him as someone other than the child Elliot from *E.T.* Those people ought to go back and look again at *E.T.* Thomas delivered an amazing performance which covered the gamut of human expression. Further proof of his range is evident in his other, more recent work, such as the teenage Norman Bates in *Psycho IV*.

A great source of humor and camaraderie was Noble Willingham, who played Sheriff Blake Davis. He kept everybody in stitches, as with his difficulty in pronouncing "Mogollon" on camera.

It was great meeting the director's wife, Marilu Henner, Best known for her work on two hit series, *Taxi* and *Evening Shade*, and for the film *L.A. Story*. I saw her on a television news-magazine during the time *Fire in the Sky* was in production. She is a really talented dancer, amazingly fit. My wife Dana, who teaches aerobics at our local college, shares her interest in dance and aerobics. Dana was delighted when Marilu presented her with a copy of *Marilu Henner's Dancerobics*, her exercise video.

We attended "dailies," which is the screening of "rushes," film just back from special processing in L.A. Even this raw, uncut footage without music was impressive. We also spent some time in the editing room with Steve Mirkovich, who kindly gave us a quick overview of the process and showed us how he had matched one segment with a specially prepared trial soundtrack. Fascinating work.

Our on-location driver, Pete Kozak who was also Robert Patrick's driver, was a really interesting person. He is a brother of actress Harley Kozak. I don't know what he was doing working as a driver, because the guy has brain and talent. I noticed that during the periods he spent waiting around, he was reading some pretty heavy intellectual books. He also would play his guitar or mandolin. When his mandolin was stolen, the cast got together and bought him a new one.

I'd heard he'd written a song called "Fire in the Sky." As we were preparing to leave we finally had a chance to hear it. I videotaped Kozac's impromptu performance while our first driver, the young English fellow, who made the longer hauls to Eugene, wrung his hands and checked his watch. It was his job to make sure he got us to our plane on time. We'd stopped off in Oakland, where the film company had gone back for one last scene at Rae's Cafe. Peter Berg was there listening to the song with us while he waited for his call.

"FIRE IN THE SKY"
by Pete Kozak

Let there be lightnin'
*   Let there be thunder*
*   Let the heavens rage on high.*
What is this thing burnin' through the darkness?
Just a fire in the sky.
Out on the backroads
*   High in the timber*
*   Hardworkin' man, just gettin' by.*
*   Then somethin' changed my life forever—*
Just a fire in the sky.
*   I saw what I saw*
*   Just can't explain it*
*   Don't you think I haven't tried?*
But who'd take the word of anybody
*   Who speaks of fire in the sky?*
It seems my people
*   They don't know me*
*   They turn away when I pass by.*
Yet anymore I ain't too sure of nothin'
*   But that fire in the sky.*
Flames of damnation, saith the preacher,
*   Consume the wicked when they die.*

What saith thou, Preacher,
Where on earth was the wicked
In that fire in the sky?
I'm not dreamin' and I'm not crazy
I can look you in the eye
Then swear as God almighty is my witness
Been rainin' fire in the sky, fire in the sky, fire in the sky . . .

His lyrics had depth and revealed a perceptiveness and understanding of some of the subtleties of the script. But this mere transcript of his lyrics can't convey the feeling his voice and his music created. We were really moved. I tried unsuccessfully to get people interested in using the song in the movie. I'd still like to get someone interested in signing Pete Kozak to record it.

Maybe it's just me, but it seems there's been an unusual amount of irony and coincidence in connection with my experience. One of my first television appearances was with Leonard Nimoy, on a show produced by David Wolper, who is grandfather to one of Dana's cousins. The official still photographer on the set was Greg Schwartz, who is the son-in-law of—Leonard Nimoy.

Georgia Emelin has some friends who used to live in Snowflake. Working in the town where the movie was shot, thousands of miles from Snowflake, is former Snowflake sheriff Marlin Gillespie's oldest son. One of the extras, the local fire chief, bore a striking resemblance to former Snowflake town marshal Sanford Flake, and the chief has friends he had recently visited in Snowflake.

In the film, the doughnut girl's mom is played by a local woman named Nancy Neifert who turned out to be a second cousin of mine who I'd never met! She just happened to be living where the movie was being made and had signed on as an extra without even connecting the movie to stories she'd heard about me through relatives. Months later, when I finally got time to make a call to verify this family connection, her father, my great-uncle Oakly Rogers, answered the phone. He'd ordered a book about his family's genealogy that very day. My grandmother's maiden name was Rogers. Who knows, maybe Mike is my tenth cousin or something.

The incident happened on November 5, 1975—which was Robert Patrick's seventeenth birthday! Seventeen years later he took on the role of Mike Rogers. In researching his role, Robert Patrick discovered he had relatives from Snowflake. *Then* he learned that he is related to Mike and Dana! Robert Patrick's cousin is married to Tony Willis, the grandson of Mike and Dana's great-aunt (and, like them, a descendant of more than one of

Snowflake's founding families). Mike's grandmother is a sister of Tony's grandmother, and on top of that, Mike's grandfather is a cousin to Tony's grandfather. Which, I'm told, makes them double cousins.

One Snowflake resident received an article about the making of the movie (which I'd not yet announced locally) from a relative who lived in . . . tiny Oakland, Oregon. Rob Lieberman directed James Earl Jones in over twenty episodes of "Gabriel's Fire" (that *fire* word again). James Earl Jones (also the voice of Darth Vader in *Star Wars*) narrated a television documentary of my experience. He also played the part of Barney, husband of Betty Hill, the couple whose famous UFO-abduction case was depicted in the 1975 NBC television-movie *The UFO Incident.* Jones also worked with Robert Patrick's *T2* costar, Arnold Schwarzenegger, in *Conan the Barbarian.* During the making of *Fire in the Sky,* a meteorite struck in a ravine near Oakland, only the fifth recovered meteorite in Oregon's history. Just after the release of *Fire in the Sky,* Bruce Lee's son Brandon died tragically on a Paramount set, an incident surrounded by bizarre parallels with his father's death that are too numerous to list.

As interesting as these ironies and coincidences are, it is illogical to attach undue significance to coincidence. Aristotle expressed this best when he said, *"It is inevitable that the unusual will sometimes occur."* Indeed it will.

In late October we left to visit the special-effects studio, Industrial Light and Magic, located in San Rafael, just north of San Francisco. (Again, over the director's druthers.) Mike Rogers was completely over his problem with the script, so he was going with us. He'd been in touch with Robert Patrick often, which had built up a lot of his enthusiasm for the project.

Industrial Light and Magic (ILM) is the brainchild of film genius George Lucas. There's no monolithic sign saying *This is the spot.* In fact, the sign doesn't say *ILM* at all—only a business name, which I won't reveal here, that doesn't remotely suggest what goes on inside.

We arrived at just the right time to see the filming of some of the scenes where I'm held down on the table inside the UFO. In spite of the differences from what actually had happened, that was very unsettling to watch. It was interesting, but it was the least enjoyable part of our two-day visit.

Most everything happening at Industrial Light and Magic is secret, at least at first, either to maintain proprietary techniques so competitors won't copy them, or to prevent unscrupulous reporters from spoiling the magic for moviegoers. We had a couple of little tours of areas of the complex which had created different effects for *Fire in the Sky.* (The effects for *Jurassic Park* were being done there while *Fire in the Sky* was being done, but we weren't supposed to see any of that, so here I'll say we didn't.) *Fire in the Sky*'s visual-effects coordinator, Molly Naughton, was our guide on the first tour. We were supposed to stay together and only go where she took us. We took pictures only with permission. On our second tour, with Nilo Rodis-Jamero, we didn't use our cameras at all because it seemed to make our hosts uncomfortable.

Nilo Rodis-Jamero was credited as coproducer on *Fire in the Sky* because the execution of the visual look in the special-effects segment was so much his own contribution. Nilo was FX art director or designer on some of the most visually stunning, and successful, movies of all time, including *The Empire Strikes Back, Return of the Jedi, Raiders of the Lost Ark, Poltergeist,* and *Star Trek III, V,* and *VI.*

Rodis-Jamero's work is phenomenal and not confined to flights of fancy. His work looks good because there's an underlying practical sense to it. He's designed products for Oakley, the California sports-gear manufacturing company best known for sunglasses. He's designed beyond achieving a "look" in creating things as diverse as tactical fighter-pilot helmets, heavy military tanks, and automobiles, for companies ranging from General Motors to Lucasfilms. He's made film-industry innovations, from editing machines to a variety of special film-effect techniques. Nilo is one of those rare people who is so intelligent, yet so centered in his personality, that he gives off an aura of openness and calm. He is a very unusual personality—a little mysterious, but very pleasant to be around.

The work being done for *Fire in the Sky* would have been intriguing even if we hadn't had a personal interest. There were some amazingly clever techniques; a few were a bit technical for us. We agreed not to reveal what we'd seen, or even develop our photos until after the movie had opened. I've kept that promise, but even now I don't feel it would be constructive to reveal those things or include those photos here. After all, some people haven't seen the movie yet.

We went into the editing room where Steve Mirkovich was working. We got to see some rushes of a couple of segments from the special-effects shots. He put one with a temporary soundtrack from another movie, a space thriller, that really churned me up to watch. As in Oregon, he was generous in his willingness to explain things and not "talk down" to us. (His other films include *Cool World, Teenage Mutant Ninja Turtles II, Flight of the Intruder, Flashback, Prince of Darkness,* and *Big Trouble in Little China.*)

We got to say hello to D.B. again (and meet his new girl), but we didn't want to bother him too much while he was between such difficult scenes. The scenes aboard the craft are some of the most intense of the entire movie. Mike met him for the first time. It was the first time he'd met any of those people, Nilo, Rob Lieberman, Wolfgang Glottis, or the ILM crew.

He got to see one of his duplicated work-trucks there, which was quite a novelty for him.

Back home, we endured a lot of suspense while they spent weeks finishing up the soundtrack, the music, the editing, and the promotional trailers for the movie.

Then came the new polygraph tests. The results created a pronounced reaction out in California. They hadn't expected the tests, but were delighted at their publicity value.

The next big events for us were the television shows and publications like *Hard Copy, Sightings, Entertainment Tonight,* and *USA Today,* who sent camera crews and reporters to Snowflake. I don't think that, prior to our appearances on those shows, Paramount had been planning to use us nearly as much as they did. But our roles in promotion grew to become a tour after they saw how well we handled it. Surprisingly, in many instances journalists displayed more interest in speaking with us than with production people, or even the actors.

The previous years had prepared me somewhat for interviews and handling situations with the media. But as intense as it had been back then, when it was all new to me, it had never been so grueling. What in the world was I doing? In the past, single interviews had left me wrung out. What effect would such total immersion have on me? Would it soon make the topic completely intolerable for me, or would it have a cathartic effect, mercifully desensitizing me?

I gave literally hundreds of interviews. Print, radio, television—back-to-back, all day long. Part of the tour overlapped the Academy Awards. The streets of L.A. were bumper-to-bumper limos, and our hotel (strangely, located at the intersection of streets bearing the names of my first son and the place in Arizona where our outdoor wedding had been held) was host to a slew of celebrities. Shock-talk host Howard Stern was broadcasting from the lobby, but fortunately we managed to avoid him.

Our schedule was pretty tightly packed. One morning, by satellite uplink I gave over fifty separate television interviews without moving from my chair. Looking at a couple of those pieces later, I didn't realize I'd been so tired: I looked downright groggy in one clip. Never once did anyone at Paramount publicity ever coach me or try to influence anything I said in interviews. They were very hands-off in that respect, but very supportive in taking care of us and keeping us informed as to our schedule, and getting us places on time.

Although many misconceptions about our experience survived due to my long silence, time had thinned out many of the false charges. And in fact, our media experience, the new polygraph tests, and the making of a movie about the incident all contributed to creating an entirely new attitude on the part of those from the media. Although there was understandably still skepticism, it was mostly of the healthy variety.

Even after traveling all over the world doing promotional work for the movie, one of the worst hatchet jobs was done right here near home, by Dewey Webb of the Phoenix tabloid *New Times*, a paper so bad they have to give it away and get by on advertising dollars alone. They rely heavily on outrageous, "shock effect" articles.

Dewey misrepresented his intentions to get me to cooperate, and pretending that he would be objective employed all the photographic tricks I'd sit still for. More "monster lighting": an up-close, fish-eye effect was apparent in the picture of me that hit the stands. While the photographer kept me busy, Webb had taken it upon himself, uninvited, to go through papers on my mantel, which of course revealed nothing except what sort of people I'd—trustingly—allowed into my home. The folder there contained nothing but Paramount's standard press kit.

Dewey Webb wrote one falsehood after another, even when he was in possession of documented evidence to the contrary. I'd given him some documents he ignored, and Mike Rogers gave him information in a telephone conversation (during which Webb lied further about his intentions, making promises he broke resoundingly). Some of his false claims were simply parroting of the debunker nonsense, but some he came up with all on his own.

He was so careless with the facts that he wrote one sentence in which my experience was seven days long at the beginning and five days long at the end: "In the early-morning hours of November 12, seven days later, the dazed, hyperspaced hitchhiker staggered out of the woods near Heber and straight into UFO immortality with a fantastic tale of how he'd been used as an intergalactic guinea pig during a five-day game of 'Doctor.' " (I was returned on November 10, which by everyone else's arithmetic adds up to five days. By November 12 I had already been in Phoenix for more than a day.) He also falsely claimed the crew's polygraph tests had been sponsored by the *National Enquirer*, instead of by the state police.

Then Webb spiced up his piece with quotes from an unnamed "source" he acknowledged he found swigging beer on a local barstool. *New Times?*— or *Weekly World News?*

I imagine Webb thinks his vicious mockery was marvelously clever and funny. I sensed his intentions and made inquiries after the interview, inquiries which Webb distorted in his report. I'm not so humorless about the incident and its ramifications as he portrayed me, but my hunch about his concealed intent was borne out.

Probably the most fun of the shows I was on was the *Geraldo* show. I'd anticipated it would be one of the worst, but it wasn't. Robert Patrick and D. B. Sweeney appeared with Mike and me. D.B. had a practical joke planned. When he was asked if he thought we were kooks, he said: "I don't know, I can't really be objective about this"—as he brought his hand out of his pocket, wearing a rubber Halloween "alien" hand which he placed nonchalantly across my shoulders. The audience roared with laughter.

I have no problem with a little good-natured humor. D.B. had had to settle for an alien pat on the back when he was unable to locate a chainsaw anywhere in New York City. His original scheme had involved cutting a chair in half, so it's just as well that the lack of forest work in the area made chainsaws rare.

The final show of the domestic publicity tour was *Larry King Live* with Mike Rogers and myself, Larry King and . . . our number-one detractor, PJK. It aired the night our movie opened. For the first time we would appear on *live* national television with a particular critic famous for his false reasoning, filibustering, and unfair tactics. We still didn't actually *meet* him because he was brought in via monitor from elsewhere in the studio; we didn't even speak directly *to* him for the most part.

Our vindication was almost anticlimatic in its ease. We made a number of very good points; PJK, the "debunker," made none, succeeding only in giving some prime examples of the acute irrationality of his arguments. The highlight of the evening was when, displaying his ineffectual frustration, the "debunker" completely lost control and shouted a snarling epithet, taking the Lord's name in vain in front of millions on live national television. Our victory was so complete we were astounded.

Ever since that night people have come up to us, called, and written to us concerning that show. Everyone, even people who usually have no comment, felt strongly that we had come off very well and that PJK had made himself look incredibly bad. The way people reacted, you'd think Luke Skywalker had just vanquished the Emperor. And what irony of timing and place!—the night of the release of *Fire in the Sky*. And on PJK's home turf, Washington, D.C. That was a triumph we'll savor for a long, long time.

It was more than the night of the theatrical debut of *Fire in the Sky*—it was the start of the Blizzard of '93, the snowstorm of the century. As we left the CNN studios the first few flakes fell. It snowed more, and more, and more.

We were supposed to fly out the next morning, but it was not to be. Washington, D.C., seldom gets much snow, and wasn't prepared to remove snow on such a scale. Only one runway at Dulles International Airport was open. We boarded and sat on the plane for nearly two hours before everyone had to get off, get their tickets back, and leave. The next day we went back to

Dulles and again boarded. Again we waited for hours and again we had to get off, get our tickets back, and leave. Many of those trying to make connecting flights spent some crowded nights in the airport. On the third day we tried again and made it. At last we were in the air.

The promotional tour had taken a grueling few weeks, but we were finally headed home. The next available flight for the final leg of our flight home wouldn't have left until the following morning. This would have required staying over in Phoenix, so it saved us another night's hotel bill and got us home sooner to be driven the rest of the way. The four of us—Dana and I, and Mike and his lady, Bernadette—were driven back to the Show Low airport in a limousine. The car ran over something in the road and had a blowout ten miles later; fortunately, *after* we had emerged from the steep, winding Salt River Canyon. To top it off, there was no lug wrench in the car. Mike caught a ride into town to get a wrench. Meanwhile, someone with a wrench finally stopped and we got the spare on and met Mike on his return trip. After the weather delays and whatnot, it certainly felt good when we finally got home that night.

Snow in record amounts had virtually locked up the eastern third of the United States. Dealing with the snow occupied the free time of nearly everyone in the affected region, a high percentage of the country's major population centers. Who was going to think about seeing a movie in what was practically a state of emergency?

As it turned out, one heck of a lot of people. Without that storm, conservative estimates are that *Fire in the Sky* would have easily topped $10 million for its opening weekend. As it was, it made a respectable $6.4 million that weekend, which made it the number-one movie in the nation. (*Fire in the Sky* remained in the top ten for three weeks.) *Fire* beat ice, natch.

Of course, the tour and the movie brought a renewed barrage of media and personal contact, calls from various celebrities—a comedian, a basketball star, even a near brush with Charlton Heston—and many, many well-wishers. But by then I was ready to move to some mountaintop cave for a while. I may do so yet.

Naturally, the personal comments I heard concerning the film were overwhelmingly positive. *Fire in the Sky* received some very good reviews, and some not so good (although not nearly as bad as reviews I've seen of some box-office giants). One thing I knew long before I had the faintest idea my book would ever be made into a movie was that film critics' opinions are completely irrelevant to the actual worth of a movie. All my life their opinions have been as likely to differ as they are to coincide with my own reactions to certain movies.

"Come on," some will say, "you're just miffed that yours didn't get 100-percent rave reviews. Film reviews have to have *some* value, right?" Wrong.

This also goes for enthusiastically *good* reviews. No movie has ever received uniformly positive reviews, and even the most favorable usually include some negative remarks.

At present, the considerations which can prejudice a reviewer one way or the other are so many and so frivolous that to take any one of their opinions seriously is the equivalent of flipping a coin. Because *the critics* presume their personal tastes are the sole arbiter of the quality of a film, doesn't mean we need do so.

I have hundreds of reviews of *Fire in the Sky*. Nothing better illustrates the irrelevance of reviews than comparing them to each other. For any comment, I can find its opposite. The best and worst comments often can be found within the same review. Some loved the first part, but found the sequence aboard the ship unbearable to watch. Some couldn't wait to get past the beginning and get to the scene aboard, of which they said they wished there was more. Some said the movie made my experience believable, others said the opposite.

Some reviewers praised one actor and insulted another, while the next would reverse those assessments. Some said great acting survived poor direction, others praised the direction and dismissed the acting. Some people felt Hollywood had botched a great story, others said no amount of cinematic expertise could make a good film from a story so unbelievable. So many definite, unequivocal pronouncements directly contradicting each other. Amazing that a multibillion-dollar industry is subject to such an arbitrary rating system.

Some reviewers trashed everything, while what really came through was that they couldn't separate their views on the *subject matter* (UFOs) from their estimations of the story, the acting, directing, etc. A few unknowingly revealed they hadn't even seen the movie, not because of anything harsh they'd said, but because they made very basic errors concerning the movie's actual content. However, many loved it and gave measured praise that rang true by speaking directly to realities in the film with insightful analysis of what was actually depicted.

Even though it's standard procedure for promoters to select bits of the best lines from reviews of their movies and make them part of every advertisement, Paramount didn't do so with *Fire*. However, my foremost detractor culled fourteen of the most negative reviewers' remarks he could gather (absurdly referring to them as "representative") and gleefully reprinted them in his newsletter, as if such pettiness highlighted anything but his irrelevance—in effect, a review of his own character.

Plenty of approving opinions were available:

"The scenes inside the craft are really very good. They convincingly depict a reality I haven't seen in the movies before." (Roger Ebert)

"Uncommonly intelligent and deeply disturbing . . . [it] may just be among the scariest movie sequences ever. The performances are uniformly good. Particularly strong are Sweeney's Walton . . . and Patrick's foreman." (The *Kansas City Star*)

"Then is it a good movie? Yes. Why? Because it exploits our curiosity without insulting our intelligence, it is nicely crafted, respectably acted and serious about its subject, and because the movie is as much about the effect of this kind of incident on the folks involved as it is about the inherent truth of it. We will call *Fire in the Sky* three stars out of four. . . . A suspenseful curiosity piece. . . . a very well made film." (WTXF-TV/Fox film critic Bill Wine)

"I highly recommend this film. . . . We were also impressed by the quality and sincerity." (RUFOS)

"Besides a look at human behavior and the character-driven approach to telling the story, the special effects . . . are phenomenal and quite believable." (Siegler, *Entertainment Today*)

". . . well-cast, capably shot, and a fairly balanced presentation of events . . ." (Gannett News Service, the *Reporter Dispatch*)

". . . don't miss *Fire in the Sky*." *(60 Second Preview)*

"[The] fabulous alien sequence is the best bit of filmmaking on-screen. It's visceral, dynamic and frightening." *(Toronto Sun)*

". . . handsomely shot . . . and well cast." (the *Union Tribune*)

"This is a gripping film that operates on many different levels. . . . The direction by Robert Lieberman is smooth and, supplemented by *Army of Darkness* cinematographer Bill Pope, becomes quite extraordinary." *(Daily Trojan)*

Equally favorable comments were expressed in Australia:

"Fire in the Sky works as totally compelling cinema because it sticks to known facts and the actors perform with power and conviction." (*Sunday Mail*, Adelaide, Australia)

"A surprisingly plausible drama." (*Sun-Herald*, Sydney, Australia)

". . . thoroughly entertaining and thought-provoking . . . truly involving . . ." (*Countryman*, Western Australia)

". . . a sensitively drawn study of an incredible event which vastly affected the lives of the men directly involved." (*X-press* magazine, Perth, Australia)

As of this writing the U.K. release has yet to occur so reviews are not available. I won't include the Italian because I can't read the language, and our local media doesn't review movies.

In the final analysis, you don't need anyone to tell you what you like. Just go rent the video and judge for yourself. I think you'll be glad you did, because it *is* an intense and thought-provoking experience, especially for those who've read this book.

I take more seriously the average person's opinions and comments after they've actually seen the movie. Remember that the reason I finally agreed to allow my book to be made into a movie was in the hope of breaking down emotional barriers to an objective analysis of the bare facts of the matter. From all indications, the film has succeeded in doing that. I noted a profound shift in people's attitudes. People were moved to come up to me and tell me how they felt, as they had never done before. Clearly a gap had been bridged—very gratifying to me.

Unlike a documentary film, a dramatic movie, although it *can* convey facts, is best at its intended purpose—that of approximating a subjective experience. On the other hand, a book, though it can (if written dramatically) approximate experience, is best at communicating facts. This book is designed to follow up on people's readiness to reexamine the facts, which was stimulated by the film. That's my emphasis here.

In this pursuit I must now attend to the dramatic license taken with the story and try to clear up any misconceptions arising from alteration of major facts. I'm not going to try to expound minutely on every detail; that would be unnecessary and tedious. Most people understand completely that the movie was a dramatic representation of a true story—not a documentary.

Still, there were purists who felt profoundly disappointed—some even became angry—that the movie wasn't a precise re-creation of everything that happened. Carried to the extreme, such an endeavor would have cost more than the combined budgets of every movie made that year, resulting in a movie hundreds of hours long. Even though there have been many other recently made movies about real-life stories that took far greater liberties with the facts, for some reason that criticism never became an issue for any of them.

The purists seemed seriously to feel that the movie should have been shot in Snowflake; that tons of money should have been spent to restore Snowflake's appearance circa 1975; that as many as possible of the people involved should have played themselves; and, especially, that my five-day experience should have been re-created as precisely as possible.

The purists were more likely to be people close to the story—such as friends, family, and those directly involved—or people in the UFO community who were already familiar with the facts and details of the case. Still, there were those in the general public, even some journalists, who felt short-changed when they learned about the departures from reality, especially those concerning the abduction experience.

As extreme as some of the purists' positions were, I felt a degree of empathy for their views because I myself had once been there. A part of me wanted to yell, "I told you so!" But so much good is being accomplished in the net effect of the movie that I'm committed, inner reservations aside, to an apologist's position on the issue. The UFO community ought to see this film as a breakthrough, because this is the first time a major studio has been willing to take the subject seriously enough to make a movie from a real-life story.

First of all, as I've said before, a multitude of factors conspire to deem an optimum length for movies of about a hundred minutes. Obviously, in order to depict any story that actually occurred in a span of more than one hundred minutes, a certain amount of condensing is going to be necessary. Although, for me, events relevant to November 5, 1975, now span decades, *Fire in the Sky* covers only two years.

The bottom line is that in order to pack two years into a hundred minutes and keep it intelligible, it's necessary to simplify. A good part of the changes from reality were made purely from that motive.

My two brothers served the same purpose in the *story*, so they were combined into one part. The same with the law officers. So many of their real-life roles served the same purpose that they were combined. (Which allows more than one lawman to claim proudly—and accurately—that he was played by James Garner.) There were actually seven of us out there; in the movie there were six. So this is no "embellishment"—obviously, it would be great if there were *twenty* eyewitnesses. Mike Rogers actually had four daughters; in the movie he has only two. In reality I encountered two separate ufologist groups: a flaky one, and a legitimate one which sponsored much testing with corroborative results. Only the flaky group made it to the screen.

Most of these changes didn't really alter the dramatic essence of the story. They did serve to reduce the number of characters the audience had to keep track of. Time was also compressed to make events flow together and to provide emotional continuity.

The crux of the issue is that if all those things had been represented just as they were in real life, the story would basically have delivered the same message—only not as clearly. Art is life tidied up.

As mentioned, ufologists and others have taken extreme exception to what they charge is the *complete fictionalization* of the abduction sequence itself. A few even implied I had sold out, allowed the corruption of my story for gain. They seemed to blame *me* for everything they didn't like, even after learning I was allowed no say in the matter. I was given some rationalizations by the filmmakers for why the changes were made, but I can only speculate as to what considerations truly prompted this approach.

Since I never really received a complete explanation, I can only guess how much of their thinking was governed by "C.Y.A."—Cover Your Assets, just in case my story was later disproved. The explanation I was given was that the aliens' appearance had to be changed to avoid similarity to other, more cheesy and ridiculous, earlier presentations of those beings, and (from descriptions in other, less-publicized reports) to provide more visual interest than would have come from images that had been seen before.

I understood this reasoning, although I didn't feel it wholly justified the aliens' changed appearance—which wasn't all that drastic of a change anyway. After all, they didn't become tentacled octopi, hairy beasts, or insectoids. They remained four-foot-tall, hairless humanoids. The compromise, however, was that the creatures were shown to use large-eyed "spacesuits" (the only spoken word in the abduction sequence), which the filmmakers felt more closely resembled my descriptions.

But why were *events* also changed? Maybe it's simply that creative people find it hard to restrain themselves from being too creative. They may have reasoned that since I couldn't remember everything, and the fact that I couldn't remember so much of that time had filled me with great foreboding, that this justified illustrating what *could have been* the source of my anxiety. In other words, since *anything* might have happened during that unremembered time, here was a gold mine of untapped possibility, wherein they exercised the creativity they had to restrain in working on a real-life story.

A few people explained the fictionalization by suggesting that the filmmakers had become part of the conspiracy to obscure the truth about UFOs, but I seriously doubt that. It is far more likely that they simply believed, correctly or not, that their changes made the story more commercially viable.

I'm not sure where the *intentional* ends and the *coincidental* begins, but what follows are my own interpretations of how several elements in *Fire in the Sky* correspond very well, at least in a symbolic fashion, to what I remember. If I couldn't have things in the movie represented just as they actually were, the next-best thing is to have people leave the theater with the same emotional reaction they would have had if they'd been through the experience themselves.

I had gradually regained consciousness in a small, dimly lit place, with an odd taste in my mouth, in a strange, heavy atmosphere that made it very difficult to breathe. All those conditions combined with the sense of being trapped to provoke intense feelings of suffocation and claustrophobia in me. The film contained corollary scenes: one in which the actor portraying me wakes up in a sort of cocoon or pod, and another in which he's trapped, held down by a membrane, unable to either move or breathe.

I couldn't describe the details of the medical-looking instruments I had seen, but even so, seeing them certainly had made me shudder at how they were to be used—or, worse, how they might have been *already* used—before I came to. So, in the scene where I am held down, undergoing terrifyingly bizarre procedures, even though the strange instruments used in the film were not created from my descriptions, the incredible intensity of that scene succeeded in conveying my feelings to the audience.

My first book, *The Walton Experience*, related descriptions of my feelings of being loath to touch, or be touched by, the aliens. Hence all the icky goo of the film. I experienced feelings of being manipulated, of being subjected, of being powerless to control my own fate—thus the actor being dragged and slammed down onto the table like a slab of meat. I described feeling I was being examined, like a bug in a jar—the unbearableness of their gaze, their eyes seeming to see right through me, so that I felt mentally naked before them. The actor is represented as being physically naked, which also serves as a metaphor for helplessness.

My single most overpowering memory was that of their huge eyes. There was also something very striking about the eyes of the human-looking beings. After my return, people who know me were very affected by the look in my eyes, especially by how red they remained for such a long time after. The eyes of everyone were on me. It seemed the whole world was staring. Appropriately, then, the most overpowering scene in the movie (for me) concerned the things done to the actor's eyes.

The disorienting feeling of entering the automatically darkening, planetarium-like room, and being surrounded in all directions (including below me) by the appearance of empty space, translated in the film to the disorienting effect of weightlessness in a dimly lit area. In the movie, the room where the spacesuits hung was a decompression chamber, the analogue of the airlock-like room I passed through.

I lashed out at the aliens with the back of my arm and with a rodlike object; in the movie the actor kicked one of the aliens. For me, my motorcycle symbolized freedom, individuality, and self-determination, the very things I felt the greatest lack of during those five days, thus the actor risking so much to grab the motorcycle key floating by. The key symbolizes to me my search for a way out. My character being dragged down the hallway obviously was inspired by my actual dash down the hallway, propelled uncontrollably by panic. My terror that I might encounter them again around every corner was represented well on the screen.

As I said, I don't know how many of these parallels are coincidental and how many, if any, were intentional. But the odds are doubtful that that many similarities came about by chance, and it seems to point to at least a subconscious symbolism on the part of whoever created those sequences.

My experience of encountering what appeared to be living humans—rather than decomposing ones in a honeycomb of cocoons, as in the movie—is omitted. Why? Again, probably to simplify, to focus on the more sensational, core aspects. The essence of the story is my abduction by aliens. Maybe the filmmakers didn't want to complicate things with something begging so loudly for explanation. To show them would have introduced an unresolvable mystery which would have distracted from the other the mess being explored.

Purists might insist that paralleling, symbolizing, and evoking the same emotions aren't good enough; the movie ought to have shown it exactly as it was. I understand, because I had at first been very upset about it myself. My earliest concept of what this movie would be was a precise, point-by-point exposition of the evidence, charges, and countercharges. At last, it would be the proper forum I deserved, a final vindication. A chance to say what needed to be said and be heard.

However, there are two reasons, from my point of view, why some of what was done actually better achieves my goal of making people feel what I felt. First is that, if one saw an actor merely standing, breathing hard, looking panicked, one would not understand *why* he felt that way. But showing a man's face, covered as he struggles to breathe . . . the viewer not only *understands*, he identifies. In the absence of dialogue or narration, *showing* is the only way.

The second reason is that audiences have grown spoiled by ever-more-fantastic effects—both visual and auditory. No gun ever roared in the way movie soundtracks cause them almost to speak the emotion of the person firing. In real life, if a rock came through one's window, the crack and tinkle would be nothing like the shattering sound and buckets of glass-shards that flood the room in a movie.

It's gotten to the point where audiences react as if movies are more real than life. It's ironic that sometimes depicting reality exactly as it is fails to convince viewers as well as the familiar film "metaphor." Real-life events causing tremendous emotion in us would bore people seeing the same thing on film. Hype has inflated the currency of emotion, but part of the reason for this inflation is that people respond less intensely knowing "it's only a movie."

To evoke any emotion as intensely as it's felt in real life, filmmakers find it necessary to up the intensity a few notches. Nevertheless, as intense as *Fire in the Sky* is, no one can possibly fully experience what we did.

The movie prompted renewed interest in one question that was earlier often asked about my experience: Were the aliens really so malevolent? Are they good or evil? Some people claimed the aliens' representation was so bad as to be the result of influence by government propagandists. There's no question that in the movie the aliens appeared to be, if not quite bad guys, at the very least ungracious hosts.

Many people find it hard to comprehend that superior intelligences could be so evil. As I have always said, perhaps I only *experienced* them as bad, due to the traumatic circumstances. The shock of abruptly seeing intelligent creatures so unfamiliar in appearance, together with the pain, feeling trapped, and the panic of feeling suffocated, all combined to make for a totally terrifying experience—which the movie accurately relays.

However, in hindsight I've noted that I *was* returned apparently unharmed except for mental trauma; that fact suggests some kind of moral responsibility. However, who could fathom the purposes of such minds? The bottom line is, although it is not an accurate representation of the creatures I saw, the film does accurately evoke emotions like those I felt at the time. One of my chief aims in the film was to impart my emotional experience.

Some ufologists were a little offended by the scene with the fictional ufologist Jarvis Powell, and the nonexistent AFAR (American Foundation for Aerial Research). I had nothing to do with that. I'm told it was an invention straight from the film director's imagination. I don't for one second see AFAR as a representation of APRO, because APRO was completely professional and scientific at all times.

The only other ufologist group we had any contact with in the first few days was Ground Saucer Watch. It was William Spaulding of GSW who, before I was ever returned, suggested obtaining the urine sample. And it was in dealing with GSW that I first had contact with pseudoscientific nonsense and flaky people with bogus credentials. So even though the character of Jarvis Powell and AFAR were purely fictional, I know who *I* picture in that role when seeing the film. For the record, respectable ufologists needn't be concerned about having provided a model for that scene.

The scene leading up to me being hit by the beam was quite accurate; if anything, it was perhaps played *down* a bit. Differences were pretty small. We described the craft as having the glow of hot metal, fresh from a blast furnace. But we meant yellowish white or white-hot, not red-hot. The movie has the surface of the craft actually looking like flowing molten metal. And the overall shape, although generally disc-like in form, was different.

Also, when the beam hit me, it was much more dramatic. The film made it look like the beam came on and stayed on, holding me in its grip before tossing me back. What really happened was that it hit me with a brief, powerful blast much more blindingly brilliant than in the movie, and I was instantly blown backward; which was, I think, far more visually stunning than the way they did it.

Some details were fictionalized to emphasize the friendship between Mike and me—for the "buddy film" aspect of the script. My firstborn son wasn't named after Mike, but again, film better *shows* than tells. Rather than simply saying, "They were close friends," ways are sought to make people actually feel it. In reality Ken Peterson was the one to call in the report to the deputy. In the movie Mike was shown making the call, in keeping with his status as lead character in my character's absence. His doing so provided an artistic counterpoint to the phone call he receives from me on that stormy night later in the movie. That call, too, used dramatic license. The real-life call went to my brother-in-law, because neither my mother nor Mike had a telephone at that time.

There wasn't any rainstorm the evening of my return. However, odd atmospheric conditions that night did cause the smoke from the prescribed control-burn of forest debris to the north to drift along within a few feet of the earth, in the low areas between Heber and Snowflake. The wild ride out and back to rescue me gained an added dimension of weirdness, because the smoke resembled ground fog. Here is an example of truth being stranger than fiction—too much stranger. Representing conditions as they actually were would have been mistaken by audiences for a clumsy attempt to add horror by resorting to clichéd monster-movie effects. So instead in the movie, it rained. But again, this *understated* reality rather than embellished it.

Even a few nonresidents of Snowflake remarked on the way townsfolk seem portrayed as a bunch of clods and hayseeds. No, this wasn't my revenge on Snowflake for not reacting more sympathetically to our report. Nothing in the script told me how locals would look and act. And keep in mind they were depicting people from seventeen years before.

I was as surprised as anyone, but I shouldn't have been. Recall my remarks in this book's preface regarding metrocentrism. Such may explain the "hick" take on local residents, but also, the language of film relies on simplifying many things into readily identifiable concepts. Which is a nice way of saying everything gets stereotyped.

Accepted polygraph-testing methodology was not followed in the movie. Instead of "boring" people with the strict yes-or-no of proper polygraph procedure, they livened things up with "phrase" answers. In real life, only one such goof-up would ruin a test.

As far as I know, no buried dog was discovered by searchers. They did dig through piles and checked into spots of disturbed earth on the contract, looking for my body. Anyway, the suspense of digging up something dead and finding out it wasn't me was effective, even though it was in the direction of increasing suspicion of my crewmates.

It's really amazing that the movie increased people's acceptance of the reality of our experience, because nearly every single departure from reality with any bearing on support for the story came down *against* it! Many, many pieces of positive evidence were omitted, many false clues against it were added. Earlier versions of the script played up even more the murder-mystery angle from the investigator's (and the audience's) point of view.

There never was a copy of a tabloid newspaper in the crew truck. I didn't even know what a tabloid was then, and I don't know if back then there was even enough of a local market for tabloids to be sold in Snowflake. (There was a time when no alcohol was sold here and, even more recently, when no "men's magazines" were sold.)

In reality all the men returned to the site, instead of Mike going in alone as in the movie. In reality, the sheriff and his men *did* search the site the same night they received the report. In reality Allen Dalis didn't yet have his serious record of armed robbery. In reality there was no suspicious cut on Allen's hand, with the crew trying to cover up how he got it. Dalis' and my fight didn't happen that day, although the tree-felling incident did. There was no quarrel that day between Mike and me over my relationship with Dana. There were no conspiratorial "Let's stick by our story" remarks among the crew. The film exaggerated the confusion in finding the exact spot of the sighting and abduction. (The men quickly resolved that question right after they returned the first time that night, by finding my heel-prints from where I'd exited the truck.)

In the movie, the sheriff asked the men to take the tests, and at first they "flatly refused." In real life the men were hollering right off for lie-detector tests. Two tests, in fact, for comparative purposes—they feared a government cover-up. They also asked to be given sodium pentothal ("truth serum"). In the movie, after the tests they were asked to return for retesting, and refused again. In real life, the first day of tests were considered sufficient; and later we answered our foremost detractor with a challenge to have us retested. In the movie, the sheriff character, Frank Watters, said in a radio interview that "polygraphs are inconclusive" and that he believed the men were lying. In reality Sheriff Gillespie went on record with: "I gotta say they passed the tests," and that he believed the men were telling the truth.

The actor with the greatest audience popularity, James Garner, was cast as an unwavering skeptic. A scene showing the man taking Geiger-counter readings at the site was filmed, but cut from the movie (only his screen credit remains). Tons of corroborating evidence (discussed at length earlier in this book) didn't make it to the screen.

In no way could anyone accuse Paramount of taking the position of embellishing the story to improve our case, when they didn't even put the best face forward of evidence as it existed. The opening credits say "Based on [not "This is"] a true story." The closing credits end with a disclaimer: "This motion picture is inspired by actual events. However, the names of certain of the characters portrayed have been changed and certain incidents portrayed have been created or dramatized."

The film doesn't actually show the incident happening; it merely dramatizes, with a sort of third-person treatment, what the men told authorities, and what came out under hypnosis. And after each of these sequences they had Watters saying mockingly, "Do you expect me to believe . . . ?" or rolling his eyes in cynical disbelief. (Recall those indignant claims that not one single thing described in my original book, *The Walton Experience*, was used in creating the UFO-abduction experience in the movie.) My feelings aside, concerning the filmmakers' avoidance of an endorsing stance, the fact is that a straight, camera's-eye view, or "omniscient" perspective, was used only for events no one challenges.

If Paramount were interested (which they weren't) in bothering to refute the attack made by CSICOP that they had misled the public by saying "Based on a true story," they could have defended themselves easily by asserting the movie qualifies as being fact-based even in the most skeptical appraisal, because it depicts as unquestioningly factual only the events no one disputes.

In fact, Tracy Torme used exactly this defense on a few occasions. From no one's point of view could it be a matter of belief or opinion that seven men went up the mountain and only six returned; that they reported what they reported; and that there was an official police report of a missing person. It's undisputed that there was a massive manhunt, an extensive investigation, polygraph testing of the men, a worldwide media barrage, and a mix of psychosocial effects and contentions which severely disrupted a normally quiet, conservative community. Those points were the focus of the movie.

We're certain of the reality of what happened to us, but as I've admitted, no one but us can *know* as we know. So I can't find fault with the filmmakers for not going beyond what they could personally know. I've gotten beyond my disappointment that they didn't come out foursquare in unqualified confirmation of our reports. Who could fault them for facing the realities of operating in a society with the largest number of lawyers per capita of any nation in the world?—a nation with an insatiable appetite for all the public butchering a predatory media can throw to it. Even though I still feel there might have been a better way, I recognize the priorities and pressures affecting the filmmakers were not the same as mine.

As I write these words, *Fire in the Sky* is concluding its run in the theaters. My experience seems to be completing one phase and entering another. Just what the previous phase will come to mean, and what the next phase holds, only time will tell.

For the international release of *Fire in the Sky* I traveled extensively, seeing countries I'd always wanted to see. We were in London for the queen's birthday celebration and saw the sights: Buckingham Palace, the Crown Jewels, the Tower of London, London Bridge, and Piccadilly Circus. (A fax to sex author Shere Hite from her Japanese publisher was delivered to my room by mistake. Sorry, it wouldn't be ethical to reveal the message.) Rod Stewart and his wife, supermodel Rachel Hunter, had lunch at our hotel during our stay. The historic Langham Hilton, which had an all-new interior resulting from having been gutted by fire, had another fire while we were there which caused everyone to be evacuated to the street. Dana and I searched for Mike and his lady in the crowd, but we later learned they had been out sightseeing during the entire uproar. It had been such a small fire, in the kitchen, that none of the other guests had seen any smoke, either. The concierge said it had been extinguished even as the alarm went off, but that since it had triggered more than one detector in the vicinity of an elevator shaft, regulations required the full drill: taking the elevators out of service, fire trucks, and all. Before we discovered what was going on, the drill did create some anxious moments; especially when we encountered a guest in a wheelchair at the top of the stairs. I was all set to leave our bags behind and carry her, chair and all, down all those stairs. She and her companions refused, explaining she did have limited ability to move some without the chair if they assisted her.

Our reactions to the fire alarm were somewhat blunted by having experienced a false alarm some weeks earlier, in our hotel in Brisbane, Australia. On that occasion the fire alarm had been triggered by workmen who'd created a short in the wiring. The loud sound went on interminably while they searched for the cause. Mike slept through that one. In Australia we had seen all the major east-coast cities, the wildlife, the rain forest, and the Great Barrier Reef—the only living thing on earth large enough to be visible from space.

We saw the famous ancient structures of Rome; we visited the Mouth of Truth. Not long after our return home, a terrorist bomb exploded near where we had walked outside the Forum. Ironic that a symbol of rational discussion is chosen as a place for those who implicitly deny the value of rational discussion. I don't know what their grievance was, and neither do most of those around the world who heard the news of the bombing. All that really comes across is that another meaningless act of destruction has occurred somewhere. Gee, we're impressed. Won't those bozos ever learn they aren't getting attention for their views, they're only succeeding in drowning themselves out with their own blasts?

People ask me if I'm satisfied with the way the movie turned out. In the final analysis, will it have achieved what I'd hoped it would? That remains to be seen.

I'm a bit cautious, but if the afterglow that exists now remains, we're on our way. Robert Patrick, the former T-1000, has great local appeal. Snowflake being a ranching community, D. B. Sweeney's *Lonesome Dove* has a bit of a cult following and, as the star of *The Cutting Edge*, he has become a bit of a teenage heartthrob. The rest of the cast are also rising stars, except of course for James Garner, who is a legend. The whole cast were excellent spokespersons for the first shout of a message the world needs to hear. No explosions to gain a hearing for this message. But a little star power to open the channels of communication doesn't really do any harm, although it's a sad commentary that humanity is in a condition in which even such benign measures are necessary.

Tracy Torme says his next project will be a western, *Stormriders*. He's done three projects on UFOs and won't be doing any more. It just might be the last words on this subject for me, too—if they'll let me.

The song over the closing credits of *Fire In The Sky* was "Sons and Daughters (reprise)" performed by the Neville Brothers, and it went like this (lyrics courtesy of A&M Records):

> *You can't stop running water*
> *You can't kill the fire that burns inside*
> *Don't deny our flesh and blood*
> *Don't forsake our sons and daughters*
>
> *I think we're all running, thinking we can hide*
> *I think we're running, trying to get away*
> *But sooner or later we're gonna realize*
> *and meet up with the truth, face-to-face*

You can't stop running water
You can't kill the fire that burns inside
Don't deny our flesh and blood
Don't forsake our sons and daughters

Its freedom of speech,
as long as you don't say too much
Sooner or later we're gonna realize
And meet up with the truth, face-to-face.

Think about it. (T. W.)

CHAPTER 15

Conclusion

The most useful piece of learning for the uses of life is to unlearn what is untrue.

—Antisthenes, 445–365 B.C.

As I scanned the foregoing for basic threads to tie together into this overview, I took to musing. Although the idea that rural people have any inordinate interest or belief in life on other worlds was refuted, there is one good reason why they *should* have developed such a greater interest. On a moonless night, at higher altitudes, away from the haze and light pollution present over even smaller towns, the uninitiated are stunned by the view. Like a billion sapphires cast upon the blackest velvet, stars are then visible in such greater numbers and with such vivid brilliance that it seems almost possible to discern the three-dimensional reality of the vast differences in their various distances from us. It is sobering to think that anyone can view that majestic panorama and retain any illusion of our absolute uniqueness.

What is the star nearest to earth? Surprisingly few people can correctly answer that question. It's not Polaris, not Alpha Centauri, Betelgeuse, nor Proxima Centauri. The answer is, of course, the sun. My kids read this to me from a book of riddles brought from school. But the effectiveness of that question demonstrates a prevalent mind-set that I feel played a part in people's reactions to reports of our incident.

The earth, sun, moon, and stars. Such is the sequence of mention in most listings of those astronomical bodies. In everyday thought their order of apparent magnitude becomes their order of importance in the cosmos. Forgotten is that our sun, blazing unequaled in our daytime sky, is but an average star, in a peripheral position in a typical galaxy, in an infinity of galaxies without center. From out there, our star appears as much a point of light as any in our night sky—a tiny glint lost in an endless dust of similar tiny glints.

I pause, reminded here of that feeling of a "stripped ego" reported by many in our woods crew. To paraphrase my 1977 description of that emotion:

"A sort of a lost feeling permeating the entire being. Perhaps glimpsing powers and intelligence far above our own, combined with the inability to affect these vast forces, impresses us with our own lack of central importance in the overall scheme of things.

"We have been moved to closely reexamine all the basic ideas and standards by which we direct our lives. And in this examination we found them lacking in a totality of perspective. Perhaps in taking our eyes off the ground and thinking in terms of the entire creation of space, we have discovered the chink in the armor of mankind's vanity. A challenge to his egocentric concepts of the world. Man, standing in clear view of the infinite universe, finds himself fighting an insistent feeling of insignificance."

Perhaps, in another of life's ironic little backloops, that feeling we believed to be a result of a unique new perspective was merely our own forced confrontation with the very apprehensions subconsciously motivating some of the resistance to our reports.

Anyway, beyond society's tacit assumption of geocentric cosmology, a hierarchy of further egocentric thought prevails. Many think it likely our star is the only one with planets; and, if not, then it is the only one with a life-supporting planet; if that is not true, then ours is the only planet with *intelligent* life—and if not that, then such intelligent life could be no more capable of crossing the distance between us than we are.

Some educated people seriously believe our understanding of physics is so complete that if our best scientists know of no way such a journey could be accomplished, then it is impossible. Ignored is that our history of science is virtually composed of accomplishing one "impossibility" after another. There is a difference between not knowing *how* something is possible and knowing that it is *not* possible—a distinction too subtle for debunkers, and even for some pro-UFO people.

I've said quite enough about debunkers, but, on the other hand, how scientific are ufologists? My incident was subjected to intense investigation by a range of professional people applying rigorous standards. Even with my limited knowledge of the field, I don't get the impression that such standards are applied very much today.

I see the field distributed along a curve extending from a starting point of good science, then turning down much too quickly into the realm of absurd nonsense. From my present position I would never presume to express my opinion of which cases are not authentic. But I think that what goes under the heading "ufology" today is in reality several distinct phenomena, some of which are psychosocial in nature.

Some people, rather than defending a position on UFOs logically and with the scientific support that *is* available (as I have shown is possible), try to excuse the subject as a special case, exempt from normal standards. I may be at odds with a few of my own supporters, but I believe such a position is absolutely unjustified. It will only succeed in further preventing the subject from being taken seriously, and in practice could actually make solution of the entire mystery impossible.

When I write on the side of science in this book, it is science as a conceptual ideal, not as it is ostensibly practiced by some. (Especially not as co-opted by pseudorationalists.) Frustration with evidence being rejected by mainstream *people* involved in the pursuit of science has lead to faultfinding with science itself.

I broadly define science as taking the best principles of thinking and of the conduct of inquiry and applying them to analysis of the universe—the entire natural world. To imply that the elusiveness of the object of study justifies declaring the matter outside the scope of science is equivalent to saying it is something outside of nature—supernatural. "Supernatural" is a contradiction in terms. If you first describe the cosmos, universe, natural world, or whatever, as everything that exists, then there can't be anything else. No matter what it is called, whatever exists, *exists*. And is therefore a proper object of study.

Science is not perfect; rather, it is forever unfinished, and rightly so. It is by definition tentative in structure and content—contingent and conditional in its perpetual refinement of methods and that which it holds as "facts." Inevitably there will continue to be radical new reorderings, "paradigm shifts." But encountering great problems in studying rare and inaccessible phenomena isn't a warrant to abandon your tools, it is a call to refine them.

We have before us in these pages mere fragments of some of the most profound issues ever faced by the human species. And so few realize it. Discovering who or what is behind this grandest of all mysteries will inevitably reflect much light on what and who *we* are. If handled properly it could have a far more enhancing and unifying effect on humanity than anything yet experienced. But if we are unprepared it could have the most destructive effect imaginable.

Our own earthbound history of contact made with isolated societies by cultures even minimally more advanced than those contacted has been largely a saga of the "less-advanced" cultures' near obliteration. Is this ultimately the result of flaws in the visitors—or in the visited? Alfred North Whitehead said that the major advances of humanity have all but wrecked the societies in which they occurred. But is this a given? Is it even accurate? There also have been many cases of first contact between differing peoples which fueled golden ages of cultural refinement, long periods of mutually enriching trade, and explosive advances made possible by the exchange of new knowledge.

It is for new knowledge that so many in this technological age yearn when anticipating contact with an advanced civilization. They dream of the problems that could be solved with higher technology, never considering what great new problems might come with it. Our arrogance could be our undoing.

People seem always to envision help from otherworldly visitors simply as elaborations of our own technology. I've been amused by artists' renderings of alien spacecraft assisting the ancients in erecting their various massive stone monuments. A far more likely speculative scenario lies in science fiction's creation of the various credos—the "non-interference directive" sort—concerning principles of conduct by spacefaring peoples. Many cultural anthropologists already subscribe to similar concepts. If advanced beings really are of a nature to desire to help us, they are certainly advanced enough to know that direct infusion of raw technology would be harmful. Humanity can't even handle the technology it already possesses. Or rather, that *some* possess. Our so-called high technology is really only an aspect of life in the developed nations. There are still peoples on this planet living essentially in the Stone Age. The majority of the world's population doesn't live very far above that level.

We continually hear how we are being outpaced by the enormous flood of new data our "information society" constantly pours forth. Channeling off the repetition, the error, the deceptive, the outdated, the irrelevant, and the false could throttle that flood to a flow which is manageable, if not by any one person, at least by the society creating it.

What we need right now is not a gift of new knowledge, but of new *understanding* (a type of assistance more conceivably permissible under a hypothetical noninterference directive). As Mark Twain said, "It isn't what you don't know that hurts you, it's what you know that ain't so."

Day after day throughout my own life I've had opportunity to observe people around me doing things that are actually causing many of their own problems, when they are fully aware of what would alleviate them. The same situation exists in national politics and world affairs. The knowledge to solve most problems is already there.

So, what we need even more than the crucial skills to properly evaluate and apply real knowledge is the *will* to do so. Who must provide that?

There it is. I don't have all the answers. Of course, it's too early to tell if my aspirations will at all succeed, but I have tried very hard to elevate the level of discussion above what it has been. Perhaps others will continue in that vein. These could be my last words on this subject. I'll keep my agreement with my publisher to make appearances to get the word out about this book, but once that's accomplished, I think I'm done. I don't mind people writing, although I can't guarantee a reply. I used to try to answer every last letter, but I should apologize because I'm still not caught up with all the mail that arrived in the wake of the movie. Now that this is done, perhaps I can get to that.

This book will certainly provoke much discussion. The computer networks have already been buzzing about issues herein, and that's sure to increase. Above all, I sincerely hope to make people *think*.

As much attention as I gave to the controversy issue, I would not want the most beneficial consequences of all this to be overlooked. The tremendous insight into humanity I believe I've gained from my experience is but one of these benefits. It's when we resolve the *meaning* of all this, the phenomena in general and my experience in particular, that I believe we will have finally hit the pay dirt, acquired the ultimate point of it all.

CHAPTER 16

Epilogue

Covert Disinformation and Cover-up Conspiracy Theories Reconsidered

Never think you can turn over any old falsehoods without a
terrible squirming of the horrid little population that dwells
under it.

—Oliver Wendell Holmes, Sr.

For a long time I was only moderately impressed with various hypothetical scenarios concerning secret efforts by certain powerful agencies to suppress the truth about UFOs, and to discredit by devious means those making such reports. However, developments have accumulated, especially recently, which force me seriously to reconsider these possibilities.

There's a joke that goes something like this: You know you're becoming paranoid when you can't even trust those who are out to get you. Seriously, however, I believe I've been pretty cautious about reading too much into circumstances (as I described in chapter 13) regarding unfavorable occurrences in my life on the local level. I've tried to give the benefit of the doubt. I wouldn't want to commit the same fallacies I've suffered from having used so unfairly against me. As previously mentioned, *Post hoc ergo propter hoc* (after this therefore because of this) is the error of assuming the *necessity* of a causal relationship between two events merely because one follows the other chronologically. Long before the incidence of such things reaches the critical level of *proof*, by sheer numbers or the character of the evidence, they rise into the significant range of strong *likelihood*. So when too many such "coincidences" begin to accrue, matching up unsettlingly in character and detail, it is time to reconsider.

In my case there has been an accumulation of suspicious happenings, some of which I won't yet make public. Some are still being investigated; revealing others simply might not be wise at this point.

Some of my earlier, milder suspicions began right after my return, hearing about my crewmates' apprehensions concerning government cover-ups while awaiting their state-police polygraph tests. I received some additional information on this question from the Aerial Phenomena Research Organization (APRO), which was conducting tests on me at the time. The outcome of the McCarthy polygraph episode and surrounding events intensified our suspicions to some degree, although I primarily suspected bias and incompetence as causes.

When my first book was published, I was annoyed that a whole page was somehow deleted from it. At the time I just chalked it up to some kind of Murphy's Law irony that, out of the entire book, it just so happened that the omitted page was the one that, to many, would have perhaps the single most direct bearing on the veracity of the incident—the conclusion of the polygraph test I passed!

The book had a large initial printing, which sold out almost immediately. I began getting word from people from all over the country who couldn't get copies anywhere, including directly from the publisher. I contacted the publisher concerning a second printing. I'd had a very amiable working relationship with them. The suggestion was put forth in writing and in a cooperative manner. But suddenly things grew a little cool. The publisher claimed there were still books available out there, yet I kept getting reports to the contrary. A lengthy wait ensued, all the while getting unmet requests from those eager to obtain the book. Then I repeated the request for another printing. No straight answers. No second printing. No books available, and yet when I requested that my rights be returned to me, as provided in the contract under such circumstances, they said they couldn't understand why I would want a reversion of rights when the book had "much selling life left." I wanted to believe that maybe it was just due to some kind of internal problems with the company. They had been going through a merger with another publishing company at that time, so maybe that was it—financial flux and changes in personnel and priorities. Still, they were a big company and their actions seemed to run counter to their own interests. I eventually succeeded in obtaining a reversion of rights, but the whole thing left me quite perplexed.

PJK and CSICOP have been known to attempt to discourage the publication of material they oppose by applying pressure and campaigns directed at editors and publishers. It has been said that a censor is a man who knows more than he thinks you ought to.

In the process of getting this new book published I acquired the services of a certain prominent literary agent. In the course of preliminary discussions with him I was a bit taken aback that he brought up PJK all on his own, prior to seeing the manuscript. PJK is not *that* well known. The way this came about caused me to feel a little cautious about proceeding without asking about the nature and extent of his involvement with PJK. The agent said it was minimal, explaining it away sufficiently to where I did continue with him for a while. (I subsequently found a less known but more effective agent in John White.)

However, he later contacted me and asked for certain pages he claimed had not been included with the manuscript. I was perplexed. My wife and I each had gone through the manuscript at least twice prior to shipping it, making certain not a single page was missing or out of sequence. I became more than a little suspicious when I learned that the missing pages were nothing more or less than those dealing with PJK! His claims of never receiving those pages rang quite hollow when I reviewed documentation wherein he had already commented to me on the contents of those pages. Confronted with this discrepancy, the agent revised his claim to say that those key pages must have been lost, probably at the manuscript photocopier's business.

I seriously wondered if the agent, or perhaps someone in his office, a professional reader, or someone else took those pages to obtain an advance copy for someone—maybe even a government official or PJK. It didn't make sense. Why wouldn't such a perpetrator avoid raising suspicion by simply copying those pages? Perhaps it was the result of a very brief opportunity, a hasty act by an outsider. Unless the entire episode was just another odd coincidence of circumstance.

An incident which provided an interesting postscript to PJK's "Forest Service Contract Motive Theory" occurred some while after the book was published. A man arrived in Snowflake who identified himself as a federal criminal investigator. He flashed a badge, but refused to reveal who or what had initiated his investigation. He first showed up at Mike Rogers' family reunion, interviewing people there. He hung around for weeks, questioning Mike's business associates. He demanded information from Mike's financial records. At the Forest Service office he went through Mike's contracting records. He interrogated and cross-examined Mike for hours. His demeanor was intimidating and hostile, actually expressing his intention to put Mike behind bars.

Ultimately, over a month later, the investigator tried to intimidate Mike into signing a statement that the investigator had written as if he were Mike. When Mike refused, the investigator became enraged. Mike stuck to his guns but, not knowing any better, agreed instead to write his own statement and sign it.

The bottom line was Mike was squeaky clean; the investigator left completely frustrated. But Mike had been wrung out and put through hell for what eventually proved to be a fishing expedition. Who had sent this guy? What was behind it all? Mike still doesn't know for certain. (But, had there been anything to PJK's contract theory, the "investigator" certainly would have discovered it.)

Certain aspects of that episode were suspicious enough at the time, but information recently has come to light which substantially strengthens an "ulterior agenda" interpretation. For example, this agent even gained access to Sheriff's Gillespie's file concerning the UFO incident!

We do not have proof that PJK was behind that encounter, but there's no doubt PJK will resort to tactics involving authorities as surrogates of his aims. PJK tried to turn the Forest Service against Mike. He tried to woo Snowflake town marshal Sanford Flake. He tried very hard to induce the sheriff and county attorney to prosecute us crewmen, with an avalanche of repeated phone calls, letters, and "white papers." One white paper resorted to a number of unique falsehoods apparently especially tailored to achieve that end; as far as I know, no one else received that particular publication.

PJK has instituted such "sic 'em" use of authorities against UFO proponents in the past. Anecdotes of such activities abound, beginning in the late 1960s with "the Treatment" leveled against Dr. James E. McDonald, a highly regarded physicist at the University of Arizona's Institute of Atmospheric Physics. For his pro-UFO stance—but perhaps in retaliation for the devastating critique (partly in testimony given by him and a number of other top scientists during a 1968 congressional inquiry into UFOs) of PJK's book, *UFOs—Identified,* as pseudoscience—PJK launched a vociferous (but ultimately ineffective) campaign against McDonald in government circles, with the allegation McDonald was misusing navy funds to investigate UFO reports. Still, the evidence here is mostly circumstantial. We are investigating this further in an effort to confirm or refute this hypothesis.

Then there are the conjectures I raised earlier in chapter 12. Readers may wish to return to page 175 to review the various theories attempting to explain UFO crafts as being of this earth.

The belief in government suppression of ufology is widespread, goes back to the beginning of the modern era of the phenomenon, and is more alive today than ever. A 1995 national survey conducted by Scripps-Howard News Service and Ohio University found that 50 percent of Americans think it is likely that the federal government is hiding the truth about UFOs from the public. Tales from former government personnel breaking orders not to speak out, and rumors of sightings of strange vehicles flying in and out of certain military installations seem to support this belief. Documents have been leaked, Freedom of Information Act suits have netted tantalizing leads, investigative journalists have dug and published books, groups have petitioned and picketed the government.

As I said in chapter 12, my witnessing the presence of beings who appeared to be human but who were not actually human would seem a challenge to the tremendous odds against such similarity of form arising by coincidence, unless their form, and ours, is a result of some common causality beyond our knowledge or understanding. Still, why the conspicuous absence of the human type from my nightmares? Could that simply be due to the fact that I didn't experience so great a terror from them? Or could it be due to the origin of, or controls upon, my recall? Again, what if my entire conscious memory of what happened during the five days is *an implanted memory*, and not what happened at all? What if certain humans from right here on earth are either partially or completely responsible for what happened to me?

It would certainly require advanced knowledge to create such a craft. But given America's huge "black budget" and the fact that seemingly futuristic capabilities of recently revealed top-secret stealth aircraft actually represent thirty-year-old technology, it's not a question of *whether or not* we have advanced technology, but only of just how advanced it is. Other than somehow simulating alien creatures by Hollywood special-effects methods, or by some kind of hypnotic or mind control, such a scheme would not be beyond the capacity of people with virtually unlimited funding. As I noted earlier, perhaps one reason the Pentagon's internal newspaper, *Pentagram*, gave *Fire in the Sky* a four-star review and called it a "must see" is because they have an interest in my experience beyond entertainment. Maybe my case is an inside joke to certain people there. I don't know, maybe I'm reaching a bit here, but subsequent developments make such speculation appear not quite so far-fetched.

In gathering data for the filmmakers and in anticipation of researching this book, I went to those in possession of the APRO files. After the deaths of Jim and Coral Lorenzen (recall the contemporaneous deaths of Jim Lorenzen and Dr. J. Allen Hynek from the same cause—a bit of a coincidence in itself), the board of directors voted to place the voluminous files of the Aerial Phenomena Research Organization into the custody of ICU-FOR, the International Center for UFO Research, an organization Hynek founded shortly before his death. In accord with the Lorenzens' last wishes, the files were to be maintained there for free access by researchers.

The trustees showed me a room jammed with filing cabinet after filing cabinet, stuffed with records of cases going back decades. Coral Lorenzen had told me personally, early in their investigation of the case, that my file was the largest in their records, already over a foot thick. But now, the curators, Brian Myers and Tina Choate, were able to locate nothing more than a thin manila folder containing only a few letters of minor pertinence and some newspaper clippings, most of which I already had or could have gotten from the library. They told me they had looked around right where it was supposed to be, and searched extensively elsewhere. No other records appeared to have been tampered with. But, apparently, sometime after the death of APRO's founders and before my quest, the only copies of a huge collection of the best data on my case ever assembled had disappeared without a trace! Hmmm. We're also looking into that disappearance.

Paramount researchers sought to obtain a copy of the original police report on the incident, with no success. They asked us to try. As the subjects of the file, and since it was no longer an active file, we have a legal right to access that file. Our right was acknowledged, our inquiry was met with verbal approval. But a series of promises to return calls and to produce the file ended with nothing but the final statement that the file could not be found. The clerk admitted it had been there up until around the time of the first request. Then, after all these years, it had disappeared. Double hmmm.

I do not believe former sheriff Gillespie would be in any way party to an illicit cover-up. In fact, he later provided us with copies of some of the desired documents from copies in his personal records. However, he may have been the recipient of higher official contact or queries concerning that which he is not at liberty to speak of. I make that suggestion based on a comment he made in an interview for an Australian television program: "I believe that there's unanswered questions out there from outer space. I think there's probably some occurrences happening that our government may be aware of that they're not telling us." This candor was a surprising departure from his prior public comments. Since the show was to be broadcast only Down Under, he apparently spoke more freely than usual. He may have been talking purely from his own personal musings. On the other hand, due to his role in the Turkey Springs affair, he may have become aware of things that cause him to at least *suspect* that such is the case.

As the release of the movie neared, there was an unexpected, exciting development. A man called to confess to me that he had been an independent eyewitness at Turkey Springs the evening of November 5, 1975! He was contrite over not having come forward sooner. He seemed rational and sincere, not flaky at all. He said he and his wife had been on a hunting trip in the area, and *both* had seen the craft; he gave good descriptions of appearance, motion, etc. He said that when all hell broke loose, he had refrained from involving himself.

The man said he had been in military intelligence and had been advised by his superior officer to keep quiet unless my crewmates were on the verge of being convicted of murder. I was very cautious and questioned him in detail, but he gave the right answers, including accurate topography of the surrounding terrain.

I called Tracy Torme and had him talk to the guy. We agreed: he sounded genuine. The man said he had confided what he'd seen right after the incident to a friend, a known public official who would attest to that. So this didn't look like an afterthought, a scheme inspired by the movie publicity, I asked Tracy to check into it. Things were really falling into place. At last, independent corroboration was at hand!

Unbeknownst to me, Paramount flew him to L.A. and interviewed him. But somehow, Paramount's suspicions were aroused. He volunteered to take a polygraph test and Paramount agreed to sponsor one.

Right before the *Larry King Live* show with PJK, I learned that Cy Gilson had tested the newfound "witness." The results were very strange—with some truly sinister implications. Not only had the man done very badly, things came to light which gave indications of deceit and suggested possible intrigue from high levels in our government! He failed especially badly on a question pertaining to his previous ties with *PJK*! Mike had predicted that because of the movie, and especially after the Marchbanks affidavit and the new polygraph tests, PJK would try something desperate. This sure looked like an example of it to us. Astounding! A bombshell.

If it is as it appears, this is evidence which may blow the lid off the government coverup scenario once and for all! Previously I'd not had complete confidence in the popular "covert disinformationist" explanation of PJK's activities. But here was evidence in that vein I couldn't dismiss.

Clues I had previously dismissed: PJK's Washington, D.C., address; his military/aerospace contacts as editor of *Aviation Week* and *Space Technology;* his extensive use of standard propaganda techniques; his constant reiteration of the politically correct establishment party line about UFOs; and his obsessive persistence. All now seem to take on new significance. Especially noteworthy now is the fact that in his book (titled with unintentional aptness *UFOs: The Public Deceived*), in which he devotes a substantial portion of text to attacking me, he devotes a similar amount of space—the introduction and more than five chapters—to a fervent attempt to refute the idea that the government has withheld any information concerning UFOs or engaged in any cover-up. He's produced a great deal of other material in zealous and dogmatic denial of such charges.

I don't know precisely what aroused suspicion of that new-claimed "witness" at Paramount, but Paramount is an organization of considerable resources. Perhaps they'd employed some of the same "researchers" they'd discreetly sent to check facts around Snowflake prior to the start of production on *Fire in the Sky*. They were certainly aware of the efforts of PJK and CSICOP to discredit the film prior to its release, with some of those broadsides in the media leveled directly at the studio.

That witness was administered two separate series of test questions on March 11, 1993, at Cy Gilson's Phoenix offices. In Series #1 he was asked if he had been truthful in saying (1) he had been present at Turkey Springs on November 5, 1975; (2) that he had seen aerial lights in the trees there; (3) that he had seen a blue beam; and (4) that he was then in U.S. Army Intelligence with a top security clearance. He responded yes to all four questions.

In Series #2 he was asked (1) if he had had any prior communication or correspondence with PJK or the head of CSICOP; (2) if he had conspired with anyone to discredit Travis Walton and his UFO story; (3) if he was currently attached or working for any branch of the U.S. military; and (4) had he been advised by a military supervisor to keep quiet about what he had seen at Turkey Springs in 1975. He answered no to the first three and yes to the final question. (In the pretest he admitted only to having *heard of* PJK, but denied ever having heard the name of CSICOP's head man.)

The examiner's numerical score on Series #1 was a +9 (+6 and up is considered truthful). The computer-based analysis of Series #1 returned a posterior probability of truthfulness of .930, or 93%.

The examiner's score of Series #2 was −12 (−6 is considered conclusive deception)! The computer analysis of the second series gave a posterior probability of deception of .890, or 90%!

However, it's less cut-and-dried than those results seem to indicate. What really complicated the examiner's analysis is the fact that Cy Gilson was able clearly to detect "a deliberate attempt to produce countermeasures" on "directed lie" questions! In his report Gilson also wrote: "The tracings are not natural. These odd response-tracings only appeared at these directed-lie questions. Deceptive responses did occur at other control and relevant questions but these tracings are normal in appearance."

In spite of the reliability of some clearly truthful and deceptive responses, Cy Gilson was unable, based on the tracings recorded, to establish a clear resolve concerning both series in their entirety. That inability was not due to any such nonsense as one truthful series canceling out one deceptive series. The attempt to produce countermeasures, and some other anomalies, forced Cy Gilson to rule "inconclusive" in his overall report, although his clearest conclusions were that the subject "was being truthful when he answered questions #R1 and #R2 in Series #1"; and that "in Series #2 the predominant deceptive responses occur to questions #R1 and #R4." The fact that the results were drawn from *four* separate runs through the charts of all eight questions gives them even greater weight.

To some, the above will be a startling revelation with implications of shockingly major proportions, although to many they are only long-awaited confirmation of what they'd always suspected. What concrete conclusions can we draw from the above information? And from them, what can we further surmise as likely? What yet-unanswered questions will be raised?

The definite information is that someone with at least *prior* (if not current) Army Intelligence affiliation, with prior contact (which he attempted to conceal) with PJK tried to insinuate himself into the case, soon after the announcement of the new polygraph tests, and just prior to the release of *Fire in the Sky*.

Why would this man admit to a top security clearance and a military-intelligence background? He must have figured it would enhance his credibility and make him seem more like a star witness, in spite of the fact that this information might also raise some mild suspicion. Moreover, it would raise less suspicion to be up front about it, than to risk having investigators discover it after he tried to hide it.

How was he able to pass the part of the test concerning witnessing the incident? Besides his residence in the western region of the nation, he may have been chosen for the mission because of having received specialized countersecurity training in beating polygraph machines (if such is possible), in which case it's been demonstrated that even the elite preparation "spooks" might receive is insufficient to beat Cy Gilson and modern polygraph testing.

Another possibility is that, while even now involved in some covert scheme, he actually *did* witness the abduction! Recall my earlier speculation that what happened to me may have resulted from the action of some earth agency; or, at least, might coincide with the popular idea that aliens are involved in some ongoing covert interaction with certain humans. The man's failure to "pass" the last question (asking if he truly had been advised by a military supervisor *not* to get involved by speaking up about what he saw in the Turkey Springs area in 1975) may have been, on the contrary, due to his actually acting under direct orders in his attempt to deceive.

The intent of the scheme seems to have been to fool Paramount into believing they had a corroborating witness, while deliberately providing enough incorrect details to justify claiming later that Paramount had disregarded accuracy to a negligent or even to a conspiratorial degree. The corollary plan was apparently to deceive Cy Gilson, then confess later to discredit the rigorousness of his methodology, and therefore discredit his tests on all seven of us. I must admit that, had it worked, the resulting public delusion would have completely succeeded in achieving the objectives of those attacking the incident and the upcoming film.

Mike and I learned of the test right before appearing on the *Larry King Live* show, which justifiably prompted our remarks about PJK being "a disinformation specialist from Washington, D.C.," and our asking: "How much is some covert agency paying you for your activities?" Curiously, although we had expected some attacks emphasizing polygraph tests such as he had made in his writings, PJK avoided the issue as carefully as if it were a pool of molten lava. The unassailability of our recent new tests may explain his retreat; but could it be that PJK was afraid even to broach the subject, because to do so would be opportunity for us to bring up the polygraph failure by the fake witness and that witness's possible link with PJK?

Even though Larry King's show is broadcast from the city where PJK resides, Washington, D.C., we heard that PJK had flown in just before the show from CSICOP headquarters in New York. Perhaps from a panicked strategy rehearsal, a hasty tactical session? The show had been scheduled for some time; but maybe the testing of the phony witness had been timed to make a big splash on Larry King's live national television program in order to do maximum damage to the case and the movie by exploiting it on the day of the movie's debut. When things unexpectedly went awry, perhaps an emergency damage-control meeting was called.

Just the tip of a colossal cover-up conspiracy showing through like an iceberg? Considering everything, I believe this information is as close to a "smoking gun" as anyone's ever uncovered. But even the best polygraph isn't absolute proof. I can't see how the above events could reflect a chance alignment of circumstance; but when dealing with deception of such caliber, one can't overlook the possibility that even what appears to have been revealed inadvertently by the false witness was actually deliberate, not a slip-up, in order to point suspicion toward PJK for some unknown reason. However, only in such an unlikely case can I envision a scenario that wouldn't appear to be a very strong indictment of PJK.

While we still don't have absolute proof, if PJK did not play a role, either as the mastermind or as a major player, I don't know what other explanation would fit the evidence. It is certainly very much stronger evidence against PJK than the polygraph "evidence" he claimed exposed me as a fraud—even had that so-called evidence been every bit as valid as PJK claimed. If PJK *was* behind the scheme, the irony would be that the polygraph, which he has used so extensively in his campaigns and whose veracity he upholds (citing the fact that, "Controlled tests have demonstrated that polygraph tests by experienced examiners are correct more than 90 percent of the time.") has now finally exposed *him*.

Exactly what our alleged witness was hiding concerning communication with PJK we never learned. No confession, nor, as far as I know, any explanation followed his test. I understand he received a stern communication from representatives of Paramount, but I'm not aware of its precise content. No one I know ever heard from him again. It was a disappointing episode, a dashed hope that we'd finally found independent corroborating witnesses.

I'd been contacted by a number of deer hunters with significant reports who were in the area at that time. We even discovered a sworn statement from another hunter among the papers in the police file we obtained. But we'll scrutinize any new forthcoming testimony very closely after the foregoing episode.

However, one ultimate benefit from the affair proved as good, or better. Picture the consternation of the architect(s) of such machinations. Not only did the plot fail completely on all counts, but actually ended up adding credibility to all they sought to discredit. Further, it flies back in the face of those behind it by showing the lengths to which they'll go in an effort to suppress public acceptance of this. Which henceforth impeaches every such effort from the same source. They inadvertently provided a situation in which Paramount could spontaneously demonstrate great vigilance and responsibility, and a situation in which Cy Gilson demonstrated both keen ability and complete objectivity.

My fear is that my revelations here will provoke a redoubling of cover-up and disinformation activities. Completely discrediting their first agent may simply cause them to send someone better cloaked and more cunning in his stead. The unrestricted budget and methods available to whomever is behind them may make the ability to neutralize me all but unstoppable. However, my *hope* is that my high visibility and making the facts public will afford me some safety. Future attacks on this incident will be greeted with new understanding of where they originate—and with whom. Any "accidents" befalling an extremely healthy and safety-minded person such as myself will certainly receive microscopic scrutiny. I'm taking serious security precautions.

Now, isn't all this beginning to sound paranoid? Time to lighten up. It's pretty bad when you can't even trust those who are out to get you.

Cumulatively, the incidents in this epilogue add up to a pretty strong case of something covert and unfriendly behind the scenes. Who, having watched such a series of events unfold over the years, wouldn't be moved to agree?

Nevertheless, in spite of the weight of evidence, a rational, fair-minded person must acknowledge the possibility of a phenomenally long series of incredibly unlikely coincidences and freak accidental circumstances, somehow happening to fall together, all pointing in one direction. Only further objective investigation will conclusively resolve the question one way or the other. *"Tempus omnia revelat."* ("Time reveals all things.") —Erasmus.

In the meantime, the conclusion—the bottom line as far as this book is concerned—is entirely up to you. It's all on the table. What do *you* think?

Truth, *whose center is everywhere*
and its circumference nowhere,
whose existence we cannot disimagine;
the soundness and health of things,
against which no blow can be struck
but it recoils on the striker.

—Emerson

PART 4

Appendix

APPENDIX

PJK: *Propaganda Job Krumbles or Perfidus Janus Kalumnior*

Facts do not cease to exist because they are ignored.
—Aldous Huxley

Marketing and public-relations wisdom would advise against including much of the following material. I'm perfectly aware that I could carefully knit a brief summary of my best evidence together with exposure of only my critics' most blatant deceits and actually have a much greater effect discrediting them and persuading people of the reality of the Turkey Springs incident. Indeed agents, editors, publishers, and others have urged just such an abbreviation.

However, my purposes go far beyond those goals. "Never explain. Your friends won't ask and your enemies won't believe you." There is wisdom in that observation. But I include this material for neither friends nor enemies. Scant possibility exists, even in the face of such overwhelming evidence, of persuading any of those entrenched against me to change their view. Friends are concerned that merely bringing up some of these charges will create doubts which would not otherwise occur to many readers who don't know me as my friends do. And they are right.

But I will not resort to a slanted presentation such as my critics employ. Remaining true to an objective philosophy demands a fuller and more balanced accounting. Gaining acceptance on the basis of emotional sway would be of no value to me; evoking a fair, rational examination of the facts, even if it somehow *didn't* result in belief, would be a far greater accomplishment. Recall again that I open both this topic and this entire book with my greatest criticism directed not at disbelievers, but at those who were content to form *any* opinion without looking at the facts.

I heartily commend those reading these words. By turning to this appendix and, as Socrates admonished, "following the argument wherever it leads," you have distinguished yourselves from less thinking individuals. Contrary to well-meaning advisors, I believe many more of you will value this material than they—or the debunkers—suppose. It is for such persons that I once more delve so deeply into a past containing such hurt. Not for enemies, not even for those friendly to me, but for anyone interested in pursuing a more logical, rational approach to *any* of the pressing issues of our day. For it is with them I hope to achieve the greatest good, and from among them that I will be able to add to those I call true friends.

The best-known UFO "debunker," Philip Julian Klass (hereinafter referred to as PJK), is also the principal attacker of the Turkey Springs incident. He's the author of four anti-UFO books and a huge number of self-published "white papers" (up to a dozen or so photocopied sheets stapled at the corner) attacking people reporting UFOs and the researchers who study UFO data.

He has devoted considerable parts of two of his books and numerous white papers to attacking me in particular. (I say "attacking me" because he tends to ignore the facts of the cases he writes about in favor of personal character attacks. I don't know the exact number of white papers because, as is typical with his victims, he's never sent any to me; undoubtedly I've missed having many of them passed on from those so blessed.)

PJK is closely associated with CSICOP, the Committee for the Scientific Investigation of Claims of the Paranormal. As a founding fellow he is an executive councilman, Chairman of the UFO Subcommittee, a member of the editorial board of the CSICOP journal the *Skeptical Inquirer*, and a frequent speaker at CSICOP functions.

CSICOP was founded not long after the Turkey Springs incident by a group headed by Paul Kurtz, president and editor of the publishing house Prometheus Books. Some charter members left CSICOP over disagreement with policies which they complained eschewed a genuinely scholarly and scientific analytical approach to the issues, in favor of militant, media-oriented goals. CSICOP's *Manual for Local, Regional and National Groups* devoted seventeen pages to "Handling the Media" and, revealingly, only three to "Scientific Investigations."

They claim to be advancing reason and science. But rather than sticking affirmatively to advancing ideas and principles, they (like PJK) more often attack people and institutions with mockery, ridicule, and innuendos against their character. A sad subrogation of nobler purposes.

CSICOP—if the unacknowledged intention was to suggest psych-cop or thought police (shades of Orwell's Ministry of Truth!), I can't think of a more arrogant acronym. But "arrogant" is one perception that recurs in critiques of CSICOP.

What about PJK himself? He's devoted a huge amount of time, effort, and print for many years to attempt to discredit UFOs. What fuels his frenzy? Nuclear physicist Stanton Friedman, who points out that PJK is a technical journalist and not a scientist, was moved to write: "Over and over again one finds in these writings an unwillingness to do adequate research, false statements, character assassination, very selective choice of data. One gets the feeling that [PJK] is following orders to attack at any cost."

In 1983 PJK telephoned a University of Nebraska administrator to protest a planned conference on unexplained phenomena at the university. He asked angrily what the university would do "if the American Nazi Party came in and said they [sic] wanted to hold a conference?" (What a comparison! It gives you an idea where he's coming from.) He went on: ". . . as a patriotic American, I very much resent the charge of cover-up, of lying, of falsehoods, charged against not one Administration, not two, but eight Administrations going back to a man from Missouri named Truman, a man named Dwight Eisenhower. Because if this charge is true—Cosmic Watergate—then all of these Presidents were implicated, and all of their Administrations. . . . [In making this charge, ufologists] seek what the Soviet Union does—to convey to the public that our Government can not [sic] be trusted, that it lies, that it falsifies. Now I'm not so naive—remembering Watergate—to say that never has happened in history. But from my firsthand experience (i.e., seventeen years in the field of Ufology), I know this charge is completely false. And I resent it as an American citizen."

PJK devotes a prodigious amount of his "spare" time (reportedly up to fifty hours a week)—incurring what must be a truly staggering telephone bill—to what he insists is his "hobby." He has compiled dossiers on leading UFO proponents; sometimes conducting extensive background checks, questioning relatives, employers, associates, and especially anyone from whom he can elicit potentially embarrassing information or an ill word for his quarry. He sifts and sorts through his collection of his targets' recorded and written statements for anything that might be remotely construed as contradictory or damaging.

PJK's ties to military/aerospace sources—as editor of *Aviation Week* and

Space Technology; his Washington, D.C., address; his prosecutorial, muckraker approach; and his extensive use of propagandist techniques—have led people in the UFO community for many years to speculate that he is a paid operative of some covert agency interested in promulgating disinformation about UFOs. As one would expect, whether it's true or not, he's always denied it.

Having heard the theory often, what do I think of it? It's plausible, but so far I see no conclusive proof for or against it. If it is true, conclusive proof probably would be unobtainable. If it is false, what evidence could possibly convince a dyed-in-the-wool, post-Watergate conspiracy buff?

If some high-level agency were going to choose someone for such a purpose, it would seem they would pick someone more able. On the other hand, government officials aren't known for choosing the most able—sometimes other qualities, such as blind loyalty, are of greater worth to them. Fooling most of the people most of the time is good enough for their purposes. Personally I think a more likely explanation for PJK's obsession is suggested by PJK's CSICOP affiliation.

CSICOP's founder, Paul Kurtz, is also founder and head of another organization, CODESH, the Council for Democratic and Secular Humanism. CODESH is a humanist organization that publishes material attacking religion and belief in God. CODESH and CSICOP have considerable overlap in membership and leadership. They are housed in the same building—the Center for Inquiry—where they share facilities including audio-visual equipment and an extensive library.

(Since CODESH is so much less compatible with mainstream views than CSICOP, it was once treated a little like an ugly stepsister kept in the cellar lest she stigmatize her sibling. However, they've abandoned their careful public segregation and begun to bring her out—to the point of sponsoring joint Institute for Inquiry seminars by "two nonprofit educational organizations dedicated to the advancement of science and critical thinking.")

CSICOP's journal, the *Skeptical Inquirer*, has begun straying into the religious area, with articles about satanic cults, the shroud of Turin, creationism, angels, and the Rapture, but CSICOP's leadership claims to be resisting the trend: "The issues we address must have some scientific content—or pretend to it—or benefit from an understanding of human psychology. Many readers want us to critique religion *as such* or skewer some ideology they disfavor. That's not our interest and it's not our intention." Such were CSICOP's words concerning their "statement of mission" in a past issue.

It's no coincidence that Paul Kurtz's publishing house, Prometheus, publishes PJK's books. An examination of the title index in Prometheus' trade catalog provides some interesting insights. Forty-some anti-paranormal titles; another forty-odd titles dealing almost exclusively with issues relating to: paraphilia, sadomasochism, bisexuality, transvestites, child sex abuse, porn actors, prostitution, adultery, and asphyxiophilia.

There are other peculiar titles, such as *Infanticide and the Value of Life*, *Qaddafi's Green Book*, *Prescription—Medicide: The Goodness of Planned Death* (by Dr. Jack Kevorkian), *Tin Star Tyrants: America's Crooked Sheriffs*, *In Pursuit of Satan*, and *The Lotus Lovers: The Complete History of the Curious Erotic Custom of Footbinding in China*.

The biggest category, however, is composed of books concerning secular humanism and atheism, with well over a hundred titles extolling humanist values or attacking religion, a number specifically devoted to anti-Mormonism. This humanist/atheist category includes titles such as *Atheism: The Case Against God*, *The Darker Side of Virtue: Corruption, Scandal and the Mormon Empire*, *Some Mistakes of Moses*, *Funerals Without God*, *Did Jesus Exist?*, and *The Dead Sea Scrolls and the Christian Myth*. There were over fifteen books by Kurtz himself, primarily on humanism, including *A Secular Humanist Declaration* and *Humanist Manifestos I & II*.

The pertinent titles in the list are those linking the CODESH and CSICOP agendas of anti-religion and anti-paranormal: *Science Versus Religion*, *A Second Anthology of Atheism and Rationalism*, and *The Supernatural, the Occult, and the Bible*. PJK's friend and fellow "debunker" Robert Sheaffer (who writes for both organizations' periodicals) authors both *The UFO Verdict* and *The Making of the Messiah*.

Paul Kurtz's *The Transcendental Temptation: A Critique of Religion and the Paranormal* is the clearest link between the two organizations he founded, between CSICOP's anti-paranormal aims and the anti-religion stance of CODESH. Kurtz's book sums up belief in ESP, UFOs, ghosts, "fringe" science, and belief in religion as manifestations of the same irrational human flaw. Little distinction is made between psychic phenomena and religious visions, between the ghosts of the paranormal and the spirits of religion.

If those humanists don't believe in religion, why don't they simply turn away from it and focus on what they *do* believe? Why do they devote so much of their periodicals to harping obsessively on *dis*belief, to personal attacks on advocates and believers, instead of promoting their approach to life affirmatively? They give lip service to that goal, but don't appear to actually pursue it in their publication.

It should be noted that CODESH does not speak for all humanists, and that CSICOP does *not* represent the views of other skeptics who consider that organization extremist (in fact, they don't even represent the views of everyone *within* the organizations).

Rather than confining their efforts to verbal opposition solely on the merits of the issue, CSICOP has been accused of attempts to pressure conference sponsors and media people into censoring views CSICOP opposes. CSICOP has billed itself in its promotional and fund-raising literature as "the lone voice defending rationality." Talk about arrogance—psych-cop, thought police, indeed.

Journalist Jerome Clark wrote: "For CSICOP it is not enough to say that those with whom it disagrees are wrong. It must also depict them as loathsome human beings. In the eyes of this Shiite-skeptic sect, proponents of anomalies and the paranormal are agents of the Great Satan of irrationality, defined as any view, however arrived at, whatever the supporting evidence, that differs from CSICOP's."

In the interest of fairness, I should mention that CSICOP has claimed to have severed ties with the person advocating "getting dirty" with "anything short of criminal activity." Credit is also due CSICOP for being one of the few organizations at least to give lip service to the idea of promoting scientific examination and a logical approach to issues. Also, in an effort to avoid committing the fallacy of attributing guilt by association, it should be pointed out that there are a few (too few) well-meaning CSICOP members and *Skeptical Inquirer* contributors who seem to do a pretty good job of practicing what they preach. Their credible exposures of some popular nonsense should be acknowledged.

However, the question remains: How effective can they be at increasing the rationality of the public, when they don't seem able to inculcate that virtue in members of their own upper echelons? As an active CSICOP participant, PJK has read and sat through countless expoundings on the tenets of good science and valid reasoning. Yet he repeatedly violates the most basic of those principles throughout his writings on the subject of UFOs.

The tone of CSICOP's writings and speeches is often very arrogant and elitist, as if they're the rare few who see the truth and can truly think. Their meetings are publicized primarily among their own membership; the $125 admission fees do not seem intended to bring in the public, but rather to preserve the exclusivity of their cloistered inner circle. Speeches relying heavily on derision of the views they oppose, and the self-laudatory ceremonies annually bestowing awards on their fellows—"In Praise of Reason," "Distinguished Skeptic," and others—suggest more the activities of a mutual admiration society than of an organization for public education.

A number of popular books have been based on the observation that by some ironic quirk of human nature, people will often choose as their life's work the one thing they are worst at, that whatever personal qualities draw a person to a particular field seem to be the qualities making them least suited for it. As William Penn said: "Truth often suffers more by the heat of its defenders than from the arguments of its opposers."

I point out the parallels, affiliation, and alliances between CSICOP and CODESH without implying their moral equivalence, or intending to blur distinctions between them which do exist.

I do not attempt to suggest guilt by association—which would be a logical fallacy (and one of PJK's common tactics). Whether or not PJK himself shares his cronies' every belief is irrelevant here. The point is not one of belief nor even one of tactics, but of *motivation*. In the interest of evenhandedness, I'm trying to establish a plausible alternative to the "covert disinformationist" theory for PJK's motivation. To truly understand any dogma you need to understand the mind-set from which it comes. In the absence of additional data, PJK's likeliest motivation seems to me to be fanatical disbelief—obsessive, overzealous, monomaniacal disbelief. Perhaps the nonreality of UFOs has become linked in his mind with the very survival of his ego. By some contortion of reasoning, somewhere in his psychological makeup it has become vitally, desperately important to PJK that UFOs not exist. How else to explain such irrational arguments in the name of rationality? It's a theory which explains PJK's approach, his tactics, and his obsession. Read on and see what I mean.

One thing I earnestly request of readers, in the interest of objectivity, is that no matter what you may think of PJK personally for employing such tactics, please judge the validity of his arguments solely on their own merit. I am certain they are *without* merit; my aim here is to provide you with justification for the same belief. But the judgment is up to you, so please base that judgment on the facts, not on character.

One might think that in referring to a man who has dragged my name through the mud for decades, I'm being surprisingly charitable with the admonition above. Not at all. My respect is for the principles of reasoning. This just isn't the place for feelings, mine or anyone else's. To use emotion in place of reason would be to commit the same error and logical fallacy PJK so regularly commits. His case falls on its own lack of merit. The first of PJK's books attacking me is titled *UFOs: The Public Deceived*. When I'm done here, I'll leave it to the reader to decide who has deceived the public. Persons unfamiliar with what PJK did to me over the years may be a bit taken aback by my intensity, and may wonder why such thoroughness is even necessary. Persons who *are* familiar with his campaign may be surprised by my restraint and by the degree to which I've managed to remain objective.

People who are ignorant of the rules of logic, debate, and public discourse may be unable to appreciate the distinctions between PJK's tactics and my own. For the record: Efforts to refute someone's statements by use of ridicule, name calling, attacks on their character or that of their advocates, family, friends, etc. are personal attacks and are logically irrelevant at best. If I have somehow inadvertently committed this error anywhere here, I am wrong to have done so and on that point I've failed to make my case, so that thread of my argument should be disregarded. Granted, to refute someone's statements might well result in their lowered status (at least temporarily, on that particular issue), but that is *not a personal attack*. However, as long as one offers compelling evidence, sound reasoning, or in some way demonstrates defensible grounds for assertions germane to the issue, it makes no difference how thoroughly one rebuts *statements*, it is *not a personal attack*.

PJK and his mutual admiration society promote him as the "Sherlock Holmes of ufology" and now, incredibly, the "Socrates of ufology." He allegedly possesses "unassailable logic" and "reason." Supposedly he applies "rigorous," "thorough," "objective" "scientific methodology," dealing in "hard facts," possessing "an impressive array of scientific and technological knowledge," and is "honored . . . for his accuracy as a technical journalist."

In regard to my case, he has demonstrated none of the above. He is not objective. His reasoning is so flawed that in his writings about me he repeatedly commits every major, classic logical fallacy. He is neither thorough nor accurate. He deals not in hard facts but in distortion, supposition, innuendo, and assumption, reaching one unjustified conclusion after another. He is as far from scientific as one can get. About me, he is simply dead *wrong*.

Where applicable I provide the necessary references to back up my refutations of PJK's specific charges against me. Keep in mind that as I write, I do so fully aware that my detractors will go over my words with a sharp dental pick and microscope. I invite anyone interested to check out the documentation I cite. No one need rely on my word, it's there for all to see for themselves.

In order to see just how logical and scientific PJK's "investigation" really is, a few words about logic and science are in order.

Scientific methodology has gradually become quite sophisticated in its procedures to enhance the accuracy of its end products, but some fundamentals are so basic that any work done contrary to them is considered worthless. First, those making the inquiry must begin with *no* conclusions concerning the question being investigated, refrain from drawing conclusions until *all* data is in, and make *no* conclusion at all unless the data is sufficient.

Throughout science great pains are taken to eliminate effects of investigator bias; blind and double-blind studies, careful avoidance of loaded survey questions, controls, placebos, mechanical stand-ins, neutral judges, remeasurements, independent verification, the criterion of replication, and repeatability of results, etc. Science journals tend to consider as possibly tainted the work of any scientist who displays a fervent position on a question prior to doing the work on it. I don't list these criteria to suggest they all should have been applied to my case, because many of these criteria apply to statistical surveys or experiments, which this is not. (But it was supposedly a "scientific investigation.")

My point is simply that science puts such elaborate emphasis on safeguards against investigator bias because of the awareness that bias is so pervasive in human thinking that only constant attention to its elimination can elevate the enterprise above the level of the tangled muddle in the average person's head.

Applying relevant criteria is crucial, but so is consistency of criteria: You don't treat data one way, then another, and get intelligible results. You treat data impartially and objectively, you separate fact from opinion, data from conjecture. Consistency, consistency, consistency: its presence does not guarantee validity, but its absence guarantees error.

One key principle of good science is to report *all* data gathered. This is probably the chief source of tainted work in science. Scandals regularly hit the news about fudged or doctored data, but more common is when the experimenter withholds data failing to support a preferred outcome. Probably because this is easiest to rationalize, the easiest about which they can deceive themselves as well as others. Ninety-nine-percent truth with one crucial detail omitted can result in radically different (false) conclusions. The "truth," without the whole truth, is not the truth.

Logic is the science of the formal principles and criteria of validity in reasoning, an ancient discipline going back to the time of Aristotle and beyond. Throughout time, in all cultures and languages, the human proclivity for certain errors of reasoning have become familiar. Certain false reasoning patterns are so common that lists of these classic logical fallacies have been compiled. Because of their historical roots in ancient Greece and classical intellectual circles they have been given Latin names such as *ad hominem, ad vericundium, post hoc ergo propter hoc, petitio principii,* and *ad populum.*

Don't be put off by the Latin words. Their plain English descriptions make them recognizable as common errors we have seen used all our lives. *Argumentum ad hominem* means "argument to the man," rather than to the issue—appealing to prejudice, as with personal attacks, character assassination. *Ad vericundium* is merely "appeal to authority," in other words, "I'm right because Joe Blow with credentials says so too." *Post hoc ergo propter hoc* means "after this; therefore because of this"—which is claiming a causal relationship necessarily exists between two events merely because one follows the other in time. *Petitio principii* is "begging the question" or assuming the conclusion in your initial premises. *Ad populum* is "appeal to the crowd," popular prejudice, or "I'm right because everybody else thinks this too."

Right out of the starting gate, PJK began his "investigation" with professed certainty that the incident had not happened as reported. Before learning any details, he set out to pursue the prior intention he had expressed to APRO and reporter Richard Robertson—to prove the incident a hoax.

His very earliest writings on the case were completely hostile to us, even though he initially knew so little about it, that he made errors he later had to correct or retract. All those early claims were quickly proven false, but they illustrate that even when so hazily informed of the facts as to make errors so basic, PJK was already totally committed to discrediting the incident.

PJK's campaign in no way fits the definition of an investigation, scientific or otherwise. Objectivity was absent from the very beginning. A genuine investigation seeks to determine what has transpired. PJK wasn't interested in discovering what happened, he was obviously concerned only with creating belief in his preestablished position. That makes his work worse than mere proselytizing; it is best described as propaganda.

Contrast PJK's opening volley against the Turkey Springs incident with the last of six points in CSICOP's statement of mission, published on the back cover of each issue: ". . . the Committee . . . does not reject claims on a priori grounds, antecedent to inquiry, but examines them objectively and carefully."

Quite a number of people with various perspectives, including skeptical ones, looked into this case. They made personal visits to the site, and spoke face-to-face with those directly involved in the incident, or at least made contact with them by phone or mail. Only PJK is the exception. He's what Dr. Hynek termed an "armchair investigator." He did *all* his work by mail or by phone; an absolutely incredible amount of it. Yet *never once* did he speak or write to me!

Astounding. Presuming to second-guess hands-on researchers out in the field, he makes what he represents as the definitive judgment on my experience and my character, and yet to this day has never met me. There is no excuse for this because he was able to locate some pretty obscure "witnesses" when looking for muck. I was in the phone book back then, and even during my years with no phone I received phone messages through neighbors and relatives from a variety of people determined to contact me. I have received mail from all over the world containing no box number, city, state, or zip code; no better address than my name and "Snowflake, Arizona, U.S.A."; "White Mountains, Arizona"; or "Sitgreaves National Forest, U.S.A." The latter two don't even refer to a single place; the White Mountains are a large area spread across three or four counties and Apache-Sitgreaves straddles two states. Snowflake isn't even quite within the forest boundary. (Who says the post office doesn't do a great job?)

In all those years of attacking me in a torrent of published material PJK never once attempted to verify with me the accuracy of what he had written about me. Over the years PJK has done the same to many others, a campaign they've come to call "the Treatment"—an enormous outpouring of calumny and character assassination, with, usually, no personal contact at all.

I find this peculiar. Why would he pass up the opportunity to be able to say he had actually made a complete investigation? Why miss the chance of getting the actual target to trip himself up or say something PJK could distort to make him look bad? The best raw material for his smears would come straight from the horse's mouth. Where else could you gather better dirt? He depends so heavily on *ad hominem,* yet is content to rely on secondhand sources for it. Why?

Some suggest cowardice, inability to face those he accuses, or simply arrogantly regarding the target as beneath personal notice. Maybe behind all the bluster and bombast is fear of rejection. (Admittedly, at this stage *I* would be indignant at such a belated attempt.) Perhaps it is to avoid putting a human face on the opposition, much like the wartime expedient of dehumanizing perceptions of the enemy to make it easier on the conscience to destroy them.

Insulating himself from unwanted information may be nothing more than the old standby, "Don't confuse me with the facts." Perhaps "the Treatment" puts PJK in a position where his contrived scenarios and weakly knitted "evidence" could fall apart or become a legal liability—if it were proven he possessed contrary information, yet knowingly omitted it from his publications. It's easier to use misinformation if he sticks to indirect sources. Then he doesn't have to find an excuse for ignoring its correction.

That legal point may apply especially to his use of *ad hominem.* He may have deluded himself into believing there is a legal defense if, for some character attacks, he substitutes an accurate quote for accurate information. "I published it, but they said it, I didn't," would justify nothing. Being able to prove a statement was actually made in many cases doesn't relieve the responsibility also to ascertain if it was true in fact. And the writer is especially culpable when he has reason to believe the statement is false, particularly if the false impression can be shown to be deliberately created by careful omission of essential context. Although truth is sometimes part of a legal defense against charges of libel, relevance (that is, the necessity of its inclusion), and the motive evident in its distillation and promulgation are key points. Besides, some of the most vicious things he says are in his own words.

Whatever the legal defense, there is no moral defense for character assassination, nor especially for the lack of intellectual integrity in extensive use of a logical fallacy in what is passed off as "scientific investigation."

I reemphasize that the volume and intensity of his barrage, and the desperation of some of his tactics, actually reveal his regard for my case and constitute a perverse endorsement of it. You won't see him writing books and a snowstorm of white papers about those phony front-page tabloid photos of aliens posing with presidential candidates. He unleashes his greatest efforts on the case which poses the greatest threat to his dogma of the nonexistence of UFOs.

One of PJK's particularly desperate—and despicable—tactics is "creative quotation." On the telephone and even in person, he tape-records nearly everything when he's "on the case," and often when he's not. Snip, snip; cut and paste. Somehow, he can take an offhand comment here, a partial quote there, juxtapose them with some unrelated supposition, and—*voilà!*— people are stunned at what he's made out of it. Similar anecdotes of this practice abound among those he quotes regarding my experience and the UFO field in general.

For many years PJK has been criticized for heavy use of the tactic of quoting out of context. Quoting out of context wouldn't be an illegitimate tactic if it were nothing more than what the phrase literally describes. A quotation *is* an excerpt. Ultimately every quote is out of context. Otherwise, carried to the absurd, you'd be obligated to include all the person ever said and all surrounding circumstances, ad infinitum. However, the phrase "quoting out of context" refers to distortion created by omission of other *pertinent* remarks or *relevant* circumstances required to transmit fully the true or intended meaning.

If the quotation PJK selects doesn't say exactly what he wants said, he feels free to add (in brackets) whatever words he thinks are lacking. In other hands this practice can be a legitimate clarifying device, but in his hands it becomes a subtle instrument of revision.

He has a habit of referring to his version of things with the redundant phrase "the true facts" of the case. As opposed—we're to surmise—to "the untrue facts" of those he attacks.

Adding emphasis by underlining, italicizing, capitalizing, or boldfacing is a related tactic, one easily subject to becoming a tool of distortion. PJK has an incredible compulsion to the overuse of such devices. Like a type-setter's nightmare, nearly every page and sometimes entire pages contain a mixture of three or four of those forms. I have samples where, in the midst of a page comprised of all the other forms of added emphasis, he actually underlined *and* italicized an all-capital-letters section set off in quotation marks!

When this underlining, italicizing, capitalizing, and boldfacing is done to selected passages of *quoted* material it has the effect of changing the speaker's emphasis and therefore his intended meaning—a bit like putting words in his mouth. It has a way of transforming the most innocuous remarks into what appear to be self-betraying slips, confessions of grave wrongdoing.

When the italicizing and capitalizing is done to his own words it gives the impression he is screaming for attention, yelling as if terrified that he'll be ignored. As if afraid his words don't have enough clout on their own, that his point will be missed. As if he feels the need to add volume to make up for lack of substance. All of which actually makes him appear quite im-potent.

Ironically, PJK's own group, CSICOP, printed in the Spring 1990 issue of their *Skeptical Inquirer* an excerpt from Jeremy Bernstein's book, *Science Observed*, which made a reference to the proclivity for this form of hyperbolous expression: "A hallmark of crank manuscripts is that they solve everything. . . . A second hallmark of cranks is that they are humorless. A third hall-mark of the crank is that he is sure everyone is out to steal his ideas. A fourth hallmark of the crank is that he is determined to bring the newspapers in somehow. A fifth hallmark of cranks is that they use a lot of capital letters."

How ironic. PJK is forever complaining that when he sends his copy-righted "white papers" to the media, they are ignored. He implies that the unfair irrationalists of the media are either a bunch of gullible fools who need to be led out of their delusion, or cynical purveyors of pap, pigheadedly fail-ing to heed their would-be savior.

Actually, I think the real reason PJK's reports and press releases are so often ignored is that journalists know a stacked deck when they see one. The recipients see them as the sender's self-promotion, and are unimpressed with their lack of adherence to journalistic standards in their failure to represent "evidence" or "proof" outside the mind of their author. In other words, they appear to be the product of a crank.

As time goes on, PJK comes off more and more like a crank. He contin-ually complains of the refusal of various media, UFO experts, and witnesses even to respond to his letters, to permit him to appear with them on tele-vision, or invite him to speak at conferences. Such frequent lamenting about being ignored is a feature common with some of the martyrs-of-the-mind at CSICOP, those with "the lone voice defending rationality." His writings and utterances increasingly meander off into obscure irrelevancies—so that people scratch their heads and say: "Even if true, so what?" (If readers find themselves occasionally asking that question about this part of this book, it's because that's the sort of material it falls to me to rebut. As the philosopher said, we must follow the argument wherever it leads.)

When is PJK going to understand that the reason so many professionals refuse to listen, assist, correspond, or debate with him has absolutely nothing to do with their fear that he is right, that his imagined razor-sharp astuteness will leave them exposed as incompetents or frauds? He's apparently oblivious to the fact that they simply don't wish to lower themselves to his level. When people disdain to expose themselves to—or legitimize—his obnoxious tactics, PJK writes as if they've conceded victory and proven his position.

He constantly attempts to settle disputes concerning matters of fact by issuing pointless challenges, often with the outcome to be resolved by polygraph, or by some authoritative body (the fallacy of *ad verecundium*—appealing to authority) which, if asked, would likely not even involve itself.

PJK's most effective publicity gimmick was a supposed $10,000 offer he first issued back in the 1960s. He likened it to his boyhood challenge to his peers: "Talk is cheap. Put your money where your mouth is." PJK said, "This is precisely what I have done to demonstrate my own confidence that there are no spaceships from other worlds in our skies. . ." Upon reading the actual contract one discovers that he does not put his money where his mouth is, he merely *promises* to pay the sum (if he lives) at some future point after the U.S. National Academy of Sciences announces it has proof of extraterrestrial visitation or after an alien appears live before the U.N. or on national TV.

In the first place, the absence of these events is not disproof of the existence of UFOs. Not only is it not a given that any of those things would happen if the existence of a UFO were openly proven (presumably a *dead* alien fails to qualify), but the contract only requires "the party of the second part" (not PJK) to put up real money—at $100 a year for ten years. The taker bets on PJK's integrity, his continued solvency, and his longevity.

PJK, however, bets only on the previously demonstrated consistency of scientists to continue officially to deny the phenomenon, and on the already demonstrated consistency of the phenomenon to avoid open contact and leave little trace. In other words, he begs the question, while pretending to boldly confront it.

In April 1987 he issued a similar absurd offer of $10,000 to anyone reporting their UFO abduction to the FBI and the bureau publicly confirming it. How many people's first thought would be to turn to the federal government in such a situation? In light of many Freedom of Information Act documents on UFOs, which are extensively blacked out before release, and in light of repeated government denials and a longstanding belief by UFO proponents in official suppression of the subject, PJK again begs the question mightily. But it makes for good press.

PJK has received a lot of media attention for his Ten Ufological Principles; which, of course, are all one needs to solve the entire UFO mystery single-handedly. Without repeating them all here, six of them (numbers 1, 2, 3, 5, 6 and 9) are basically variations on one idea, which can be summarized as: People don't really see what they think they see, because they are either incapable of accurate perception, or psychologically indisposed to it.

Principle Number 10 basically says that the cases ufologists fail to explain away simply haven't been given sufficiently rigorous effort. Read on, for examples of PJK's "rigorous effort."

Principle Number 4 says the news media are biased, in that they give great attention to UFO reports when first received, but then ignore later prosaic explanations. His criticism of the media is slanted by his skeptical bias. Much of the initial coverage of my experience was false evidence *against* it, the subsequent disproof of which the media gave little or no space or time to. If I were as biased as PJK, I would claim the opposite of what he claims. However, my own view, which I think a more objective perspective, is that those in the media, for reasons often unconnected with any "slant," don't always give equal time to rebuttals, retractions, or information contrary to an earlier story.

Principle Number 8: "The inability of even experienced investigators to fully and positively explain a UFO report for lack of sufficient information, even after a rigorous effort, does not really provide evidence to support the hypothesis that spaceships from other worlds are visiting the Earth." (Translation: "Even if I can't prove it, I'm right anyway.") So much for the namesake of "the Sherlock Holmes of ufology."

An oft-quoted saying of Holmes was that when you have conclusively eliminated every other possible explanation, the one that remains, no matter how unlikely, is the solution. If you summarized Number 8 as "Failure to disprove isn't evidence in favor," I would have to disagree. But actually, if you were to interpret it as "Failure to disprove isn't *proof* in favor," I would agree.

Our legal system may equate a man who is proven innocent with one whose guilt was failed to be proved beyond a doubt, but such reasoning wouldn't get one far in normal pursuits. The preference to err in the direction of freeing ten guilty men lest one innocent be punished has no corollary in logic or science. We certainly can't accept a methodological trade-off of criteria that have us believing ten false things to avoid the risk of disbelieving one true thing.

Evidence is merely something which suggests that a particular proposition is more *likely* to be true; *proof* is something that makes that proposition *necessarily* true. Because PJK confuses evidence with proof, Principle Number 8, as it is written, simply isn't necessarily true. (I considered including here ten principles I wrote in parody of PJK's ten, describing what he actually practices in the course of his "investigations," but I think I'll spare readers the black humor.)

I've held PJK's Ufological Principle Number 7 till last, because it is actually far more germane to his modus operandi than the others. It reads: "In attempting to determine whether a UFO report is a hoax, an investigator should rely on physical evidence, or the lack of it where evidence should exist, and should not depend on character endorsements of the principals involved."

Sounds okay. This principle is most pertinent to PJK's technique, not because it is the one he follows most consistently, but because it is the one he *violates* most often. Nearly every one of PJK's many critics list his propensity for distorting or ignoring physical evidence as second only to his misuse of character assessment in his tactics against UFO cases.

PJK launched a virtual torrent of personal attacks on my character, my fellow crewmen, my family, and every one of the many researchers who voiced corroborative opinions. He concealed all positive data he acquired concerning our characters, yet heaped compliments on the character of anyone who attacked me even when he had full access to negative information about them. (I'll cite specific examples later.)

At the same time, he entirely ignored every bit of physical evidence in support of the case. In his many white papers and in his two books attacking my case there was *not a single mention* of the recorded magnetic anomalies, ozone traces, Geiger-counter readings, or strange "metal" fragments found at the very site of the incident! Not a peep about the reports of outages of power and television reception in the nearest towns at the time of the incident! He was well aware of those reports, yet not a word about them. That's his "relying on physical evidence"? That's "rigorous," "objective" "scientific methodology"?

Another part of Ufological Principle Number 7 PJK abuses continually is "the lack of [physical evidence] where evidence should exist." He is forever building "straw men," which he can then knock the stuffing out of by arbitrarily presuming the necessity of some piece of evidence.

(Here we see illustrated something I call the fallacy of "absence of evidence equals evidence of absence," or the error of negative proof; i.e., "since the presence of Joe's fingerprints would prove he was there, the absence of prints proves he wasn't there." What if Joe touched nothing, wore gloves, or wiped everything off? When you take PJK's repeated use of the "absence of evidence is evidence of absence" fallacy, and consider it alongside his disregard of facts, what can we expect? GIGO—the old computer acronym for "Garbage in, garbage out." Those who are fooled by his paralogism and are unaware of the evidence he ignores, would naturally be duped into perceiving his case to be as airtight as it was made to appear.)

For example, PJK contends that the absence of burn marks and bruises on my body is proof that I was not struck by a beam of energy and knocked back through the air. He presumes to possess a complete understanding of the nature of an energy beam produced by incredibly advanced technology. He presumes that since the woods crew said it looked like a flame or lightning bolt, that it would behave precisely as if it were one or the other. Where is his science? Humans use microwave beams in industry that can either clean delicate parts, set glue, cook food, or transmit phone calls. We use ultraviolet energy to grow plants or to kill bacteria. Infrared light is used to remote-operate your VCRs, and to cure new paint, or strip off old paint. We use laser beams in one form to weld delicately in place detached retinas in the eye, or in another form to slice precise holes through blocks of metal (potentially, to blast incoming ballistic missiles out of the sky). Various combinations of specific colors (frequencies) and energy levels of lasers have marked differences in effect. In medicine we use ultrasound waves that can harmlessly view a living fetus, or can be used to pulverize kidney stones, leaving nearby bones unaffected. PJK admits to prior reading of my 1978 book in which I wrote, "That beam behaved in many ways like a bolt of lightning or electricity, but it might have been some other form of energy entirely." Yet he prefers to ignore that concept in favor of his straw man.

PJK is indeed a master of the arrogant assumption. Who is he to presume why the beam didn't blow away the nearby pine needles? Accuracy alone would account for that. The absurdity of his presumption that any beam powerful enough to knock me down would also necessarily blow away or ignite the surrounding debris and leave marks on me is demonstrated by comparison with a mere earth invention used by police: the stun gun (which *does* operate on electricity). Powered by batteries as modest as those used to operate a Walkman, makers of stun guns say their devices are effective through heavy clothing, able to knock down a three-hundred-pound man while leaving him and his clothing unmarked.

PJK claims that if I really had been knocked back through the air to hit the rocky ground on my shoulder, "there should have been bruises." Perhaps PJK has not been very physically active in his life. I've taken numerous hard blows in sparring matches which never left a bruise. All the guys on the crew have had limbs and small trees fall on them in the course of a workday, leaving no bruises. It can take a lot to bruise a healthy, fit young man. It's unlikely that landing after being thrown ten feet would be sufficient to cause a mark which would last five days, especially through a work shirt and denim jacket.

First PJK claimed I should have been bruised by the "hard rocky earth"; in the very next paragraph he claimed the same ground was covered with "a thick carpet of dry pine needles" which should have burst into flame! You may laugh at the absurdly obvious self-contradiction, but his CSICOP cronies read it and applauded. And these guys call themselves skeptics.

But what renders all this discussion moot is that whatever damage might have occurred to my body at that moment could have been somehow repaired by my captors during the five days. So any subsequent biological or medical assessment must take into consideration the possibility of exceptional intervention or manipulations of the natural system that would render *any* data or observations unreliable.

I believe that if I had been returned with a big bruise on my shoulder, PJK would have argued that *that* was proof the incident was fraudulent, because "surely" such an advanced race would have healed it.

Tighten up your critical faculties anytime you see PJK, the mind-reading "debunker," use words like "surely," "should," "certainly," or "would naturally." "Surely" so-and-so would think or do such-and-such. Usually there's really no reason whatsoever to think that so-and-so would act by these imaginary norms. Often it would be ludicrous for people to respond that way.

If there had been ketones in my urine specimen, PJK would have read imaginary significance into it such as calling it evidence I had wandered through the forest, dazed and starving for five days, because "surely" beings considerate enough to return me unharmed would be considerate enough to prevent the effects of starvation. Such schizophrenic interpretations permeate his writings.

PJK employed a bizarre array of arguments against the Turkey Springs incident, many of them contradicting the others. He seemed reluctant to leave out any possible theory. I remember hearing from Jim and Coral Lorenzen that in one of his earliest shots, PJK had tossed out the idea of a plasma phenomenon. Later, the suggestion of the misidentified planet Jupiter surfaced, then drug hallucinations and transitory psychosis, among many others. Postulating a coherent theory of an alternative scenario wasn't his goal; his aim was to create doubt any way he could. But his pet theory, the one he put the most effort into, was his Forest Service Contract Motive Theory.

The Forest Service Contract Motive Theory begins with the charge that the crew boss, Mike Rogers, wanted to get out of his Turkey Springs contract long before the UFO incident, because it was, supposedly, an unprofitable contract. The theory holds that Mike could quickly obtain his 10-percent hold-back money on the job if he could get the contract defaulted; that he needed an "act of God" excuse to achieve that result; and that he got his six crewmen to make up a UFO story that would supposedly fulfill the "act of God" requirement.

The facts are: that Turkey Springs was not a bad contract; and that nothing, not even an "act of God" contract clause, could achieve an early release of held-back funds. Regardless of cause, all defaults follow the same procedure and have the same result, except that to invoke the obscure "act of God" clause would involve the comptroller general, *adding* a number of very lengthy steps to the process instead of shortening it; quite apart from it being quite dubious that the government would ever allow a UFO incident to qualify as an "act of God." (Perhaps PJK's obsession with this "act of God" scenario is because his atheist cronies love the irony they see in it.)

According to PJK, Mike Rogers saw the NBC-TV movie, *The UFO Incident,* which aired several weeks before our Turkey Springs encounter, and was inspired to make up a similar tale. However, not one of the seven of us saw that movie. I didn't have a television; Mike says he turned his off a few minutes into the program. How could he be inspired by a story he didn't see? If Mike had anything to hide he would have denied any knowledge of the program. PJK tries to twist minor admissions of irrelevancies into full-blown confessions.

This TV-show angle is actually an example of the logical fallacy of *post hoc, ergo propter hoc*—"after this, therefore because of this." A necessary causal relationship cannot be inferred merely because one thing follows another in time. In today's media-drenched world, is it likely that a UFO incident could *ever* happen at a time when you couldn't point to some book or movie release, TV show or news story, within several weeks prior to the event and claim such inspiration by it? Saturday-morning cartoons alone would guarantee such a window of "suspect" exposure.

PJK devotes a major part of his last book to the premise that most of what's being reported about UFOs today was inspired by images from that very TV movie becoming embedded in the national psyche. Why would a TV program with unimpressive ratings have a greater effect on the world's subconscious mind than any number of more spectacular theatrical movies seen by far more people? (PJK also predicted a massive "flap" of UFO reports would follow the movie *Close Encounters of the Third Kind*, a movie seen by zillions—far more than ever saw *The UFO Incident*. Such a flap never materialized. Spielberg's *E.T.*, the most successful movie of all time, was seen by over seven hundred million people worldwide, but there were no global reports of huggable aliens showing up in children's bedrooms. People aren't quite so suggestible as he claims.)

The Turkey Springs contract was a good one. PJK claims Mike was "delinquent" on Turkey Springs because he'd been "moonlighting" on other, "better-paying" contracts. (Jobs paying less than half the acre-price of Turkey Springs were supposedly "better-paying.") It is normal procedure for contractors to have several jobs running simultaneously, actually quite common. Yet, PJK foolishly calls this "moonlighting." The Forest Service doesn't even consider it any of their concern what other work a contractor may have. Some contractors have completely different lines of work in addition to their forest jobs. For full-time contractors it is necessary to have more than one contract at a time to avoid "dead time" between jobs, which would result in a contractor having his better crewmen go elsewhere to maintain steady employment. And since the same Forest Service personnel award, inspect, and issue payment for subsequent contracts to the same contractor, it's absurd to term it "moonlighting."

Mike had received an extension on his completion deadline for Turkey Springs, not because the actual work being done on it was unproductive, but only because he had been finishing up some other contracts and didn't get back to it full-time until after mid-October, when much of the contract time on it had elapsed. Turkey Springs was the more lucrative contract of the lot, but since it had the latest completion date, he was finishing it up last. It would likely take us three weeks or so, but we could reasonably expect another five or six weeks of workable weather. We had worked on Turkey Springs in December and January the previous winter.

In an apparent attempt to deceive the public about prior progress on the job, PJK misquoted the Forest Service record to read "working days" instead of "calendar days," thus eliminating weekends and other normal time-losses from his distorted calculations. PJK also misreported that the days elapsed on piling (work that can be three or four times slower than the thinning part of the job) were representative of the progress on the job as a whole. We did most of the piling and a lot of the thicker areas of the job first, because the other part of the job lay along the main Rim Road, which would be more accessible if bad weather came early. What remained was mostly the higher daily-acreage-rate work, the easier, "gravy" portion. That assessment was borne out by the crew who finished the job.

Why would a contractor stick with a job for a year and a half, then drop it weeks from completion? Why would anyone who planned to get out of a job leave the easiest for last? They'd go cut the easiest parts for a quick payday.

Contract time extensions are a common procedure. Every other contractor on the forest has received extensions a number of times. Mike was not facing some immutable cutoff point with his remaining time. If he had needed more time, he could have obtained another extension. In fact, another extension was offered to him after the UFO incident, but Mike declined because by then he had no crew.

After what they'd been through with the incident and the murder accusations, none of the men were interested in returning to work in those woods. Fear and the psychological impact of what they'd been through were deciding factors, plus the fact that most of them had already made other plans to solve their employment problem.

PJK has been forced to distort many facts to sustain his scenario. He also had accused my mother and brother of helping to carry off the alleged hoax to get Mike out of his contract. Although not enemies, neither my brother nor my mother were very close to Mike. Anyone familiar with their relationship (or lack of one) would find it laughable that either of them would lie to help Mike. And why would Dwayne Smith, who had only been working three days, go to such great trouble for Mike's sake? Dwayne, Allen, and John had come up from the southern part of the state, and Ken had come all the way from Mexico to find work. Why would they become part of an insane plan that would cost them their jobs?

If Mike had wanted to get out of his contract, all he would have had to do was simply walk away from the job and do nothing more. He did not need any wild UFO tale to be released from his contract. The core of PJK's Forest Service Contract Theory depends on the absurd idea that Mike would believe a standard default would be severely damaging to his reputation with the Forest Service, while a default due to a report of something so bizarre and popularly ridiculed as a UFO abduction would be well received! Mike certainly wouldn't have thought either of those things. Neither his prior default, nor most of those defaults received by other contractors, had had any catastrophic consequences.

Mike's Turkey Springs contract was defaulted when his crew would not return to work; it cost him money, as any default would, whether or not it had been caused by a UFO incident. Actually it cost him more than a default under ordinary circumstances. He was never paid for his last four and a half weeks' work, because he didn't find out until after the default that the completed acreage failed inspection—due to searchers having moved and torn apart many of the piles, looking for my dead body.

PJK claimed Mike had seriously underbid the price-per-acre on Turkey Springs. Of course Mike had underbid the other contractors: that was how he had been awarded the contract. His price was considerably less than the other bidders', but still well *above* the official Forest Service Estimate. (To provide a general idea of an acceptable price range, the Forest Service Estimate is established for each contract prior to advertising the job for bid, but remains confidential until after the opening bid.) Mike has profitably finished many contracts that were bid below the Forest Service's estimated acre-price.

PJK acts as if the dollar-per-acre offered by the highest bidder for the job was indication of the true worth of work on Turkey Springs. Nonsense. Bidding is open to all. There are sometimes absurdly low and high bids from novices who couldn't tell one end of a chainsaw from the other. Often a variety of factors determine why different bidders with equal performance ability would require different acre-prices to achieve the same profit margin. For example, if a contractor is located at a great distance from a job, he will add travel and sometimes even crew lodging expenses to his bid, and must take into account that travel will reduce the amount of actual time his crew will spend on the job site. It is also common practice for some contractors, after they get enough contracts to stay busy, to throw in inflated bids on every other contract let out for bidding, just in case they get lucky and no other qualified bidder makes it past the selection process.

Turkey Springs was the best contract, profitwise, that Mike had ever been awarded. In fact, it was the highest price-per-acre he had ever received on any job he had ever bid in his previous ten years of TSI (Timber Stand Improvement, or "thinning").

PJK makes a big deal out of the one-dollar-per-acre cost of time extensions, as if this were the last straw against Mike's "already too-low price" of $27.40. (Mike finished Candy Mountain *profitably* at $11.85 per acre). The contract was defaulted and reawarded to another bidder (coming all the way from Luna, New Mexico) at a still lower price-per-acre ($3.40, or nearly 12.5 percent, lower than Mike's!) and finished easily and profitably with a smaller crew in a number of man-hours not appreciably greater than the two to three weeks Mike had estimated. With the cost of time extensions, this still would have been at a price that would have been at least $1.40-per-acre higher than the price paid to John Hammond, the contractor who did finish it. PJK must have been aware of those facts.

An example of the kind of progress Mike was actually capable of achieving on Turkey Springs is demonstrated by documentation of work (exclusively on Turkey Springs) completed between August 28, 1974, and September 5, 1974. As documented by Forest Service Payment Estimate #3 of September 5, 1974, Payment Invoice #3 of September 7, 1974, pay stubs, and other instruments, a crew of seven full- and part-time workers put in a total of 210-1/3 man-hours to cut 115 acres in those 6 working days: 4.4 acres per man per day. The 238 acres remaining after November 1975 was of similar or lesser density, so at that rate it would have only taken our six-man crew (with Rogers supervising) nine working days to finish it. However, since a certain percentage of calendar days inevitably will be lost to weekends, rain, mechanical breakdowns, and perhaps another day due to an on-the-job injury, it might have taken as many as seventeen calendar days *profitably* to complete the remainder of the Turkey Springs contract: precisely the midpoint of the offhand estimate Mike gave PJK. Yet the man persisted in barging ahead with his twisted numbers.

(Incidentally, even after deductions of the 10-percent hold-back, etc., for those six days' work, Mike was paid $2,772.88—an amount greater than the total of the 10-percent retention fund ($2,638.00) Mike supposedly was so desperate to be paid early.)

PJK never checked his conclusions with Mike Rogers before publicly advancing his senseless theory. He has continued to publicize it widely, in total disregard of the contrary facts Mike pointed out, and in the face of Forest Service Contracting Officer Maurice Marchbanks' statement that: "There was no way such an alleged hoax could benefit Rogers." Even Forest Service Contract Supervisor Junior Williams said, "He had no reason—I didn't see that he had anything to gain, as far as his contract was concerned, or anything else, to conjure up a story of this kind." PJK knew, or had access to, all of the preceding contract-related information (he had obtained a copy of Mike's contracting file), yet does not mention it to his readers.

In a July 10, 1976, paper PJK sent to Sheriff Gillespie, he put his own words—"UFO-infested area"—in quotation marks to give the false impression that Mike had uttered them in claiming his crew wouldn't enter such an area to work. In fact, Mike *never* mentioned the incident in the process of the contract's termination. PJK also wrote: "Rogers was paid his previously withheld $2,638 by early 1976 without an outright default."

That was an outright falsehood: There most certainly *was* an outright default. This untruth was needed as part of PJK's pretense that there was something about the default following the incident (and more advantageous to Mike) different from a default occurring in the absence of the incident. There was absolutely no such difference, as PJK either knew or could have learned. It's a fact, that Mike never attempted to invoke any "act of God" clause (as Marchbanks confirms) during the default proceedings, which were finalized months *prior* to PJK's publicizing his theory. The above is only one of a number of indisputable key facts which, even taken singularly, completely refute the "Contract Motive Theory."

By the way, that figure was correct: $2,638. That's right; all this sound and fury, PJK's saying that the "INVESTIGATION REVEALS THAT THERE WAS A MOTIVE, A STRONG FINANCIAL MOTIVE, FOR ALL OF THEM TO COLLABORATE ON A HOAX," is referring to a lousy $2,638! This would come to a mere $293.11 for each of nine "conspirators" ($376.85, if you go by the claim of seven conspirators which PJK was supposedly forced to retreat). Laughable.

He alleges this monumental effort was put forth not to gain unearned money, but only to get already-earned money early. Except that, without the hoax scenario, *all* that money would have been Mike's. PJK's theory is that Mike needed that entire sum to get him through the winter. People are expected to believe that, just to get it early (which any experienced contractor would know was impossible anyway and which *did not happen*), Mike would settle for a seventh or a ninth of the original amount. PJK essentially claims that Mike needed only $376.85 (or less) to support himself and his large family for a period of several months. Otherwise, what becomes of PJK's contract-linked motive for the rest of us six or eight? You can't have Mike getting the whole amount to himself to get him through the winter, *and* have his "coconspirators" receive their paltry shares. Either way it's sliced, it's a scenario without any sense.

The crew was only a few days away from our next payday, and Mike had over a month's work he hadn't yet had inspected for payment. Why would we want to leave that immediately available money on the table? And, because of the default, most of the crew didn't get the pay they would have received that following Friday until over three months later, when the 10 percent was paid in early February. (PJK's July 20, 1976, paper to Sheriff Gillespie claimed: "After the new contractor's bid of $24.00 per acre was received, Rogers was paid his full 10-percent retention [$2,638], providing funds to tide him over the winter." This gave the false impression that payment immediately followed the November default, when in fact it came over three months later, after much of the winter weather limiting access to the woods was past.)

Some people might get lost in the complexities of PJK's distortion of contractual fine print. Creating such confusion in the casual reader is something PJK counts heavily on. He takes advantage of the fact that the average person unfamiliar with his modus operandi will tend to take him at his word and succumb to the false notion that, "If it wasn't true, he couldn't say it in print." But no one can be fooled by the bottom line. The aforementioned insignificant dollar amount is all the Forest Service money PJK has ever claimed there was to be gained. He asks his readers to believe that seven men would subject themselves to great legal risk, loss of their jobs, charges of murder, ridicule, and years of suspicion, for less than $377 each.

PJK's writings are so worded that his readers would be led to assume that he obtained the basis for his erroneous concepts and twisted interpretation of contracting procedure through the Turkey Springs contracting officer, Maurice Marchbanks. Marchbanks is as far from prejudiced in the matter as one can be. He gave PJK his opinion of the incident itself: "I didn't believe it then, and I don't believe it now."

Yet Marchbanks says there is absolutely nothing in the Turkey Springs record or in Forest Service contracting procedure to support PJK's theory. Period. And he has been telling PJK so from the beginning, which fact PJK hides from his readers.

There's no more authoritative source in the world on the Contract Motive Theory than Maurice Marchbanks. So, to put the question to rest in irrefutable fashion, Mike Rogers recently sent the retired contracting officer the following letter and questionnaire.

January 28, 1993

Maurice Marchbanks
(address)
Logan, New Mexico

Dear Mr. Marchbanks:

As per our telephone conversation a few days ago, I am enclosing a brief questionnaire as to knowledge you can easily provide to the absurd allegations made by the infamous UFO investigator, [PJK].

The reason I never took the time or interest to completely refute [PJK's] nonsense before this is because he is really small potatoes in the area of UFO research and his books don't sell well enough to reach very many people and most of those who have read some of his stuff are generally unimpressed with his lack of rationality. The reason I am taking the time to refute [PJK] now is because of the quickly approaching release of the movie *Fire in the Sky*. This major movie is going to create an all-new interest in our incident and the [PJK] nonsense is bound to come up somewhere along the line.

The most lengthy (tiresome—six chapters) of [PJK's] tirades against me is in his recent book *The Public Deceived,* in which his basic scenario boils down to the following: that I wanted out of the Turkey Springs contract long before the UFO incident as he presumes it was a bad contract; that I could quickly obtain my 10% retention money if I could get my contract defaulted, that I needed an "act of God" excuse to have my contract defaulted, and that I got my six crewmen to help me get out of the supposedly bad contract. He also presumes to have proved that I am capable of producing false stories with his claim that I was dishonest in my dealings with the Forest Service by "moonlighting" on other contracts during the Turkey Springs contract.

I know that you find this long line of add-on assumptions to be laughable even from the first as any knowledgeable contracting officer would. You have been quoted by several reputable investigators as having said that there was no way such an alleged hoax could benefit me as far as my contract was concerned. I also know that any contracting officer could easily point out the obvious fallacies in every one of [PJK's] assumptions, but you were my contracting officer at the time of the incident and it is most appropriate that you be the one to help me set the record straight.

There is also something else which comes forth in [PJK's] writing which should be of concern to you personally. The twisted and clever way in which [PJK] writes deliberately leads his readers into assuming that he obtained all his totally wrong concepts of Forest Service contracting procedure directly from you. I'm sure you don't like being made to look the fool any more than I do.

This upcoming new movie will have its written companion, a book which is also titled *Fire in the Sky*. I have been promised that your responses on the questionnaire will be included in the book in a chapter which will put [PJK] in his rightful, notorious place. In doing this, we will both have the opportunity to vindicate ourselves completely from the [PJK] trash.

It is good to be hearing from you again. I hope your new life of retirement is filled with the best.

Sincerely,

Michael H. Rogers

And here is the questionnaire:

FOREST SERVICE CONTRACTING OFFICER FOR THE TURKEY SPRINGS CONTRACT OF 1975, MAURICE MARCHBANKS, HAS AGREED TO ANSWER THE FOLLOWING QUESTIONS FOR THE RECORD:

1. Is it necessary for a contractor to provide an "act of God" excuse to a contracting officer before the Forest Service can proceed with a termination of that contract for default?
   Answer: NO
2. Is it necessary for a contractor to provide any excuse to a contracting officer before the Forest Service can proceed with a termination of that contract for default?
   Answer: NO
3. Assuming that Rogers did want out of his Turkey Springs contract, via termination for default, is it true that Rogers could have easily accomplished this at any time by simply walking off the job and not coming back?
   Answer: YES

4. Was it your normal course of action, after a contract had been defaulted, that the Forest Service would readvertise that contract for new bids and that the original contractor would only receive his 10 percent retention money if the new low bid was equal to or lower than the original bid price, and only then would the original contractor receive that money after the entire process was complete (a process not uncommon to last four months or more) and only then after the additional time needed for the check to be processed and sent?

    Answer: YES

5. Would you consider it to be "dishonest" or "deception" if a contractor of yours had other working contracts, other than the one held with you, even if you were not personally aware of those other jobs?

    Answer: NO

6. Is it true that [PJK] called and talked to you upwards of ten times during the year of 1976 and that you grew quite weary of his persistent hectoring?

    Answer: YES

7. Is it your honest appraisal of the real situation on the Turkey Springs contract that Rogers had nothing to gain by a UFO story as far as his contract was concerned?

    Answer: YES

signed *Maurice Marchbanks,* February 5, 1993

So there it is. No need for a crash course in complex contract law. No need to go into PJK's obscure, convoluted hypothesizing. No need to go into all the multitude of little tricks he used: the partial quotes, the distortions, clever omissions, self-contradictions, or even his misuse of excerpts from written contract documents. Each of PJK's basic Forest Service Contract Motive Theory claims are here, each totally and succinctly refuted.

Marchbanks, a skeptic about the UFO incident itself, has nothing to gain from calling it as he sees it. But if his facts were not in line with what every one of his many other contracting-officer peers know, it would tarnish the honorable record of his long and respectable career.

Mike has returned to logging and contracts TSI from the Forest Service, maintaining an excellent reputation with them to this day. Recently, in 1992, Mike's situation was fairly typical, and similar to his contracting situation back in 1975. He had three contracts running simultaneously, received a time extension on each of the three, even a second time extension on one of the contracts—normal operating procedures, not "delinquent," not "moonlighting." All were completed satisfactorily. His present contracting officer, Violet Mills, considers him one of the better contractors now operating in those woods.

PJK's attack on the Turkey Springs incident is a real scattergun assault. Outside of character assassination, he stakes the core of his campaign on two things: the confabulated contract theory we just put out of its misery, and his hyped-up version of my initial encounter with a polygraph examiner. If you think the contract theory has been blown completely out of the water, wait till you see the McCarthy "test" hype go down in flames.

PJK appears to regard his "theory" of the thinning contract as the crowning achievement of his investigation. Without it, he might have considered the McCarthy polygraph experiment his "case breaker," except for the fact that public knowledge of my complete success in passing another polygraph test preceded his "revelation."

However, PJK's pride notwithstanding, the public seemed less impressed with his convoluted "contract theory" concoction than with my "failed" test. That "test" was so incredibly flawed that a number of highly regarded polygraph examiners invalidated it solely on the basis of the transcript of a tape of it, without needing to examine the actual charts. As a matter of fact, I'll wager one couldn't find a single reputable polygraph examiner who, after reading the following analysis of the many fundamental errors in that "test," would be willing to stake his reputation on upholding its propriety.

First, a basic sketch of the underlying principles of the polygraph. In that pursuit I will quote from testimony given before the United States House of Representatives' Committee on Government Operations from the 93rd Congress, on June 4, 1974, concerning "The Use of Polygraphs and Similar Devices by Federal Agencies."

Testimony quoted is from Cleve Backster, Director of the Backster School of Lie Detection. Mr. Backster is recognized as one of the top experts in the world in his field, with forty-five years of experience. He has served as training director for scores of advanced-work conferences and seminars, and for more than 140 basic polygraph-examiner training courses, administered chiefly to law enforcement personnel at the state and municipal level. He has worked as an interrogation instructor in the U.S. Army Counterintelligence Corps, as an interrogation specialist with the CIA, and been a guest instructor at Fort Gordon, the U.S. Department of Defense Polygraph School, the Canadian Police College Polygraph Examiner School, and the FBI Academy. He has held numerous high-ranking posts in polygraph professional associations, and made major contributions to his field, with achievements in basic scientific research on polygraphy and improvements in procedure adopted throughout the field. Mr. Backster had also testified before Congress as an expert witness ten years earlier, in 1964. An excerpt from his 1974 testimony reads as follows.

Of utmost importance in a polygraph examination is the psychophysiological chain of events occurring in response to a strong relevant question. For example, during deception:

1. Subject answers the polygraph examiner's relevant question with a lie.

2. The lie stimulates the fear of detection of deception.

3. The fear of the detection of deception stimulates a variety of psychophysiological changes within the subject's body.

4. Certain of these psychophysiological changes are recorded upon a moving chart.

5. The polygraph examiner then evaluates the relevant question reaction.

The procedure stated, thus far, brings up an important consideration. Can the polygraph examiner safely identify one emotion from another by merely looking at a relevant question reaction on a polygraph chart? It is my belief that the answer is that he cannot—with any degree of consistency.

It is extremely important that this problem be overcome by the use of a carefully structured procedure that is designed to allow the examiner to isolate not only "fear" as the emotion involved, but also to distinguish "fear of the detection of deception" from the other varieties of "fear."

The principal solution in most modern polygraph techniques, regardless of minor variations, is the use of a carefully structured and reviewed control-question procedure.

At times polygraph evidence pertaining to our experience has been unfairly criticized for the examiners' wording their conclusions to state that the tested person "believed" such-and-such to be the case; which, the scoffers point out, doesn't necessarily mean that it was so. Nevertheless, there is nothing tentative about such conclusions. The limit of what can be inferred from polygraph-equipment measurements is whether or not the subject believes he or she is telling the truth. But this is quite sufficient.

Admittedly, if you believed you could fly, a polygraph would confirm your belief, and only something such as successful arm-flapping could confirm the reality of what you believed. Ultimately you have to acknowledge that anytime you speak the truth, it is the truth as you know it, as you believe it to be. We're human, so who could ask for more than that when you ask a person for the truth?

The McCarthy test experiment was attempted only a few days after my return, when I was still in a deeply anxious state. My condition was so serious that APRO personnel had already advised me, as they subsequently stated in a November 14, 1975, press release, to delay taking a test from the state police examiner until I had recovered. But APRO's investigation was being bankrolled by the *National Enquirer*, and the *Enquirer*'s principal concern was to gain precedence over the other media. They were not inclined to wait even one day if it might jeopardize their scoop.

APRO's Dr. James Harder warned the *Enquirer* crew and the examiner John McCarthy (in the presence of witnesses) at great length that I was in no condition to be tested. The *Enquirer* crew leader, Paul Jenkins, pressed, arguing there was nothing to lose because the test would be given in strict confidence and the results wouldn't be released without my permission. APRO finally agreed to a test as an experiment, a gauge of my condition. If it turned out well, they would publicize it, but if it went as Dr. Harder predicted, they would forget the test and write their account without it.

When the test yielded stressful readings, as Dr. Harder had warned, Mc-Carthy reneged on his assurance that he would take my devastated psychological condition into consideration. He was plainly quite angry at having his opinion overridden by other experts. Having my brother Duane tell McCarthy to his face in explicit language what he thought of McCarthy's reversal must have contributed greatly to McCarthy's subsequent attitudes and actions.

PJK made a big deal out of the fact that the test was kept secret. But there was no sinister cover-up. McCarthy had agreed to absolute confidentiality on the phone *before* the test, before he'd even seen me. The condition of confidentiality was made partly to maintain the *Enquirer*'s exclusive, but was in anticipation of confirmation that I was not yet sufficiently recovered to be testable.

I have never in my entire life been in such a desperate mental state, either before or after. I was in a constant state of terror. In spite of what was going on inside, I struggled to present coherent behavior, not always successfully. APRO director Jim Lorenzen: ". . . Travis' demeanor at the time resembled that of a caged bobcat. He seemed to be poised for flight even though he was lying in a semireclining position . . ." Psychiatrist Dr. Jean Rosenbaum: ". . . this is a person who has been going through a . . . life crisis . . . , for example, a death or divorce. . . ." And, "he was like a wild animal in a cage." Reporter Jeff Wells: "Our first sight of the kid was at dinner in the motel dining room that night. It was a shock. He sat there mute, pale, twitching like a cornered animal." Interesting how they were all moved separately to use a similar metaphor.

I was even struggling with my grip on reality at times. One theory Sheriff Gillespie was pushing was that my coworkers had slipped me drugs, hit me on the head, and put on masks or something to guide my "trip." I was aware that the press had been speculating wildly in search of alternative explanations for the entire incident.

My own resistance to accepting what my memories were telling me had me looking for a way out myself. McCarthy only made things worse. He referred to the alcohol-influenced, drug-hallucination angle. He asked if I had been "hypnotized," "programmed to forget"—if maybe I had really been in a "hospital" or "building" somewhere. I was asking myself, had my mind slipped a cog? McCarthy was nurturing my seeds of doubt and planting some of his own in the midst of my temporary reality-testing. During the first few days of this most critical period of adjusting to the reality of what I'd been through, I was cut off from the reassurance of the corroboration of my crewmates, who had also seen what I had.

American Polygraph Association members agree to abide by nineteen minimum guidelines of performance, titled *Standards and Principles of Practice*. Standard Number 4 requires that "A member shall not conduct an examination of any person whom the member believes to be physically or emotionally unsuitable for testing."

I had heard about the uproar, before Cy Gilson's tests of my crewmates in Sheriff Gillespie's office, over the suspicion of a government cover-up. Allen Dalis' inconclusive test had me wondering. Government hush-ups had long been a basic belief with ufologist organizations like APRO; they did nothing to lessen my misgivings. I had quite an inner dialogue running back and forth about this, some of my thoughts uttered aloud and captured on tape. (I have a clear tape of the entire pretest interview and test proceedings, and a complete transcript, without the omissions and errors of the transcript published by APRO. Keep in mind when reading quotations here or any references to what happened during the test that I am prepared to document each of them precisely.)

McCarthy's condescending, sarcastic, and hostile attitude was only the beginning of the ordeal. My alarm bells were going off constantly. He tried to put words in my mouth; he'd *tell* me how I felt instead of asking me. He wouldn't let me finish, interrupting me *twenty-eight times* during those scant ninety minutes. I saw the situation developing, but felt trapped.

When he told me Dr. Harder had told him I was fine, I figured he was lying since I had just discussed my condition with Dr. Harder and heard his remarks to the others. He made me sign a consent/waiver form, over my objections that the statement acknowledged certain things had occurred which had not. I was badly disoriented as to time, but McCarthy spent over five minutes hazing me about time and dates, at one point snapping: "Where have you been, in a vacuum?" Yet he stated in his report that I was "lucid."

A polygraph examiner is *not* supposed to antagonize or deliberately upset a test subject. He is supposed to create a calm, neutral atmosphere so that the subject reacts to the *questions*, not to any other agitating stimulus. To be so negative in the pretest reveals more than the absence of proper technique; it exposes a strong bias.

A recognized text of polygraphy, *Psychological Methods in Criminal Investigation and Evidence*, states in chapter 8, "Polygraph Techniques for the Detection of Deception": "It is critical that the polygraph examiner's demeanor and behavior be professional and objective. If the subject is suspicious of the examiner or feels that the examiner is not competent or is biased, the accuracy of the test is compromised. Some examiners are psychologically insensitive and abusive, and they sometimes convey an impression of disbelief in the subject's version of the events or attempt to interrogate the subject prior to the completion of the test. Such behaviors on the part of the examiner are likely to increase the risk of a false positive error." ("False positive" means judging a truthful person as deceptive.)

Dr. David C. Raskin, author of the passage quoted above, is a professor of psychology at the University of Utah, and author or coauthor of many respected texts. He has performed scientific research on polygraphy and published recognized papers on his widely adopted innovations in the refinement of technique. Dr. Raskin has twenty-three years' experience in polygraphy, and is a frequently consulted, court-recognized expert in the U.S. and Canada. He has been involved in well-known cases such as the Howard Hughes will, Jeffrey *(Fatal Vision)* McDonald, serial killer Ted Bundy, the DeLorean affair, and the McMartin preschool spectacle. As an internationally known expert, Dr. Raskin has testified before British Parliament, the Israeli Kineset, and the Judiciary Committee of the U.S. Senate—having been called in by the latter four times, with regard to cases including Watergate and Iran-Contra.

The Spring 1990 issue of the CSICOP journal PJK edits, the *Skeptical Inquirer*, published an article critical of the polygraph, by Elie A. Shneour, called (appropriately) "Lying About Polygraph Tests." I could get quotations similar to the following from many other sources, but these, coming from PJK's own outfit, are hardest for PJK to deny. Shneour says: "Although few examiners will admit it, a good judge of human behavior will override the polygraph charts and generate a report that is more heavily weighed by the examiner's own perception of the subject." And certainly a *poor* judge of human behavior would be just as—if not more—prone to such departure from objective measurement.

The CSICOP article goes on: "The central premise of polygraph testing, the psychological assumption that guilt can *always* be inferred from emotional disturbance, is considered to be implausible by the majority of knowledgeable psychologists in the field." While this comment acknowledges that there are many mental states other than deception that can produce stressful polygraph charts, it is *not* true that polygraph examiners act under a premise which ignores that fact, as evidenced by Backster's congressional testimony. In fact, a great part of their training and methodology is directed solely at making certain they know the category of stimulus for any emotional disturbance recorded on their charts, and to avoid getting certain categories entirely. That was one of several areas where John J. McCarthy failed miserably.

Let's look again at the last part of the excerpt of congressional testimony I quoted above: "It is extremely important . . . to distinguish 'fear of the detection of deception' from the other varieties of 'fear.' The principal solution in most modern polygraph techniques, regardless of minor variations, is the use of a carefully structured and reviewed control-question procedure." The concept of control-question tests (CQTs) was introduced in 1939 and refined in 1947. In 1974 CQTs were considered (and still are) the accepted modern technique. (The state police polygraph examiner, Cy Gilson, used CQT on the six witnesses.)

However, McCarthy was still using a straight "relevant/irrelevant" test method, considered over twenty-seven years out of date even in 1975! This type of test has generated as high as 80 percent false positives in controlled test research where verification was independently certain. The straight relevant/irrelevant test can be worse than worthless—it violates some states' regulations governing the use of polygraphs. In states where polygraph results are admissible evidence in court, such as New Mexico, this method is *not* admissible. It is prohibited procedure in Nevada, where they use Backster Zone of Comparison methodology in conjunction with (as their manual specifies) CQT methodology. In Utah an examiner could lose his license for using the relevant/irrelevant method without special prior approval (which has never before been requested or granted). The Utah Department of Public Safety Bureau of Regulatory Licensing says, "Irrelevant and relevant tests without controls will not be recognized by the Bureau as approved techniques." I didn't personally verify the fact, as I did for all states bordering Arizona, but I've been told by experts that the same situation concerning methodology prevails throughout the rest of the country.

The reason people were getting away with not updating their training and still using the simpler, old "relevant/irrelevant" method in Arizona, when it is prohibited in all the surrounding states, is that in 1975 Arizona had no official licensing or regulation of the profession.

PJK tried to point to McCarthy's application of the so-called "stim test," which he did *between* his two runs through the questions, as being proof of my suitability for testing. The stim test consists of the examiner unerringly identifying (supposedly by use of the chart tracings) a card "secretly" chosen by the subject, to convince the subject of the infallibility of the machine. Since the stim test (which Shneour's *Skeptical Inquirer* article so criticizes) often relies on deception on the part of the examiner (as prescribed by the method's school), using marked cards, most modern examiners reject the technique. Although I cannot show that McCarthy rigged the stim test, it is suspicious that he didn't actually show me the chart that supposedly gave him his answer. To legitimate the assay he should have done so to reinforce the effect.

This old method's reliance on trickery has led some people to assume erroneously that modern polygraphy depends on bluff for its success, and that simply seeing through this will allow people to beat the test. On the contrary, I'm quite certain that modern methods (*sans* stim test) could easily determine the amount of change in your pocket, if you knew it yourself, to the penny, without the examiner knowing the sum in advance.

None of the studies claiming to support the accuracy of the relevant/irrelevant test in field applications meets the reasonable scientific standards for internal or external validity set by the government's Office of Technology Assessment.

Most of the criticism of the reliability of polygraph in general is actually due to the obsolete relevant/irrelevant methodology. Misconceptions such as those contained in the CSICOP article come in large part from practices that are now no longer used. But, since its information applies to my archaic "test," I'll quote again from the article PJK's crony wrote: "But the ultimate irony lies in the well-established observation that polygraph examinations tend to err on generating substantially more false positive than false negatives. This means that truthful persons incriminated as liars by the polygraph will outnumber actual liars." This was seconded by Scott Lilienfeld in the Fall 1993 *Skeptical Inquirer.* ". . . the polygraph typically yields a high rate of false positives." (That article also pointed out the portion of false positives that paradoxically includes "excessively guilt-prone individuals, who are probably among the least likely of all people to prevaricate"; and decried the prospect that we might "penalize particularly moral individuals, many of whom may be the 'guilt-grabbers' erroneously detected by the polygraph test."

You won't hear PJK making use of the above knowledge because it overturns his position on my case. His tunnel vision on "lie detectors" (being an extreme reverse of what research has shown) is that failed tests concerning UFOs are always flawless; passed tests on the subject can never be right.

I didn't defend myself with the above information in my book in 1977 because I wasn't aware of it then. All I knew was that McCarthy wasn't right. In fact, I didn't discover most of this material until after I passed the last polygraph tests I'll ever take on this subject, in 1993. (See chapter 11.)

Modern polygraph testing has become an extremely refined science, replete with highly technical terms I don't completely understand: climax damping, double cross-validation, zone of comparison (ZOC), electrodermal burst frequency, peak of tension (POT), and "vasomotor univariate point-bisarial correlations."

The reliability and sensitivity of modern equipment is also vastly improved. Besides using a completely discredited method, John McCarthy was using an early three-trace polygraph machine. It used the unreliable, old-style finger-paddle, passive galvanic system, a glitch-prone method which simply measures fluctuations in skin conductivity. Modern equipment utilizes a steady microcurrent through the hand which gives a constant reference baseline of comparison, eliminating spurious conductivity changes.

(Compared with my other tests, McCarthy spent a lot of time fussing with attaching the galvanic terminals to me, the wires to which had noticeably frayed insulation. He adjusted, readjusted, and fretted about my exact hand position. At one point on the tape he exclaimed aloud in angry frustration: "I can't get this thing . . . I can't get the instrument tuned in to you if you keep jumping around in the chair!" I apologized, but I didn't think I'd been moving at all. Part of the *APA Standards and Principles of Practice* reads: "A member shall not knowingly conduct an examination using any instrument which at the time of the examination is not functioning properly as designed."

I've learned that the construction of McCarthy's machine required that the air in the blood-pressure cuff directly, physically, move the chart needle. That design yielded much less sensitivity and required higher pressures, therefore greatly increasing the discomfort on the subject's arm (which also raises those unwanted extraneous stress levels). I complained of the pain it was causing in a recent injury inflicted to my elbow in a sparring match with my karate instructor, but McCarthy brushed my complaint aside. Pain, like stress, can register on the charts and further confuse an appraisal.

Who was this relic McCarthy, anyway? PJK touts him as "the most experienced and one of the most respected polygraph examiners in Arizona." I've uncovered information indicating he was probably neither. For one thing, he wasn't even a member of the Arizona Polygraph Association. One might guess why he might want to distance himself from knowledgeable examiners from what follows.

On the tape of the pretest interview, McCarthy claims to have had twenty-five years of experience. On KOOL-TV's August 12, 1976, *Face the State*, he said he had *fifteen* years' experience. The *NICAP Bulletin* wrote he was first licensed in Illinois in 1964, which, without prior unlicensed experience, would give him eleven years at that time. PJK read the test and pretest transcript with its "twenty-five years" claim. Yet even he embellished his boast of McCarthy's being "the most experienced examiner in the state of Arizona," only to the extent of claiming McCarthy had "nearly twenty" years of experience at the time of the test. Later PJK changed that claim to "for nearly twenty years he . . . practiced in Phoenix." Twenty-five, fifteen, eleven, nearly twenty total, or twenty in Phoenix alone—which is it? Why the inconsistencies?

Figuring McCarthy wouldn't be any more forthright with me than he had been in the past, in 1993 I asked Mike Rogers to telephone McCarthy and ask him directly about the matter to see if he could get a straight answer. Mike told McCarthy who he was, about the film *Fire in the Sky* coming out soon, and that he wanted to nail down some facts, to be completely accurate. From the start McCarthy backtracked and hedged:

Mike: *. . . the only thing we can find for your earliest licensing is Illinois in 1964.*
JMc   *Um-hm.*
MR   *Were you licensed or practicing prior to that?*
JMc   *No. Illinois was my first, uh, uh, license. When Illinois got the licensing law, I applied and got, obtained, one of their licenses.*
MR   *So that was your first—that's when you first started practice, then?*
JMc   *No, no, not when I first started practicing. I first started practicing in 1949.*
MR   *Okay.*
JMc   *In C.I.D.*
MR   *What is C.I.D.?*
JMc   *Criminal Investigation Division—*
MR   *Is this in the military? [both speaking]*
JMc   *Of the army. [both speaking]*
MR   *Oh, the military, okay.*
JMc   *Uh-huh, right.*
MR   *Yeah, that was what I was trying to find out, okay. Uh, I think that's all I have here. Now in this military, even though that wasn't private practice, that was actual polygraph practice? That wasn't your training or anything like that, was it?*
JMc   *It was all criminal work.*
MR   *Okay. Okay, but "It wasn't training?" is what I'm trying to say.*
JMc   *Training?*
MR   *Yeah, training.*
JMc   *Nope. That's uh—*
MR   *When, do you know, do you remember, when you received your training? I understand that was at Fort Gordon or something.*
JMc   *That's right. It was at Fort Gordon.*
MR   *Do you remember the years on that?*
JMc   *Ahh, I think that was, um, uh, '50.*
MR   *1950?*
JMc   *'Fifty, I believe, yeah.*
MR   *Just the one year, 1950?*
JMc   *Yeah, right.*

Mike then mentioned the movie, the need for accurate dates, and the fact that this information might be used in a book of the same title as the movie. Then Mike said: "So you say that you were— Oh, I just noticed something here. You might have these years backwards. You said you were actually in practice in 1949, and you said you got your schooling in 1950."

JMc *No, that's not— I was not actually in practice in, in, at that time in '49 and '50 and those years, I was commander of a Criminal Investigation Detachment and we, uh, obtained the first polygraph examiner, uh, with his equipment in the area of jurisdiction that we covered at that time. And, uh, so we sorta got OJT just like every other piece of equipment in the detachment. I, uh, wanted to familiarize myself with it so I knew, uh, what was goin' on, just like you, uh—*

MR *Okay.*

JMc *Uh, recording equipment, uh, wiretap equipment, uh, fingerprint, uh, latent-fingerprint-lifting equipment, photography, the use of the speed graphic that was, uh, uh, you know, operational at that time. So my, my interest was getting to know everything that I—was in my outfit.*

MR *Okay, well I guess the precise question is, when did you actually receive your own personal schooling on the polygraph?*

JMc *Uh, let me see. [aside] When did I go to polygraph school, do you remember? Hm? [background voice: " 'Fifty-eight"] 'fifty . . . [then, to Mike] I don't know it was someplace in the late fifties.*

MR *Late fifties?*

JMc *Yeah, somewhere around there.*

MR *Okay, okay, so, see, the question I'm asking is not "When did you first become familiar with it and start working with it in your department?" but "When did you personally get your schooling and when did you first actually start using a polygraph as a schooled polygraph examiner?"*

JMc *Uh, oh yeah, I know when it was now, that was when we were at Huachuca. Um, it was 'fifty-seven.*

MR *[simultaneously] Okay, you first, uh, okay, 'fifty-seven is when you received your schooling?*

JMc *[simultaneously] 'Fifty-seven is when I went to school. Um-hm. 'Fifty-seven to 'fifty-eight, my wife says.*

MR *'Fifty-seven to 'fifty-eight. Okay, did you start actually practicing polygraph in the military after 1958?*

JMc *Yes. Um-hmm.*

MR *Okay, so then you could say that you've been in actual practice as a schooled examiner since 1958.*

JMc *Right.*

MR *Okay, all right, I just wanted to make certain of that. Uh, I guess that's all I have, so I really appreciate your talking to me.*

People who presume to undertake the business of separating truth from fiction ought to be scrupulous in their own statements.

On *Face The State,* McCarthy made several untrue statements. He claimed my brother Duane bodily threw him out of the hotel where the APRO/*Enquirer* investigation was taking place. There were many witnesses to his departure, and Duane never touched him. McCarthy also claimed on the show that during the pretest interview I told him that I, my brother, and mother had often speculated about riding in UFOs.

PJK repeats those charges in his writings, despite having read the transcript of the pretest interview and therefore knowing the claim to be false. Nowhere in the tape (which is the *total* of my words with McCarthy other than on "Face The State") did I refer to a belief in UFOs by anyone else in my family. And, in complete contradiction of McCarthy's and PJK's claims, I absolutely did not say on that tape that I'd "often" thought of riding in a UFO. Quite the contrary. McCarthy brought up this question entirely on his own, apparently coming into the situation prejudiced by false rumors he'd heard in the news media. (For PJK it is quite a routine tactic to change "ever" to "often," "some" to "all," etc.)

I did explain to McCarthy, attempting to be absolutely accurate in response to a question of "ever" thinking of such a thing, that seeing something on TV makes the viewer, in a sense, live the filmmaker's fantasy. (Again, I don't think anyone in our society could claim they'd never seen such images.) But in spite of his badgering on this issue, I answered, "It was no burning desire, nothing I've thought about at all." He pressed on: "You never thought of riding in a UFO?" I answered: "No."

By pressuring me on that point he got me to change my answer several times in the course of the pretest talk, due to my effort to be absolutely accurate. But, my condition being what it was and having hardly slept in days, I was confused by his emphasizing the absolute term "ever" but his manner suggested he was seeking to interpret it as an obsession or fixation. He got me so confused about this question I actually answered no on the first test chart and yes on the second chart! Such a discrepancy would invalidate the question (and therefore the entire test) for an examiner going by accepted procedure. Yet McCarthy (who, PJK said, specified that as the only relevant question I answered truthfully) didn't appear to have noticed I had given opposite replies to the same question.

The American Polygraph Association's *Standards and Principles of Practice* item Number 5 states: "A member shall not provide a conclusive decision or report based on chart analysis without having collected at least two (2) separate charts in which each relevant question is asked on each chart. (A chart is one presentation of the question list.)"

I reason that if McCarthy had really looked at the charts he would have caught the mistake, since there would have been contradictory tracings. And if there *weren't* contradictory tracings the charts would have been either *both* truthful, which would invalidate the question (by showing my confusion) and therefore the entire test (good examiners will always toss such a tainted series and start fresh—APA Standards require it); or *both* stressful, which would invalidate the test as a clear demonstration of stress reactions to both truth and untruth.

It's one thing for APRO's volunteers who prepared their version of the transcript from poor-quality equipment to have missed that compromising discrepancy; but I thought it too incredible that a present polygraph "expert" who was actually present could miss something so obvious as differing answers to the same question. I at first believed McCarthy had overlooked this, perhaps because the charts were nothing but an unreadable mass of generalized stress reactions and he hadn't based his conclusion on the charts at all. Then I noticed something peculiar. Of the eight relevant questions, that is the only one McCarthy didn't list or make any reference to in his written report.

This led me to notice another irregularity. PJK (referring to what he said McCarthy told him) wrote of the question: "In the past, have you ever thought of riding in a UFO? "Travis answered: 'Yes'. The resulting polygraph chart indicated that Travis was being truthful."

Note that PJK said *"chart"*—in the singular! I could find no other place in any of his writings where polygraph "*charts*" were referred to in the singular. Does PJK share McCarthy's knowledge of a test-invalidating blunder?

Accepted modern polygraph procedure requires *a minimum of three charts* during specific examinations. Some examiners consider two runs adequate on a nonspecific test concerning routine matters such as a preemployment clearance, but the better examiners consider even this to be substandard. No question could possibly be considered validly determined by a single chart; APA's *Standards and Principles of Practice* forbids it. The state police tests on the six witnesses in my case were CQTs and were three, and in some cases four, charts long. That's a minimum of three separate runs through the questions. Three runs are required by regulators in states like New Mexico and Utah, which also require a *minimum* 20-second interval between the end of one question and the beginning of the next.

McCarthy ran *only two charts* on me, and none of his time intervals were as long as 20 seconds; they averaged only 14 seconds, going as low as 10 seconds. For two runs of 12 questions, McCarthy spent a mere 7 minutes on my charts—a test both PJK and CSICOP tried to hype by labeling it as "lengthy." Seven minutes out of a total of less than 88 minutes for the entire interview and test, interruptions included. It's a small point but the regulations in Utah require tests to be at least 90 minutes long. So, "lengthy"? (McCarthy's report claims that "the examination commenced at 1425 and was concluded at 1615 hours," which would have made it ten minutes short of two hours in length. The tape conclusively proves that simply was not the case. But hey, if you're going to grab your verdict out of thin air, why not the time span, too?)

McCarthy asked three "relevant" questions which required me to answer on the basis of assumption or speculation rather than direct personal knowledge. This is considered a very basic and serious error by polygraph operators. *Psychological Methods in Criminal Investigation and Evidence* states, "Any relevant question that is ambiguous or that requires the subject to make interpretations can cause problems in drawing inferences about truth or deception, regardless of the actual guilt or innocence of the person tested."

My tendency to give literal responses stems from what Jim Lorenzen referred to as "philosopher syndrome." Readers have commented on the curiously sparse use of metaphors in my first book, *The Walton Experience* (which I try to remedy in this one). In my recent college philosophy class we had discussed all those nature-of-reality concepts: *Cogito ergo sum*—if a tree falls in the forest and no one hears it, does it make a sound? Etcetera. My interest in martial arts had me thinking about an episode of *Kung Fu* in which Master Po asks Caine, "If I fall asleep and dream I am a butterfly, how can I be certain when I awake that I am not a butterfly dreaming I am a man?" Prior to the incident our woods crew had had several rap sessions during break time on the job about such ideas.

The three questions about which I had no direct perceptual knowledge were (1) Was I actually in a spacecraft? (2) Was I actually taken aboard? and (3) Was I actually somewhere in Arizona during the five days I was missing? I told McCarthy: "All I can say is, to the best of my knowledge I assume that's what it was. I can only tell you what I saw; I can't say it was a spacecraft." I hadn't even been conscious, either going in or out, and I was saying that I did not know where I had been. I also said, "Now I'm going to answer them the way I *see* it, because you know if you ask me if I know for sure that some something— I'll tell you what I perceive. And I'll say yes to those kinds of— If you say, do you know positively that what this was, was what it appeared to be? I can't answer questions like that, but I will." My condition kept me from being very coherent, but these statements should have been a red flag for the need to clarify questions. But McCarthy just passed it by.

McCarthy falsely claimed in his report that I had stated I could answer each question with a yes or no. It is critical to proper testing that such understanding be clearly established. The tape distinctly shows I never made such a statement. As a matter of fact, the telephone rang at that point in the pretest; there was an interruption, with people coming into the testing room. That key element was skipped on resuming the pretest interview.

A polygraph examiner must take into account individual physiological differences. I have had a nurse take my pulse and comment in amazement on the slowness of my resting pulse. She asked if I was some kind of pro athlete. I told her not really, but that hard work at high altitude can condition one in a similar manner. The relevancy to my polygraph test is that if the examiner doesn't know the examinee normally has a low resting pulse rate, he will be unable to note the significance of an elevated pulse rate caused by general agitation. There is something else atypical about my cardiorespiratory system, which may result from a high degree of conditioning. I have a low resting respiratory rate, and sometimes skip a breath or two when physically inactive. Also at such times I sigh frequently, usually following a breathing lapse.

McCarthy claimed in his final report that I "was deliberately attempting to distort" my respiration pattern. If he really referred to the charts at all in rendering his verdict, I believe he had merely detected my respiratory quirk. My sighs are clearly audible throughout the tape, even in the test portion (but do not bear any relation—negatively or positively—to statements germane to the issue in question).

In any event, why would anyone *distort* their breathing if they were trying to defeat a test? Wouldn't normal breathing be the desired thing? I was bewildered by McCarthy's claim and thought it must be a fabrication. Then APRO's Jim Lorenzen noticed my breathing peculiarity and pointed it out to others before telling me about it. Lorenzen observed: "I have noticed the respiratory pause that Travis has. I have one, too, more pronounced if I'm nervous. It's as though I forget to breathe." Several interviewers noticed it as well, and one observed that "a year after Travis was unhooked from McCarthy's polygraph machine, he was still doing it."

McCarthy's biggest error was a blatant violation of one of the most fundamental principles of the polygraph profession; the violation was so overt that it is almost impossible to believe anyone with any training at all could do such a thing unintentionally: He created a strong mental link between the number-one key question on the test and the single most guilt-ridden memory of my life. He had to know better, because elaborate precautions are woven into the entire methodology in the effort to avoid the very problem of inadvertently provoking responses stimulated by such extraneous issues. (Even though many might think my early misdeed relatively minor, I won't specify it here, thereby serving PJK's ends by further disseminating it.)

During the interview McCarthy pushed persistently (for ten minutes—longer than the test itself) into areas in my past over which I held deep regrets and lingering guilt. On the tape he claimed this probing as merely "background" for irrelevant questions. However, there wasn't a single question based on that material. I've learned that some examiners might use such information (especially on a CQT, which this wasn't) to know what to be careful to avoid bringing up, but McCarthy had used it for an apparently opposite purpose.

The central question of the entire test, the one he referred to in his conclusion, was first asked in the pretest interview: "Have you acted in collusion with others to perpetrate a UFO hoax?"

I answered: "No."

Then McCarthy said: "Do you know what I mean when I say 'Have you acted in collusion with somebody?' "

I said, "No. What does collusion mean? Abnormal?"

McCarthy: "No, no. That means acting in concert with somebody else, one or more people to perpetrate a hoax, you know."

I understood and said, "Okay." If McCarthy had stopped there, he'd have remained within proper procedure with this particular question.

But he added: "Acting in collusion with somebody else, you know, to set this thing up. Just like you acted in collusion with this friend of yours to [blank, blank, and blank], right? That's collusion, 'cause you're acting in concert with somebody else. Now, have you acted in collusion with others, either one or more people—others—to perpetrate a UFO hoax?"

I had asked for the meaning of an unfamiliar word in the key question of the test, and he defined it solely in terms of what he knew was the one thing concerning which I felt the very greatest shame and guilt. What I had done might be far from the worst thing a person could do, but it had been *my* worst. He was in effect saying: "Now, when you hear this new word, *collusion*, I want you to recall the worst wrong you've ever done in your life."

At that point he could have asked me if I had acted in collusion to have breakfast that morning and obtained a powerful reaction—whether I answered yes or no! How could he not know this, if he's really had polygraph training? It appears almost contrived, just too much of a direct contradiction of one of the most basic tenets of polygraphy to be an accident. In between the two runs through the questions I told McCarthy: "My mind wandered to something that was upsetting me." He just brushed my remark aside.

PJK boasts that prior to my case he had "acquired some understanding of the use of the polygraph." Yet the "collusion" passage of the transcript I quoted above is nonchalantly quoted in his book with nary a raised brow. The obvious reason he chose to repeat the passage was the opportunity to gratuitously recite, for their *ad hominem* effect, the references to my misdeed from years before.

To get me to talk, McCarthy had assured me of confidentiality; then he was very evasive when I asked twice more about confidentiality, when he kept dwelling on my past mistakes. Talk about creating an atmosphere of distrust! However, if I had been someone who thought he could lie through a polygraph test, why would I have provided any information about my past misdeeds? I had no criminal record; there was no way he could know of the other, more minor things unless I told him. He was simply taking advantage of my efforts to be completely honest with him.

An examiner is not supposed to ask any unreviewed questions or change the wording (or even *the order*) of any test questions once they are reviewed with the subject, not even the irrelevant questions. This is partly to enhance some kind of "anticipation effect" for possible "guilty knowledge" items; another reason is to avoid introducing the possibility of eliciting a surprised response that would be mistaken for deception.

McCarthy changed one question from "Did you lie . . . ?" in the pretest, to "Have you lied . . . ?" on the first run, and then back to "Did you lie . . . ?" on the second run. I don't put a great deal of weight on the idea that a relatively small technical error of this sort completely invalidates a test, although in theory one could. Overall, the test is completely invalid solely on the basis of the obsolete method used, or based on any one of a number of major errors. I go farther in cataloging lesser errors to demonstrate that the test was generally riddled with one deficiency after another. One can therefore surmise there are very likely other errors I can't perceive, that would be obvious to a polygraph expert.

Long after I slammed the door on all the controversy which followed the incident, the battle continued, among ufologists, in my absence. I found out later that in 1981 Allen Hendry, on behalf of Dr. J. Allen Hynek's Center for UFO Studies, asked the internationally recognized polygraph expert Dr. David C. Raskin for his opinion of the McCarthy test, based on its transcript. Dr. Raskin provided him with the written opinion that the techniques used in the examination were seriously deficient, "unacceptable," and "more than thirty years out-of-date."

Cleve Backster, of the Backster Research Foundation in San Diego (whose congressional testimony was quoted earlier), was sent a tape and transcript of the McCarthy test. On February 22, 1993, he wrote a letter which said, ". . . I have carefully reviewed the material received. Based on the outdated technique utilized by Mr. McCarthy, even at that time, along with a significant number of other observations—it is my opinion that the result reported by John McCarthy following that November 15, 1975, polygraph examination should not be considered valid."

Mr. Backster and Dr. Raskin, although they differ strongly on various technical points of polygraph theory, and have perhaps a less-than-congenial professional relationship, are recognized as the top two experts in the entire world on the polygraph. And they are in total agreement about the nonvalidity of McCarthy's test. The test was not reviewed on the basis of the charts themselves. As I said at the outset of this passage, the test was so flawed that chart tracings weren't even necessary to disqualify it.

In going over the transcript I made a most stunning observation. It hit me so hard I stared at it, to make certain I was reading what I thought I was reading. Why hadn't anyone seen it before? Passing rigorous *new* polygraph tests and having the McCarthy test invalidated by the top experts in the world were as much in the way of vindication as I'd thought I could get. But what I'd never expected was to have the McCarthy polygraph overturned by McCarthy himself!

McCarthy didn't spend any time analyzing or poring over the charts. Immediately after I answered the last question, he spent a little over two minutes rolling the charts up, putting them away, and removing the machine's sensors from my body. Then he said: "Travis, your responses are deceptive."

I was stunned. I told him there had to be a mistake, that I was telling the truth. Then I said very emphatically, "*This* is what happened to me, as I see it, to the best of my knowledge."

That's when he slipped. John J. McCarthy said: "Could it be that you have just, uh, made yourself *believe* that this happened to you?"

A bombshell! Absolutely astounding! All a polygraph can possibly reference is what one *believes*. He had barely finished saying I was not truthful. If McCarthy was sincere and confident in his verdict, how could he, even for a second, entertain the idea that I "believed" my story true? *This*, ladies and gentlemen of the jury, is the true "smoking gun" concerning the polygraph examination administered by John J. McCarthy to Travis Walton on November 15, 1975.

With the charts destroyed, all the analyses of conduct, invalidation by top experts, my cataloging of one procedural blunder after another, total discrediting of the method itself—although each is devastating by itself, none is as abruptly enlightening in its effect as that one spontaneous remark by McCarthy himself: "Could it be that you have just, uh, made yourself *believe* that this happened to you?"

There's simply no way to rationalize the implication of his question away. He certainly wasn't trying to be nice to me; he was unceasingly hostile throughout our encounter. Evidently something in those charts, which we'll never see, told McCarthy something he could not reconcile with whatever conviction he had when he'd entered that testing room. I have a feeling it was different from the conviction he left with.

McCarthy had promised complete confidentiality before he was ever hired. He reaffirmed that promise on tape during the pretest. Also, he signed an explicit agreement to that effect.

However, his word of honor notwithstanding, he broke his promise. He made public more than his baseless conclusion. McCarthy even felt it necessary to reveal details of the pretest interview, an interview in which he pressed for and received personal information about my past that was in no way related to the UFO experience he was hired to test me for. He misused privileged information of mistakes I had made as a juvenile to malign me to the public, in a clear abuse of professional confidence.

McCarthy claimed in the *Arizona Republic* of July 12, 1976, that he "decided to break silence because the *National Enquirer* is involved in complicity which is detrimental to our profession." If this was true, why had McCarthy pledged his silence in the first place? Or why didn't he break his word soon after the testing date? It shouldn't have taken him *nine months* to leap to the defense of his profession. Why hadn't he spoken out thirty days after the test, when the *Enquirer* came out with their December 1975 issue on the UFO event with no mention of the test? Why not when the results of my second test were publicized in February 1976? McCarthy's "decision" to go public actually came about on March 15, 1976, during a telephone conversation with PJK. If anything, that breach and his ensuing mudslinging in the media were detrimental to the public's perception of the polygraph profession. This man's signature on a document was meaningless.

McCarthy was bound to confidentiality by his American Polygraph Association membership, even if his verbal and written agreements had never been made. Item Number 15 of the *APA Standards and Principles of Practice* specifically states: "To protect the privacy of each examinee, no member shall release information obtained during a polygraph examination to any unauthorized person. This shall not preclude the release of polygraph charts for the purpose of quality-control review."

"McCarthy had badgered me during the pretest interview about my disorientation in regard to time and dates. ("Where have you been, in a vacuum?") Yet, for my test's sponsors he signed an agreement which gave the incorrect date! The document contains his written confidentiality agreement ("I have conducted the test in absolute secrecy and will not divulge the results to anyone but Mr. Jenkins and Mr. Cathcart at any time.") His promise was repeated orally on the tape of the pretest discussion. Nevertheless, PJK has tried to claim that this acknowledged typographical error (wrong month) made it legally non-binding." Such preference for cynical manipulation of "the letter" rather than straightforward adherence to "the meaning and spirit" of the law testifies as to the code PJK operates by. To claim that such a technicality (even if the dubious legalistic point were valid) could relieve one of the obligation to perform as promised seems to me to be outrageously unethical.

True to form, PJK has taken every opportunity to disseminate as widely as possible the privileged information he obtained from McCarthy. My pretest disclosures to McCarthy have no bearing on the UFO incident at all. Distorting and publicizing them comprise the worst-spirited and least relevant of all PJK's blatantly *ad hominem* attacks.

I do not think I myself am guilty of same in expressing my disgust and contempt, in pointing out PJK's total lack of intellectual integrity. The *ad hominem* fallacy does not arise from a negative appraisal of a person; it arises from invalid reasoning, which attempts either to state or imply that *because of this* negative appraisal, *therefore* what you are saying is invalid.

I explicitly state once more that the despicable nature of PJK's tactics is not what invalidates his conclusions. His conclusions are not valid due to his use of tailored data, false premises, and faulty reasoning.

One of the experts hired by the *National Enquirer*, Dr. Jean Rosenbaum, had testified in court as an expert on the validity of polygraph examinations. He had witnessed the regressive hypnosis performed on me by Dr. Harder, had reviewed the results of a number of other tests, and was perfectly aware of McCarthy's pseudograph. In a television interview with ABC-TV News 3 in Phoenix on the afternoon of November 18, 1975 (three days *after* McCarthy's test, of which Rosenbaum was fully informed), Rosenbaum stated: "Our conclusion, which is absolute, is that this young man is not lying, that there is no collusion involved, no attempt to hoax or collusion of the family or anyone else." In dismissing the validity of McCarthy's test, Rosenbaum certainly could not be considered prejudiced in my favor, since he doesn't believe that UFOs exist, but it's a nice touch that he used McCarthy's term, "collusion."

Rosenbaum had arrived shortly after the test was concluded. To ensure that his opinion would be uninfluenced by McCarthy's, APRO asked Rosenbaum's opinion about the suitability of my condition for a polygraph test *before* informing him it had already been performed. He strongly recommended against my taking any test while in such a condition. PJK tried to imply that APRO's delay in telling Rosenbaum of the test had been somehow deceptive when in fact it had been the best way to get an unbiased opinion, in the tradition of the best science in "blind" reports.

APRO has been highly criticized, especially by PJK (who has withheld all positive data pertaining to APRO's investigation), for not immediately publicizing McCarthy's conclusion. I think such criticism is highly unfair. Responsibility for the decision not to publicize the test lies with the *National Enquirer*; that publication paid for the test, and the results were its property—not McCarthy's, not APRO's, and not mine. Their decision was justified by the testimony of their expert consultants who expressed the opinion that *no test* given at that time could be valid, due to my emotional condition. Since the *Enquirer* knew the test was invalid, it chose (in this instance) to prevent the dissemination of misleading information. Their ostensible perspective (unlike the ostensible perspectives of PJK, as well as APRO) is one of journalism rather than science.

PJK asked hypothetically: If Walton had passed, would they have kept it confidential? The answer is a candid no, because as previously stated, many variables can elicit stressful readings from an honest subject; but only honesty will result in a passed test. I might ask hypothetically: If I'd passed, would PJK be touting McCarthy as the most experienced examiner in the state? I think instead he would have characterized him as just the oldest guy doing lie detection in Arizona, hired by some sensationalist tabloid. I think PJK would have preempted the comments by APRO's Jim Lorenzen, that the test was "badly botched," "unbelievably incompetent," and that "sometimes long years of experience can serve to crystallize bad habits." McCarthy retired in 1990, having used the same outdated military method—the relevant/irrelevant questions—throughout his entire career!

A recent telephone interview with McCarthy confirmed that even after all these years he never switched to modern methodology. McCarthy apparently doesn't even understand the polygraph terms "CQT" and "relevant/irrelevant" as defined by the rest of the polygraph profession. Every other examiner who has seen the McCarthy test or its transcript knows it was a relevant/irrelevant test. In its earliest form there wasn't even a stim test. This explains why, on the tape of the test, he erroneously referred to his tricky little stim test as a "control test"! He is apparently so ignorant of the methodology that he has confused that tiny little improvement in the archaic relevant/irrelevant test—the "stim"—with the major advancement of modern Control Question Test methodology. He actually refers to his ancient relevant/irrelevant method as Control Question Test methodology!

Since APRO and the *Enquirer* had solid professional opinions dismissing the validity of the test, they would have been in the wrong to prematurely put forth invalid data, which would not have added to understanding of what happened, but instead would only have fueled the momentum of the tide of prejudice against it. However, it definitely was a public-relations dilemma. Frankly, it became a PR debacle because of how the information finally did come out. But it also would have been a PR debacle if they'd publicized it immediately.

I have gone on record as characterizing good science as necessitating the ultimate disclosure of all relevant data. I can think of a number of complete exceptions to this which are less extreme than the publication of data on making improved nuclear warheads. However, I stand by that principle for most everything, even though there are times when it's best to delay that objective, at least temporarily. For example, Pons and Fleischmann were criticized for *not* withholding the preliminary data of their cold-fusion experiments until they had further confirmed it with better testing.

I'll concede in hindsight that probably the best thing APRO could have done would have been to hold back on reporting the McCarthy test only until (with their sponsor's permission) they could conscientiously report it as a minor footnote to the properly conducted test I did pass later. As long as they avoided publicizing preliminary conclusions as anything more than tentative, such an approach would have satisfied all the various ethical considerations involved. APRO would have kept their members fully informed while satisfying the desire to avoid "muddying the waters." A problem with scientific ethics arises, not from withholding data until an investigation is properly completed, but from publishing a *conclusion* while withholding data—as PJK does.

After the results of McCarthy's abortive test, it was decided that I would be allowed to calm down for a period before attempting a serious test.

Due to his close involvement and his protection of me from the media, my brother Duane had been accused by PJK of conspiring with me to perpetrate an alleged hoax. A week after my birthday, on February 7, 1976, APRO arranged a polygraph examination for him with the Ezell Polygraph Institute of Phoenix, which performed all the polygraph work for the Pinal County Sheriff's Office.

I felt sufficiently recovered from the emotional trauma of my experience, and drove the 180 miles to Phoenix from Snowflake to make use of the opportunity to be tested. I was interviewed by APRO representatives Jim Lorenzen, Hal Star, Dr. R. Leo Sprinkle, and Dr. Harold Cahn. They judged my condition as sufficiently stable and agreed that I was ready. The examiner was informed of my availability before Duane's testing ended.

Testing was performed on Duane and me by George Pfiefer, a charter member of the Arizona Polygraph Association and a full member of the American Polygraph Association. He had been a detective-sergeant with the police department of Miami, Florida.

Pfiefer's report:

Mr. Travis Walton was given a polygraph examination at this office at 3:00 P.M., February 7, 1976. The purpose of this examination was to determine the truth in his statements regarding a UFO incident that occurred on November 5, 1975, and lasting until the early morning hours of November 11, 1975, as reported by Travis. This examination was performed by using a Lafayette Polygraph Model #76056-B.

During the pretest interview it was determined that Travis Walton was well rested and cooperative, was feeling physically fit and preliminary tests indicated he was a suitable subject for the examination.

A discussion was held and we mutually designed questions for this examination. Prior to the examination all questions were again reviewed with him. He agreed to answer all and signed the consent waiver form.

Question formulation was of the relevant/irrelevant type. Following is a list of the relevant questions used in this examination:

#3. Are there approximately only two hours you recall during your experience?
Answer: YES.
#4 Did you find yourself on a table inside a strange room?
Answer: YES.
#6. Did you see strange-looking beings inside the room?
Answer: YES.
#7. Have you been reasonably accurate in describing your experience?
Answer: YES.
#9. Did you conspire with another to perpetrate a hoax about this matter?
Answer: NO.
#10. Were you struck by a blue-green ray on the evening of November 5, 1975?
Answer: YES.
#11. Since November 1, 1975, have you used any illegal narcotic drugs?
Answer: NO.
#13. Before November 5, 1975, were you a UFO buff?
Answer: NO.
#14. Have you been completely truthful with Mr. Lorenzen in this matter?
Answer: YES.
#15. Did you see a UFO on the evening of November 5, 1975?
Answer: YES.

It should be noted that questions numbered 9, 10, 11, 13, and 15 were used in this examination exactly as Mr. Travis Walton dictated them to this examiner. [Questions numbered 1, 2, 5, 8, and 12, are omitted here because they are the irrelevant questions: those which ask my name, residence, etc.] Mr. Walton was completely cooperative during this examination.

There was some slight response regarding #10. After the first chart was run it was determined that Travis had not actually seen a "blue-green ray" coming from the alleged UFO. He did see the area illuminated with a "greenish light."

After a very careful analysis of the polygrams produced, there are no areas left unresolved and it is the opinion of this examiner that Travis Walton has answered all questions in a manner that he himself is firmly convinced to be truthful regarding the incident commencing November 5, 1975.

George J. Pfiefer, Jr.

Examiner

I believe in being objective and evenhanded with criticism; so, for starters I will acknowledge a couple of minor errors George Pfiefer made in writing up his report. In the first part of his report he wrote: "A discussion was held and we mutually designed questions for this examination." That was correct; but he was in error when, later in the report, he wrote that "questions numbered 9, 10, 11, 13, and 15 were used in this examination exactly as Mr. Travis Walton dictated them." This was incorrect, as Pfiefer now verifies.

I did not "come in with the questions" I wanted to be asked, as PJK alleges. Of the five test questions supplied by APRO, wording was worked out by Jim Lorenzen, Hal Star, Dr. Cahn, and Dr. Sprinkle, whose specialty is testing: he is the Director of Counseling and Testing at the University of Wyoming. The four APRO people had worked out questions numbered 3, 4, 6, 7, and 14 before I arrived; I did discuss and accept them with the examiner. However, I did not feel they were direct enough. I offered half a dozen *areas* I felt should be covered, but did *not* specify wording of questions. (In using the word "dictate," I believe Pfiefer was trying to emphasize my cooperativeness, in my having suggested the more specific questions.) Notice that the second five we ended up with are the more direct questions. The questions I suggested did not replace the questions APRO had planned as the complete test; they simply added to them.

I was in error myself in suggesting one question, number 10, which required me, the literalist, to answer on the basis of assumption rather than experience. So Pfiefer wrote, correctly, that I "had not actually seen" the ray; but added that I'd seen the area light up with a "greenish glow." That addition was incorrect. I said I had seen the greenery in the area lit by the glow from the craft, but that the light had been of a peculiar pale golden color. This occurred *before* I was hit. I felt only a numbing shock and blacked out at the same instant that my coworkers later told me they had seen the ray strike. This may have caused a last-minute twinge of doubt. Or perhaps the sharp pain associated with the memory of this psychologically intense peak in my experience could have triggered this "slight response."

Pfiefer confirms that he *reworded every single question* suggested to him for all the tests. PJK nevertheless has repeatedly claimed that my input into the question formulation was a violation of proper polygraph procedure of such a magnitude that my positive test results from the Pfiefer test should be considered invalid.

Not only is the above-mentioned practice not condemned by experts, it's recommended! One more brief quotation from Elie A. Shneour's article in CSICOP's *Skeptical Inquirer,* "Lying About Polygraph Tests" (an article, by the way, which refers to Dr. David Raskin as one of the "leaders in the field"):". . . the examination begins with the subject being cuffed and strapped to the device. The considerable resulting discomfort is eased every fifteen minutes or so while the examiner changes charts.

"These interludes provide the examiner with opportunities to ask the subject about his reaction to the questions posed and allow refinement of the questions to be asked next."

More accurate concerning actual polygraph procedure, and much more to the point on the issue, is the following excerpt from Cleve Backster's 1974 congressional testimony.

Congressman: *Mr. Backster, on page 3 of your testimony you say here at the bottom: 'It should be noted that all the questions are reviewed word-for-word, in advance of the beginning of the chart concerned.' Is that reviewed with the subject?*

Mr. Backster: *Yes, with the subject. In fact, the subject is allowed an opportunity to help formulate the questions so that he certainly will have a basic understanding of each one to be asked . . .*

If we don't review questions and particularly the control questions, ahead of time, we don't know what psychological "button" we may be touching as far as the subject is concerned, if he hasn't had an opportunity to talk with us about such questions.

I think it is extremely imperative that questions are reviewed ahead of time.

If the subject taking the test is apprehensive that surprise questions may be interjected, he may be apprehensive to all questions. He may be attuned to some kind of outside issue that very much bothers him as compared to the relevant issue.

In fairness to the subject and in fairness to the technique, Mr. Chairman, in my opinion, it is absolutely essential that the questions be carefully reviewed in advance.

George Pfiefer was interviewed by Mike on December 29, 1992, concerning his examinations on myself, my brother, and my mother. Here's what he had to say:

Q: *Are you firm on your conclusions on the Walton test?*
A: *Certainly!*
Q: *You are?*
A: *Sure!*
Q: *What I was wondering personally is if your opinion had changed since, so I guess it hasn't, then?*

A: *Nope, no way, no way!*

Q: *So I would assume then that your tests on Travis's mother and his brother, your conclusions on all of their tests are as firm as they were originally?*

A: *Absolutely!*

Q: *It has been said that Travis dictated the questions to you that he wanted.*

A: *No. You see, this is another one of those things. Now, you had a polygraph examination, right?*

Q: *Right.*

A: *Now, the examiner had made out questions. Before the test started, he read you those questions, didn't he?*

Q: *Right.*

A: *And, if you didn't like something about a question you could ask him to change it, correct?*

Q: *That's correct, that's the way ours went.*

A: *That's exactly what we're talking about, just exactly.*

Q: *So, that's the way Walton's went?*

A: *Yes.*

The only examination solidly scheduled in advance for February 7, 1976, was my brother Duane's. I had been discussing my readiness to be retested with APRO, and had given them a tentative agreement to be tested along with Duane. I was having problems with my car. If, through no fault of my own, I didn't manage to make my appointment, how would another missed appointment look in the wake of the abortive arrangements for the sheriff's test? So, since APRO wasn't certain I'd make it, they only made an appointment for Duane.

Naturally PJK reads sinister intrigue into that fact, alleging a plan to "test the waters with Duane" before agreeing to have me tested, alleging a conspiracy which excluded the examiner but included all the APRO personnel present. This is absurd—how could one person's reactions to a test have any bearing on the outcome of a different person's test with completely different questions?

The fact is I arrived while Duane's testing was still under way (interrupting a test in progress isn't allowed), and committed myself to being tested to the APRO personnel there, without receiving the slightest hint of how my brother's testing was going, since nobody had any idea at that point. (I never saw Duane that day at all. That evening I did talk to him about the tests, by telephone, on my way out of town.) While Duane was being tested I went across the street for a walk in the park with Dana. While we were gone the examiner was asked about testing me during a break between test series (Duane actually took two separate tests in a row, one with six relevant questions and one with eight relevant questions), prior to the examiner giving his conclusion on Duane's tests. Duane finished and left to return to his work before I returned from the park.

The irrelevant questions, which ask for name, residence, etc., are not listed and are only asked in order to provide a yardstick of "known truth" responses for comparison. Also, Duane initially took the "Known Lie Test," which showed him a strong responder. Some of the fourteen relevant questions (the others were variations or subissues of these) on my brother's polygraph test were:

#2. Did you participate in a hoax to pretend that Travis was missing?
#3. Do you believe that Travis participated in a hoax to pretend that he was missing?
#4. Do you know where Travis was located during the several days that he was missing?
#5. Do you believe that Travis is sincere in describing his experience while he was missing?
#6. Would you lie to help Travis in this matter?
#7. Did Travis hide on the Kellett Ranch?
#8. Prior to November 5, 1975, had you read a book on UFOs?

The examiner, George Pfiefer, wrote in his report: "After a careful analysis of the polygrams produced, along with information gained during pretest and post-test interviews, it is the opinion of this examiner that Duane Walton has answered all questions truthfully according to what he believes to be the truth regarding this incident and has not attempted to be deceptive in any area."

When Duane was protecting me from being grilled by the press, the sheriff's men, and the curious, he said things to throw people off the scent. Then, when PJK called and tried to pry into mistakes I'd made when I was younger, and asked if I had taken a test prior to Pfiefer's, Duane denied any such knowledge. PJK contrasts that fact with Duane's being judged truthful on question number 6 above, and tries to claim a disparity which overturns the validity of the entire test.

Duane had learned prior to the call of PJK's reputation for being rabidly anti-UFO, unfair, devious, prone to twisting people's words to suit his purposes. In fact, Duane ignored advice not even to speak to him. But PJK arrogantly presumes that people should respond to him as if he were a federal special prosecutor, with as much openness, fullness, and precision as if testifying under oath before a full session of both houses of Congress. However, surveys show that when confronted with a person one considers shady, or believes intends one harm, most honest people consider themselves justified in speaking at odds with the facts to whatever extent is necessary.

Naturally Duane interpreted question number 6 to mean, would he lie to help me falsify a UFO incident?—that was the reason he was taking the test. The sponsors of the test knew of Duane's shielding me from being mobbed, because they themselves at first had been deflected by him in their efforts to investigate the case. They wouldn't have framed a question to encompass falsehoods originating in brotherly protectiveness. Psychologists observe that there are no perfectly truthful persons; modern polygraph methodology actually *counts on* this fact, even to establish innocence.

PJK has gotten so carried away in attacking the Turkey Springs incident that he has even made allegations against my mother! I brought her along when I was in Phoenix to meet with Dr. J. Allen Hynek on March 22, 1976. As mentioned, the late Dr. Hynek was an astronomer at Northwestern University, and, as head of the Center for UFO Studies, was a leading national authority on unidentified flying objects. Hynek was probably best known to the general public for his Project Blue Book work for the U.S. Air Force and acting as scientific consultant in the making of the movie *Close Encounters of the Third Kind.* The renowned scientist made a press release the next day endorsing the validity of my experience, saying I was "not hoaxing" and "had been made the subject of a lot of unnecessary and unfounded accusations."

APRO arranged for my mother to take a polygraph test while we were there. Her testing was uneventful, performed more as a matter of course than from serious questioning of her integrity. Some of the thirteen relevant questions on her test were:

> #3. Did you ever conspire with Travis or any person to perpetrate a hoax to pretend that Travis was missing?
>
> #4. Were you deeply involved in the UFO subject before Travis' disappearance?
>
> #6. During the period of November 6, 1975, to November 10, 1975, did you actually know where Travis was?
>
> #7. Did you conceal Travis from public contact between November 5, 1975, and November 11, 1975?
>
> #9. Do you believe that Travis is truthful in this matter?
>
> #10. Have you yourself ever seen a flying saucer?

The examiner's judgment of her truthfulness was written in his report as follows: "After a very careful analysis of the polygraphs produced and comparing the polygraph tracings with the Known Lie pattern, it is the opinion of this examiner that Mrs. Mary Kellett has answered all the questions truthfully according to the best of her knowledge and beliefs."

Observant readers will have noticed in the report on my test that it says "Question formulation was of the relevant/irrelevant type." That was also the method used on my brother and mother's test. In the interest of being consistent with the criteria I've been using concerning polygraph tests, wouldn't the validity of these tests have to be disqualified on the same basis that experts disqualified McCarthy's test? (Readers won't find such candor or balance in PJK's writings.)

The experts disqualified the McCarthy test on the basis of two aspects. One aspect was the multitude of what would have been judged to be procedural errors even by those who accepted its methodology. The other disqualifying aspect was its discredited methodology, which implicitly included the fact that it was a "failed" test! Whoa, you say. That sounds like the reverse of PJK's biased criteria of accepting all flunked tests as proof and claiming all passed tests are flawed.

I know it's ironic, but with the relevant/irrelevant methodology it really is the case that failed tests are the only area in which the research showed such gross unreliability! (As we can conclude from information given in PJK's fellow CSICOP member's article, in a situation using modern methods where you have one test pass and one fail, the pass has considerably greater weight. But the research shows that with relevant/irrelevant it is overwhelmingly so.)

In the same research study (Horowitz, 1988) which demonstrated the method yields 80 percent false positives (that is, only 20 percent of the independently established innocent subjects were correctly classified), quantitative chart evaluations yielded 100-percent correct outcomes on guilty subjects! Again, this refers to independently proven and confirmed guilt. (Of course, this percentage would drop below 100 percent in actual field use to where it would actually be a bit less than the upper ninetieth percentile of accuracy shown for polygraph in general. Averaging the innocent and guilty together naturally gives the method an accuracy rate far lower than that of polygraph in general.) But if the method is so skewed it calls 80 percent of innocent subjects liars, it's no surprise it gets the last few percent of the guilty ones—it's probably by accident! Sounds like that old mercenary soldier's saying, "Kill 'em all, let God sort 'em out." Evidently your reactions have to be extremely innocent to pass a relevant/irrelevant test, but when you do pass, it's pretty solid.

Also Pfiefer was not using an old machine like McCarthy's, he was using a more modern four-trace machine. (PJK never mentions this but knew about it, since he put pictures of both machines in his book.) And Pfiefer didn't make the numerous violations of accepted procedure that McCarthy committed.

When PJK sought to discredit the Pfiefer test, he called Pfiefer's employer, Tom Ezell. APRO, in the interest of full disclosure, had informed George Pfiefer of the McCarthy test, so there was no suppression of that information where disclosure was relevant and proper. That information was given to Ezell and Associates in confidence; but according to PJK Tom Ezell *vol-*

unteered it to him, in violation of professional confidence and flouting item number 15 of *APA Standards and Principles of Practice.*

If true, Tom Ezell shares responsibility with McCarthy in the release of privileged information; a wrong McCarthy severely compounded by confirming the test results, and in going on to repeat personal information about me acquired in the confidential pretest interview. I have been told I have a solid legal case against all involved here, including the clerk who illegally supplied PJK with details, but right now I'd be satisfied if they would cease and desist their malicious campaign.

In that first, March 13, 1976, call, Ezell told PJK that Pfiefer had returned to independent practice. Apparently Ezell was quickly cornered into trying to distance himself from the tests he himself had arranged with APRO by saying he'd been out of town. The tests took place on February 9, 1976, and PJK's call came on March 13, 1976, more than a month later. Why hadn't Ezell been moved *immediately* to "reassess" Pfiefer's work? He claimed to already have had doubts from talking to Pfiefer after hearing the verdicts on returning to town. Why is it that only after being contacted by PJK more than thirty days later did Ezell mention his "doubts" and "offer" to make a reappraisal within ten days? What really happened during that first phone call? What really motivated Ezell to volunteer the information he did—including some words of praise for McCarthy?

Perhaps it's no wonder Ezell gave such praise of McCarthy, since they had been both still using the same outdated method. But is Ezell now still using relevant/irrelevant? His answer: "No! No no. No no! We use Control Question Technique now!" Why did he abandon the old method tests? "Because I found out those were making too many mistakes." Recall that McCarthy used the relevant/irrelevant method for his entire career.

Tom Ezell, who had originally been scheduled to administer Duane's and my tests, had to be out of town that day, but informed APRO that Pfiefer was "as qualified as I am. He's up on all the latest methods."

Ezell evidently remained of that opinion until he was goaded by PJK into disavowing my test. (Shortly after which he, like McCarthy, destroyed the corresponding charts!) In the March 22, 1976, phone call, Ezell did not say that the test was failed; in fact, in PJK's own version, Ezell avoided using the word "inconclusive." Either he didn't want to commit so firmly to contradicting a conclusion he'd already received payment for; or he may have used the word, with PJK omitting it as too neutral for his purposes. Its absence could be evidence that Ezell was only looking for a face-saving neutral position to back into. Maybe PJK edited Ezell's actual words so thoroughly that Ezell's meaning has been greatly altered. A complete and accurate transcript of PJK's calls to Ezell and an unexpurgated copy of his letter would likely throw enough light to give a whole new interpretation of their exchange.

The March 22, 1976, phone call PJK quotes has undergone the usual curious metamorphosis. In his June 20, 1976, white paper PJK quoted Ezell: "You would not be able to say if [Travis Walton] is telling the truth or if he's lying." Even though PJK attacks Duane and his test extensively in that same seventeen-page report, not a single word was mentioned about Ezell's "reassessing" Duane's test. However, by the time the conversation appeared in PJK's book, "reassessment" was embellished to include Duane's test.

When APRO heard about that unofficial new conclusion, APRO wrote to Ezell inquiring as to whether he would be interested in making the revision official by returning the money his firm had received as payment for two valid polygraph tests. Ezell didn't reply. But if he was confident in second-guessing Pfiefer, why did he destroy the charts?

People have suggested Ezell was cooperating with a government cover-up, but I don't think so. When another skeptical UFO investigator recently brought up Ezell's disavowal, I told him I believed it was all a PR job because Ezell figured the flak in the news media would hurt his business. I've heard that people around Tom Ezell observed that for days ("days" perhaps being those after PJK's first call, rather than after hearing Pfiefer's verdict) he became deeply upset and depressed about the effect the UFO stigma from the media controversy would have on his business.

I bet the ufologist that if Ezell were asked again to test someone claiming a UFO experience that he would refuse the business just on the basis of the subject matter. If his problem was only disbelief in UFOs, he could test them and prove it. He couldn't imagine there was stigma attached to flunking such subjects, only in substantiating their reports. So we asked him. Sure enough, he said, "I'd rather not get mixed up in that, I'd rather not." Due to the subject matter? "Yeah."

PJK carefully stacked his description of Pfiefer's and McCarthy's credentials in a very biased fashion I will specify later. PJK's main point was that Pfiefer was less experienced; therefore, years of experience became the ultimate standard of the comparative skill of polygraph examiners.

In the wake of the controversy after the two polygraph tests, Jerome Clark, then associate editor at Clark Publishing Company, sponsored a PSE (psychological stress evaluator) examination of a taped interview of me and also tapes (provided by APRO) of my two polygraph examinations by Pfiefer and McCarthy; the PSE charts were analyzed by two independent PSE experts.

PSE was an electronic "lie-detection" technique in use at that time which had been developed in the previous ten years by three retired Army Intelligence officers: Allan Bell, Jr., Wilson Ford, and Charles McQuiston. The PSE is an instrument which was said to detect *inaudible* frequency changes in the human voice caused by emotional stress.

Inevitably the PSE, like all "lie-detecting" techniques, has generated controversy, partly because stress does not automatically equal lying, and because of competition between businesses employing differing types of "lie detection"—principally, the PSE and the polygraph.

Enough security experts, law enforcement officers, industrial investigators, and other such professionals approved PSE at that time (proponents claimed it was more than 90-percent accurate) that the method grew widely in use; a dozen states admitted it as evidence in court. But the technique has languished from lack of further development, and has never gained the status or level of use of the polygraph. In fact, even though these tests corroborated my story, in the interest of objectivity I must admit—based on what I've learned about its level of development at that time—that I don't believe the PSE should be given much weight. I only include it because I heard that William Spaulding of GSW claimed to have taken a PSE which supported his position. However, for whatever it's worth, my PSE results follow.

One expert, Ann B. Hooten of Mid-America Laboratory in Minneapolis, concluded her January 30, 1978, final report of my PSEs thusly: "The opinion of this office and staff is that Travis Walton is sincere in believing his UFO experience was genuine."

Several weeks later the other expert, one of the PSE's developers himself, Charles McQuiston, concluded his thirty chart evaluation with, "His stress factors indicate to me there is little if any possibility of a hoax involvement in telling the story. His patterns are varied. He's under varying degrees of stress ranging from extreme stress almost to the panic point in describing certain traumatic elements of his experience. I don't think this would be possible if it was any kind of a hoax being perpetrated on his part. The patterns are consistent with [those of] other subjects of UFO sightings that I have run in terms of where they display the stress. . . ."

"For this reason I believe it's pretty consistent with a subject who had a traumatic experience and is recalling this experience which is causing his trauma [in the sense that he is] reliving the trauma he was under. He really believes that he lived this, that he saw the creatures in question."

After reviewing and running PSE analysis on the PSE evaluations by Ann Hooten, McQuiston stated, "Both that test—the PSE taken during the [McCarthy] polygraph examination—and the subsequent PSE test taken by Ann Hooten are NDI: no deception indicated. He did *not* fail those tests."

PJK has made arrogant and unjustified accusations of lying against nearly everyone he attacks, which has included respected scientists, police officers, priests, and professionals of every sort. We're in the midst of many examples of PJK's statements that are at odds with the truth; these are but a fraction of his falsehoods in this matter if we include the vast multitude of lies of omission, which I'll be getting to.

In looking back over PJK's writings on UFOs, a gradual change in his approach becomes evident. His first book takes witnesses at their word and tries to explain what people report as honest mistakes of sightings of what he considered to be a real phenomena (plasmas).

His second book touches on the hoax explanation, but mostly in regards to young kids and college students as pranksters. But in this second book he still specifically says that reports do not come only from "kooks" and that many "come from seemingly honest, intelligent and often well-educated citizens." And his second book also lists his Ten Ufological Principles of which only one refers to hoax while the other nine refer to visual or mental misperceptions by "basically honest and intelligent persons" or honest (if inept) oversight by newspersons and investigators.

Then in his third book on this topic, he largely forgets ufological principles, includes a few cases of honest misperception, but for the most part sees hoaxes and liars everywhere.

His fourth anti-UFO book takes the final step: Ufological principles are completely omitted and proponents are all either liars or mentally deluded people and their cynical exploiters who are now downright dangerous and a threat to society.

Even the titles of his books follow the evolving pattern of his increasing obsession: *UFOs Identified, UFOs Explained, UFOs—The Public Deceived,* and then, *UFO Abductions—A Dangerous Game.*

This evolution of PJK's growing obsession with lying and lie detectors (while his own distortions of the truth accumulate monumentally) has paralleled his increasing hostile irrationality and behavior resembling that of a crank. To his writings he adds quotes about lying taken from famous persons of the past. "One falsehood treads on the heels of another" (Terence). "He who permits himself to tell a lie once, finds it much easier to do it a second time and a third time, till at length it becomes habitual" (Thomas Jefferson). "Half the truth is often a great lie" (Benjamin Franklin). "He who does not bellow the truth when he knows the truth makes himself the accomplice of liars and forgers" (Charles Peguy). These last two are especially good advice—too bad he doesn't follow it, instead of withholding every bit of favorable evidence.

PJK made so much noise about the validity of the tests on the six witnesses, and the validity of the tests on me, my brother, and my mother, that the nine of us threw down the gauntlet. We threw his "Talk is cheap, put your money where your mouth is" challenge back at him. The nine of us challenged him to have us all retested according to standards he would first agree would yield valid results. He would not have to pay a cent if any tests were failed, we would. However, *he* would have to pay for all tests passed. If he was sincere, how could he refuse?

One might think a proposition so straightforward would come to quick resolution. Not with PJK. Our correspondence was undertaken publicly, so he finally agreed, "in principle" only, to save face. But we were just entering the most ridiculous spectacle of evasion, equivocation, nit-picking, stalling, ducking, and dodging from him one can imagine.

Our first mistake was letting him get away with redefining the issue. His reply never said, "I accept your *challenge*"—something you simply either accept or reject. His reply termed it a "proposal"; in subsequent letters it was downgraded to "agreement," then to "equitable agreement," then "negotiations for a mutually acceptable agreement."

The decision to negotiate would not have been a mistake with a normal, fair-minded individual. With PJK it turned into a preposterously aggravating, tangled nightmare.

He worded his response to include a list of those persons challenging, but sneakily dropped my mother from the list of test subjects. Then, after initially agreeing to a list that included Duane, a little while later he also dropped my *brother* in the same sneaky way—a casual relisting of the test subjects with another name deleted, again with no comment.

When we caught the alteration and took him to task about it, he made the lame excuse that since they weren't present during the incident, they didn't need to be tested! After publishing pages and pages of accusations and insinuations against them, he dug in his heels and refused to include them. So, one clear, early victory achieved by our "challenge" was, in effect, to force PJK to admit for all to see that he really believed at least Duane and my mother were innocent of his charges. Since then, however, he has hypocritically continued to repeat those charges, even though he wouldn't put his money where his mouth was when it counted.

After including Duane and reneging, PJK made a qualified acceptance of a choice of polygraph examiner, then reneged. The proposed examiner was none other than the eminent Cleve Backster. PJK backed out on Backster because Jim Lorenzen had spoken with him first, implying, absurdly, that whoever spoke to Backster first would corrupt him.

Backster had at one time performed research involving primary perception at the cellular level in plants and animals, which he had gotten into serendipitously when using one of his polygraph machine's sensors to measure an office plant's rate of water uptake. After PJK had rejected Backster as examiner, he dug up an inaccurate old newspaper clipping about his plant inquiries and made a futile attempt at *ad hominem* ridicule. Backster has done probably every investigation imaginable with a polygraph, hooking it to everybody and everything around him; it's not surprising that in all his years of research he ventured into an area somewhat less well received by restricted thinkers than his more conventional research.

PJK's excuses for all his backtracking were ridiculous. We couldn't seem to make real headway. As soon as we thought we had one of his objections resolved, he would find another.

One of PJK's delaying tactics was to demand signatures from all of us on each piece of correspondence. This mischief had us driving all over the state to gather signatures. (We'd organized by phone.) So we had to insist on being represented by the signature of our erstwhile crew chief, Mike Rogers.

Before this, PJK kept taunting us about the missing signatures of Smith and Dalis. He mistakenly believed we didn't know that PJK knew Dalis was in jail. He secretly assumed that, as he later admitted, this meant Dalis would be unable to be tested. That may have been the only reason PJK agreed, even "in principle," to our challenge, thinking Allen Dalis' inability to test would provide PJK a loophole for escape, and simultaneously serve to make it look as if we had challenged him in bad faith.

After his stealthy elimination of my mother and brother, he took elaborate care to word each tentative, qualified reference to acceptance to clearly state "you, and the other six members of your crew." However, we had already checked with Dalis' lawyer and at the jail to make sure that he could be tested there or at his lawyer's office. PJK's attempt to trick us by pretending not to know of Dalis' troubles didn't work, but he did resurrect the old "guilt by association" component of his *ad hominem* tactic.

Niggling refinement of terms went on for nearly a year before we'd had enough. The agreement had become seven typed, single-spaced, pages long; it was beginning to look like a piece of three-committee legislation. It was fair, and as refined as we cared to get. We issued a final, unequivocal, put-up-or-shut-up *challenge*. Again he tried to quibble and harangue, hedge and qualify.

After eleven months (with a frustrated pause or two) of exasperating and sincere negotiations on our part, we realized we never would actually get him to end his filibuster and follow through. He never acted as if he comprehended the definition of a challenge—a sham, from one always issuing challenges himself. Has he ever negotiated the terms of *his* challenges? PJK had, in effect, rejected our challenge and we published that fact. He had failed, clear and simple, to seize an opportunity to "put his money where his mouth is" and prove he was unafraid to stand behind his accusations.

PJK denies that he declined the final challenge (which he refers to as an ultimatum), but his last reply really didn't differ in tone from his first, nearly a year earlier.

If one wishes not to rely on my synopsis of the matter, beware of relying on the selective quotations PJK publishes. I can provide the opportunity to examine complete, unexpurgated copies for serious, respectable investigators, if any are *that* interested, of the whole frustrating exchange, with commentary (it amounts to an entire book in itself), so that a fully informed judgment can be made. Nearly everyone who followed the exchange (carried out publicly, with many copies of letter after letter going to polygraph examiners McCarthy and Pfiefer, Sheriff Gillespie, newsmen, and interested investigators) said it was plain to them that we were sincere and PJK was not.

Our final words on the subject:

Mr. *(PJK):*
Just as we expected, your decline of our final challenge was buried in pages and pages of convoluted exhortations intertangled with selective repetitions of all your ridiculous old assertions. But just as we said in our challenge-letter, we are not the slightest bit interested in your excuses.

The definition of a challenge is not "an equitable agreement," as you would prefer. A challenge is a *challenge.* You have *failed to accept* ours—pure and simple. Our challenge to you was to (in your own words) "put up or shut up." You have failed to "put up" and unfortunately will probably not "shut up" either. Therefore, we turn a deaf ear to your rabid tirades. Since you don't have anything important to say, no one listens to you anyway. Anyone who has had anything to do with you knows that anything you say is nothing but character assassination, negative proofs, misrepresentation of material quoted out of context, innuendo, false logic, selective mention and omission of data, etc., etc. In short, the tools of shyster lawyers and propagandists.

The incident at Turkey Springs did, in fact, happen and perhaps someday you will admit it. But your aberration is so extreme that it is doubtful that even a long ride in a UFO could cure you.

This is our very last correspondence with you. Do not bother writing anymore, as all mail from you will be returned unopened.

Sincerely,

The Nine Test Subjects

(PJK sneakily circumvented our ban on his endless letters by sending Mike one in an American Airlines envelope with no return address.)

Just like PJK's force-fit of UFO data into his plasma theory, PJK's "investigations" would be laughed out of real science. And speaking of shyster lawyer tactics, since PJK fails in his claimed arena of science, how would he pan out in the legal arena? That which would be laughed out of science would likewise be thrown out of court.

However flawed in the logical sense, the legal system is an institution which, like debate and science, is yet another forum for arriving at "truth." PJK uses all the discredited tactics in this arena, too. When PJK quotes biased and unreliable witnesses, he equates the accuracy of his quote (unreliable in itself) with the factuality of the statement. For someone whose father was a lawyer, he should know better than to use character assassination, hearsay, withheld evidence, leading questions, innuendo, etc. He sent this collection of pettifoggery to Sheriff Marlin Gillespie in an effort to get him to prosecute the nine of us. The sheriff turned PJK's material over to the county attorney, who, together with the sheriff, told reporters that although they'd certainly prosecute anything solid, PJK's material didn't amount to anything more than a collection of opinions, theories, and unsubstantiated supposition. Many people were fooled by his writings until they saw the other side, but Sheriff Gillespie and Navajo County attorney Bob Hall were astute enough that they could clearly see this *without* having heard our rebuttals.

Earlier I mentioned an attempt to pay Steve Pierce to disprove the UFO incident. Several aspects of the episode made it appear that PJK was behind the offer. The offered amount of $10,000, for one, an amount PJK has offered a number of times in various challenges, added to that suspicion.

However, PJK denies any involvement, claiming that the first time he knew about the offer was when he read Bill Barry's account of it. PJK implied that only on hearing that Steve was "considering repudiating the incident" did he become interested in making contact with him. This supposedly led him for the first time to make contact with the officer who had taken the offer to Steve.

If that is true, why, in his report of talking to the deputy, didn't PJK mention what the deputy had to say concerning the $10,000 offer? If PJK were innocent, one would expect that in the face of such a damaging charge he would be highly motivated to obtain exonerating quotes with which to clear himself to his readers.

PJK wrote of Barry's account in *UFOs: The Public Deceived.*

Clearly Rogers feared that at least one member of his crew would fail the test, regardless of who was accepted as the examiner. Barry's book quotes Rogers as saying: "Steve told me and Travis that he had been offered ten thousand dollars just to sign a denial. He said he was thinking about it. . . . So I told him, 'Then you'll spend the money alone, and you'll be bruised.' " The latter suggests that Rogers was threatening Pierce with physical harm if he recanted.

Beware the *ellipses,* those three dots so often found in PJK's quotes. They frequently stand in for information he wishes to hide in order to falsify the speaker's true meaning.

Here's what that passage on page 160 of Barry's book actually said:

According to Mike Rogers, "Steve told me and Travis that he had been offered ten thousand dollars just to sign a denial. He said he was thinking about taking it. We asked him, 'Even though you know it happened, would you deny it just for the money?' He said maybe he would; he was thinking about it. So I told him, 'Then you'll spend the money alone, and you'll be bruised.' "

PJK only used one set of ellipses to make two omissions—his chief aim to omit deliberately the key phrase "Even though you know it happened, would you deny it just for the money?"—an obvious effort to deceive his readers into believing that Mike was threatening Steve to keep him from "recanting" or revealing the truth, rather than threatening retribution for knowingly giving false testimony for money! What a sneaky trick! How fraudulent can he get? PJK also said this indicated Mike was afraid Pierce wouldn't pass the test we had challenged PJK to provide; the full quotation proves quite the contrary.

Bafflingly, PJK quotes Steve as telling him: "If I could ever prove it was a hoax I'd damn sure do it," contradicting PJK's hypothesis that Steve already knew the incident to be a hoax. I could say the same and still not be denying my perceptions and memories. If I found out that some earth organization or government was responsible for what has happened to me, I, too, would damn sure try to prove it.

I have reason to believe that if PJK could be induced to turn over the entire tape of the withheld portions of his conversation with Steve, the public would have something else to raise eyebrows about. PJK's vague reference to this undisclosed portion was: "But I could not gain any meaningful details about what had transpired."

Knowing PJK's tactics, "any meaningful details" could refer to a great deal of positive testimony. Another example of such use of words was his reference to a blood sample (which, in opposition to his charges, contained *no trace of any drug*): "[D]etailed examination . . . included analysis of a blood sample, which revealed nothing unusual." He was not pointing out that it was a drug-free sample. It was actually a sly way of getting around that glaring disproof of his charge, by emphasizing that the sample displayed no bizarre characteristic or unknown substance which would constitute an indisputable artifact of alien abduction.

In the February 1993 issue of the *MUFON Journal* I wrote of PJK: "When his contrived edifice first started to crumble as I began refuting him, he was already showing signs of wavering and edging away from his prior claims. When I'm done, I predict he'll be forced to make a full retreat from the collapsing ruin of his previous 'convictions.' And I predict that he'll come to act as if he never really said any of those things. After some vain attempts to defend the old nonsense, he'll espouse some new nonsense with the same fervent certainty."

My words apparently touched a nerve. Our "debunker" issued a $1,000 challenge wager in his March 1993 newsletter concerning my prediction, listing six points which he claims to be unassailable. Most of the six points were obscure in their bearing on the principal facts of the case. They referred to a couple of hearsay quotes (which are false, but ultimately unprovable either way, since they weren't taped); the McCarthy test; the out-of-context quote from Steve Pierce; and an excerpt from the Sylvanus tape of Sylvanus' interview with Duane and Mike at the forest site.

Well, the ink was barely dry on his words before PJK was issuing a retraction on one of his unassailable points. He had claimed in one of his books that I had said in a TV interview that I had been "bleeding heavily" during my experience. He then went on about the subsequent absence of wounds on my body or blood on my clothes, as if he were the only person astute enough to catch what would have been an astoundingly obvious contradiction. He subsequently was forced to admit that I had indeed said "breathing heavily" not "bleeding heavily." He said he'd publish his retraction accordingly.

(He didn't fully keep that promise. In his newsletter, *SUN*, he wrote: "The Editor of *SUN* wishes to clarify its editorial policy which firmly adheres to the following principles: (1) *SUN* never errs. (2) When *SUN* does err, it never admits it. (3) However, there may be times when some 'clarification' is appropriate." He then gave his retraction as "Clarification #1," and repeated his intention so to correct future editions of his book. Contrast this "never admit it" policy with his Ufological Principle Number 4, criticizing the media for not correcting pro-UFO errors.)

What actually prompted PJK to publish his correction was the fact that CSICOP's executive director, Barry Karr, had heard about his misquoting of me and asked PJK about it. So he was faking good for his cronies, but PJK made no such effort to correct another such "error" exposed on national television a few days later.

Was this "bleeding"/"breathing" thing a deliberate trick? Or just an error, another example of the "careful investigation" and "accuracy" PJK boasts about? It's hard to see how he could have sincerely made such a mistake, because the tape (contrary to his excuses) is quite clear; even his own published transcript of it shows that right after the phrase in question I added: "I couldn't catch my breath."

Speaking of breath, I didn't hold mine waiting for his $1,000 check, which I've yet to receive.

The account above is just a typical example of the quality of his work and the flimsiness of his case—and just the beginning of the fulfillment of my predictions.

Jeff Wells, an Australian member of the team of *National Enquirer* reporters who worked on my story, later left that paper and wrote some articles about what he represented as his experiences as part of the *Enquirer*'s coverage of the UFO incident. There doesn't seem to be any low to which those lacking in ethics, journalistic and otherwise, will not stoop in printing anything that will serve their ends.

After years of heaping scornful criticism on the tabloids, PJK and CSI-COP apparently felt no hypocrisy in reprinting the ex–tabloid writer's article in the Summer 1981 issue of the *Skeptical Inquirer*. (The *Skeptical Inquirer* was evidently named to take a backhanded slap at the tabloids by playing off the *National Enquirer*'s name, to make clear that CSICOP considered themselves the antithesis of the tabloid mentality.) The article was riddled with tabloid-style hyperbole, distortion, and pure fiction. But PJK, as "UFO editor," added remarks taking issue with only two falsehoods, which he judged to err in the direction of supporting our case's validity. It seems to me there's no muck so rank that PJK won't suck it up and spew it out to the public; but, again, not without what I'll call "creative enhancement" in the direction of what he wishes it *had* said, as I shall here elucidate.

There were so many outrageously baseless lies in Jeff Wells' article (which could be easily refuted since the proceedings were taped and there were many others present) that I won't even bother to refute them individually. (The coincidence is ironic, but *this* freelance writer Jeff Wells is apparently *not* the same freelance writer Jeff Wells who has been embroiled in so many accusations of outrageously false reporting about Schwarzenegger's film *The Last Action Hero*, Clint Eastwood, and other entertainment-industry figures.)

PJK passed the *Skeptical Inquirer* version off as a "reprint." However, apparently it offered an excess of sleaze-appeal which PJK felt compelled to tidy up with a little undisclosed erasing. I came into possession of a copy of

the photocopies of the original newspaper article which PJK had been circulating among ufologists. Since they didn't match, his hand was tipped.
Some of his changes were irrelevant: reparagraphing, changing Australian
spellings to American usage. But other alterations were designed to make
the piece look more respectable, thereby misleading readers as to its reliability.

The original newspaper version of the article begins: "The characters in
this UFO story are real even if they appear more like the inventions of a
Hollywood hack." They *weren't* real, they were the inventions of a *tabloid*
hack. He continues: "A haunted young man, a ruthless cowboy, a hard-
drinking psychiatrist, a bunch of reporters and a beautiful girl with a kinky
sex problem."

PJK's *Skeptical Inquirer* version read as follows: "A haunted young man, a
ruthless cowboy, a strange professor, a hard-drinking psychiatrist, and a
bunch of reporters." No editor's note here, no ellipses, only a seamless, air-
brushed flow of words, with no reference to the beautiful girl with a kinky
sex problem. Wells may have been referring to the only female present, Dr.
Rosenbaum's attractive psychologist wife, Dr. Beryl Rosenbaum. Of course
the kinky sex problem was fiction. (And Wells had the gall in his article to
refer to *60 Minutes* as a "muckraker TV show.")

PJK's sanitized reprint then changed the phrase "shack up with us in a luxury motel" to "hole up with us in a luxury motel." The only payoff on the sex-
ual bait at the top of the article was when Wells wrote later on in the fiction:

> . . . the psychiatrist put the cowboy and the kid through a long session
> of analysis.
> Their methods were unique. The next day the four of them disap-
> peared into a room, and soon a waiter headed in there with two bot-
> tles of cognac.
> At the end of it the psychiatrists were rolling drunk, but they had their
> story and the brothers were crestfallen.

PJK left that imaginary scene undoctored because no one would read sex-
ual suggestion into it without the earlier material he had deleted.

PJK so indiscriminately seized on anything, regardless of the source,
which he could use against me, that he stooped to borrowing from tabloid
writers, a group he and CSICOP had previously so often derided. It didn't
even bother him that the article stated: "Our first sight of the kid was at dinner in the motel dining room that night. It was a shock. He sat there mute,
pale, twitching like a cornered animal." True, but, incidentally, refuting
PJK's claim that I had been in a proper state to take a polygraph test. Wells
continued with this embellishment:

But suddenly the strain began to tell on the kid and he lapsed into sobbing bouts. He was falling apart and so was his story.

It necessitated flying in a husband-and-wife team of psychiatrists from Colorado to tranquilize the kid and keep the cowboy from exploding. The kid was a wreck, and it was all the psychiatrists could do to get him ready for the lie detector expert we had lined up. [Wells' recollection of the chronology of events is in error. The polygraph test was given by McCarthy in the early afternoon of November 15, 1975, and the two Colorado psychiatrists did not arrive in Phoenix until that evening.—Ed.]

(I was not tranquilized. Also, PJK didn't actually put his name to the article—except as "Ed." However, since PJK is the UFO editor of the *Skeptical Inquirer,* and the chairman of CSICOP's UFO subcommittee, and since my experience was his territory at CSICOP, and because it was he who circulated the newspaper article from which the alleged "reprint" was taken, I felt it reasonable to assume that PJK is "Ed."—but any such assumption like this should be so labeled.)

Wells not only gets the basic chronology wrong, he describes events he *couldn't* have seen. Yet the editors at CSICOP praised the "significant insights" of the tabloid writer's article, respectfully referring to him as a "journalist." (I might also point out that, as fantastical and exaggerated as Wells' account was, he didn't claim that Duane had thrown McCarthy bodily out of the motel, which Wells would surely have done—with avid embellishment—if McCarthy's charge had been true.)

There is another interesting sidelight to this. Jeff Wells wrote a second version of his same tale for *Omni* magazine's March 1982 "Antimatter" column. I was not then aware of the earlier *Skeptical Inquirer* article, but took great offense at the multitude of gross misrepresentations in the *Omni* column: so many they almost crowded out all truth. Except for some of the names and dates and places, and except for his description of the shape I was in, there was not one completely true and accurate sentence in it.

At that time Carol Burnett had just won a huge judgment against the *National Enquirer* for false reports of supposedly drunken public antics. Her story, widely reported in the news media, had an underlying parallel to my situation, with Wells' false claim of drunkenness. I made reference to her case as an implied warning concerning *Omni*'s responsibility to truth in the matter.

March 15, 1982

Omni
909 Third Avenue
New York, NY 10022

Omni Letters/Dialogue:

Jeff Wells' "UFO Update" in "Antimatter," March '82 was the most ludicrous pack of lies yet written about my November 1975 experience. There are so many distortions and outright fabrications in that half page that I can't begin to rebut them all. Wells' years at the *National Enquirer* have left him with some bad habits.

Wells did not ever see me or my brother "staggering" drunk. I am a 100% abstaining, teetotaling non-drinker. My brother and I *did not* and *do not* drink alcoholic beverages of any kind.

The idea of my having a transitory psychosis involving a UFO cultist father who abandoned me is an absurd invention. I am now told that my father had no such interest, but I could not have known *anything* about my father because he divorced my mother and left for good when I was only fourteen months old!

As a small part of a detailed investigation by the Aerial Phenomena Research Organization I underwent a battery of psychological tests by a number of independent experts which indicated "normality and no deviations that would point toward psychosis," "a normal pattern of scores," "no indication of a neurotic or psychotic reaction" and concluded with, "a picture of a healthy young man, with a good sense of self-awareness, a tendency toward skepticism, and an inner strength or emotional stability."

Jeff Wells did not request that the story be killed as he claims; it was published with his byline and with more of his typical distortions such as claiming that the ray which struck me made me vanish into thin air, as if the story needed any sensationalizing.

"Antimatter" has been good for laughs but I'm not laughing at this one. *Omni* has a lot of fine writers to fill its pages without resorting to yellow contributions from ex-*Enquirer* reporters. Carol Burnett I'm not, but I sincerely hope you will allow me to refute this gratuitous slander against me.

Sincerely,

Travis Walton

I wasn't aware of the wide liberties allowed to magazine editors in rewriting letters for publication. In their defense, they cite space limitations, justifying their changes by claiming they preserve the intended meaning. You be the judge of whether my intended meaning was preserved. In the June 1982 "Letters" column *Omni* printed:

No Laughing Matter

Jeff Wells's UFO Update ["Antimatter," March 1982] was the most ludicrous pack of lies yet written about my November 1975 experience. Wells did not see me or my brother "staggering" drunk. My brother and I did not—and do not—drink alcohol.

I underwent a battery of psychological tests by a number of independent experts that indicated no neurosis or psychosis.

"Antimatter" has been good for laughs, but I am not laughing at this one. I am not Carol Burnett.

Travis Walton

Snowflake, Ariz.

Enormous compression, but the abridgment held up—until the Carol Burnett line. They took my remark, in which I was saying in effect that "I don't have Burnett's financial power or star clout to do to you what she did to the *Enquirer,* but please correct this offense by printing my letter," and changed it to "I am not Carol Burnett"! To me it looks as if *Omni* were trying to make me look nutty, as if I had an identity delusion, or believed Wells had called me Carol Burnett or was trying to say "Carol Burnett is guilty of this but I'm not." Unintentional, or not? You be the judge.

Anyway, the main point relevant to the present discussion is that in Jeff Wells' *Skeptical Inquirer* version, he describes Duane as a "total abstainer" (true) and claims "the psychiatrists were rolling drunk" (untrue). In his *Omni* version he repeats, almost word for word, his florid description of Duane from his newspaper article:

He was one of the meanest and toughest-looking men I've ever seen— in his late twenties, a rodeo professional and amateur light-heavy- weight fighter, a total abstainer, broad shouldered, T-shirt packed with muscle, chiseled-down hips, bow legged, eyes full of nails, tense, unpredictable. He leaned against a pick-up truck with a gun rack in the cabin and raked us with beams of cunning and hatred as strong as the flash from the spaceship that had pole-axed his brother as the wit- nesses fled in terror.

Except, in *Omni,* he carefully omitted "total abstainer." Then Wells creatively edited the part about the two psychiatrists from the earlier version which, to repeat, went: "Their methods were unique. The next day the four of them disappeared into a room, and soon a waiter headed in there with two bottles of cognac. At the end of it the psychiatrists were rolling drunk, but they had their story and the brothers were crestfallen." In the *Omni* article he changed it to: "Then a psychiatrist flew in from Colorado. He locked himself in a room with Travis, the cowboy and a bottle of cognac. When the three staggered out hours later, he had his story."

These stories came out more than five years after the event, but only months apart. In that short interval the two bottles of cognac became one, the two psychiatrists reduced to one, and Duane and I went from "total ab- stainer" and "crestfallen" to staggering drunk. (And, of course, the beautiful girl with the kinky sex problem vanished without a trace.) Gives one a notion of his journalistic accuracy, doesn't it? I wouldn't be surprised to learn of the existence of more bizarre recyclings of the article published elsewhere.

Such are the sorts of sources PJK relies on. But then what else would you expect in a smear campaign?

PJK draws many unjustified conclusions from a taped interview with my brother Duane and Mike Rogers, conducted by ufologist Fred Sylvanus out near the site during the search for me. PJK sees sinister implications in my brother's repeated assertions: "they don't kill people"; "he'll be all right"; "he's having the experience of a lifetime"; "he'll turn up"; "I don't believe he's hurt"; "I refuse to put the beings or the craft or whatever you want to call it in the role of villains"; "if they wanted to make war they'd of destroyed us long ago."

In light of Duane's character, anyone can see that he was *not* talking like a UFO buff. He sounded as anyone might if he was trying to convince himself that someone he cared greatly for was all right. Particularly when he contradicts himself by showing concern about the effectiveness of the ground search.

The context PJK ignores is that this was after three exhausting days of fruitless searching and unsolicited advice from ufologists and UFO buffs. My brother had grilled my coworkers, and he'd had days to face the facts of the situation. So, astounding as the conclusion was, the only alternative was to accept that I'd been taken.

PJK implies my family could only have avoided PJK's suspicion (actually he would've seen every possible reaction as suspicious) by steadfastly disbelieving it. But that would've been irrational. Remember Sherlock Holmes: "When you've eliminated all other possibilities, whatever remains, however unlikely, is the answer."

Duane sounded more like someone at a funeral repeating that their dearly departed is safe in the hands of angels, free at last, at least not feeling pain any longer, gone to a better place, etc. A relative pacing a hospital waiting room might have a similar tone to their remarks. The parent of a missing child often takes the position, "She's safe, I just know it," or "I wish I was with her." If his reaction had occurred in any similar situation, not involving UFOs, his optimism would not be questioned even for a second. Granted, different people take things differently, some might wail and scream, but would Duane? In a sense, Duane's bravado was exactly what PJK claims was lacking—a show of concern. If he were truly unconcerned about my well-being, he wouldn't have kept bringing up the subject in that way.

Another factor of the context of this tape that PJK ignores is that after three days of endlessly talking about the same subject, people's areas of emphasis naturally change. Every single conversation would not cover the entire range of their thoughts and feelings on the subject. Their first words about it might be most representative of their reaction. But, after a while, each conversation would add a fresh perspective, not be a repetition of their first words.

This is especially true of heavy emotional content. Three or four sleepless nights and tension-filled days alone would tend to make people a little numb. In several instances where friends have lost a close loved one and I was unable to go offer support for several days, I was surprised at how unemotional they had already become. People get cried-out, and if they don't cry, they get grieved-out, or worried-out. But rarely do people maintain their peak of emotional expression for days on end. Especially people prone to withholding emotion and avoiding the betrayal of anything that might be construed as weakness.

When Sylvanus asked Duane if he'd read much about flying saucers, from the context one can tell that Duane felt his knowledge was being challenged by the ufologist, that justification for all his rationalizing and philosophizing about me being okay was being questioned. Duane had quite a swagger to him in those days, and he wasn't one to be outdone, especially when challenged. He had an expression he used, whenever people asked him how he was doing—with a big confident grin he'd shoot back, "Better'n anybody!" Duane was a boxer, and Muhammad Ali's braggadocio was widely known, so it was something people took as a kind of half-jesting style that was understood. So, although Duane hadn't ever read a single book on the subject, he answered, "As much as anybody," but then quickly qualified it with, "It's just one of those things."

In his "analysis" of the Sylvanus tape PJK wrote (underlined, all caps): *"BUT AT NO TIME DURING THE HOUR-LONG INTERVIEW DID ROGERS EXPRESS THE SLIGHTEST CONCERN OVER WHETHER TRAVIS MIGHT HAVE BEEN INJURED OR KILLED ..."* And, in his book: *"Yet never once during the sixty-five-minute interview did either Duane Walton or Rogers express the slightest concern over Travis's well-being. Quite the opposite!* [emphasis PJK's] Nor did Rogers ever voice any regret that he decided to drive off and abandon his good friend Travis, leaving him to a supposedly strange fate. When Rogers described the appearance of the UFO to Sylvanus he never once used words like 'frightening' or 'ominous.'"

No, and he didn't use words like *xenophobia* or *inauspicious*, either. But he did use the word "scared" repeatedly. PJK deceives again.

People are so often tricked by PJK quoting or citing some clear documentation like a tape because they don't expect there's a need to question the accuracy of his quotations and summations. Mike's references to being afraid are scattered all through his account: ". . . a deep, throbbing feel to it—that's what scared me more than anything." "Nobody ever got out of the truck but Walton, we were all too scared to do anything. . . ." ". . . I looked away because I was scared and a couple of the guys had already said, you know, let's get the hell out of here." ". . . I drove the truck too fast, I panicked and I almost wrecked the truck." "We were scared, everybody was yelling, everybody was shouting, my fingers turned numb, my feet were numb, my stomach was in a ball. . . ." These are just a few examples, clear proof that PJK deliberately misrepresented what was actually said.

Mike's description of the craft as something perfect and beautiful reminds me of the sort of hypnotic, deadly fascination I've read about in descriptions of someone staring transfixed at some brightly colored poisonous serpent or something else of complex, yet imposingly dangerous, appearance. The paradox of the combination of beauty and danger was what prompted Mike's musing.

Mike expressed concern for my well-being many times in the interview, and in a variety of ways. Although the issue of his driving off and leaving me behind was a touchy one between him and Duane, who was present, he even commented on that.

Mike's expression of being aggravated because he believed (mistakenly) that his repeated suggestion to use bloodhounds had been ignored until it became too late to use tracking dogs, and his dissatisfaction with the effectiveness of the search, certainly implied concern. (To prove that my ellipses are not tricky, like PJK's, doubters can arrange to listen to a copy of the tape.) Scattered all through the tape, in no particular order, are the following: ". . . we better go back in case he's hurt and bleeding . . ."; ". . . we're going to have to go back. I agreed, you know, we couldn't leave him over there if he was hurt, which he certainly looked to me like he received some kind of [*pause*] something, some kind of injury, I don't know if it just stunned him or hurt him. Since we haven't found him we don't know but [*big sigh, pause*] . . ."; ". . . no tracks, no pieces of clothing, no blood, no nothing. I mean there was no trace of it, and there was no trace of him. Some of the guys started crying; I remember I started crying . . ." Again, just a few examples from among others.

No fear, "concern," or regret? Of course, it wasn't enough for PJK to tell his readers blatant falsehoods about the part of the Sylvanus tape he *didn't* transcribe. PJK's partial transcript contained a passage in which Duane said, ". . . he got directly under the object and he's received the benefits for it." PJK then quotes Sylvanus as saying, "You hope he has!"—after which PJK interjects this comment: "Listening to the foregoing portion of the tape-recorded interview, it is clear from the tone of Sylvanus's voice that he is much more concerned over Travis's well-being than either Rogers or Duane Walton." Or so you would be led to believe. Except for the fact that it was *not* Sylvanus's voice expressing this concern. The one who said, "You hope he has!" was in reality Mike Rogers!

PJK's transcribing and "analyzing" the tape was supposed to prove Mike and Duane were suspiciously unconcerned, and talking like UFO buffs. The one comment that PJK judges to be "clear from the tone of . . . voice that he is much more concerned" actually came from Mike, proving quite the opposite of PJK's whole point! The few remarks Duane did make about UFOs did *not* show how "well-versed in UFO lore" he was, but were in fact sufficiently inaccurate to prove again the opposite of PJK's contention.

After days of unsuccessful searching my mother logically concluded that I wasn't on this earth and agreed with termination of the search. PJK criticizes this by implying it was something only a true believer (or, variously, a conspirator) would do. Then he contemptuously criticizes as a waste the action Duane and Mike took in getting the search reinstituted, instead of seeing it as an expression of concern, which he had claimed was lacking. He repeatedly switches back and forth between characterizing the people involved as either conspirators or true believers. He uses whatever most negative depiction seems to work best at the moment, in total disregard of the inconsistency with his other representations.

How could this attributing of Mike's words to Sylvanus be a mistake? PJK had read Bill Barry's accurate transcript of this passage, which properly attributes that comment to Mike. And I've listened to the tape—it's clear. There is no mistaking the voice of a twenty-eight-year-old Mike for the voice of the elderly Sylvanus (now deceased).

If these aren't tricks, if his switching the attribution of concern, and the "bleeding"/"breathing" accusation, were both actually errors, it speaks volumes about PJK's mind-set (and lack of accuracy) throughout his work. His penchant for misattribution even extends to videotape, where he can see people's lips move. He published a transcript of a portion of the *Larry King Live* where he attributes to Mike a remark that *I* made. How many of the transcripts he publishes of his recorded phone calls have similar "convenient" errors? PJK's words "accidentally" ending up coming from the mouth of those called in his telephone "research"? Without originals we may never know.

It is ironic that so many of his Ten Ufological Principles boil down to say that people see what they expect to see, what they want to see, what they're psychologically predisposed to see. I believe that these observations about human nature are often accurate. The irony lies in the extent to which this appears to dominate PJK's own thinking on the subject. His mind fills in the blanks and "quickly supplies the details"—as he says of UFO witnesses.

If he'd applied his Ufological Principle Number 7, he wouldn't have been attacking the characters of Mike and Duane, and would have focused on the tape portion where Mike describes witnessing the government man taking radiation readings at the site. Yet PJK has never written a single word about such physical traces, not even to attack them. The tape also contains references to concern about a government cover-up, two days before the polygraph tests, which they were calling for on the tape, along with other tests like sodium pentothal ("truth serum"). An objective investigator would have focused on signs like these, and the call for tracking dogs, instead of ignoring them to carp about a fictional lack of concern.

PJK keeps harping on the nonsense that the "entire Walton family are UFO buffs," when he is very poorly informed concerning my family. He calls Duane the "oldest son" when he is the second oldest son and the third oldest child. He put a photograph in his book with a caption identifying my sister, Alison, as Duane's wife. Except for a passing reference, in one of his less circulated papers, to Don tearing apart the slash-piles looking for a body, he has never made a single specific mention of my other three siblings, yet writes repeatedly of the whole family's alleged obsession.

Speaking of photos, he has a habit of publishing uncomplimentary photos of his targets, often taken from video footage, where you can catch a bad frame. Apparently, he especially prefers mid-blink, which gives just the impression he's after. The odds would be much against catching that many people in mid-blink purely by chance.

The phoniest photo PJK uses in his book is one of McCarthy with a deceptive caption that says, in part, that McCarthy ". . . examines the original charts from the lie detector test he gave Travis Walton shortly after he reappeared." (Yeah, *too* shortly.) The single *chart* McCarthy is looking at could not be my original chart*s*. The chart he is looking at is still in the machine with the ink-tracing needles still on the lines, and the paper still attached to the main roll. Immediately after my test, McCarthy removed the charts from the machine, rolled them up and put them away, and *no photos were taken* (as PJK specifically mentioned on page 186 of the same book!). McCarthy's machine in the photo is desk-mounted in a built-in mode. When he tested me it was in portable mode, which is a suitcase-like accessory used for carrying and mounting the device for road jobs. The photo was taken in some office, not the motel room where the test actually took place. The picture is just a transparent attempt at a tabloid-style dramatization of McCarthy's "gross deception" claim quoted in the bogus caption.

Riddled with deliberate alterations of the truth as his case is, numerous as these examples are, his most-used tactic is still the omission of data. We will probably never know the full extent of what lies on his cutting-room floor, but there are many more examples of things kept just barely out of frame of the picture he portrays to his readers.

PJK scratched deep in efforts to dig up dirt on those he attacked. I learned that he telephoned all the bars in town, looking for bad stories about me, but when they told him I *never* went in there, PJK hid this fact. He called neighbors and former employers. When these people told PJK good things about me, he withheld this information, too.

In a November 8, 1976, white paper criticizing Jim Lorenzen of APRO's handling of my case, PJK wrote, "An investigative reporter, or a UFO investigator, has a duty to report *all significant facts* [emphasis his] he uncovers, even if some run contrary to his own beliefs." Recall the line of Peguy's that PJK is so fond of quoting: "He who does not bellow the truth when he knows the truth makes himself the accomplice of liars and forgers." And one he takes from Ben Franklin: "Half the truth is often a great lie."

He would never bring himself to mention that my mother was several times nominated and once voted Woman of the Year by the chamber of commerce for her volunteer work and community service. But he kept digging until he found someone who, jealous of our family's use of the Bear Springs cabin, was willing to make spurious attacks on my mother's character. Oh, he "ignored character endorsements of the principals involved" all right—if, and only if, they were on the affirmative side of the issue.

But on the other hand, he actively and enthusiastically *went looking for* character attacks. He was aware of my scholarship grants from three universities, but kept quiet about it. Others, like Mike's Forest Service associates, gave positive testimony that went no farther than PJK's ears. People had loads of good things to say about Ken Peterson's character, but PJK never repeated any of it.

"He who does not bellow the truth when he knows the truth makes himself the accomplice of liars and forgers."

Nowhere is PJK's one-sided reporting as demonstrable as in his treatment of credentials. He hypes the credentials of my critics and plays down the credentials of my advocates.

PJK falsely claimed that George Pfiefer had only two years' experience, instead of his actual five years. He played up Ezell's four years of polygraph experience and his brief work for the police, and completely omits the fact, known to him, that Pfiefer had for years been a detective-sergeant with the Miami Police Department in Florida, from which he later retired. Pfiefer had been honored by being specially selected from among the department's seven hundred–plus employees, as best-qualified for assignment to the Bureau of Scientific Investigation, and to the Identification Bureau. Part of his duties involved participating in the training of police recruits—one of whom went on to become Miami's chief of police.

Subsequently Pfiefer was Director of Security in the state of Arizona for the large corporation National Convenience Stores, before entering private practice. His reputation caused him to be immediately swamped with business, thus prompting the merger with Ezell and Associates. PJK omits reporting that Pfiefer was a charter member of the Arizona Polygraph Association, and a full member of both the American Polygraph Association and the California Association of Polygraph Examiners. His membership in the American Polygraph Association was sponsored by both vice presidents of that organization; and his membership in the California organization was sponsored by its president.

Yet, for McCarthy—who wasn't even a member of the Arizona Polygraph Association—PJK doesn't fail to mention McCarthy's American Polygraph Association membership. He writes respectfully of "McCarthy's Arizona Polygraph Laboratory," but refers to Pfiefer as "operating under the business name of Associated Polygraph," as if *Pfiefer's* company's name were some flimflam alias.

In one of his books PJK attacks self-proclaimed UFO witness Dan Fry's credentials, putting his title—"Dr."—in quotation marks. PJK goes into detail about checking on the source of Fry's Ph.D., the difficulty in actually finding what turned out to be a "correspondence school" and his discovery that, "From their standard application form I learned that anyone could apply for a Ph.D. by simply submitting a ten-thousand-word thesis and paying a modest fee which amounted to less than one hundred dollars."

APRO's investigation of "Dr." Lester Steward's academic credentials, which PJK read, followed an almost identical course. However, instead of discrediting Steward as he did Fry, PJK ignores the fact that Steward had tried to pass himself off as an M.D. (he impersonated an M.D. not only to Duane and me, but also to reporters). And, merely because Steward attacked me, PJK continues to treat him respectfully as the "drug expert" Steward claims to be, when PJK *knew* Steward had no such formal training at all.

PJK discounts the testimony of Dr. Kandell in his dismissal of the drug-trip scenario because Kandell's specialty was pediatrics, even though Kandell was a bona fide M.D. with years of legitimate training and experience. How much drug-addiction experience or training could PJK's "drug expert," Steward, truly have, when the school from which he supposedly obtained his training had been in existence for only two years? As Steward so grossly misrepresented his academic credentials, how could anyone honest prefer Steward's pronouncements to those of a reputable, genuine medical doctor? If Steward had been one of my advocates, rest assured PJK would have declared Steward's "expert opinion" as bogus as his credentials. He'd have skewered Steward. PJK discounts the witness reliability of astronauts and experienced pilots but takes the word of flakes at face value if he thinks they support his case.

PJK omits mentioning Dr. Rosenbaum's status in court as an expert witness on the validity of the polygraph, when Rosenbaum rejects the validity of the McCarthy test. (PJK does quote Rosenbaum's statement, but then claims that my book, *The Walton Experience* (which he falsely and repeatedly implies was ghostwritten), "omits Dr. Rosenbaum's other conclusion; that Travis 'did not go on a UFO.' ") Another PJK falsehood. What he claims I omitted appears on page 139.

PJK recounts Rosenbaum's "transitory psychosis" theory for the opportunity to reflect negatively on my mental status, even though he ultimately (correctly) discounts it as flawed because the theory fails to account for the witnesses, the ray, and my urine sample. (PJK is very equivocal about the urine sample: If there are no drugs in it, then it can't be mine; but if there are no acetones in it, it *is* mine and proof that I wasn't aboard the craft because I have no conscious memory of being fed.)

APRO performed two psychiatric examinations on me, ruling out any kind of psychological abnormality (a fact PJK was aware of but, again, carefully omits). Dr. Harold Cahn, a physiologist and APRO's consultant in parapsychology, administered the Rorschach (inkblot) test and filed a report with APRO which indicated I was "not highly suggestible" and possessed a good, normal, basic personality structure. The Minnesota Multiphasic Personality Inventory, conducted by Lamont McConnell (who holds an M.S. in psychology), indicated "normality and no deviations that would point toward psychosis."

The results of both tests were reviewed for further interpretation by Dr. R. Leo Sprinkle, who was APRO's Consultant in Psychology and also Director of the Division of Counseling and Testing at the University of Wyoming. In his report he wrote in summary: "The profile is viewed as a normal pattern of scores; there is no indication of a neurotic or psychotic reaction." And in conclusion: ". . . the MMPI profile of Travis Walton provides a picture of a healthy young man, with a good sense of self-awareness, a tendency toward skepticism, and an inner strength or emotional stability."

The real reason PJK discounts Rosenbaum's theory is not its contradiction of the facts, but that at its core it depends on my *belief* in what happened to me: acceptance of which would overturn the McCarthy test, the Forest

Service Contract Motive Theory, and all that vast web of interrelated innuendo.

PJK rejects Rosenbaum's two major points: his spurious psychosis theory and the invalidation of the McCarthy test. Then he hypocritically uses Rosenbaum's claims that "the Waltons are UFO freaks," a notion Rosenbaum got from the media. *Then* PJK reprints an article falsely claiming Rosenbaum was rolling drunk when gathering this "reliable" data. He quotes from Rosenbaum's recounting of my childhood history, which doesn't remotely match up with any of the easily verified facts about where I really lived, when I moved, facts about my father, his work, my mother, her work, etc. Had PJK admitted checking enough to find out how ridiculously erroneous the false childhood history was, he wouldn't have been able to use the other Rosenbaum statements he selectively included. Flip flop flip flop. Sift and sort. Cut and paste.

It really wouldn't hurt my case if Rosenbaum's *entire* testimony were rejected as unreliable, because the validity of the McCarthy test has been rejected by about a dozen other experts of much higher standing.

PJK drew similar "family of UFO buffs" stories from Dr. Kandell, who PJK quotes as saying he heard me say such things *during* his medical examination of me—an examination for which he wrote an official report wherein he stated that discussion was confined to the medical aspects of my condition. In his June 20, 1976, paper PJK said, ". . . I asked him whether Travis or Duane had indicated any previous interest in UFOs during his November 11 discussions and examination. Dr. Kandell replied: 'They admitted to that freely, that he [Travis] was a 'UFO freak,' so to speak. . . . He had made remarks that if he ever saw one, he'd like to go aboard.' "

I certainly never said any such thing to Kandell. This is another example of the sneaky quote out of context. Don't believe PJK's quotes for one second. I discover deception has occurred nearly every time I get access to the context of his quotes or the material substituted for by his three-dot ellipses. An actual (to the extent it can be trusted, since it was written by PJK), little-circulated transcript of the conversation from which the quote above was taken proves that PJK knew all along that Dr. Kandell was like McCarthy and Rosenbaum in simply repeating what the newspapers and TV had been screaming. The quote sounds certain, without qualification, right? Look what was trimmed off after PJK's question about the family's prior interest:

Dr. Kandell: *They admitted to that freely, that he was, you know, a "UFO freak,"*
                 so to speak. He's interested in it.

PJK: *Which one?*

Dr. Kandell:	*Travis. He had made remarks before that if he ever saw one, he'd like to go aboard, this and that. So, yes, that was mentioned. That was out.*
PJK:	*When was that? Was that when you and Dr. Saults were there or when more of the people were there?*
Dr. Kandell:	*No, that was, I think, subsequently, it came out. I don't know whether it was that Friday night, or it could have been that I, that it was in the newspapers, that somebody else might have mentioned it.*
PJK:	*But you heard it from their own lips?*
Dr. Kandell:	*I think so. I think so. I can't be 100-percent positive. But if I didn't, it was discussed. They didn't deny that. That wasn't denied.*

PJK was putting pressure on him to say he heard these things directly from me. But still Dr. Kandell essentially admitted that he'd heard it elsewhere, from the newspapers or something and ends lamely with the statement that no one specifically spoke to the contrary. Tricky.

Anyone writing to PJK would be well advised to be certain to keep a carbon copy. If you can't tape it yourself, anyone speaking to him in person or on the phone needs to be certain to speak like a paranoid politician—in precise sound bites. Make sure that if you qualify your statements, do it within the sentence, not as an afterthought.

Of course, as with the Bill Barry quote, it's nearly impossible to speak in a way that will prevent distortion by those three little dots, the ellipsis. Imagine what could be done to "I admit that I was shocked when someone robbed Fort Knox" by substituting an ellipsis for the middle four words.

Also one must be constantly aware of how their words will look bare, devoid of the richness of inflection, tone, and emotion normally used to communicate so much of what we really think. Take any one of PJK's quotes and read it aloud with various emotions: cagey hesitancy, prosecutorial stridence, offhand carelessness, emphatic certainty, hollow insincerity, a mocking or questioning tone implying "someone else believes this but not me."

To further illustrate how a mere transcript can strip away meaning, repeat the sentence, "I never said I saw him steal money," and one at a time emphasize the first word, the second, the third, and so on until the stress has been placed on each of the eight words. Shows you what's lost in a transcript, doesn't it? Reading song lyrics doesn't make us feel like dancing. And this doesn't begin to show how an infinite variety of things said in a surrounding context can dramatically alter, even reverse, the meaning of those few words enclosed in quotes.

But wait, there's more. In PJK's book, *UFOs: The Public Deceived,* he refers to that very same November 11 medical examination, this time trying to build the *opposite* case—that the Waltons were being closemouthed and secretive, rather than freely speaking of eagerness for a UFO ride: ". . . Duane asked that the doctors limit themselves to a cursory examination and not to ask Travis for any details of his UFO experience, and the doctors complied. Kandell told me that Travis would reply cryptically to questions 'but he really did not expound on anything voluntarily.' " ("Cursory" is PJK's word, not Duane's and not accurate.)

Apparently PJK was moved by criticism of his earlier Kandell "quotes" (ironic that for PJK we have to put "quote" in quotation marks) to retreat to a position closer to the truth. Somehow, though, in his descriptions of the same encounter we went from raving on about UFOs, to saying almost nothing at all. The truth is, Kandell *did* ask a little about the experience aboard the craft but only so far as it related to my condition, as mentioned in his medical report.

Kandell also wrote: "He appeared anxious, though calm; spoke slowly and showed no emotions at all, i.e. his affect [*sic*] was extremely flat." "A drug screen run by the Maricopa County Medical Examiner's Office, Toxicology Division, revealed no detectable drugs in that initial specimen submitted." "His emotional state suggested that he had been through a disturbing experience."

Consistent criteria? Or flip flop? PJK points with great suspicion to the fact my mother failed to invite the town marshal into her Snowflake home at one time during the search, implying she was hiding me there. (She'd just become fed up with reporters and law officers—many of whom, including Flake, had already been allowed in—getting her very upset and invading her privacy.) Yet PJK also attacked her for being too believing in her remarks. Which is it, PJK, was she a wide-eyed believer, or was she in on some kind of conspiracy?

Then elsewhere PJK turns around and claims I was hiding twenty-five miles away at Bear Springs. PJK saw it as very suspicious that, in the crisis, my mother left the remote cabin which had no phone, to return home to be near her family and word of what was going on. If she had stayed at Bear Springs I'm certain that PJK would have seen that as suspicious, too.

Both his conflicting claims ignore the fact that the Navajo County Sheriff's Department *knew for certain* from the telephone operator's tip, that my call for help had come from Heber, miles from either alleged hideout. PJK knew this—he reported it elsewhere in his book. (Sheriff Gillespie's wife was a former telephone operator and in the early days of his career the Sheriff's Department had no dispatcher but instead had a big red light on top of the phone-company building up on the hill, which they would turn on as a signal to call in.) And my mother passed a polygraph test as to her innocence of all PJK's charges, which also included specific questions concerning this issue. Recall that he declined her polygraph challenge, obviously not really believing his charges against her.

I guess the man's attitude could be summed up as the logical fallacy of black-or-white. Everyone who has any part of upholding the validity of a UFO case is black, and anyone who attacks it is white, and there is no gray area.

PJK speculated (before release) that the movie would contain elements concerning genetic experimentation described in other recent cases which were not present in my original account. His prediction missed; the movie contained no such "angles." But if it had, it would have been a false hit. Because it's simply untrue that my first book made no such mentions, there *were* references to implants, fetuses, reproduction, and genetic engineering.

One of his favorite words was "eager." When abducted, I was "eager." If any pro-UFO person appears on television, they do so "eagerly." He continually accuses Pfiefer, me, and many other witnesses and investigators, of wanting to become "celebrities." Contrast this with his constant plying the media with his mailings and his continual requests to be interviewed, to rebut this or comment on that.

He just as frequently accuses witnesses and investigators of deceiving the public, not just for attention, but for *profit*. With his four books, lectures, newsletter, etc., we can see that PJK's position has not left him unsullied by gain. I've been told that he owns an apartment complex, a big, oceangoing boat, and makes frequent trips to places like the Bahamas. With the many falsehoods exposed here, Mike has said publicly that in a sense it is PJK who has been shown to be a UFO hoaxer.

Actually, humor aside, it is completely invalid from a logical standpoint to make the test of virtue for someone on any side of any issue be whether they profit from their position. Like everything, it bears examination, but it's no acid test. Such a standard falls apart if some Hitleresque zealot preaches genocide and asks nothing for himself from his followers, while a dedicated physician earns a very comfortable living for himself and his family. This is America, we believe in capitalism, free enterprise, and all that. If PJK has made some money, fine. The key is that he not be hypocritical in applying a standard to others he doesn't want applied to himself.

I want to repeat my request that the facts of this matter be evaluated solely on the merits of the data and reasoning. No matter what the personal estimation is of a person who resorts to such tactics and reasoning patterns, the truth must be determined independently of such considerations. I don't think I'd have a great deal of trouble whipping up such emotion, if that's what I wanted, because he already does this to himself. The more objective ufologists actually have a sort of grudging respect for some of the other major skeptics and debunkers, but not for PJK. No one else seems to engender the kinds of strong negative feelings he does.

Even those with initially sympathetic ears wind up becoming quite disaffected: skeptical people like Town Marshal Sanford Flake, Forest Service contracting officer Maurice Marchbanks, reporter Richard Robertson, and several others I could name, came to develop strong negative reactions to his approach. As negative as these people have been about my case, they came away using words like "biased" and "unfair" about PJK's modus operandi.

Bill Barry described it thusly: "His method of dealing with their evidence was harsh, smug, superior, unfair, and sometimes worse. And when push came to shove, and evidence could not be impugned, [PJK] simply ignored it and omitted it from consideration. So his investigation of UFOs finally suffered from several interrelated defects: there was a personal taint of obnoxia about it; it failed to deal with the complete subject; its conclusion was no more substantial than the premise that had spawned it."

Perhaps it's his habit of badgering people who thought they were on his side. Even people completely neutral end up shoved one way or the other by the feeling of being cornered, cross-examined like a hostile witness, everything for the record, everything for that isolated quote, trapped into choosing sides in a battle that wasn't theirs. Those shoved to my side are sometimes surprised to find themselves upholding an idea of a sort they never would have expected they could ever back up. Those shoved to his side seem vaguely guilty or to faintly resent it somehow, like they feel used or manipulated. Yet PJK criticizes modern UFO researchers for supposedly doing this very thing in surveys, interviews, or even during hypnosis: leading, suggesting, pressuring subjects for the desired answers.

The rational mind is neither credulous nor skeptical—it is *objective*. Objectivity means having no bias either for or against an issue. Our only "bias," if you wish to call a priority or goal a "bias," should be for the truth—things as they are, to the best of our ability to determine it.

If we are objective we believe only those things proven true and we only disbelieve those things proven false. In the real world these extremes are rare; those indeterminate things in between have to be assigned relative weight on the basis of defensible criteria. The error of both the gullible and the skeptical is to try to lump too much into one of the absolute categories at the extremes.

We can't logically categorize the unproven as necessarily untrue, any more than we can categorize everything that is not disproved as necessarily true. With this understanding, the term "skeptic" is as derogatory as the term "gullible." Both suffer a form of blindness. Each is a side of the same coin—the error of the criteria for belief.

Ironically, the burden of proof lies with my critics. I am perfectly aware, and agree, that extraordinary claims require extraordinary proof. So ordinarily the situation would be reversed. But I am the one who has been pursued in this. By the time I was returned, the choice of going public about it or not was out of my hands. I have never sought out an interview in my life. They've come to me. And so have my attackers. It is they who claim. They who draw conclusions. They who make pronouncements that prove to be without foundation, without justification, without logical defense.

Years ago, from the very start, I frankly acknowledged the lack of indisputable proof. I informed my readers that I basically laid the material on the table, to judge as they saw fit. It was my critics who claimed to provide them with answers and conclusions—even proof.

And again, over two decades later, I put the same limits on what I ask. I don't ask for belief. For someone not privy to my perspective, such a conclusion might not be justified by the data available to you. You have to first allow *any* possibility. (This means considering all things that are possible—not considering that all things *are* possible, because they aren't.) Then I ask only for a fair appraisal of the facts.

I have pointed the way for those looking for more facts, more documentation. You can find it here if you wish to rely on my word, or go on and verify it for yourself if you want. Please take a minute to scan back through all the half-truths, distortions, and false charges leveled against me. Then ask yourself if you would ever trust their source as reliable concerning *any* information.

In looking over the case presented by my critics, do the words *thorough, accurate, scientific, fair, rational,* or *consistent* spring to mind? It is they who claim science and logic as their yardstick. I have tried to apply these values as best I can, but in reality it is their claim. Just as they claim to judge by these standards, it is their burden to be judged by them.

I am no logician and I'm no scientist. And the reader of these words is also unlikely to be either. But everyone has the right—no, the obligation—to use the best available standards and criteria in judging anything in life. The more important the answer, the more stringent your criteria better be.

Look back at the hail of hot barbs that have been fired at me, raining down on my life for decades. Want to trade places? The miracle is, I'm still standing.

Trial by fire. I've gained some unique and precious insight, but at a price I doubt anyone could begin truly to comprehend or willingly pay. It's no exaggeration when I say that people's reaction to what happened nearly overshadows the experience itself. That's saying a lot, but I could yet drop the word "nearly." Ironically, PJK's second book attacking me began with: "This book is dedicated to those who will needlessly bear mental scars for the rest of their lives because of the foolish fantasies of a few."

I've always been struck by the extraordinary incidence of irony in situations arising out of my experience. One is that my experience, which has come to be known as *Fire in the Sky,* was attacked in two hardcovers published by Prometheus Books. PJK and company have more in common with Procrustes than with Prometheus. Prometheus was the Titan of Greek religion who stole fire from heaven and gave it to man. And, for having brought this metaphorical gift of fire to mere mortals, Zeus sentenced him to be bound to a big rock on Mount Caucasus and be endlessly tormented by a vulture daily ripping at and consuming his liver, which would then regrow.

I leave it to history to decide who is truly the Prometheus in this episode of my life story, and who are the vultures.

I present these issues to the public for *their* judgment. My statements include a rebuttal of PJK's charges, but it is not a reply *to* him. Not after decades of vicious and unfair attacks, with never a single direct word from him. He has had ample opportunity to prove himself completely unworthy of debate. Conspicuous in this is the ugly prominence of his use of personal *ad hominem* attacks on me that are completely irrelevant to the issue. PJK's unworthiness of a fair and open discussion is due to his demonstrated lack of fairness, right on the face of it, by publishing and sending his baseless assertions to almost everyone. Everyone except the person they were about, the one person in the best position to most easily show they were wrong, if he'd been the least bit interested in prior verification or fact-checking. This is not a matter of pride, or of wanting to avoid "dignifying by reply"—it's simply a matter of not wasting time on something so utterly futile. You can't teach a pig to sing—it wastes your time and annoys the pig. In his exchanges with my proponents and his writings in general, he has amply demonstrated his abysmal lack of intellectual integrity and adherence to even the most rudimentary standards of rational discussion. It's far too late to undo the harm done. It is far too late for a chat.

While PJK deliberately hid favorable data and ducked confrontation of my strongest points, I have openly confronted his best; each has evaporated under full illumination. Space prohibits specific refutation of the minutiae of his maelstrom of misrepresentation (although more thorough and detailed analyses may be published on a smaller scale). Yes, believe it or not, the foregoing is far from being exhaustive of every last detail of his attacks. However, not one point in his prosecutorial campaign can stand up to rational analysis, to weigh objectively against the incident's authenticity.

An honest response by PJK would involve his publicly acknowledging these points, and conceding that he hasn't made his case—even if he wishes to persevere in advocating his underlying premise that there are no such things as UFOs. However, I predict that in PJK's public rantings he will flatly ignore my most decisive points, try to rebut some trivial points, and pound away at points of still greater obscurity and irrelevance. Perhaps, out of desperation he'll come up with new, more convoluted ad hoc scenarios he'll tailor to fit the data (or tailor the data to fit the scenario). And when all else fails, the measure of his ineffectuality will be proportionally reflected in even greater reliance on *ad hominem* character attacks.

He'll completely sidestep my examples of how he conducted his campaign, my exposure of his falsehoods, deceptive omissions, and distortions. He'll continue to beg the question of the strongest evidence: physical traces, consistent testimony from seven eyewitnesses, unassailable polygraph tests.

He'll rave on. Only this time, among those who now have the facts, no one will be listening.